THE HEART OF GEORGE MACDONALD

Rolland Hein, editor

A one-volume collection of his most important
- fiction - essays - sermons - drama
- poetry - letters

Harold Shaw Publishers
Wheaton, Illinois

Copyright © 1994 by Rolland Hein

Cover art and design © 1994 by David LaPlaca

ISBN 0-87788-371-8

Library of Congress Cataloging-in-Publication Data

MacDonald, George, 1824-1905.
    The heart of George MacDonald : a one-volume collection of his most important fiction, essays, sermons, drama, poetry, and letters / Rolland Hein, editor.
      p. cm.
    Includes bibliographical references.
    ISBN 0-87788-371-8
    I. Hein, Rolland. II. Title.
PR4966.H4 1994
823'.8—dc20   93-53-28
                                 CIP

99 98 97 96 95 94

10 9 8 7 6 5 4 3 2 1

"A stronger desire to do the will of the Father . . .
is surely the best thing God himself can kindle in
the heart of any man. For what good is there in
creation but the possibility of being yet further
created? And what else is growth but more of the
will of God?"

—George MacDonald, *Far Above Rubies*

CONTENTS

Drama

Sermons

ACKNOWLEDGMENTS

I would like to thank the following libraries for permission to quote the George MacDonald letters in their possession:

The Beinecke Rare Book and Manuscript Library, Yale University, New Haven, Connecticut:

> To [Louisa] "My dearest wife, Preston,
>   Sunday Afternoon, 28 October 1853"
> To "Dear W____, Bordighera, 31 January 1886"
> To "My dear Andy, Bordighera, 20 April 1888"
> To "My very dear Eva, Old Palace, Richmond, 28 September
>   1889"
> To "My dear Adelaide, Bordighera, 8 February 1890"
> To "Dearest Child, C.C.B., 4 January 1891"

The Huntington Library, San Marino, California:

> To "My dear Susan, Bordighera, 12 January 1888," HM 6349

The Trustees of the National Library of Scotland, Edinburgh:

> To "My loved and honoured old friend, Bordighera, 11 November
>   1894." MS. 2640, ff. 109-10

I would also like to thank the Wade Center, Wheaton College, for reproducing from their collection the text of the 1883 edition of *The Princess and Curdie* (Philadelphia: J.B. Lippincott and Company) and the text of the 1867 edition of *The Golden Key,* found in *Dealings with the Fairies* (London: Alexander Strahan).

The sermons entitled "The Child in the Midst," "The Consuming Fire," "The God of the Living," and "The New Name" are abridged from *Unspoken Sermons* (London: Alexander Strahan, Publisher, 1867); "The

Truth in Jesus," "Abba, Father," "The Word of Jesus on Prayer," and "The Last Farthing" from *Unspoken Sermons: Second Series* (London: Longmans, Green, and Co., 1891); and "The Creation in Christ," "The Knowing of the Son," "Light," "Justice," "The Truth," and "Freedom" from *Unspoken Sermons: Third Series* (London: Longmans, Green, and Co., 1889). The excerpt from "The Imagination: Its Functions and Its Culture," is taken from *Orts* (London: Sampson Low, Marston, Searle, & Rivington, 1882), and "The Fantastic Imagination" from *The Light Princess and Other Fairy Tales* (New York: G.P. Putnam's Sons, 1893).

INTRODUCTION

A man of vivid imagination, George MacDonald wrote in a great variety of literary genres, excelling in the creation of fairy tales, as he said, for children from seven to seventy. This anthology aspires to sample the best of his writings from each of these genres, with a view to conveying what C. S. Lewis praised most in the writer he considered his master: his genuine holiness. Among MacDonald's gifts is the ability to make goodness attractive and Christian living seem the only sensible course for one's life.

His vision is infectious. Discursively, it is cogently presented in his *Unspoken Sermons,* from which we have selected and abridged several. A part of its attraction lies not in the hope for an endless perpetuation of what one presently is, but in the expectation of becoming quite a different person, to whom life in God is endless bliss. He writes in one of the novels:

> He is not the greatest man who is the most independent, but he who . . . sees in his Self the one thing he can devote, the one precious means of freedom by its sacrifice, and that in no contempt or scorn, but in love to God and his children, the multitudes of his kind. By dying ever thus, ever thus losing his soul, he lives like God, and God knows him, and he knows God. This is too good to be grasped, but not too good to be true.

The larger one's hope, the larger one's nature, the more effective present relationships will be, and the larger the glory of the desired fulfillment. "It can not be selfishness to hunger and thirst after righteousness, which righteousness is just your duty to your God and your neighbor."[1]

To the objection that his system represents simply the human mind deceiving itself with its own dreams and desires, MacDonald insists that a person can know such is not the case only by practicing obedience to Christ's commands. Conviction will issue only from the doing, never from argument. When a person does the truth one sees, that person will grow to see further truths. To master a system of doctrine with no intention of obeying it is spiritually disastrous:

But the more familiar one becomes with any religious system, while yet the conscience and will are unawakened and obedience has not begun, the harder is it to enter into the kingdom of heaven. Such familiarity is a soul-killing experience, and great will be the excuse for some of those sons of religious parents who have gone further toward hell than many born and bred thieves and sinners.[2]

Truth, he felt, was something impossible for anyone entirely to comprehend short of that final revelation when the soul stands in the presence of its Maker. God's work is revelation; the universe exists for the unveiling of the Father in the Son. All things tend to this end, at constant cost to God—hence Calvary. But not only so: the entirety of creation represents an ongoing sacrificing of himself for the good of his children.

All people have the potential to grow towards final fulness of knowledge, but truth is apprehended bit by bit, and each person is capable of apprehending that truth that is appropriate to his present spiritual state and needs. To those who care not to be true in their innermost beings, "the truth itself must seem unsound, for the light that is in them is darkness."

At the heart of his writings, therefore, is a passionate belief in God, and the purpose of his writings is to induce a similar belief in his readers. But he insists that the God in whom he believes is not the God in whom the great majority of Christians believe. He exclaims to the skeptic, "But hear me this once more: the God, the Jesus, in whom I believe, are not the God, the Jesus, in whom you fancy I believe: you know them not; your idea of them is not mine. If you knew them you would believe in them, for to know them is to believe in them."[3] He says earlier in the novel that he would rather have no God than the God whom people casually think of when they think of Christianity.

George MacDonald was born on December 10, 1824, the second son of a strong-willed but gentle Scottish tenant farmer, at Huntly, in the Scottish Highlands. His rural upbringing, amid the measureless blessings of a lovingly disciplined and joyous home, instilled within him a fervent love of nature, of the Christian virtues, and of the God who is over all. He was educated in King's College, Aberdeen, and Highbury Theological College, London. In 1851 he married Louisa Powell, daughter of a prosperous

London merchant. Deeply feeling a call to present the gospel to his age but uncertain what form his servanthood should assume, he began his career by accepting a call to serve the Trinity Congregational Church at Arundel.

In this quiet village on the southern English coast he assumed his duties with conviction and compassion, but his desire to minister to people through writing kept growing. Then he began hemorrhaging from the lungs—a threatening indication of tuberculosis. Epidemic in his day, the dreaded disease had already taken many family members and would in the years to come take many more. During his immediate convalescence on the Isle of Wight, he composed a dramatic poem of some forty-five hundred lines, which he entitled *Within and Without*. Its melodramatic plot presents many of the insights into spiritual realities that would become his hallmark in future years. Its publication in 1855 established his name in contemporary literary circles as a young poet whose work was to be watched.

When many of the more influential members of his Calvinist congregation became disgruntled with his emphasis upon practical godliness and his larger vision of God's compassion extending to all people, he left, taking Louisa and their two daughters, Lilia and the newly born Mary, to the northern industrial city of Manchester. In utter poverty but complete trust in God, he undertook an independent ministry of preaching and lecturing from rented quarters.

No sooner had he found another congregation, however, when the hemorrhaging recurred and would not be stopped. A doctor friend, seeing him close to death, undertook with extreme daring to halt his loss of blood through bleeding from the arm. Miraculously, the scheme worked, but MacDonald lay in utter frailty for weeks, his strength refusing to return.

His poem *Within and Without,* however, became the means by which his health was returned to him. When Lady Byron, the poet's widow, read it, she determined to find the young writer whose work seemed to her so profoundly helpful in regard to the deep needs of the human spirit. Discovering him in his debility, she afforded him a trip to Algiers. After several months in the African sun, his strength returned.

Circumstances now indicating he should not return to a pulpit ministry, he settled in Hastings and gave himself to his writing. His early attempts at writing drama, fantasy, and novels, however, aroused little public enthusiasm. *Phantastes,* a book-length fantasy for adults published in 1858, occasioned so little public interest that publishers were reluctant to issue any more of his works. Some seventy years later C. S. Lewis would purchase a used copy in a railroad station and, as he was later to say, find it "baptized" his imagination. It was one of the chief factors effecting Lewis's conversion.

Sensing the possibility of conveying his convictions to a larger popular audience by writing novels, MacDonald worked persistently until in 1863 he was at last successful in finding a publisher for *David Elginbrod*. Its success among the reading public marked the beginning of his prolific novel-writing career, in which he published some thirty. Each novel embodies in the narrative a vision of the loving Father God manifesting himself in the lives of men and women through nature and circumstance. MacDonald's running commentary of poignant spiritual observations upon the characters and action remains a rich source of Christian insight into why people think and behave the way they do.

He felt that such basic themes as heroic exploits, evil overcome, and suffering that leads through restoration to triumph offer paradigms for the entire story of the human race, viewed from the standpoint of its denouement and ultimate resolution. A part of his interest as a novelist lies in his ability to discern and present these patterns in realistic settings, and to create believable characters in whose experiences they are evident. Since these archetypal patterns are not synonymous with plot, MacDonald's work must be assessed somewhat differently from the manner one assesses the fiction of a writer with exclusively naturalist and aesthetic concerns.

"He had yet to learn," MacDonald wrote about one of his characters, "that through 'the heartache and the thousand natural shocks that flesh is heir to,' people become capable of the blessedness to which all the legends of a golden age point."[4] The exigencies of plot are not ends in themselves, but they serve to illustrate spiritual effects. "No story ends in this world," he said; he viewed his characters in the light of eternity. When he commented that his novel *St. George and St. Michael* was "a story of hearts rather than fortunes," he was in essence speaking about all his fiction.[5]

Provocative as one may find his novels to be, his talents have their highest expression in his fantasies and fairy tales, such as *The Golden Key, The Princess and the Goblin, The Princess and Curdie,* and *At the Back of the North Wind.* In them his imagination, roaming unfettered by any considerations other than the moral and spiritual ones with which he is preoccupied, achieves a yet purer vision of mythic patterns. Such scenes as Curdie being asked by his great-great grandmother to thrust his hands into the fire of flaming roses, or Tangle being told by the Old Man of the Earth that she must throw herself into a great dark hole, for "there is no other way," are among his most memorable. These moments may well grip the imagination and reside in the reader's memory as strongly as any scenes from the great literature of the past.

Much of their strength lies in their symbolism. Their significances may seem ineffable, more compellingly real than words can capture. The principles they suggest may perhaps be stated abstractly—that painful trials are necessary for the good they yield, and that one must by faith die into life—but to no one's satisfaction. The term *allegory* is commonly applied to stories whose images have values that may be readily contained in abstract statement, but he invariably bristled when his fantasies were spoken of as allegorical. One "must be an artist indeed," he observed, "who can . . . produce a strict allegory that is not a weariness to the spirit." He affirmed that a fairy tale may contain allegory, and indeed there are moments in his work when his symbols veer close to becoming allegorical in the definiteness of their abstract significances, but their strength lies in the dynamic of their symbolic suggestions. They have an imaginative power that indeed dismisses weariness.

George MacDonald was very like the prior romantics Blake, Wordsworth, and Coleridge—whose thought influenced him appreciably—in his view of the necessity of the imagination in the pursuit of truth. "It is God who gives thee thy mirror of imagination," he wrote, "and if thou keep it clean, it will give thee back no shadow but of the truth."[6] He nevertheless recognized the necessity for abstract thinking, offering in his sermons and essays a comprehensive and coherent system of his own (although he was careful not to systematize it). He felt that intellectual and rational approaches to experience concern themselves mainly with the look of things and give us analytical explanations leading to systems of reality that are only abstract; imaginative visions of the pure in heart alone perceive what eternally is. In order to reach to ultimate truth, the intellect is obliged to work through the imagination.

Truth to MacDonald was a Person, not a creed. When Christ, the Spirit of Truth, is received and his words obeyed, the individual participates in the process of becoming a true person. All aspects of experience may nurture this process, for the Spirit of God is present throughout his world; his truth is organic and dynamic. The first significance of the physical world is that it incarnates the spiritual. Existence itself is the embodiment of God's thought; it is what it is because God is thinking it. Further, God offers all experience to people as sacrament. Grace comes through it, according to one's need.

A person is able to view life rightly as one succeeds in discerning the thoughts of God that are resident in things. To do so requires a reorientation of mind to the world of spirit. For the world that a given individual sees is that individual's mind turned inside out. If MacDonald read Blake's proverb that a fool does not see the same tree that a wise man sees, he agreed with it. The person who wills God's will sees in a tree something of the glory God is investing in it, and profits spiritually. The person who sees it only as a botanist would, or a lumberman, may have a practical view of its structure or of its uses, but does not see the truth of the tree.

Human experience itself, in a world so conceived, constantly has eternal significance. Story, therefore, which imaginatively contemplates the experience and behavior of people, can portray a vision of the true nature and import of life with power and insight. Thoughtfully presented and shaped by the deeper patterns of human existence, it has a much larger capacity to contain truth than does pure exposition.

He blended such latitudinarian attitudes with some stern insistences. Although he saw spiritual energies as flowing through the physical, he also saw the world as fallen and the natural tendencies of human nature as inclining to evil. In the beginning of *The Princess and Curdie,* Curdie discovers he had been "always doing wrong, and the wrong had soaked all through" him, so that his spirit must be awakened in order to see the mysterious Princess Grandmother, and his hands conditioned in the rose fire before he can do her bidding. At the ending, after Irene and Curdie as king and queen have died, the people of Gwyntystorm rapidly revert to their former wickedness. No one knew better than MacDonald that the central reality of life is that of spiritual struggle between the forces of good and evil. And the realm of the spirit is a realm of paradox: one dies into life; the way down is the way up; and the meek alone will inherit the earth. One must meet God through the struggles of fallen human experience; a mere rational understanding of him will not suffice. Genuine spiritual growth is hard-won.

With self-deprecation, self-discipline, and something of a Scottish sternness, he sought for personal holiness that issued from conscientious obedience in the midst of the struggles of life, together with a constant cultivation of a sense of the Divine Presence. His *Book of Strife in the form of a diary of an old soul,* at least in part the product of the all but overwhelming grief he and Louisa felt at the deaths, within a year, of their children Mary and Maurice, is one of the most remarkable records in all literature of an earnest soul's diligent and painstaking wrestling with the inexorable aspects of experience in order to discern God's presence and purpose.

One of the most revealing chronicles of the inner life of the MacDonald family is their *Dramatic Illustrations of Passages from the Second Part of The Pilgrim's Progress.* When their children had been quite young, the parents read them fairy tales dramatically, MacDonald on occasion on all fours among the children acting out parts along with them. They were pleased to see how quickly the children themselves assumed different characters and thoroughly enjoyed the roles. Louisa rewrote their favorite stories as children's dramas, even making simple props to accompany the presentations.

When many of the children were teenagers, the family moved to The Retreat in Hammersmith, a western suburb of London. There they converted a part of the coachhouse in the yard into a small theatre. The boys exercised their flair for construction by building a movable outdoor stage; the girls sewed costumes and painted curtain backdrops. Their own favorite among their productions was their version of the "Beauty and the Beast."

During a period of especial financial hardship in 1876, Louisa conceived the idea of going public with their family acting troupe and charging a small fee from the viewers. When they presented a farce entitled "Obstinacy" to the Working Women's College in London in May, they were elated to find it enthusiastically received. Their hope to incorporate their Christian concerns into this activity prompted Louisa's adapting for the stage the second part of John Bunyan's classic.

She reworked his imaginatively vivid rendition of the Christian life as a perilous journey toward the Celestial City, staying remarkably true to Bunyan's text but investing the dialogue with MacDonald's own emphasis upon Christian experience, as opposed to Bunyan's insistence on a rational grasp of Calvinist doctrine. With MacDonald as Greatheart and their highly talented oldest daughter Lilia as Christiana, the effort was so successful that several entire summers were given to their presenting their work in churches and public halls all across Britain and the Italian Riviera, where they lived after 1877.

MacDonald rose to become in his own time an immensely popular religious writer among the laity in both Britain and America, publishing altogether some fifty-two volumes. Many of his novels passed through numerous editions, some up to a dozen in his own lifetime. He also lectured widely, touring the United States in 1873. Afflicted with a weak constitution and sickly during much of his long life, with first tuberculosis, then asthma and eczema—and almost constantly poor—he always faced adversity with courage and faith. "So sure am I that many things which illness has led me to see are true, that I would endlessly rather never be well than lose sight of them," he remarked. His anagram, based on the letters of his name, was "Corage, God mend al." He spent many of his later years in Italy, and died in 1905.

MacDonald was singularly unconcerned with his own "image" among his fellow men, preoccupied rather with championing his vision of the reality of the world of the spirit. "Perhaps the highest moral height which a man can reach," he wrote, ". . . is the willingness to be *nothing* relatively, so that he attain that positive excellence which the original conditions of his being render not merely possible, but imperative. It is nothing to a man to be greater or less than another—to be esteemed or otherwise by the public or private world in which he moves." He determined to leave his reputation and destiny in the hands of his God.

ENDNOTES

1. *Paul Faber, Surgeon,* chapter 30.
2. Ibid., chapter 17.
3. *Paul Faber, Surgeon,* chapter 54.
4. *Alec Forbes of Howglen,* chapter 39.
5. Ibid., chapter 41.
6. *Paul Faber, Surgeon,* chapter 7.

THE LIFE OF GEORGE MACDONALD

1792   Father, George MacDonald Senior, born.

1822   Father marries Helen MacKay. Louisa Powell born to James and Phoebe Powell, 5 November in London.

1823   Brother Charles born.

1824   George MacDonald born 10 December.

1826(?) Brother James born. Dies at age of eight.

1827   Brother Alexander born.

1829   Brother John MacKay dies in infancy.

1830   Brother John Hill born.

1832   Helen MacDonald dies.

1839   Father marries Margaret McColl.

1840   MacDonald attends Aulton Grammar School, Aberdeen. Wins bursary to King's College, Aberdeen.

1843   Misses a session at King's. Teaches Latin, Greek, and arithmetic at Aberdeen Central Academy. Free Church of Scotland formed.

1844   Louisa's brother Alexander marries George's cousin Helen MacKay, occasioning his introduction to Powell family.

1845   Receives Master of Arts degree in April. Becomes a tutor in Fulham, London.

1847   Has deepening Christian experience and begins to feel call to Christian ministry.

1848   Visits Huntly. Enrolls in Highbury Theological College, Highbury Park, London. Proposes to Louisa.

1849   Has apprentice pastorate at Whitehaven, Cumbria. Louisa's mother dies. Takes apprentice pastorate in Cork, Ireland.

1850   Completes his theological course at Highbury in June. Receives call to Trinity Congregational Church in Arundel, Sussex, on 3 October. Experiences severe hemorrhaging from lungs in November and convalesces on Isle of Wight. Begins composition of long dramatic poem, *Within and Without*.

1851   Resumes pastoral responsibilities in January. Marries Louisa on 8 March in Hackney. Ordained to the Congregational ministry in June, John Godwin, a professor at Highbury, presiding.

1852   Lilia Scott born 4 January. Alec, afflicted with tuberculosis, visits in March. MacDonald's congregation, dissatisfied with his preaching, reduces his salary by almost two-thirds.

1853   Alec dies in March at Huntly. MacDonald publishes article on Robert Browning's "Christmas Eve" in *The Christian Spectator* in May. Resigns from his church in May. Mary Josephine born 23 July. Family moves to Manchester, where A. J. Scott is Principal of Owens College. Performs marriage of John Godwin to Charlotte Powell in August. Brother John goes to Moscow to teach. Applies unsuccessfully for post of librarian at Owens College.

1854   Stricken with severe hemorrhaging from lungs. Family moves to Alderly Cross, then to 3 Camp Terrace, Lower Broughton. Teaches English literature in his home. Grows a beard. Preaches from rented quarters on Renshaw Street, Manchester. Publishes "The Broken Swords" in *The Christian Spectator*. Caroline Grace born 16 September. Attends a lecture by Frederick Denison Maurice in London.

1855 *Within and Without* published by Longman's. Receives laudatory reviews. Lady Byron is much impressed with it. Visits Huntly in July. Isabella, his half-sister, dies in August. Accepts call to congregation at Bolton. Almost dies from hemorrhaging from lungs in November.

1856 Greville born 20 January. Convalesces at Kingswear. Family visits Huntly in June. Leaves with Louisa and Mary for Algiers in November, a trip sponsored by Lady Byron for MacDonald's health.

1857 Returns to London in May. Moves to Huntly Cottage, Hastings. Visits Huntly. *Poems* published in July. Irene born 31 August.

1858 *Phantastes* published by Smith and Elder. John visits, ill with tuberculosis; returns to Huntly; dies 7 July, followed by George Senior on 24 August. Both buried in Drumblade churchyard. Winifred Louisa born 6 November.

1859 Begins travelling lecture tours. Composes a drama, "If I Had a Father," then turns it into a novel, *Seekers and Finders,* with no publisher interest in either. Meets Charles L. Dodgson (Lewis Carroll). Assumes chair of English literature at Bedford College, London, and moves to 18 Queen Square, Bloomsbury.

1860 *The Portent* appears in *Cornhill Magazine*. Submits article on Percy Bysshe Shelly for 1860 edition of *Encyclopedia Britannica*. Lady Byron dies in May. Moves to Tudor Lodge, Regent's Park. Ronald born 27 October. Meets John Ruskin.

1862   Moves to 12 Earles Terrace, Kennsington.

1863   *David Elginbrod* published. Praised by reviewers.

1864   *Adela Cathcart* published. Maurice born 7 February.

1865   MacDonald and two friends take trip to Switzerland in July. Applies unsuccessfully for professorship of rhetoric and belles lettres at the University of Edinburgh. Meets Thomas Carlyle. Bernard Powell born 28 September. *Alec Forbes of Howglen* published.

1866   Becomes member of the Church of England at Chapel of St. Peter's, Vere Street. Begins lecturing to evening classes at King's College, London.

1867   *The Disciple and Other Poems, Dealings with the Fairies, Annals of a Quiet Neighbourhood,* and *Unspoken Sermons* published. George MacKay born 23 January, completing the family. MacDonald takes a parish for the summer at Kilkhampton. Family moves to The Retreat, Upper Mall, Hammersmith.

1868   *Robert Falconer, Guild Court,* and *The Seaboard Parish* published. Family begins giving dramatic and musical "entertainments" regularly for the London poor, MacDonald being involved with the housing projects of John Ruskin and Octavia Hill. Resigns his post at King's 27 March. Awarded LLD degree by University of Aberdeen.

1869   Becomes editor of *Good Words for the Young.* Falls deathly ill on yachting trip to Lofoten Islands; recovery long and slow.

1870   James Powell dies 20 June. Family secures auxiliary residence at Hastings for their health. *The Miracles of Our Lord* published. Louisa publishes *Chamber Dramas for Children.*

1871   *At the Back of the North Wind, Works of Fancy and Imagination,* and *Ranald Bannerman's Boyhood* published.

1872   *Wilfrid Cumbermede, The Vicar's Daughter,* and *The Princess and the Goblin* published. In September arrives in America for nine-month lecture tour.

1873   Return from America in May. *Gutta Percha Willie* published. Mary becomes engaged to Ted Hughes.

1875   *Malcolm* published. Tennyson visits at The Retreat. The family moves to Great Tangley Manor at Wonersh, and in the fall to Corage at Boscombe for MacDonald's and Mary's health.

1876   *Exotics, St. George and St. Michael, Thomas Wingfold, Curate,* and *A Double Story (The Wise Woman)* published. MacDonald involved in religious conferences at Broadlands. Family begins public performances of plays.

1877   *Pilgrim's Progress, Part 2* performed at Christchurch, Hampshire, 8 March, with Princess Louise present. *The Marquis of Lossie* published. Moves to Italy for Mary's health, settling at Nervi. Greville passes medical examinations. Queen Victoria awards MacDonald a Civil Lists Pension.

1878   Mary dies 27 April. William Morris takes The Retreat. MacDonalds move to Villa Barratta at Porto Fino.

1879   Maurice dies 5 March. *Paul Faber, Surgeon,* and *Sir Gibbie* published. Spends summer at Corage.

1880   *A Book of Strife in the form of the diary of an old soul* published. Family settles at Bordighera, Italy, and builds Casa Coraggio.

1881   *Mary Marston* published. Grace married to Kingsbury Jameson in Rome.

1882   *Warlock O'Glenwarlock, Weighed and Wanting, Orts, The Princess and Curdie,* and *The Gifts of the Child Christ* published. Grace gives birth to Octavia Grace 17 March.

1883   *Donal Grant* published.

1884   Grace dies 5 May. Greville attempts medical practice in Florence.

1885   *The Tragedie of Hamlet* published.

1886   *What's Mine's Mine* and *Unspoken Sermons, Series Two* published.

1887   Earthquake occurs at Bordighera 27 February, damaging Casa Coraggio. *Home Again* published.

1888   Greville marries Pheobe Winn, and Ronald marries Louise Vivenda Blandy. MacKay and Bernard attend Cambridge. *The Elect Lady* published.

1889   *Unspoken Sermons, Series Three* published. Ronald emigrates to America, becoming headmaster of Ravenscroft School in Asheville, North Carolina.

1890   Completes first manuscript of *Lilith*. Lilia visits Ronald and Vivenda in Ashville. Vivenda dies. Bernard marries Belinda Bird.

1891   *A Rough Shaking, The Flight of the Shadow,* and *There and Back* published. Octavia Grace dies in February. MacDonald gives final lecture series. Lilia dies 22 November.

1892   *A Cabinet of Gems* and *The Hope of the Gospel* published.

1893   *Scotch Songs and Ballads, The Poetical Works of George MacDonald,* 2 vols., and *Heather and Snow* published.

1897   *Rampolli* and *Salted with Fire* published. Winifred marries C. Edward Troup 2 January.

1899   *Far Above Rubies* appears in Christmas issue of the *Sketch* (published 1899 by Dodd, Mead).

1900   Moves to St. George's Wood, near Haslemere.

1901   Fiftieth wedding celebration, 8 June.

1902   Louisa dies, 13 January.

1905   MacDonald dies 18 September at Winifred's home, Ashtead, Surrey. Cremated, his ashes buried in Louisa's grave in the Stranger's Cemetery, Bordighera.

Letters

INTRODUCTION

George MacDonald wrote literally thousands of letters during his life. His activities often took him away from his family, and he established many friendships across the United Kingdom. Writing was the only means of communication when one was at a distance. Feeling deeply the momentous significance of the truths that mattered most to him, he wrote freely about them. In times of distress, he possessed the ability to enter imaginatively into the needs of those with whom he was corresponding. His letters are a powerful record of his mind and spirit.

He must first be understood in terms of the religious climate in the churches of his day. A rigid intellectualism prevailed. Christianity was too often a religion of the head rather than the heart; doctrinal precision was highly esteemed, and the spirit of sectarianism was rife. MacDonald as a young pastor confronted this dominant attitude, feeling that most churches had replaced the spirit of devotion to Christ and the desire to live in obedience to Christ's precepts with a spirit of cold rigidity, combined with material preoccupations.

The first letter below shows him in the throes of this confrontation. It arises from a period of uncertainty and stress in his early married life. He had just left the Trinity Congregational Church in Arundel because of insurmountable differences between his view of the essence of the Christian life and message and theirs. He was reluctant to take another church, yet he felt the call to Christian ministry; he desired to be a poet and writer, yet could by no means make a living from his pen.

To Louisa
28 October 1853

In October of 1853 he visited the northern industrial city of Manchester at the invitation of his brother Charles, who was in business there, to see what possibilities might exist for him. After preaching on a Sunday morning to an unresponsive congregation, he wrote to Louisa from the home of his host. She was back in Arundel with their two small daughters.

Portions of the letter show his attitudes toward his situation, the state of his own spiritual life, the message he was convinced he had from God, and the vibrancy of his hope. The material that follows his signature is from that written across the letter, on top of and at right angles to the primary text (to save postage), suggesting how full his mind was with that which he was saying.

Preston, Sunday Afternoon
28 October 1853

My dearest wife,

I have left the mamma and four children in the dining room and come here—to the study to write to you—which is more interesting than sitting with another man's wife and children. It is *very* cold and I am surprised I did not suffer more in the chapel—for it has not been warmed yet—especially as I had a less interested, or perhaps interesting congregation then usual, though a large one. They were not listless at all, but I was not quite satisfied with their countenances, so though I was not at all embarrassed in preaching, my sermon was more didactic than sympathetic. I saw Mr. Spence before he left last night, and found him *very much* improved. The change of feeling on many points of common belief spreads much among the ministers, although of course most can only follow in the wake of the few. . . .

How have you spent the day, dearest? It is a very good thing for us to be parted sometimes. It makes us think more, both more truly about each other, and less interruptedly about our God. He is the Truth, and all that we can see to be beautiful and true is in Him and we were taught by Him to see it. Perhaps it is a very bad want of faith in him to doubt whether he means what we see. But he knows too that it is impossible for us to be good all at once, and to be good at all without him. So we must seek him. We may however say to ourselves—one day these souls of ours will blossom into the full sunshine—when all that is desireable in the commonness of daily love, and all we long for of wonder and mystery and the look of Christmas time will be joined in one, and we shall walk as in a wondrous dream yet with more sense of reality than our most waking joy now gives us.

How is my Lily? and my sweet Blackbird. She laughs as the bluebird sings. I hope dear love your cold is better. You are a dear good wife—and your husband loves you.

I am your own
George MacDonald

. . . . A true Revival is springing up, and kept down I suppose in other quarters besides Arundel by those who cry most for it. But our great danger is of acting on feeling as a party. I wish to ignore and forget all opposition and be in a condition in which I can do my work for the Truth's sake, without any reference to others as opposing my teaching. We ought never to wish to overcome because *we* are the fighters. Never feel—there is *my* Truth—the hardest lesson to learn. Every higher stage of Truth brings with it its own Temptation like that in the Wilderness, and if one overcomes not in that, he overcomes not at all. The struggle may be hard. I would I could be sure of the struggle, and then I should of the victory. But Jesus overcame in the truest spiritual fight—So shall we overcome, too. Our God will surely help us to attain to that which he himself loves most. Oh dearest, whatever you may feel about our homeless condition at present, I hope it has helped to teach your husband some things. Pray for him that he may not forget them but that he may be all God's and then let God give him what he will. We may wait a little for a home here, for all the universe is ours and all time and the very thought of God himself.

Again, dearest, your Husband.

To "W"
31 January 1886

Although he deeply opposed every vestige of the sectarian spirit, Mac-Donald knew what he believed as to the great essential verities of the Christian faith. His convictions—which he formed early and essentially held intact throughout his lifetime—were the result of much careful thought and prolonged consideration, as he had a need constantly to rethink his positions, but he never wavered from his characteristic conclusions. Neither did he feel it his mission to argue with his fellow Christians concerning them. One of his favorite texts was: "If any man will do his will, he shall know of the doctrine . . ." (John 7:17, KJV); God gives to believers who put obedience to his precepts above all else, truth sufficient for their practical needs. One's obedience to the divine commands is essential to the quality of one's Christianity; a sense of certainty concerning one's intellectual positions is not. Arguments about them distract one's energies and arouse rancor in one's spirit.

He therefore loathed argument, refusing to become involved in discussions on doctrinal issues treated as ends in themselves. The positions he took in his many writings were, however, controversial, and on rare occasions in spite of his firm intentions he found himself in verbal exchange. On one occasion, staying overnight in a home while on a lecture tour, his overbearing host forced him into such a conversation. After returning home, he received from his host a letter underscoring the latter's view of doctrinal truths. MacDonald responded with the following letter. It is as precise a statement of his attitudes as exists among his writings.

Bordighera
31 January 1886

Dear W_____

When I had the pleasure of being your guest I entered with you into a conversation such as I am in general far from favourable to, believing it not at all conducive to profit. Had you been a stranger, I should have avoided or declined the argument. But in answer to your letter, I reply thus far, that your presentation of your opinions, which are the same as from childhood I was familiar with, I refuse entirely as the truth, holding them as the merest invention of the human intellect in the attempt to explain things which the spirit of the Son of Man alone can make any man understand for his salvation.

If however any man ask me, as you do in your letter, to give in its stead the attempt of my intellect to explain the same things, I answer, far be it from me to do so! I am not going to replace in the same kind in dried and petrified form, what I see of the truth, favouring thus the idea that anything else whatever than a vital union with

5

Christ, as of the members with the body, as of the branches of the vine, is of any avail to the well-being of a man. It is in no sense what we believe about Christ, or what way we would explain his work, that constitutes or can be the object of faith. No belief in the atonement, for instance, whether that atonement be explained or understood right or wrong, no belief in what the theologians call the merits of Christ, is in the smallest degree or approximation what the Lord or his apostles meant by faith in him. It is to take him as our Lord and Master, obey his words, be prepared to die for him; it is to take on us the yoke his father laid on him and regard the will of God as the one thing worthy of a man's care and endeavour—as indeed our very life—that, and nothing less than that, is faith in the Son of God.

Then as to all things that are necessary for our growth in the Divine life, that is, for growing like to him in whose image we are made, he promises to teach us by his spirit everything. Nor even if a man could, which is impossible, know with his understanding the deepest mysteries, would these avail him the least, that would not constitute the knowledge of them after the true fashion: they must be spiritually discerned—in a way that no man can by any possibility teach his neighbour, but which only the Spirit of God can teach. I think and believe that the mischief done to the kingdom of Christ by teaching of what is called doctrine by theologians, and calling that teaching the Gospel, instead of presenting Christ as he presented himself, and took a whole life of labour to present himself, is enormous, and the cause of a huge part of the infidelity in the world. Let us follow the Lord, studying the mind of him, and not what the scribes and the elders teach about him.

If any man come to me with theological questions, if I find that they are troubling him, and keeping him from giving himself to God, I do my best to remove any such obstructions as are the result of man's handling of the eternal things: what I count false, I will not spare. But if the man come to me only for the sake of conference on the matter, I will hold none. Let him get what teaching he is capable of receiving from his knowledge of Christ, and the spirit given him. If he is satisfied with the theology he has learned, I should give myself no trouble to alter his opinion. I should do him no good either by success or failure in the attempt. I have other things altogether to do.

I have to take up my cross and follow the master first, and then persuade him who will be persuaded to come with me. He is the atonement, and through him, through knowing him and being every day, every hour, every moment taught by him, I shall become pure in heart, and shall at length see God. No doctrine shall come between me and him. Nor will he come between anyone and God save to lead him home to the Father. The whole mischief has come of people setting themselves to understand rather than to do, to arrange God's business for him, and tell other people what the Father meant, instead of doing what the Father tells them, and then teaching others to do the same.

If I am told that I am not definite—that something more definite is needed, I say your definiteness is one that God does not care about, for he has given no such system as you desire. But, I ask, is not the living man, the human God, after his 3 and 30 years on earth, poor and scanty as are the records of him, a definite enough object of faith for your turn? He is not, I grant you, for the kind of definiteness you would have, which is to reduce the infinite within the bounds of a legal document; but for life, for the joy of deliverance, for the glory of real creation, for the partakings of the divine nature, for the gaining of a faith that shall remove mountains, and for deliverance from all the crushing commonplaces of would-be teachers of religion, who present us with a God so poor and small that to believe in him is an insult to him who created the human heart—the story of the eternal Son of God, who knew and loved his father so that he delighted to die in the manifestation of him to his brothers and sisters, is enough, triumphantly enough. To have to believe in the God of the Calvinist would drive me to madness or atheism; to believe in the God of our Lord Jesus Christ, is to feel that, if such God there be, all is well, he may do with me as he pleases. I am blest.

Thus, or somehow thus, I would answer any man who pressed me to be more definite. Not that I could not give what seemed to me the best of reasons why the Lord should die, but if I set them out, it shall be in a vital fashion, and not in a *hortus siccus* of heavenly flowers.[1]

[1. Latin for "a dry garden."]

So far, my dear sir, I have answered, so far I have declined to answer your letter. I have other reasons also, the result of a long life's experience in these regions, for doing as I have done. But the day will come for saying anything. May we be of those who walking the streets of the New Jerusalem hold sweet counsel together without danger of being misunderstood.[2]

To Andrew Pym
20 April 1888

The following letter was written to Andrew Pym, a brother of Eva, who was a close friend of the MacDonalds' oldest daughter, Lilia. Eva spent much time with them in their Italian home and died there of tuberculosis in 1891. A close friend of her parents, George MacDonald evidently was less well acquainted with Andrew, a sailor who came home ill. Perhaps prompted by Eva's concern for her brother's spiritual state, he wrote the following letter to him. It illustrates his manner in approaching the unconverted.

Bordighera
20 April 1888

My dear Andy,

We are all concerned to hear that you are not so well, though after such a journey and in such weather we cannot be surprised. If it were not for your father and mother who have the right and the joy to have you I could say wish you were here, for the weather is now growing balmy, and the best of the year is coming in. But so I hope it is with you also.

You have seen ever so much more of the outside world than I have, and when you are lying awake at night, or ill in the day, I suppose many scenes strange to me will come back to you with familiar looks: but there is another, the inside world, of thought and

[2. Being a copy contained in a family album in the MacDonald Collection at the Beinecke Rare Book and Manuscript Library, the letter is unsigned.]

feeling and need and longing, into which, being so much older than you, I must have withdrawn more than you—like a snail to the inside of its shell; and I have learned to be sure that even if I had everything I could wish for in the outside world: if even I were strong enough to meet with delight the storms you know so well, and have battled with so often, there would be something wanting inside, in that other world, if I did not feel that the Power by which I am here, a glad human soul, was there present with one, and telling me he is my father, my friend, far too grand and good ever to forget the being he has called into life, and who cannot keep himself alive or do anything by his own power.

If I had made but a sparrow, I would be very careful over that sparrow; and the Lord who knows his father perfectly tells us that he cares for the sparrows he makes, and much more for us. You see what I am driving at, Andy: I want you to think over and again, for my sake, however often you think it for yourself, that God is just the one haven you have to make for in this storm. Say to him, My Father, I belong to thee, and I am ill, and I cannot help myself; be my Father and keep near me, and do what thou wilt with me, only take care of thy child, and let him know thou art taking care of me.

You know me, Andy, and would hardly expect me to be able to write to you without saying something about the only things I care for. I cannot tell you how happy the thought of God makes me. When I was a child, and was hardly able to breathe for pain, I felt all right when my father came to me; and so now I am a man I feel of my higher father, the father of all fathers, and that without thinking any less but far more of my earthly father, to see whom again is one of the greatest joys I expect when I have to follow him—as cannot be very long now.

Eva is pretty well for her, though sad because she loves you, and you are not so well. We all love you, and would do anything we could for you. Madre in especial sends you her love. And I should like to send mine in particular to your father. We fathers know a thing or two that you young ones don't.

But Willie is come to fetch my letter—so good night for the present. I hope we shall hear soon that you are more comfortable.

Yours affectionately
George MacDonald

Andy Pym never read this letter, as he died before it reached him.

To Susan Scott
12 January 1888

Among the most moving of MacDonald's letters are those of condolence. He often wrote these several weeks after the loved one's demise, knowing well the sense of emptiness and longing that may afflict those who mourn increasingly for some time after the event. His understanding of such sorrow was hard-earned, having, by 1888, lost his parents, two brothers, a half-sister, and three of his own children (most to tuberculosis), to say nothing of numerous close friends. The first was written to Susan Scott, daughter of A. J. Scott, a teacher and friend whom MacDonald greatly admired.

Bordighera
12 January 1888

My dear Susan,

You will be missing your mother more now than when first she went away! As the days go on and the common look gathers again upon the things round you, and the Kingdom of heaven seems no nearer, we are apt to feel more of a separation. There seems sometimes to be nowhere beyond, because no voice comes back from the beloved. This parting seems so complete at times. Why is all so dumb? Why no personal revelation of the world to which they are gone?

God knows and cares, and uses for us a means of education for our hearts and spirits which we do not ourselves understand. It is not needful that we understand the motive power in the processes that go on within us. It is enough to him who believes it that the Lord *did* rise again, although after that he was hidden from their sight. Yes, I will believe that I shall hold my own in my arms again, their hearts nearer to mine than ever before.

It is a blessed thing to be children and to be parents of children. So God binds us all together. You and I have much to thank God for that we came of such parents. And we shall see them again and our hearts shall rejoice. For what is true of the Lord is true of all his, for they are one with him.

I need not say to you that I owe your father and mother more than I can tell. I looked up to your father more than to any man except my own father, who did not know half so much, but who was worthy of knowing whatever God taught him. We *shall* see them all and love them more and more in all eternity . . . .

Yours affectionately
George MacDonald

To Eva Pym
28 September 1889

To Eva Pym:

Old Palace
Richmond
28 September 1889

My very dear Eva,

I write to you but I mean you all when I write. If you saw how occupied I have been you would not wonder much that I had not written to you before. But indeed I often put off writing to such as are in your sorrow, because I know that a time comes, worse than the first, and a word then is sometimes more of a help.

I wish I could just flash into your minds all I think about these partings! only perhaps you are thinking better things than I am thinking, and find the same impossibility of showing them.

I loved and love your father and look forward to having many talks with him yet. He is out of our sight, but God sees him alive—and many who love him also see him alive; and when our time comes to go—not like the demons out into the void, but home, home, home! we also shall see and love him more than ever.

For God goes on to be good. He never changes, nor cares less, for his children one time than another.

We come into the world to learn to love, and have done with taking care of ourselves; and he whose one desire is to have his children love, cannot take them from each other after they have learned to love each other. The thing is not to be reasoned about; it does not need it.

Now for your outlook into the future, I send you a word I wrote since coming here:

> Go not forth to call thy sorrow
> From the dim fields of tomorrow;
> Let her roam there all unheeded;
> She will come when she is needed;
> But when she draws nigh the door,
> She will find God there before.

You, my dear Eva, I shall see in a month or so. I wish I could say the same for more of you.

But God be with you all, and then all is well. None of us will know, or I think will ever know, though we go on learning it for ever, how perfectly gloriously good and unselfish our Father in heaven is. We might let him have his way with us.

Your loving friend
George MacDonald

To Adelaide Pym
8 February 1890

To Adelaide Pym:

Bordighera
8 February 1890

My dear Adelaide,
Let my heart come near to yours, and talk a little bit to it. If you are not able to listen, you can easily say to my messenger, "Wait till I can hear you."

We are all just children in our Father's nursery. Some of us are taken before others away from it, and we are left without our playmates. But we know the father has them, and though we must miss them constantly, we must remember that we shall be sent for by and by, and must by patient waiting be ready to go. You know all this as well as I do, but let us think it together.

What is all this life but a waiting? You who have suffered so much, must know that better than most! For myself, I have never been content with this world as a place to live in. I mean it has always, more and less, had the feel of a foreign land. The feeling has not been caused by much suffering, neither by any sense of outside failure. No doubt the world has been less satisfactory because of my own evil and great lack; but allowing for all that, there remains a something that indicates that it was never intended to be our home, and we were never intended to feel at home in it.

We must not then be unhappy when one of us goes to make the others happier who have gone before, and were waiting for them, and are now waiting for us to join them! The very notion of heaven is to have all we love with us, and God is just carrying out that notion for us, by gentle recurrent removals as we are ready to go. It seems so commonplace when said to a sore heart—missing heart—but surely what you and anyone like you, and in such sorrow, needs is to "have your pure mind stirred up by way of remembrance."

But God has a marvellous bliss, and yet a very homely one, waiting for us. Be sure it will run in the old grooves, but the grooves will be of gold and gems, not of iron and clay. I think we shall talk of all the old times with the hearts of divinely glad little ones—and sometimes wonder that we made such a work about certain things. We shall have everything, for the father who loves us, and is himself, as Dante calls him, "the glad creator," will see that his dear little ones are happy indeed, and have all they want. It will be safe then to give us all we want, for we shall not forget him, or forget that he gives us EVERYTHING.

And then what a thing it will be to feel our bodies as free, as little held down and oppressed, as our better part! Of course the great joy of heaven will be the same as that of this world—to know God and to be what he is; but we shall know him so much better then, and know how foolish it was of us to be troubled about anything when HE was looking after everything! There will be no question whether life is worth living to those who know what life means.

Things are just as right as they could be, so far as God is concerned, for the making us capable of his own joy in life. The only thing amiss is that we put our hope in other things than God, and wish things that are not worth giving us, and which therefore he does not care to give us, and so we do not work along with him for what he wants us to be and thereby delay the success of his work with us. For there is nothing good but being one with him in every desire and hope and joy.

My heart says these things to your heart, dear Adelaide, because they are life to it—or rather He who makes them truth, and is the truth, is life to it. He is our elder brother, watching ever for our good. We know what it is to have brothers to love; what is it to have a brother to love perfectly because he is a perfect brother!

So you must love Beatrice more than ever, and more yet, and wait in strong expecting patience: she will be more lovely still by the time we see her again—though that cannot be very long. Day runs so swiftly after day, and our "salvation" is nearer than when we believed. . . .

Affectionately the friend of so many of you
George MacDonald

To Lily
4 January 1891

George and Louisa had eleven children. Their family life was close and affections were strong. In 1890 Lilia, their oldest, went to visit her brother Ronald and his wife Vivenda in Asheville, North Carolina, where he was teaching. While she was there—for her fortieth birthday—her father penned her the following letter.

MacDonald held tender feelings for all his children, but especially for his first-born. A highly talented woman, she was in many ways the emotional center of family life because of her kind and selfless ways. As it happened, Lilia returned from America in May, shortly thereafter to be diagnosed with tuberculosis, and died in her father's arms that November. Already having lost three of their children—Mary, Maurice, and Grace—Lilia's death was an immense grief, requiring all the resources of his faith to endure.

C. C. B.
4 January 1891

Dearest Child,

I could say so much to you, and yet I am constantly surrounded by a sort of cactus-hedge that seems to make adequate utterance impossible. It is so much easier to write romance, where you cannot easily lie, than to say the commonest things where you may go wrong any moment. Even this is not the kind of way I meant to write to you. It is all wrong. I can only tell you I love you with true heart fervently, and love you far more because you are God's child than because you are mine.

I don't thank you for coming to us, for you could not help it, but the whole universe is "tented" with love, and you hold one of the corners of the great love-canopy for your mother and me. I don't think I am very ambitious, except the strong desire "to go where I am" be ambition; and I know I take small satisfaction in looking on my past, but I do live expecting great things in the life that is ripening for me and all mine—when we shall all have the universe for our own, and be good merry helpful children in the great house of our father. I think then we shall be able to pass into and through each others very souls as we please, knowing each other's thought and being, along with our own, and so being *like* God. When we are all just as loving and unselfish as Jesus; when like him, our one thought of delight is that God is, and is what he is; when the fact that a being is just another person from ourselves, is enough to make that being precious—then, darling, you and I and all will have the grand liberty wherewith Christ makes free—opening his hand to send us out like white doves to range the universe.

Have I not shown that the attempt to speak what you mean is the same kind of failure that walking is—a mere, constantly recurring, recovery from falling. . . .

Tell Ronald from me that Novalis says: "This world is not a dream, but it may, and perhaps ought to become one." Anyhow, it will pass—to make way for the world God has hidden in our hearts.

Darling, I wish you life eternal. I daresay the birthdays will still be sparks in its glory. May I one day see that mould in God out of which you came.

Your loving Father

To "My loved and honoured old friend"
11 November 1894

MacDonald characteristically combined in his attitudes a deep appreciation for this life and the richness of its experiences with a yearning for a better life to come. As he grew older, the expectation increased. The following letter, written when he was seventy years old, summarizes well his attitudes:

Bordighera
11 November 1894

My loved and honoured old friend,

I was glad to have your letter, and would have written sooner but have been much occupied. I am sorry to hear of your suffering. I know what asthma is, but that, with all other troubles of the breathing apparatus has long left me.

The shadows of the evening that precedes a lovelier morning are drawing down around us both. But our God is in the shadows as in the shine, and all is and will be well: have we not seen his glory in the face of Jesus? and do we not know him a little? Have we not found the antidote to the theology of men in the Lord himself? I may almost say I believe in nothing but in Jesus Christ, and I know that when life was hardest for him, he was still thoroughly content with his father, whom he knew perfectly, and whom he has laboured and is labouring to make us know. We do know and we shall go on to know him. This life is a lovely school-time, but I never was content with it. I look for better—oh, so far better! I think we do not yet know the joy of mere existence. To exist is to be a child of God; and to know it, to feel it, is to rejoice evermore. May the loving father be near you and may you know it, and be perfectly at peace all the way into the home-country, and to the palace-home of the living one—the life of our life.

Next month I shall be 70, and I am humbler a good deal than when I was 20. To be rid of self is to have the heart bare to God and to the neighbour—to *have* all life ours, and possess all things. I see, in my mind's eye, the little children clambering up to sit on the throne with Jesus. My God, art thou not as good as we are capable of imagining thee? Shall we dream a better goodness than thou hast ever thought of? Be thyself, and all is well with us.

It may be that I shall be able to come and see you, if you are still within sight, next summer. But the hand of age is upon me too. I can work only four hours a day, cannot, only I never could, walk much, and feel tired. But all is not only well, but on the way to be better.

I need hardly tell you how truly I am in sympathy with the sonnet you were so good as to send me. It seems to me that the antidote to party-spirit is church history, and when the antidote itself has made you miserably ill, the cure is the gospel pure and simple—the story and words of Jesus. I care for no church but that of which every obedient disciple of the Lord, and no one else, is a member—though he may be—must be learning to become one. Good bye—for a little while anyhow. I have loved you ever since I knew you, for you love the truth. Please give my love to your wife—from of old time also.

Yours always
George MacDonald

Fantasies

INTRODUCTION

George MacDonald's fantasies are the purest expression of his artistic talent. Those that follow—perhaps his masterpieces in this genre—appeal to both children and adults. He was fond of the saying of Christ, "Except ye be converted, and become as little children, ye shall not enter into the kingdom of heaven" (Matthew 18:4), and he undertook to speak to the child in all of us, helping to cultivate those attitudes that make for spiritual health.

Children are captivated by the simple, vivid characterization and action; adults by the symbolic reaches of the imagery. MacDonald was fully committed to the principle that imaginative perception is capable of reaching higher toward transcendent truths than is discursive statement, but the imagination and reason both must work closely together in pursuing truth. He found in symbolic fantasies the readiest vehicle for conveying his spiritual insights.

THE PRINCESS
AND CURDIE

Chapter 1

The Mountain

Curdie was the son of Peter the miner. He lived with his father and mother in a cottage built on a mountain, and he worked with his father inside the mountain.

A mountain is a strange and awful thing. In old times, without knowing so much of their strangeness and awfulness as we do, people were yet more afraid of mountains. But then somehow they had not come to see how beautiful they are as well as awful, and they hated them, —and what people hate they must fear. Now that we have learned to look at them with admiration, perhaps we do not always feel quite awe enough of them. To me they are beautiful terrors.

I will try to tell you what they are. They are portions of the heart of the earth that have escaped from the dungeon down below, and rushed up and out. For the heart of the earth is a great wallowing mass, not of blood, as in the hearts of men and animals, but of glowing hot melted metals and stones. And as our hearts keep us alive, so that great lump of heat keeps the earth alive: it is a huge power of buried sunlight—that is what it is. Now think: out of that caldron, where all the bubbles would be as big as the Alps if it could get room for its boiling, certain bubbles have bubbled out and escaped—up and away, and there they stand in the cool, cold sky—mountains. Think of the change, and you will no more wonder that there should be something awful about the very look of a mountain: from the darkness—for where the light has nothing to shine upon, it is much the same as darkness—from the heat, from the endless tumult of boiling unrest—up, with a sudden heavenward shoot, into the wind, and the cold, and the starshine, and a cloak of snow that lies like ermine above the blue-green mail of the glaciers; and the great sun, their grandfather, up there in the sky; and their little old cold aunt, the moon, that comes wandering about the house at night; and everlasting stillness, except for the wind that turns the rocks and caverns into a roaring organ for the young archangels that are studying how to let out the pent-up praises of their hearts, and the molten music of the streams, rushing ever from the bosoms of the glaciers fresh-born. Think too of the change in their own substance—no longer molten and soft, heaving and glowing, but hard and shining and cold. Think of the creatures scampering over and burrowing in it, and the birds building their nests upon it, and the trees growing out of its sides, like hair to clothe it, and the lovely grass in the valleys, and the gracious flowers even at the very edge of its armour of ice, like the rich embroidery of the garment below, and the rivers galloping down the valleys in a tumult of white and green! And along with all these, think of the terrible precipices down which the traveller may fall and be lost, and the frightful gulfs of blue air cracked in the glaciers, and the dark profound lakes, covered like little arctic oceans with floating lumps of ice. All this outside the mountain! But the inside, who shall tell what lies there? Caverns of awfullest solitude, their walls miles thick, sparkling with ores of gold or silver, copper or iron, tin or mercury, studded perhaps with precious stones—perhaps a brook, with eyeless fish in it, running, running ceaseless, cold and babbling, through banks crusted with carbuncles and golden topazes, or over a gravel of which some of the stones are rubies and emeralds, perhaps diamonds and sapphires—who can tell?—and whoever can't tell is free to think— all waiting to flash, waiting for millions of ages—ever since the earth flew off from the sun, a great blot of fire, and began to cool. Then there are caverns full of water, numbing cold, fiercely hot—hotter than any boiling water. From some of these the water cannot get out, and from others it runs in channels as the blood in the body: little veins bring it down from the ice above into the great caverns of the mountain's heart, whence the arteries let it out again, gushing in pipes and clefts and ducts of all shapes and kinds, through and through its bulk, until it springs newborn to the light, and rushes down the mountain side in torrents, and down the valleys in rivers—down, down, rejoicing, to the mighty lungs of the world, that is the sea, where it is tossed in storms and cyclones, heaved up in billows, twisted in waterspouts, dashed to mist upon rocks, beaten by millions of tails, and breathed by millions of gills, whence at last, melted into vapour by the sun, it is lifted up pure into the air, and borne by the servant winds back to the mountain tops and the snow, the solid ice, and the molten stream.

Well, when the heart of the earth has thus come rushing up among her children, bringing with it gifts of all that she possesses, then straightway into it rush her children to see what they can find there. With pickaxe and spade and crowbar, with boring chisel and blasting powder, they force their way back: is it to search for what toys they may have left in their long-forgotten nurseries? Hence the mountains that lift their heads into the clear air, and are dotted over with the dwellings of men, are tunnelled and bored in the darkness of their bosoms by the dwellers in the houses which they hold up to the sun and air.

Curdie and his father were these: their business was to bring to light hidden things; they sought silver in the rock and found it, and carried it out. Of the many other precious things in their mountain they knew little or nothing. Silver ore was what they were sent to find, and in darkness and danger they found it. But oh, how sweet was the air on the mountain face when they came out at sunset to go home to wife and mother! They did breathe deep then!

The mines belonged to the king of the country, and the miners were his servants, working under his overseers and officers. He was a real king—that is one who ruled for the good of his people, and not to please himself, and he wanted the silver not to buy rich things for himself, but to help him to govern the country, and pay the armies that defended it from certain troublesome neighbours, and the judges whom he set to portion out righteousness amongst the people, that so they might learn it themselves, and come to do without judges at all. Nothing that could be got from the heart of the earth could have been put to better purposes than the silver the king's miners got for him. There were people in the country who, when it came into their hands, degraded it by locking it up in a chest, and then it grew diseased and was called *mammon,* and bred all sorts of quarrels; but when first it left the king's hands it never made any but friends, and the air of the world kept it clean. About a year before this story began, a series of very remarkable events had just ended. I will narrate as much of them as will serve to show the tops of the roots of my tree.

Upon the mountain, on one of its many claws, stood a grand old house, half farmhouse, half castle, belonging to the king; and there his only child, the Princess Irene, had been brought up till she was nearly nine years old, and would doubtless have continued much longer, but for the strange events to which I have referred.

At that time the hollow places of the mountain were inhabited by creatures called goblins, who for various reasons and in various ways made themselves troublesome to all, but to the little princess dangerous. Mainly by the watchful devotion and energy of Curdie, however, their designs had been utterly defeated, and made to recoil upon themselves to their own destruction, so that now there were very few of them left alive, and the miners did not believe there was a single goblin remaining in the whole inside of the mountain.

The king had been so pleased with the boy—then approaching thirteen years of age—that when he carried away his daughter he asked him to accompany them; but he was still better pleased with him when he found that he preferred staying with his father and mother. He was a right good king, and knew that the love of a boy who would not leave his father and mother to be made a great man, was worth ten thousand offers to die for his sake, and would prove so when the right time came. For his father and mother, they would have given him up without a grumble, for they were just as good as the king, and he and they perfectly understood each other; but in this matter, not seeing that he could do anything for the king which one of his numerous attendants could not do as well, Curdie felt that it was for him to decide. So the king took a kind farewell of them all and rode away, with his daughter on his horse before him.

A gloom fell upon the mountain and the miners when she was gone, and Curdie did not whistle for a whole week. As for his verses, there was no occasion to make any now. He had made them only to drive away the goblins, and they were all gone—a good riddance—only the princess was gone too! He would rather have had things as they were, except for the princess's sake. But whoever is diligent will soon be cheerful, and though the miners missed the household of the castle, they yet managed to get on without them.

Peter and his wife, however, were troubled with the fancy that they had stood in the way of their boy's good fortune. It would have been such a fine thing for him and them too, they thought, if he had ridden with the good king's train. How beautiful he looked, they said, when he rode the king's own horse through the river that the goblins had sent out of the hill! He might soon have been a captain, they did believe! The good, kind people did not reflect that the road to the next duty is the only straight one, or that, for their fancied good, we should never wish our children or friends to do what we would not do ourselves if we were in their position. We must accept righteous sacrifices as well as make them.

Chapter 2

The White Pigeon

When in the winter they had had their supper and sat about the fire, or when in the summer they lay on the border of the rock-margined stream that ran through their little meadow, close by the door of their cottage, issuing from the far-up whiteness often folded in clouds, Curdie's mother would not seldom lead the conversation to one peculiar personage said and believed to have been much concerned in the late issue of events. That personage was the great-great-grandmother of the princess, of whom the princess had often talked, but whom neither Curdie nor his mother had ever seen. Curdie could indeed remember, although already it looked more like a dream than he could account for if it had really taken place, how the princess had once led him up many stairs to what she called a beautiful room in the top of the tower, where she went through all the—what should he call it?—the behaviour of presenting him to her grandmother, talking now to her and now to him, while all the time he saw nothing but a bare garret, a heap of musty straw, a sunbeam, and a withered apple. Lady, he would have declared before the king himself, young or old, there was none, except the princess herself, who was certainly vexed that he could not see what she at least believed she saw. And for his mother, she had once seen, long before Curdie was born, a certain mysterious light of the same description with one Irene spoke of, calling it her grandmother's moon; and Curdie himself had seen this same light, shining from above the castle, just as the king and princess were taking their leave. Since that time neither had seen or heard anything that could be supposed connected with her. Strangely enough, however, nobody had seen her go away. If she was such an old lady, she could hardly be supposed to have set out alone and on foot when all the house was asleep. Still, away she must have gone, for of course, if she was so powerful, she would always be about the princess to take care of her.

But as Curdie grew older, he doubted more and more whether Irene had not been talking of some dream she had taken for reality: he heard it said that children could not always distinguish betwixt dreams and actual events. At the same time there was his mother's testimony: what was he to do with that? His mother, through whom he had learned everything, could hardly be imagined by her own dutiful son to have mistaken a dream for a fact of the waking world. So he rather shrunk from thinking about it, and the less he thought about it, the less he was inclined to believe it when he did think about it, and therefore, of course, the less inclined to talk about it to his father and mother; for although his father was one of those men who for one word they say think twenty thoughts, Curdie was well assured that he would rather doubt his own eyes than his wife's testimony. There were no others to whom he could have talked about it. The miners were a mingled company—some good, some not so good, some rather bad—none of them so bad or so good as they might have been; Curdie liked most of them, and was a favourite with all; but they knew very little about the upper world, and what might or might not take place there. They knew silver from copper ore; they understood the underground ways of things, and they could look very wise with their lanterns in their hands searching after this or that sign of ore, or for some mark to guide their way in the hollows of the earth; but as to great-great-grandmothers, they would have mocked him all the rest of his life for the absurdity of not being absolutely certain that the solemn belief of his father and mother was nothing but ridiculous nonsense. Why, to them the very word "great-great-grandmother" would have been a week's laughter! I am not sure that they were able quite to believe there were such persons as great-great-grandmothers; they had never seen one. They were not companions to give the best of help towards progress, and as Curdie grew, he grew at this time faster in body than in mind—with the usual consequence, that he was getting rather stupid—one of the chief signs of which was that he believed less and less of things he had never seen. At the same time I do not think he was ever so stupid as to imagine that this was a sign of superior faculty and strength of mind. Still, he was becoming more and more a miner, and less and less a man of the upper world where the wind blew. On his way to and from the mine he took less and less notice of bees and butterflies, moths and dragon-flies, the flowers and the brooks and the clouds. He was gradually changing into a commonplace man. There is this difference between the growth of some human beings and that of others: in the one case it is a continuous dying, in the other a continuous resurrection. One of the latter sort comes at length to know at once whether a thing is true the moment it comes before him; one of the former class grows more and more afraid of being taken in, so afraid of it that he takes himself in altogether, and comes at length to believe in nothing but his dinner: to be sure of a thing with him is to have it between his teeth. Curdie was not in a very good way then at that time. His father and mother had, it is true, no fault to find with him—and yet—and yet—neither of them was ready to sing when the thought of him came up. There must be something wrong when a mother catches herself sighing over the time when her boy was in petticoats, or the father looks sad when he thinks how he used to carry him on his shoulder. The boy should enclose and keep, as his life, the old child at the heart of him, and never let it go. He must still, to be a right man, be his mother's darling, and more, his father's pride, and more. The child is not meant to die, but to be for ever fresh-born.

Curdie had made himself a bow and some arrows, and was teaching himself to shoot with them. One evening in the early summer, as he was walking home from the mine with them in his hand, a light flashed across his eyes. He looked, and there was a snow-white pigeon settling on a rock in front of him, in the red light of the level sun. There it fell at once to work with one of its wings, in which a feather or two had got some sprays twisted, causing a certain roughness unpleasant to the fastidious creature of the air. It was indeed a lovely being, and Curdie thought how happy it must be flitting through the air with a flash—a live bolt of light. For a moment he became so one with the bird that he seemed to feel both its bill and its feathers, as the one adjusted the other to fly again, and his heart swelled with the pleasure of its involuntary sympathy. Another moment and it would have been aloft in the waves of rosy light—it was just bending its little legs to spring: that moment it fell on the path broken-winged and bleeding from Curdie's cruel arrow. With a gush of pride at his skill, and pleasure at its success, he ran to pick up his prey. I must say for him he picked it up gently—perhaps it was the beginning of his repentance. But when he had the white thing in his hands—its whiteness stained with another red than that of the sunset flood in which it had been revelling—ah God! who knows the joy of a bird, the ecstasy of a creature that has neither storehouse nor barn!—when he held it, I say, in his victorious hands, the winged thing looked up in his face—and with such eyes! asking what was the matter, and where the red sun had gone, and the clouds, and the wind of its flight. Then they closed, but to open again presently, with the same questions in them. And so they closed and opened several times, but always when they opened, their look was fixed on his. It did not once flutter or try to get away; it only throbbed and bled and looked at him. Curdie's heart began to grow very large in his bosom. What could it mean? It was nothing but a pigeon, and why should he not kill a pigeon? But the fact was, that not till this very moment had he ever known what a pigeon was. A good many discoveries of a similar kind have to be made by most of us. Once more it opened its eyes—then closed them again, and its throbbing ceased. Curdie gave a sob: its last look reminded him of the princess—he did not know why. He remembered how hard he had laboured to set her beyond danger, and yet what dangers she had had to encounter for his sake: they had been saviours to each other—and what had he done now? He had stopped saving, and had begun killing! What had he been sent into the world for? Surely not to be a death to its joy and loveliness. He had done the thing that was contrary to gladness; he was a destroyer! He was not the Curdie he had been meant to be! Then the underground waters gushed from the boy's heart. And with the tears came the remembrance that a white pigeon, just before the princess went away with her father, came from somewhere—yes, from the grandmother's lamp, and flew round the king and Irene and himself, and then flew away: this might be that very pigeon! Horrible to think! And if it wasn't, yet it was a white pigeon, the same as it. And if she kept a great many pigeons—and white ones, as Irene had told him, then whose pigeon could he have killed but the grand old princess's? Suddenly everything round about him seemed against him. The red sunset stung him: the rocks frowned at him; the sweet wind that had been laving his face as he walked up the hill, dropped—as if he wasn't fit to be kissed any more. Was the whole world going to cast him out? Would he have to stand there for ever, not knowing what to do, with the dead pigeon in his hand? Things looked bad indeed. Was the whole world going to make a work about a pigeon—a white pigeon? The sun went down. Great clouds gathered over the west, and shortened the twilight. The wind gave a howl, and then lay down again. The clouds gathered thicker. Then came a rumbling. He thought it was thunder. It was a rock that fell inside the mountain. A goat ran past him down the hill, followed by a dog sent to fetch him home. He thought they were goblin creatures, and trembled. He used to despise them. And still he held the dead pigeon tenderly in his hand. It grew darker and darker. An evil something began to move in his heart. "What a fool I am!" he said to himself. Then he grew angry, and was just going to throw the bird from him and whistle, when a brightness shone all round him. He lifted his eyes, and saw a great globe of light—like silver at the hottest heat: he had once seen silver run from the furnace. It shone from somewhere above the roofs of the castle: it must be the great old princess's moon! How could she be there? Of course she was not there! He had asked the whole household, and nobody knew anything about her or her globe either. It couldn't be! And yet what did that signify, when there was the white globe shining, and here was the dead white bird in his hand? That moment the pigeon gave a little flutter. *It's not dead!* cried Curdie, almost with a shriek. The same instant he was running full speed towards the castle, never letting his heels down, lest he should shake the poor wounded bird.

Chapter 3

The Mistress of the Silver Moon

W hen Curdie reached the castle, and ran into the little garden in front of it, there stood the door wide open. This was as he had hoped, for what could he have said if he had had to knock at it? Those whose business it is to open doors, so often mistake and shut them! But the woman now in charge often puzzled herself greatly to account for the strange fact that however often she shut the door, which, like the rest, she took a great deal of unnecessary trouble to do, she was certain, the next time she went to it, to find it open. I speak now of the great front door, of course: the back door she as persistently kept wide: if people *could* only go in by that, she said, she would then know what sort they were, and what they wanted. But she would neither have known what sort Curdie was, nor what he wanted, and would assuredly have denied him admittance, for she knew nothing of who was in the tower. So the front door was left open for him, and in he walked.

But where to go next he could not tell. It was not quite dark: a dull, shineless twilight filled the place. All he knew was that he must go up, and that proved enough for the present, for there he saw the great staircase rising before him. When he reached the top of it, he knew there must be more stairs yet, for he could not be near the top of the tower. Indeed by the situation of the stair, he must be a good way from the tower itself. But those who work well in the depths more easily understand the heights, for indeed in their true nature they are one and the same: mines are in mountains; and Curdie from knowing the ways of the king's mines, and being able to calculate his whereabouts in them, was now able to find his way about the king's house. He knew its outside perfectly, and now his business was to get his notion of the inside right with the outside. So he shut his eyes and made a picture of the outside of it in his mind. Then he came in at the door of the picture, and yet kept the picture before him all the time—for you can do that kind of thing in your mind,—and took every turn of the stair over again, always watching to remember, every time he turned his face, how the tower lay, and then when he came to himself at the top where he stood, he knew exactly where it was, and walked at once in the right direction. On his way, however, he came to another stair, and up that he went of course, watching still at every turn how the tower must lie. At the top of this stair was yet another—they were the stairs up which the princess ran when first, without knowing it, she was on her way to find her great-great-grandmother. At the top of the second stair he could go no farther, and must therefore set out again to find the tower, which, as it rose far above the rest of the house, must have the last of its stairs inside itself. Having watched every turn to the very last, he still knew quite well in what direction he must go to find it, so he left the stair and went down a passage that led, if not exactly towards it, yet nearer it. This passage was rather dark, for it was very long, with only one window at the end, and although there were doors on both sides of it, they were all shut. At the distant window glimmered the chill east, with a few feeble stars in it, and its light was dreary and old, growing brown, and looking as if it were thinking about the day that was just gone. Presently he turned into another passage, which also had a window at the end of it; and in at that window shone all that was left of the sunset, a few ashes, with here and there a little touch of warmth: it was nearly as sad as the east, only there was one difference—it was very plainly thinking of to-morrow. But at present Curdie had nothing to do with to-day or to-morrow; his business was with the bird, and the tower where dwelt the grand old princess to whom it belonged. So he kept on his way, still eastward, and came to yet another passage, which brought him to a door. He was afraid to open it without first knocking. He knocked, but heard no answer. He was answered nevertheless; for the door gently opened, and there was a narrow stair—and so steep that, big lad as he was, he too, like the Princess Irene before him, found his hands needful for the climbing. And it was a long climb, but he reached the top at last—a little landing, with a door in front and one on each side. Which should he knock at?

As he hesitated, he heard the noise of a spinning-wheel. He knew it at once, because his mother's spinning-wheel had been his governess long ago, and still taught him things. It was the spinning-wheel that first taught him to make verses, and to sing, and to think whether all was right inside him; or at least it had helped him in all these things. Hence it was no wonder he should know a spinning-wheel when he heard it sing—even although as the bird of paradise to other birds was the song of that wheel to the song of his mother's.

He stood listening so entranced that he forgot to knock, and the wheel went on and on, spinning in his brain songs and tales and rhymes, till he was almost asleep as well as dreaming, for sleep does not *always* come first. But suddenly came the thought of the poor bird, which had been lying motionless in his hand all the time, and that woke him up, and at once he knocked.

"Come in, Curdie," said a voice.

Curdie shook. It was getting rather awful. The heart that had never much heeded an army of goblins, trembled at the soft word of invitation. But then there was the red-spotted white thing in his hand! He dared not hesitate, though. Gently he opened the door through which the sound came, and what did he see? Nothing at first—except indeed a great sloping shaft of moonlight, that came in at a high window, and rested on the floor. He stood and stared at it, forgetting to shut the door.

"Why don't you come in, Curdie?" said the voice. "Did you never see moonlight before?"

"Never without a moon," answered Curdie, in a trembling tone, but gathering courage.

"Certainly not," returned the voice, which was thin and quavering: "*I* never saw moonlight without a moon."

"But there's no moon outside," said Curdie.

"Ah! but you're inside now," said the voice.

The answer did not satisfy Curdie; but the voice went on.

"There are more moons than you know of, Curdie. Where there is one sun there are many moons—and of many sorts. Come in and look out of my window, and you will soon satisfy yourself that there is a moon looking in at it."

The gentleness of the voice made Curdie remember his manners. He shut the door, and drew a step or two nearer to the moonlight.

All the time the sound of the spinning had been going on and on, and Curdie now caught sight of the wheel. Oh, it was such a thin, delicate thing—reminding him of a spider's web in a hedge! It stood in the middle of the moonlight, and it seemed as if the moonlight had nearly melted it away. A step nearer, he saw, with a start, two little hands at work with it. And then at last, in the shadow on the other side of the moonlight which came like a river between, he saw the form to which the hands belonged: a small, withered creature, so old that no age would have seemed too great to write under her picture, seated on a stool beyond the spinning-wheel, which looked very large beside her, but, as I said, very thin, like a long-legged spider holding up its own web, which was the round wheel itself. She sat crumpled together, a filmy thing that it seemed a puff would blow away, more like the body of a fly the big spider had sucked empty and left hanging in his web, than anything else I can think of.

When Curdie saw her, he stood still again, a good deal in wonder, a very little in reverence, a little in doubt, and, I must add, a little in amusement at the odd look of the old marvel. Her grey hair mixed with the moonlight so that he could not tell where the one began and the other ended. Her crooked back bent forward over her chest, her shoulders nearly swallowed up her head between them, and her two little hands were just like the grey claws of a hen, scratching at the thread, which to Curdie was of course invisible across the moonlight. Indeed Curdie laughed within himself, just a little, at the sight; and when he thought of how the princess used to talk about her huge great old grandmother, he laughed more. But that moment the little lady leaned forward into the moonlight, and Curdie caught a glimpse of her eyes, and all the laugh went out of him.

"What do you come here for, Curdie?" she said, as gently as before.

Then Curdie remembered that he stood there as a culprit, and worst of all, as one who had his confession yet to make. There was no time to hesitate over it.

"Oh, ma'am! see here," he said, and advanced a step or two, holding out the dead pigeon.

"What have you got there?" she asked.

Again Curdie advanced a few steps, and held out his hand with the pigeon, that she might see what it was, into the moonlight. The moment the rays fell upon it the pigeon gave a faint flutter. The old lady put out her old hands and took it, and held it to her bosom, and rocked it, murmuring over it as if it were a sick baby.

When Curdie saw how distressed she was he grew sorrier still, and said,—

"I didn't mean to do any harm, ma'am. I didn't think of its being yours."

"Ah, Curdie! if it weren't mine, what would become of it now?" she returned. "You say you didn't mean any harm: did you mean any good, Curdie?"

"No," answered Curdie.

"Remember, then, that whoever does not mean good is always in danger of harm. But I try to give everybody fair play; and those that are in the wrong are in far more need of it always than those who are in the right: they can afford to do without it. Therefore I say for you that when you shot that arrow you did not know what a pigeon is. Now that you do know, you are sorry. It is very dangerous to do things you don't know about."

"But, please, ma'am—I don't mean to be rude or to contradict you," said Curdie, "but if a body was never to do anything but what he knew to be good, he would have to live half his time doing nothing."

"There you are much mistaken," said the old quavering voice. "How little you must have thought! Why, you don't seem even to know the good of the things you are constantly doing. Now don't mistake me. I don't mean you are good for doing them. It is a good thing to eat your breakfast, but you don't fancy it's very good of you to do it. The thing is good—not you."

Curdie laughed.

"There are a great many more good things than bad things to do. Now tell me what bad thing you have done to-day besides this sore hurt to my little white friend."

While she talked Curdie had sunk into a sort of reverie, in which he hardly knew whether it was the old lady or his own heart that spoke. And when she asked him that question, he was at first much inclined to consider himself a very good fellow on the whole. "I really don't think I did anything else that was very bad all day," he said to himself. But at the same time he could not honestly feel that he was worth standing up for. All at once a light seemed to break in upon his mind, and he woke up, and there was the withered little atomy of the old lady on the other side of the moonlight, and there was the spinning-wheel singing on and on in the middle of it!

"I know now, ma'am; I understand now," he said. "Thank you, ma'am for spinning it into me with your wheel. I see now that I have been doing wrong the whole day, and such a many days besides! Indeed, I don't know when I ever did right, and yet it seems as if I had done right some time and had forgotten how. When I killed your bird I did not know I was doing wrong, just because I was always doing wrong, and the wrong had soaked all through me."

"What wrong were you doing all day, Curdie? It is better to come to the point, you know," said the old lady, and her voice was gentler even than before.

"I was doing the wrong of never wanting or trying to be better. And now I see that I have been letting things go as they would for a long time. Whatever came into my head I did, and whatever didn't come into my head I didn't do. I never sent anything away, and never looked out for anything to come. I haven't been attending to my mother—or my father either. And now I think of it, I know I have often seen them looking troubled, and I have never asked them what was the matter. And now I see too that I did not ask because I suspected it had something to do with me and my behaviour, and didn't want to hear the truth. And I know I have been grumbling at my work, and doing a hundred other things that are wrong."

"You have got it, Curdie," said the old lady, in a voice that sounded almost as if she had been crying. "When people don't care to be better they must be doing everything wrong. I am so glad you shot my bird!"

"Ma'am!" exclaimed Curdie. "How *can* you be?"

"Because it has brought you to see what sort you were when you did it, and what sort you will grow to be again, only worse, if you don't mind. Now that you are sorry, my poor bird will be better. Look up, my dovey."

The pigeon gave a flutter, and spread out one of its red-spotted wings across the old woman's bosom.

"I will mend the little angel," she said, "and in a week or two it will by flying again. So you may ease your heart about the pigeon."

"Oh, thank you! thank you!" cried Curdie. "I don't know how to thank you."

"Then I will tell you. There is only one way I care for. Do better, and grow better, and be better. And never kill anything without a good reason for it."

"Ma'am, I will go and fetch my bow and arrows, and you shall burn them yourself."

"I have no fire that would burn your bow and arrows, Curdie."

"Then I promise you to burn them all under my mother's porridge-pot to-morrow morning."

"No, no, Curdie. Keep them, and practise with them every day, and grow a good shot. There are plenty of bad things that want killing, and a day will come when they will prove useful. But I must see first whether you will do as I tell you."

"That I will!" said Curdie. "What is it, ma'am?"

"Only something not to do," answered the old lady; "if you should hear any one speak about me, never to laugh or make fun of me."

"Oh, ma'am!" exclaimed Curdie, shocked that she should think such a request needful.

"Stop, stop," she went on. "People hereabout sometimes tell very odd and in fact ridiculous stories of an old woman who watches what is going on, and occasionally interferes. They mean me, though what they say is often great nonsense. Now what I want of you is not to laugh, or side with them in any way; because they will take that to mean that you don't believe there is any such person a bit more than they do. Now that would not be the case—would it, Curdie?"

"No indeed, ma'am. I've seen you."

The old woman smiled very oddly.

"Yes, you've seen me," she said. "But mind," she continued, "I don't want you to say anything—only to hold your tongue, and not seem to side with them."

"That will be easy," said Curdie, "now that I've seen you with my very own eyes, ma'am."

"Not so easy as you think, perhaps," said the old lady, with another curious smile. "I want to be your friend," she added after a little pause, "but I don't quite know yet whether you will let me."

"Indeed I will, ma'am," said Curdie.

"That is for me to find out," she rejoined, with yet another strange smile. "In the meantime all I can say is, come to me again when you find yourself in any trouble, and I will see what I can do for you—only the *canning* depends on yourself. I am greatly pleased with you for bringing me my pigeon, doing your best to set right what you had set wrong."

As she spoke she held out her hand to him, and when he took it she made use of his to help herself up from her stool, and—when or how it came about, Curdie could not tell—the same instant she stood before him a tall, strong woman—plainly very old, but as grand as she was old, and only *rather* severe-looking. Every trace of the decrepitude and witheredness she showed as she hovered like a film about her wheel, had vanished. Her hair was very white, but it hung about her head in great plenty, and shone like silver in the moonlight. Straight as a pillar she stood before the astonished boy, and the wounded bird had now spread out both its wings across her bosom, like some great mystical ornament of frosted silver.

"Oh, now I can never forget you!" cried Curdie. "I see now what you really are!"

"Did I not tell you the truth when I sat at my wheel?" said the old lady.

"Yes, ma'am." answered Curdie.

"I can do no more than tell you the truth now," she rejoined. "It is a bad thing indeed to forget one who has told us the truth. Now go."

Curdie obeyed, and took a few steps towards the door.

"Please, ma'am,"—"what am I to call you?" he was going to say; but when he turned to speak, he saw nobody. Whether she was there or not he could not tell, however, for the moonlight had vanished, and the room was utterly dark. A great fear, such as he had never before known, came upon him, and almost overwhelmed him. He groped his way to the door, and crawled down the stair—in doubt and anxiety as to how he should find his way out of the house in the dark. And the stair seemed ever so much longer than when he came up. Nor was that any wonder, for down and down he went, until at length his foot struck on a door, and when he rose and opened it, he found himself under the starry, moonless sky at the foot of the tower. He soon discovered the way out of the garden, with which he had some acquaintance already, and in a few minutes was climbing the mountain with a solemn and cheerful heart. It was rather dark, but he knew the way well. As he passed the rock from which the poor pigeon fell wounded with his arrow, a great joy filled his heart at the thought that he was delivered from the blood of the little bird, and he ran the next hundred yards at full speed up the hill. Some dark shadows passed him: he did not even care to think what they were, but let them run. When he reached home, he found his father and mother waiting supper for him.

Chapter 4

Curdie's Father and Mother

The eyes of the fathers and mothers are quick to read their children's looks, and when Curdie entered the cottage, his parents saw at once that something unusual had taken place. When he said to his mother, "I beg your pardon for being so late," there was something in the tone beyond the politeness that went to her heart, for it seemed to come from the place where all lovely things were born before they began to grow in this world. When he set his father's chair to the table, an attention he had not shown him for a long time, Peter thanked him with more gratitude than the boy had ever yet felt in all his life. It was a small thing to do for the man who had been serving him since ever he was born, but I suspect there is nothing a man can be so grateful for as that to which he has the most right. There was a change upon Curdie, and father and mother felt there must be something to account for it, and therefore were pretty sure he had something to tell them. For when a child's heart is *all* right, it is not likely he will want to keep anything from his parents. But the story of the evening was too solemn for Curdie to come out with all at once. He must wait until they had had their porridge, and the affairs of this world were over for the day. But when they were seated on the grassy bank of the brook that went so sweetly blundering over the great stones of its rocky channel, for the whole meadow lay on the top of a huge rock, then he felt that the right hour had come for sharing with them the wonderful things that had come to him. It was perhaps the loveliest of all hours in the year. The summer was young and soft, and this was the warmest evening they had yet had—dusky, dark even below, while above the stars were bright and large and sharp in the blackest blue sky. The night came close around them, clasping them in one universal arm of love, and although it neither spoke nor smiled, seemed all eye and ear, seemed to see and hear and know everything they said and did. It is a way the night has sometimes, and there is a reason for it. The only sound was that of the brook, for there was no wind, and no trees for it to make its music upon if there had been, for the cottage was high up on the mountain, on a great shoulder of stone where trees would not grow. There, to the accompaniment of the water, as it hurried down to the valley and the sea, talking busily of a thousand true things which it could not understand, Curdie told his tale, outside and in, to his father and mother. What a world had slipped in between the mouth of the mine and his mother's cottage! Neither of them said a word until he had ended.

"Now what am I to make of it, mother? It's so strange!" he said, and stopped.

"It's easy enough to see what Curdie has got to make of it—isn't it, Peter?" said the good woman, turning her face towards all she could see of her husband's.

"It seems so to me," answered Peter, with a smile, which only the night saw, but his wife felt in the tone of his words. They were the happiest couple in that country, because they always understood each other, and that was because they always meant the same thing, and that was because they always loved what was fair and true and right better—not than anything else, but than everything else put together.

"Then will you tell Curdie?" said she.

"You can talk best, Joan," said he. "You tell him, and I will listen—and learn how to say what I think" he added, laughing.

"*I,*" said Curdie, "don't know what to think."

"It does not matter so much," said his mother. "If only you know what to make of a thing, you'll know soon enough what to think of it. Now I needn't tell you, surely, Curdie, what you've got to do with this?"

"I suppose you mean, mother," answered Curdie, "that I must do as the old lady told me?"

"That is what I mean: what else could it be? Am I not right, Peter?"

"Quite right, Joan," answered Peter, "so far as my judgment goes. It is a very strange story, but you see the question is not about believing it, for Curdie knows what came to him."

"And you remember, Curdie," said his mother, "that when the princess took you up that tower once before, and there talked to her great-great-grandmother, you came home quite angry with her, and said there was nothing in the place but an old tub, a heap of straw—oh, I remember your inventory quite well!—an old tub, a heap of straw, a withered apple, and a sunbeam. According to your eyes, that was all there was in the great old musty garret. But now you have had a glimpse of the old princess herself!"

"Yes, mother. I *did* see her—or if I didn't,—" said Curdie very thoughtfully—then began again. "The hardest thing to believe, though I saw it with my own eyes, was when the thin, filmy creature, that seemed almost to float about in the moonlight like a bit of the silver paper they put over pictures, or like a handkerchief made of spider-threads, took my hand, and rose up. She was taller and stronger than you, mother, ever so much!—at least, she looked so."

"And most certainly was so, Curdie, if she looked so," said Mrs. Peterson.

"Well, I confess," returned her son, "that one thing, if there were no other, would make me doubt whether I was not dreaming after all, for as wide awake as I fancied myself to be."

"Of course," answered his mother, "it is not for me to say whether you were dreaming or not if you are doubtful of it yourself; but it doesn't make me think I am dreaming when in the summer I hold in my hand the bunch of sweet-peas that make my heart glad with their colour and scent, and remember the dry, withered-looking little thing I dibbled into the hole in the same spot in the spring. I only think how wonderful and lovely it all is. It seems just as full of reason as it is of wonder. How it is done I can't tell, only there it is! And there is this in it too, Curdie—of which you would not be so ready to think—that when you come home to your father and mother, and they find you behaving more like a dear good son than you have behaved for a long time, they at least are not likely to think you were only dreaming."

"Still," said Curdie, looking a little ashamed, "I might have dreamed my duty."

"Then dream often, my son; for there must then be more truth in your dreams than in your waking thoughts. But however any of these things may be, this one point remains certain: there can be no harm in doing as she told you. And, indeed, until you are sure there is no such person, you are bound to do it, for you promised."

"It seems to me," said his father, "that if a lady comes to you in a dream, Curdie, and tells you not to talk about her when you wake, the least you can do is to hold your tongue."

"True, father!—Yes, mother, I'll do it," said Curdie.

Then they went to bed, and sleep, which is the night of the soul, next took them in its arms and made them well.

Chapter 5

The Miners

It much increased Curdie's feeling of the strangeness of the whole affair, that, the next morning, when they were at work in the mine, the party of which he and his father were two, just as if they had known what had happened to him the night before, began talking about all manner of wonderful tales that were abroad in the country, chiefly of course those connected with the mines, and the mountains in which they lay. Their wives and mothers and grandmothers were their chief authorities. For when they sat by their firesides they heard their wives telling their children the selfsame tales, with little differences, and here and there one they had not heard before, which they had heard their mothers and grandmothers tell in one or other of the same cottages. At length they came to speak of a certain strange being they called Old Mother Wotherwop. Some said their wives had seen her. It appeared as they talked that not one had seen her more than once. Some of their mothers and grandmothers, however, had seen her also, and they all had told them tales about her when they were children. They said she could take any shape she liked, but that in reality she was a withered old woman, so old and so withered that she was as thin as a sieve with a lamp behind it; that she was never seen except at night, and when something terrible had taken place, or was going to take place—such as the falling in of the roof of a mine, or the breaking out of water in it. She had more than once been seen—it was always at night—beside some well, sitting on the brink of it, and leaning over and stirring it with her forefinger, which was six times as long as any of the rest. And whoever for months after drank of that well was sure to be ill. To this one of them, however, added that he remembered his mother saying that whoever in bad health drank of the well was sure to get better. But the majority agreed that the former was the right version of the story—for was she not a witch, an old hating witch, whose delight was to do mischief? One said he had heard that she took the shape of a young woman sometimes, as beautiful as an angel, and then was most dangerous of all, for she struck every man who looked upon her stone-blind. Peter ventured the question whether she might not as likely be an angel that took the form of an old woman, as an old woman that took the form of an angel. But nobody except Curdie, who was holding his peace with all his might, saw any sense in the question. They said an old woman might be very glad to make herself look like a young one, but who ever heard of a young and beautiful one making herself look old and ugly? Peter asked why they were so much more ready to believe the bad that was said of her than the good. They answered because she was bad. He asked why they believed her to be bad, and they answered, because she did bad things. When he asked how they knew that, they said, because she was a bad creature. Even if they didn't know it, they said, a woman like that was so much more likely to be bad than good. Why did she go about at night? Why did she appear only now and then, and on such occasions? One went on to tell how one night when his grandfather had been having a jolly time of it with his friends in the market town, she had served him so upon his way home that the poor man never drank a drop of anything stronger than water after it to the day of his death. She dragged him into a bog, and tumbled him up and down in it till he was nearly dead.

"I suppose that was her way of teaching him what a good thing water was," said Peter; but the man, who liked strong drink, did not see the joke.

"They do say," said another, "that she has lived in the old house over there ever since the little princess left it. They say too that the house-keeper knows all about it, and is hand and glove with the old witch. I don't doubt they have many a nice airing together on broomsticks. But I don't doubt either it's all nonsense, and there's no such person at all."

"When our cow died," said another, "she was seen going round and round the cowhouse the same night. To be sure she left a fine calf behind her—I mean the cow did, not the witch. I wonder she didn't kill that too, for she'll be a far finer cow than ever her mother was."

"My old woman came upon her one night, not long before the water broke out in the mine, sitting on a stone on the hill-side with a whole congregation of cobs about her. When they saw my wife they all scampered off as fast as they could run, and where the witch was sitting there was nothing to be seen but a withered bracken bush. I make no doubt myself she was putting them up to it."

And so they went on with one foolish tale after another, while Peter put in a word now and then, and Curdie diligently held his peace. But his silence at last drew attention upon it, and one of them said,—

"Come, young Curdie, what are you thinking of?"

"How do you know I'm thinking of anything?" asked Curdie.

"Because you're not saying anything."

"Does it follow then that, as you are saying so much, you're not thinking at all?" said Curdie.

"I know what he's thinking," said one who had not yet spoken; "—he's thinking what a set of fools you are to talk such rubbish; as if ever there was or could be such an old woman as you say! I'm sure Curdie knows better than all that comes to."

"I think," said Curdie, "it would be better that he who says anything about her should be quite sure it is true, lest she should hear him, and not like to be slandered."

"But would she like it any better if it were true?" said the same man. "If she is what they say—I don't know—but I never knew a man that wouldn't go in a rage to be called the very thing he was."

"If bad things were true of her, and I *knew* it," said Curdie, "I would not hesitate to say them, for I will never give in to being afraid of anything that's bad. I suspect that the things they tell, however, if we knew all about them, would turn out to have nothing but good in them; and I won't say a word more for fear I should say something that mightn't be to her mind."

They all burst into a loud laugh.

"Hear the parson!" they cried. "He believes in the witch! Ha! ha!"

"He's afraid of her!"

"And says all she does is good!"

"He wants to make friends with her, that she may help him to find the gangue."

"Give me my own eyes and a good divining rod before all the witches in the world! and so I'd advise you too, Master Curdie; that is, when your eyes have grown to be worth anything, and you have learned to cut the hazel fork."

Thus they all mocked and jeered at him, but he did his best to keep his temper and go quietly on with his work. He got as close to his father as he could, however, for that helped him to bear it. As soon as they were tired of laughing and mocking, Curdie was friendly with them, and long before their midday meal all between them was as it had been.

But when the evening came, Peter and Curdie felt that they would rather walk home together without other company, and therefore lingered behind when the rest of the men left the mine.

Chapter 6

The Emerald

Father and son had seated themselves on a projecting piece of the rock at a corner where three galleries met—the one they had come along from their work, one to the right leading out of the mountain, and the other to the left leading far into a portion of it which had been long disused. Since the inundation caused by the goblins, it had indeed been rendered impassable by the settlement of a quantity of the water, forming a small but very deep lake, in a part where was a considerable descent. They had just risen and were turning to the right, when a gleam caught their eyes, and made them look along the whole gangue. Far up they saw a pale green light, whence issuing they could not tell, about halfway between floor and roof of the passage. They saw nothing but the light, which was like a large star, with a point of darker colour yet brighter radiance in the heart of it, whence the rest of the light shot out in rays that faded towards the ends until they vanished. It shed hardly any light around it, although in itself it was so bright as to sting the eyes that beheld it. Wonderful stories had from ages gone been current in the mines about certain magic gems which gave out light of themselves, and this light looked just like what might be supposed to shoot from the heart of such a gem. They went up the old gallery to find out what it could be.

To their surprise they found, however, that, after going some distance, they were no nearer to it, so far as they could judge, then when they started. It did not seem to move, and yet they moving did not approach it. Still they persevered, for it was far too wonderful a thing to lose sight of so long as they could keep it. At length they drew near the hollow where the water lay, and still were no nearer the light. Where they expected to be stopped by the water, however, water was none: something had taken place in some part of the mine that had drained it off, and the gallery lay open as in former times. And now, to their surprise, the light, instead of being in front of them, was shining at the same distance to the right, where they did not know there was any passage at all. Then they discovered, by the light of the lanterns they carried, that there the water had broken through, and made an adit to a part of the mountain of which Peter knew nothing. But they were hardly well into it, still following the light, before Curdie thought he recognised some of the passages he had so often gone through when he was watching the goblins. After they had advanced a long way, with many turnings, now to the right, now to the left, all at once their eyes seemed to come suddenly to themselves, and they became aware that the light which they had taken to be a great way from them was in reality almost within reach of their hands. The same instant it began to grow larger and thinner, the point of light grew dim as it spread, the greenness melted away, and in a moment or two, instead of the star, a dark, dark and yet luminous face was looking at them with living eyes. And Curdie felt a great awe swell up in his heart, for he thought he had seen those eyes before.

"I see you know me, Curdie," said a voice.

"If your eyes are you, ma'am, then I know you," said Curdie. "But I never saw your face before."

"Yes, you have seen it, Curdie," said the voice.

And with that the darkness of its complexion melted away, and down from the face dawned out the form that belonged to it, until at last Curdie and his father beheld a lady, "beautiful exceedingly," dressed in something pale green, like velvet, over which her hair fell in cataracts of a rich golden colour. It looked as if it were pouring down from her head, and, like the water of the Dustbrook, vanishing in a golden vapour ere it reached the floor. It came flowing from under the edge of a coronet of gold, set with alternated pearls and emeralds. In front of the crown was a great emerald, which looked somehow as if out of it had come the light they had followed. There was no ornament else about her, except on her slippers, which were one mass of gleaming emeralds, of various shades of green, all mingling lovelily like the waving of grass in the wind and sun. She looked about five-and-twenty years old. And for all the difference, Curdie knew somehow or other, he could not have told how, that the face before him was that of the old princess, Irene's great-great-grandmother.

By this time all around them had grown light, and now first they could see where they were. They stood in a great splendid cavern, which Curdie recognised as that in which the goblins held their state assemblies. But, strange to tell, the light by which they saw came streaming, sparkling, and shooting from stones of many colours in the sides and roof and floor of the cavern—stones of all the colours of the rainbow, and many more. It was a glorious sight—the whole rugged place flashing with colours—in one spot a great light of deep carbuncular red, in another of sapphirine blue, in another of topaz-yellow; while here and there were groups of stones of all hues and sizes, and again nebulous spaces of thousands of tiniest spots of brilliancy of every conceivable shade. Sometimes the colours ran together, and made a little river or lake of lambent interfusing and changing tints, which, by their variegation, seemed to imitate the flowing of water, or waves made by the wind. Curdie would have gazed entranced, but that all the beauty of the cavern, yes, of all he knew of the whole creation, seemed gathered in one centre of harmony and loveliness in the person of the ancient lady who stood before him in the very summer of beauty and strength. Turning from the first glance at the circumfulgent splendour, it dwindled into nothing as he looked again at the lady. Nothing flashed or glowed or shone about her, and yet it was with a prevision of the truth that he said,—

"I was here once before, ma'am."

"I know that, Curdie," she replied.

"The place was full of torches, and the walls gleamed, but nothing as they do now, and there is no light in the place."

"You want to know where the light comes from?" she said, smiling.

"Yes, ma'am."

"Then see: I will go out of the cavern. Do not be afraid, but watch."

She went slowly out. The moment she turned her back to go, the light began to pale and fade; the moment she was out of their sight the place was black as night, save that now the smoky yellow-red of their lamps, which they thought had gone out long ago, cast a dusky glimmer around them.

Chapter 7

What *Is* in a Name?

For a time that seemed to them long, the two men stood waiting, while still the Mother of Light did not return. So long was she absent that they began to grow anxious: how were they to find their way from the natural hollows of the mountain crossed by goblin paths, if their lamps should go out? To spend the night there would mean to sit and wait until an earthquake rent the mountain, or the earth herself fell back into the smelting furnace of the sun whence she had issued—for it was all night and no faintest dawn in the bosom of the world. So long did they wait unrevisited, that, had there not been two of them, either would at length have concluded the vision a home-born product of his own seething brain. And their lamps *were* going out, for they grew redder and smokier! But they did not lose courage, for there is a kind of capillary attraction in the facing of two souls, that lifts faith quite beyond the level to which either could raise it alone: they knew that they had seen the lady of emeralds, and it was to give them their own desire that she had gone from them, and neither would yield for a moment to the half-doubts and half-dreads that awoke in his heart. And still she who with her absence darkened their air did not return. They grew weary, and sat down on the rocky floor, for wait they would—indeed, wait they must. Each set his lamp by his knee, and watched it die. Slowly it sank, dulled, looked lazy and stupid. But ever as it sank and dulled, the image in his mind of the Lady of Light grew stronger and clearer. Together the two lamps panted and shuddered. First one, then the other went out, leaving for a moment a great red, evil-smelling snuff. Then all was the blackness of darkness up to their very hearts and everywhere around them. Was it? No. Far away—it looked miles away—shone one minute faint point of green light—where, who could tell? They only knew that it shone. It grew larger, and seemed to draw nearer, until at last, as they watched with speechless delight and expectation, it seemed once more within reach of an outstretched hand. Then it spread and melted away as before, and there were eyes—and a face—and a lovely form—and lo! the whole cavern blazing with lights innumerable, and gorgeous, yet soft and interfused—so blended, indeed, that the eye had to search and see in order to separate distinct spots of special colour.

The moment they saw the speck in the vast distance they had risen and stood on their feet. When it came nearer they bowed their heads. Yet now they looked with fearless eyes, for the woman that was old and yet young was a joy to see, and filled their hearts with reverent delight. She turned first to Peter.

"I have known you long," she said. "I have met you going to and from the mine, and seen you working in it for the last forty years."

"How should it be, madam, that a grand lady like you should take notice of a poor man like me?" said Peter, humbly, but more foolishly than he could then have understood.

"I am poor as well as rich," said she. "I too work for my bread, and I show myself no favour when I pay myself my own wages. Last night when you sat by the brook, and Curdie told you about my pigeon, and my spinning, and wondered whether he could believe that he had actually seen me, I heard all you said to each other. I am always about, as the miners said the other night when they talked of me as Old Mother Wotherwop."

The lovely lady laughed, and her laugh was a lightning of delight in their souls.

"Yes," she went on, "you have got to thank me that you are so poor, Peter. I have seen to that, and it has done well for both you and me, my friend. Things come to the poor that can't get in at the door of the rich. Their money somehow blocks it up. It is a great privilege to be poor, Peter—one that no man ever coveted, and but a very few have sought to retain, but one that yet many have learned to prize. You must not mistake, however, and imagine it a virtue; it is but a privilege, and one also that, like other privileges, may be terribly misused. Hadst thou been rich, my Peter, thou wouldst not have been so good as some rich men I know. And now I am going to tell you what no one knows but myself: you, Peter, and your wife have both the blood of the royal family in your veins.

I have been trying to cultivate your family tree, every branch of which is known to me, and I expect Curdie to turn out a blossom on it. Therefore I have been training him for a work that must soon be done. I was near losing him, and had to send my pigeon. Had he not shot it, that would have been better; but he repented, and that shall be as good in the end."

She turned to Curdie and smiled.

"Ma'am," said Curdie, "may I ask questions?"

"Why not, Curdie?"

"Because I have been told, ma'am, that nobody must ask the king questions."

"The king never made that law," she answered, with some displeasure. "You may ask me as many as you please—that is, so long as they are sensible. Only I may take a few thousand years to answer some of them. But that's nothing. Of all things time is the cheapest."

"Then would you mind telling me now, ma'am, for I feel very confused about it—are you the Lady of the Silver Moon?"

"Yes, Curdie; you may call me that if you like. What it means is true."

"And now I see you dark, and clothed in green, and the mother of all the light that dwells in the stones of the earth! And up there they call you Old Mother Wotherwop! And the Princess Irene told me you were her great-great-grandmother! And you spin the spider-threads, and take care of a whole people of pigeons; and you are worn to a pale shadow with old age; and are as young as anybody can be, not to be too young; and as strong, I do believe, as I am."

The lady stooped towards a large green stone bedded in the rock of the floor, and looking like a well of grassy light in it. She laid hold of it with her fingers, broke it out, and gave it to Peter.

"There!" cried Curdie, "I told you so. Twenty men could not have done that. And your fingers are white and smooth as any lady's in the land. I don't know what to make of it."

"I could give you twenty names more to call me, Curdie, and not one of them would be a false one. What does it matter how many names if the person is one?"

"Ah! but it is not names only, ma'am. Look at what you were like last night, and what I see you now!"

"Shapes are only dresses, Curdie, and dresses are only names. That which is inside is the same all the time."

"But then how can all the shapes speak the truth?"

"It would want thousands more to speak the truth, Curdie; and then they could not. But there is a point I must not let you mistake about. It is one thing the shape I choose to put on, and quite another the shape that foolish talk and nursery tale may please to put upon me. Also, it is one thing what you or your father may think about me, and quite another what a foolish or bad man may see in me. For instance, if a thief were to come in here just now, he would think he saw the demon of the mine, all in green flames, come to protect her treasure, and would run like a hunted wild goat. I should be all the same, but his evil eyes would see me as I was not."

"I think I understand," said Curdie.

"Peter," said the lady, turning then to him, "you will have to give up Curdie for a little while."

"So long as he loves us, ma'am, that will not matter—much."

"Ah! you are right there, my friend," said the beautiful princess.

And as she said it she put out her hand, and took the hard, horny hand of the miner in it, and held it for a moment lovingly.

"I need say no more," she added, "for we understand each other— you and I, Peter."

The tears came into Peter's eyes. He bowed his head in thankfulness, and his heart was much too full to speak.

Then the great old young beautiful princess turned to Curdie.

"Now, Curdie, are you ready?" she said.

"Yes, ma'am," answered Curdie.

"You do not know what for."

"You do, ma'am. That is enough."

"You could not have given me a better answer, or done more to prepare yourself, Curdie," she returned, with one of her radiant smiles. "Do you think you will know me again?"

"I think so. But how can I tell what you may look like next?"

"Ah, that indeed! How can you tell? Or how could I expect you should? But those who know me *well*, know me whatever new dress or shape or name I may be in; and by-and-by you will have learned to do so too."

"But if you want me to know you again, ma'am, for certain sure," said Curdie, "could you not give me some sign, or tell me something about you that never changes—or some other way to know you, or thing to know you by?"

"No, Curdie; that would be to keep you from knowing me. You must know me in quite another way from that. It would not be the least use to you or me either if I were to make you know me in that way. It would be but to know the sign of me—not to know me myself. It would be no better than if I were to take this emerald out of my crown and give it you to take home with you, and you were to call it me, and talk to it as if it heard and saw and loved you. Much good that would do you, Curdie! No; you must do what you can to know me, and if you do, you will. You shall see me again—in very different circumstances from these, and I will tell you so much, it *may* be in a very different shape. But come now, I will lead you out of this cavern; my good Joan will be getting too anxious about you. One word more: you will allow that the men knew little what they were talking about this morning, when they told all those tales of Old Mother Wotherwop; but did it occur to you to think how it was they fell to talking about me at all?—It was because I came to them; I was beside them all the time they were talking about me, though they were far enough from knowing it, and had very little besides foolishness to say."

As she spoke she turned and led the way from the cavern, which, as if a door had been closed, sunk into absolute blackness behind them. And now they saw nothing more of the lady except the green star, which again seemed a good distance in front of them, and to which they came no nearer, although following it at a quick pace through the mountain. Such was their confidence in her guidance, however, and so fearless were they in consequence, that they felt their way neither with hand nor foot, but walked straight on through the pitch dark galleries. When at length the night of the upper world looked in at the mouth of the mine, the green light seemed to lose its way amongst the stars, and they saw it no more.

Out they came into the cool, blessed night. It was very late, and only starlight. To their surprise, three paces away they saw, seated upon a stone, an old countrywoman, in a cloak which they took for black. When they came close up to it, they saw it was red.

"Good evening!" said Peter.

"Good evening!" returned the old woman, in a voice as old as herself.

But Curdie took off his cap and said,—

"I am your servant, princess."

The old woman replied,—

"Come to me in the dove-tower to-morrow night, Curdie—alone."

"I will, ma'am," said Curdie.

So they parted, and father and son went home to wife and mother—two persons in one rich, happy woman.

Chapter 8

Curdie's Mission

The next night Curdie went home from the mine a little earlier than usual, to make himself tidy before going to the dove-tower. The princess had not appointed an exact time for him to be there; he would go as near the time he had gone first as he could. On his way to the bottom of the hill, he met his father coming up. The sun was then down, and the warm first of the twilight filled the evening. He came rather wearily up the hill: the road, he thought, must have grown steeper in parts since he was Curdie's age. His back was to the light of the sunset, which closed him all round in a beautiful setting, and Curdie thought what a grand-looking man his father was, even when he was tired. It is greed and laziness and selfishness, not hunger or weariness or cold, that take the dignity out of a man, and make him look mean.

"Ah, Curdie! there you are!" he said, seeing his son come bounding along as if it were morning with him and not evening.

"You look tired, father," said Curdie.

"Yes, my boy. I'm not so young as you."

"Nor so old as the princess," said Curdie.

"Tell me this," said Peter: "why do people talk about going down hill when they begin to get old? It seems to me that then first they begin to go up hill."

"You looked to me, father, when I caught sight of you, as if you had been climbing the hill all your life, and were soon to get to the top."

"Nobody can tell when that will be," returned Peter. "We're so ready to think we're just at the top when it lies miles away. But I must not keep you, my boy, for you are wanted; and we shall be anxious to know what the princess says to you—that is, if she will allow you to tell us."

"I think she will, for she knows there is nobody more to be trusted than my father and mother," said Curdie, with pride.

And away he shot, and ran, and jumped, and seemed almost to fly down the long, winding, steep path, until he came to the gate of the king's house.

There he met an unexpected obstruction: in the open door stood the housekeeper, and she seemed to broaden herself out until she almost filled the doorway.

"So!" she said; "it's you, is it, young man? You are the person that comes in and goes out when he pleases, and keeps running up and down my stairs, without ever saying by your leave, or even wiping his shoes, and always leaves the door open! Don't you know that this is my house?"

"No, I do not," returned Curdie, respectfully. "You forget, ma'am, that it is the king's house."

"That is all the same. The king left it to me to take care of, and that you shall know!"

"Is the king dead, ma'am, that he has left it to you?" asked Curdie, half in doubt from the self-assertion of the woman.

"Insolent fellow!" exclaimed the housekeeper. "Don't you see by my dress that I am in the king's service?"

"And am I not one of his miners?"

"Ah! that goes for nothing. I am one of his household. You are an out-of-doors labourer. You are a nobody. You carry a pickaxe. I carry the keys at my girdle. See!"

"But you must not call one a nobody to whom the king has spoken," said Curdie.

"Go along with you!" cried the housekeeper, and would have shut the door in his face, had she not been afraid that when she stepped back he would step in ere she could get it in motion, for it was very heavy, and always seemed unwilling to shut. Curdie came a pace nearer. She lifted the great house key from her side, and threatened to strike him down with it, calling aloud on Mar and Whelk and Plout, the men-servants under her, to come and help her. Ere one of them could answer, however, she gave a great shriek and turned and fled, leaving the door wide open.

Curdie looked behind him, and saw an animal whose gruesome oddity even he, who knew so many of the strange creatures, two of which were never the same, that used to live inside the mountain with their masters the goblins, had never seen equalled. Its eyes were flaming with anger, but it seemed to be at the housekeeper, for it came cowering and creeping up, and laid its head on the ground at Curdie's feet. Curdie hardly waited to look at it, however, but ran into the house, eager to get up the stairs before any of the men should come to annoy—he had no fear of their preventing him. Without halt or hindrance, though the passages were nearly dark, he reached the door of the princess's workroom, and knocked.

"Come in," said the voice of the princess.

Curdie opened the door,—but, to his astonishment, saw no room there. Could he have opened a wrong door? There was the great sky, and the stars, and beneath he could see nothing—only darkness! But what was that in the sky, straight in front of him? A great wheel of fire, turning and turning, and flashing out blue lights!

"Come in, Curdie," said the voice again.

"I would at once, ma'am," said Curdie, "if I were sure I was standing at your door."

"Why should you doubt it, Curdie?"

"Because I see neither walls nor floor, only darkness and the great sky."

"That is all right, Curdie. Come in."

Curdie stepped forward at once. He was indeed, for the very crumb of a moment, tempted to feel before him with his foot; but he saw that would be to distrust the princess, and a greater rudeness he could not offer her. So he stepped straight in—I will not say without a little tremble at the thought of finding no floor beneath his foot. But that which had need of the floor found it, and his foot was satisfied.

No sooner was he in than he saw that the great revolving wheel in the sky was the princess's spinning-wheel, near the other end of the room, turning very fast. He could see no sky or stars any more, but the wheel was flashing out blue—oh such lovely sky-blue light!—and behind it of course sat the princess, but whether an old woman as thin as a skeleton leaf, or a glorious lady as young as perfection, he could not tell for the turning and flashing of the wheel.

"Listen to the wheel," said the voice which had already grown dear to Curdie: its very tone was precious like a jewel, not *as* a jewel, for no jewel could compare with it in preciousness.

And Curdie listened and listened.

"What is it saying?" said the voice.

"It is singing," answered Curdie.

"What is it singing?"

Curdie tried to make out, but thought he could not; for no sooner had he got a hold of something than it vanished again. Yet he listened, and listened, entranced with delight.

"Thank you, Curdie," said the voice.

"Ma'am," said Curdie, "I did try hard for a while, but I could not make anything of it."

"Oh, yes, you did, and you have been telling it to me! Shall I tell you again what I told my wheel, and my wheel told you, and you have just told me without knowing it?"

"Please, ma'am."

Then the lady began to sing, and her wheel spun an accompaniment to her song, and the music of the wheel was like the music of an Æolian harp blown upon by the wind that bloweth where it listeth. Oh! the sweet sounds of that spinning-wheel! Now they were gold, now silver, now grass, now palm-trees, now ancient cities, now rubies, now mountain brooks, now peacock's feathers, now clouds, now snowdrops, and now mid-sea islands. But for the voice that sang through it all, about that I have no words to tell. It would make you weep if I were able to tell you what that was like, it was so beautiful and true and lovely. But this is something like the words of its song:—

> The stars are spinning their threads,
>   And the clouds are the dust that flies,
> And the suns are weaving them up
>   For the time when the sleepers shall rise.
>
> The ocean in music rolls,
>   And gems are turning to eyes,
> And the trees are gathering souls
>   For the time when the sleepers shall rise.
>
> The weepers are learning to smile,
>   And laughter to glean the sighs;
> Burn and bury the care and guile,
>   For the day when the sleepers shall rise.

Oh, the dews and the moths and the daisy-red,
  The larks and the glimmers and flows!
The lilies and sparrows and daily bread,
  And the something that nobody knows!

The princess stopped, her wheel stopped, and she laughed. And her laugh was sweeter than song and wheel; sweeter than running brook and silver bell; sweeter than joy itself, for the heart of the laugh was love.

"Come now, Curdie, to this side of my wheel, and you will find me," she said; and her laugh seemed sounding on still in the words, as if they were made of breath that had laughed.

Curdie obeyed, and passed the wheel, and there she stood to receive him!—fairer than when he saw her last, a little younger still, and dressed not in green and emeralds, but in pale blue, with a coronet of silver set with pears, and slippers covered with opals, that gleamed every colour of the rainbow. It was some time before Curdie could take his eyes from the marvel of her loveliness. Fearing at last that he was rude, he turned them away; and, behold, he was in a room that was for beauty marvellous! The lofty ceiling was all a golden vine, whose great clusters of carbuncles, rubies, and chrysoberyls, hung down like the bosses of groined arches, and in its centre hung the most glorious lamp that human eyes ever saw—the Silver Moon itself, a globe of silver, as it seemed, with a heart of light so wondrous potent that it rendered the mass translucent, and altogether radiant.

The room was so large that, looking back, he could scarcely see the end at which he entered; but the other was only a few yards from him—and there he saw another wonder: on a huge hearth a great fire was burning, and the fire was a huge heap of roses, and yet it was fire. The smell of the roses filled the air, and the heat of the flames of them glowed upon his face. He turned an inquiring look upon the lady, and saw that she was now seated in an ancient chair, the legs of which were crusted with gems, but the upper part like a nest of daisies and moss and green grass.

"Curdie," she said in answer to his eyes, "you have stood more than one trial already, and have stood them well: now I am going to put you to a harder. Do you think you are prepared for it?"

"How can I tell, ma'am?" he returned, "seeing I do not know what it is, or what preparation it needs? Judge me yourself, ma'am."

"It needs only trust and obedience," answered the lady.

"I dare not say anything, ma'am. If you think me fit, command me."

"It will hurt you terribly, Curdie, but that will be all; no real hurt, but much real good will come to you from it."

Curdie made no answer, but stood gazing with parted lips in the lady's face.

"Go and thrust both your hands into that fire," she said quickly, almost hurriedly.

Curdie dared not stop to think. It was much too terrible to think about. He rushed to the fire, and thrust both his hands right into the middle of the heap of flaming roses, and his arms halfway up to the elbows. And it *did* hurt! But he did not draw them back. He held the pain as if it were a thing that would kill him if he let it go—as indeed it would have done. He was in terrible fear lest it should conquer him. But when it had risen to the pitch that he thought he could bear it no longer, it began to fall again, and went on growing less and less until by contrast with its former severity it had become rather pleasant. At last it ceased altogether, and Curdie thought his hands must be burnt to cinders if not ashes, for he did not feel them at all. The princess told him to take them out and look at them. He did so, and found that all that was gone of them was the rough hard skin; they were white and smooth like the princess's.

"Come to me," she said.

He obeyed, and saw, to his surprise, that her face looked as if she had been weeping.

"Oh, princess! what *is* the matter?" he cried. "Did I make a noise and vex you?"

"No, Curdie," she answered; "but it was very bad."

"Did you feel it too then?"

"Of course I did. But now it is over, and all is well.—Would you like to know why I made you put your hands in the fire?"

Curdie looked at them again—then said,—

"To take the marks of the work off them, and make them fit for the king's court, I suppose."

"No, Curdie," answered the princess, shaking her head, for she was not pleased with the answer. "It would be a poor way of making your hands fit for the king's court to take off them all signs of his service. There is a far greater difference on them than that. Do you feel none?"

"No, ma'am."

"You will, though, by and by, when the time comes. But perhaps even then you might not know what had been given you, therefore I will tell you.—Have you ever heard what some philosophers say—that men were all animals once?"

"No, ma'am."

"It is of no consequence. But there is another thing that is of the greatest consequence—this: that all men, if they do not take care, go down the hill to the animals' country; that many men are actually, all their lives, going to be beasts. People knew it once, but it is long since they forgot it."

"I am not surprised to hear it, ma'am, when I think of some of our miners."

"Ah! but you must beware, Curdie, how you say of this man or that man that he is travelling beastward. There are not nearly so many going that way as at first sight you might think. When you met your father on the hill tonight, you stood and spoke together on the same spot; and although one of you was going up and the other coming down, at a little distance no one could have told which was bound in the one direction and which in the other. Just so two people may be at the same spot in manners and behaviour, and yet one may be getting better and the other worse, which is the greatest of all differences that could possibly exist between them."

"But, ma'am," said Curdie, "where is the good of knowing that there is such a difference, if you can never know where it is?"

"Now, Curdie, you must mind exactly what words I use, because although the right words cannot do exactly what I want them to do, the wrong words will certainly do what I do not want them to do. I did not say *you can never know*. When there is a necessity for your knowing, when you have to do important business with this or that man, there is always a way of knowing enough to keep you from any great blunder. And as you will have important business to do by and by, and that with people of whom you yet know nothing, it will be necessary that you should have some better means than usual of learning the nature of them. Now listen. Since it is always what they *do*, whether in their minds or their bodies, that makes men go down to be less than men, that is, beasts, the change always comes first in their hands—and first of all in the inside hands, to which the outside ones are but as the gloves. They do not know it of course; for a beast does not know that he is a beast, and the nearer a man gets to being a beast the less he knows it. Neither can their best friends, or their worst enemies indeed, *see* any difference in their hands, for they see only the living gloves of them. But there are not a few who feel a vague something repulsive in the hand of a man who is growing a beast. Now here is what the rose-fire has done for you: it has made your hands so knowing and wise, it has brought your real hands so near the outside of your flesh-gloves, that you will henceforth be able to know at once the hand of a man who is growing into a beast; nay, more—you will at once feel the foot of the beast he is growing, just as if there were no glove made like a man's hand between you and it. Hence of course it follows that you will be able often, and with further education in zoology, will be able always to tell, not only when a man is growing a beast, but what beast he is growing to, for you will know the foot—what it is and what beast's it is. According then to your knowledge of that beast, will be your knowledge of the man you have to do with. Only there is one beautiful and awful thing about it, that if any one gifted with this perception once uses it for his own ends, it is taken from him, and then, not knowing that it is gone, he is in a far worse condition than before, for he trusts to what he has not got."

"How dreadful!" said Curdie. "I must mind what I am about."

"Yes, indeed, Curdie."

"But may not one sometimes make a mistake without being able to help it?"

"Yes. But so long as he is not after his own ends, he will never make a serious mistake."

"I suppose you want me, ma'am, to warn every one whose hand tells me that he is growing a beast—because, as you say, he does not know it himself."

The princess smiled.

"Much good that would do, Curdie! I don't say there are no cases in which it would be of use, but they are very rare and peculiar cases, and if such come you will know them. To such a person there is in general no insult like the truth. He cannot endure it, not because he is growing a beast, but because he is ceasing to be a man. It is the dying man in him that it makes uncomfortable, and he trots, or creeps, or swims, or flutters out of its way—calls it a foolish feeling, a whim, an old wives' fable, a bit of priests' humbug, an effete superstition, and so on."

"And is there no hope for him? Can nothing be done? It's so awful to think of going down, down, down like that!"

"Even when it is with his own will?"

"That's what seems to me to make it worst of all," said Curdie.

"You are right," answered the princess, nodding her head; "but there is this amount of excuse to make for all such, remember—that they do not know what or how horrid their coming fate is. Many a lady, so delicate and nice that she can bear nothing coarser than the finest linen to touch her body, if she had a mirror that could show her the animal she is growing to, as it lies waiting within the fair skin and the fine linen and the silk and the jewels, would receive a shock that might possibly wake her up."

"Why then, ma'am, shouldn't she have it?"

The princess held her peace.

"Come here, Lina," she said after a long pause.

From somewhere behind Curdie, crept forward the same hideous animal which had fawned at his feet at the door, and which, without his knowing it, had followed him every step up the dove-tower. She ran to the princess, and lay down at her feet, looking up at her with an expression so pitiful that in Curdie's heart it overcame all the ludicrousness of her horrible mass of incongruities. She had a very short body, and very long legs made like an elephant's, so that in lying down she kneeled with both pairs. Her tail, which dragged on the floor behind her, was twice as long and quite as thick as her body. Her head was something between that of a polar bear and a snake. Her eyes were dark green, with a yellow light in them. Her under teeth came up like a fringe of icicles, only very white, outside of her upper lip. Her throat looked as if the hair had been plucked off. It showed a skin white and smooth.

"Give Curdie a paw, Lina," said the princess.

The creature rose, and, lifting a long fore leg, held up a great dog-like paw to Curdie. He took it gently. But what a shudder, as of terrified delight, ran through him, when, instead of the paw of a dog, such as it seemed to his eyes, he clasped in his great mining fist the soft, neat little hand of a child! He took it in both of his, and held it as if he could not let it go. The green eyes stared at him with their yellow light, and the mouth was turned up towards him with its constant half-grin; but here *was* the child's hand! If he could but pull the child out of the beast! His eyes sought the princess. She was watching him with evident satisfaction.

"Ma'am, here is a child's hand!" said Curdie.

"Your gift does more for you than it promised. It is yet better to perceive a hidden good than a hidden evil."

"But," began Curdie.

"I am not going to answer any more questions this evening," interrupted the princess. "You have not half got to the bottom of the answers I have already given you. That paw in your hand now might almost teach you the whole science of natural history—the heavenly sort, I mean."

"I will think," said Curdie. "But oh! please! one word more: may I tell my father and mother all about it?"

"Certainly—though perhaps now it may be their turn to find it a little difficult to believe that things went just as you must tell them."

"They shall see that I believe it all this time," said Curdie.

"Tell them that to-morrow morning you must set out for the court—not like a great man, but just as poor as you are. They had better not speak about it. Tell them also that it will be a long time before they hear of you again, but they must not lose heart. And tell your father to lay that stone I gave him last night in a safe place—not because of the greatness of its price, although it is such an emerald as no prince has in his crown, but because it will be a news-bearer between you and him. As often as he gets at all anxious about you, he must take it and lay it in the fire, and leave it there when he goes to bed. In the morning he must find it in the ashes, and if it be as green as ever, then all goes well with you; if it have lost colour, things go ill with you; but if it be very pale indeed, then you are in great danger, and he must come to me."

"Yes, ma'am," said Curdie. "Please, am I to go now?"

"Yes," answered the princess, and held out her hand to him.

Curdie took it, trembling with joy. It was a very beautiful hand—not small, very smooth, but not very soft—and just the same to his fire-taught touch that it was to his eyes. He would have stood there all night holding it if she had not gently withdrawn it.

"I will provide you a servant," she said, "for your journey, and to wait upon you afterwards."

"But where am I to go, ma'am, and what am I to do? You have given me no message to carry, neither have you said what I am wanted for. I go without a notion whether I am to walk this way or that, or what I am to do when I get I don't know where."

"Curdie!" said the princess, and there was a tone of reminder in his own name as she spoke it, "did I not tell you to tell your father and mother that you were to set out for the court? and you *know* that lies to the north. You must learn to use far less direct directions than that. You must not be like a dull servant that needs to be told again and again before he will understand. You have orders enough to start with, and you will find, as you go on, and as you need to know, what you have to do. But I warn you that perhaps it will not look the least like what you may have been fancying I should require of you. I have one idea of you and your work, and you have another. I do not blame you for that—you cannot help it yet; but you must be ready to let my idea, which sets you working, set your idea right. Be true and honest and fearless, and all shall go well with you and your work, and all with whom your work lies, and so with your parents—and me too, Curdie," she added after a little pause.

The young miner bowed his head low, patted the strange head that lay at the princess's feet, and turned away.

As soon as he passed the spinning-wheel, which looked, in the midst of the glorious room, just like any wheel you might find in a country cottage—old and worn and dingy and dusty—the splendour of the place vanished, and he saw but the big bare room he seemed at first to have entered, with the moon—the princess's moon no doubt—shining in at one of the windows upon the spinning-wheel.

Chapter 9

Hands

Curdie went home, pondering much, and told everything to his father and mother. As the old princess had said, it was now their turn to find what they heard hard to believe. If they had not been able to trust Curdie himself, they would have refused to believe more than the half of what he reported, then they would have refused that half too, and at last would most likely for a time have disbelieved in the very existence of the princess, what evidence their own senses had given them notwithstanding. For he had nothing conclusive to show in proof of what he told them. When he held out his hands to them, his mother said they looked as if he had been washing them with soft soap, only they did smell of something nicer than that, and she must allow it was more like roses than anything else she knew. His father could not see any difference upon his hands, but then it was night, he said, and their poor little lamp was not enough for his old eyes. As to the feel of them, each of his own hands, he said, was hard and horny enough for two, and it must be the fault of the dulness of his own thick skin that he felt no change on Curdie's palms.

"Here, Curdie," said his mother, "try my hand, and see what beast's paw lies inside it."

"No, mother," answered Curdie, half-beseeching, half-indignant, "I will not insult my new gift by making pretence to try it. That would be mockery. There is no hand within yours but the hand of a true woman, my mother."

"I should like you just to take hold of my hand, though," said his mother. "You are my son, and may know all the bad there is in me."

Then at once Curdie took her hand in his. And when he had it, he kept it, stroking it gently with his other hand.

73

"Mother," he said at length, "your hand feels just like that of the princess."

"What! my horny, cracked, rheumatic old hand, with its big joints, and its short nails all worn down to the quick with hard work—like the hand of the beautiful princess! Why, my child, you will make me fancy your fingers have grown very dull indeed, instead of sharp and delicate, if you talk such nonsense. Mine is such an ugly hand I should be ashamed to show it to any but one that loved me. But love makes all safe—doesn't it, Curdie?"

"Well, mother, all I can say is that I don't feel a roughness, or a crack, or a big joint, or a short nail. Your hand feels just and exactly, as near as I can recollect, and it's not now more than two hours since I had it in mine,—well, I will say, very like indeed to that of the old princess."

"Go away, you flatterer," said his mother, with a smile that showed how she prized the love that lay beneath what she took for its hyperbole. The praise even which one cannot accept is sweet from a true mouth. "If that is all your new gift can do, it won't make a warlock of you," she added.

"Mother, it tells me nothing but the truth," insisted Curdie, "however unlike the truth it may seem. It wants no gift to tell what anybody's outside hands are like. But by it I *know* your inside hands are like the princess's."

"And I am sure the boy speaks true," said Peter. "He only says about your hand what I have known ever so long about yourself, Joan. Curdie, your mother's foot is as pretty a foot as any lady's in the land, and where her hand is not so pretty it comes of killing its beauty for you and me, my boy. And I can tell you more, Curdie. I don't know much about ladies and gentlemen, but I am sure your inside mother must be a lady, as her hand tells you, and I will try to say how I know it. This is how: when I forget myself looking at her as she goes about her work—and that happens oftener as I grow older—I fancy for a moment or two that I am a gentleman; and when I wake up from my little dream, it is only to feel the more strongly that I must do everything as a gentleman should. I will try to tell you what I mean, Curdie. If a gentleman—I mean a real gentleman, not a pretended one, of which sort they say there are a many above ground—if a real gentleman were to lose all his money and come down to work in the mines to get bread for his family—do you think, Curdie, he would work like the lazy ones? Would he try to do as little as he could for his wages? I know the sort of the true gentleman—pretty near as well as he does himself. And my wife, that's your mother, Curdie, she's a true lady, you may take my word for it, for it's she that makes me want to be a true gentleman. Wife, the boy is in the right about your hand."

"Now, father, let me feel yours," said Curdie, daring a little more.

"No, no, my boy," answered Peter. "I don't want to hear anything about my hand or my head or my heart. I am what I am, and I hope growing better, and that's enough. No, you shan't feel my hand. You must go to bed, for you must start with the sun."

It was not as if Curdie had been leaving them to go to prison, or to make a fortune, and although they were sorry enough to lose him, they were not in the least heart-broken or even troubled at his going.

As the princess had said he was to go like the poor man he was, Curdie came down in the morning from his little loft dressed in his working clothes. His mother, who was busy getting his breakfast for him, while his father sat reading to her out of an old book, would have had him put on his holiday garments, which, she said, would look poor enough amongst the fine ladies and gentlemen he was going to. But Curdie said he did not know that he was going amongst ladies and gentlemen, and that as work was better than play, his work-day clothes must on the whole be better than his play-day clothes; and as his father accepted the argument, his mother gave in.

When he had eaten his breakfast, she took a pouch made of goatskin, with the long hair on it, filled it with bread and cheese, and hung it over his shoulder. Then his father gave him a stick he had cut for him in the wood, and he bade them good-bye rather hurriedly, for he was afraid of breaking down. As he went out, he caught up his mattock and took it with him. It had on the one side a pointed curve of strong steel, for loosening the earth and the ore, and on the other a steel hammer for breaking the stones and rocks. Just as he crossed the threshold the sun showed the first segment of his disc above the horizon.

Chapter 10

The Heath

He had to go to the bottom of the hill to get into a country he could cross, for the mountains to the north were full of precipices, and it would have been losing time to go that way. Not until he had reached the king's house was it any use to turn northwards. Many a look did he raise, as he passed it, to the dove-tower, and as long as it was in sight, but he saw nothing of the lady of the pigeons.

On and on he fared, and came in a few hours to a country where there were no mountains more—only hills, with great stretches of desolate heath. Here and there was a village, but that brought him little pleasure, for the people were rougher and worse-mannered than those in the mountains, and as he passed through, the children came behind and mocked him.

"There's a monkey running away from the mines!" they cried.

Sometimes their parents came out and encouraged them.

"He don't want to find gold for the king any longer,—the lazybones!" they would say. "He'll be well taxed down here though, and he won't like that either."

But it was little to Curdie that men who did not know what he was about should not approve of his proceedings. He gave them a merry answer now and then, and held diligently on his way. When they got so rude as nearly to make him angry, he would treat them as he used to treat the goblins, and sing his own songs to keep out their foolish noises. Once a child fell as he turned to run away after throwing a stone at him. He picked him up, kissed him, and carried him to his mother. The woman had run out in terror when she saw the strange miner about, as she thought, to take vengeance on her boy. When he put him in her arms, she blessed him, and Curdie went on his way rejoicing.

And so the day went on, and the evening came, and in the middle of a great desolate heath he began to feel tired, and sat down under an ancient hawthorn, through which every now and then a lone wind that seemed to come from nowhere and to go nowhither sighed and hissed. It was very old and distorted. There was not another tree for miles all around. It seemed to have lived so long, and to have been so torn and tossed by the tempests on that moor, that it had at last gathered a wind of its own, which got up now and then, tumbled itself about, and lay down again.

Curdie had been so eager to get on that he had eaten nothing since his breakfast. But he had had plenty of water, for many little streams had crossed his path. He now opened the wallet his mother had given him, and began to eat his supper. The sun was setting. A few clouds gathered about the west, but there was not a single cloud anywhere else to be seen.

Now Curdie did not know that this was a part of the country very hard to get through. Nobody lived there, though many had tried to build in it. Some died very soon. Some rushed out of it. Those who stayed longest went raving mad, and died a terrible death. Such as walked straight on, and did not spend a night there, got through well, and were nothing the worse. But those who slept even a single night in it were sure to meet with something they could never forget, and which often left a mark everybody could read. And that old hawthorn might have been enough for a warning—it looked so like a human being dried up and distorted with age and suffering, with cares instead of loves, and things instead of thoughts. Both it and the heath around it, which stretched on all sides as far as he could see, were so withered that it was impossible to say whether they were alive or not.

And while Curdie ate there came a change. Clouds had gathered over his head, and seemed drifting about in every direction, as if not "shepherded by the slow, unwilling wind," but hunted in all directions by wolfish flaws across the plains of the sky. The sun was going down in a storm of lurid crimson, and out of the west came a wind that felt red and hot the one moment, and cold and pale the other. And very strangely it sung in the dreary old hawthorn tree, and very cheerily it blew about Curdie, now making him creep close up to the tree for shelter from its shivery cold, now fan himself with his cap, it was so sultry and stifling. It seemed to come from the death-bed of the sun, dying in fever and ague.

And as he gazed at the sun, now on the verge of the horizon, very large and very red and very dull—for though the clouds had broken away a dusty fog was spread all over him—Curdie saw something strange appear against him, moving about like a fly over his burning face. It looked as if it were coming out of his hot furnace-heart, and was a living creature of some kind surely; but its shape was very uncertain, because the dazzle of the light all around it melted its outlines. It was growing larger, it must be approaching! It grew so rapidly that by the time the sun was half down its head reached the top of his arch, and presently nothing but its legs were to be seen, crossing and recrossing the face of the vanishing disc. When the sun was down he could see nothing of it more, but in a moment he heard its feet galloping over the dry crackling heather, and seeming to come straight for him. He stood up, lifted his pick-axe, and threw the hammer end over his shoulder: he was going to have a fight for his life! And now it appeared again, vague, yet very awful, in the dim twilight the sun had left behind him. But just before it reached him, down from its four long legs it dropped flat on the ground, and came crawling towards him, wagging a huge tail as it came.

Chapter 11

Lina

It was Lina. All at once Curdie recognised her—the frightful creature he had seen at the princess's. He dropped his pick-axe, and held out his hand. She crept nearer and nearer, and laid her chin in his palm, and he patted her ugly head. Then she crept away behind the tree, and lay down, panting hard. Curdie did not much like the idea of her being behind him. Horrible as she was to look at, she seemed to his mind more horrible when he was not looking at her. But he remembered the child's hand, and never thought of driving her away. Now and then he gave a glance behind him, and there she lay flat, with her eyes closed and her terrible teeth gleaming between her two huge fore-paws.

After his supper and his long day's journey it was no wonder Curdie should now be sleepy. Since the sun set the air had been warm and pleasant. He lay down under the tree, closed his eyes, and thought to sleep. He found himself mistaken however. But although he could not sleep, he was yet aware of resting delightfully. Presently he heard a sweet sound of singing somewhere, such as he had never heard before—a singing as of curious birds far off, which drew nearer and nearer. At length he heard their wings, and, opening his eyes, saw a number of very large birds, as it seemed, alighting around him, still singing. It was strange to hear song from the throats of such big birds. And still singing, with large and round but not the less bird-like voices, they began to weave a strange dance about him, moving their wings in time with their legs. But the dance seemed somehow to be troubled and broken, and to return upon itself in an eddy, in place of sweeping smoothly on. And he soon learned, in the low short growls behind him, the cause of the imperfection: they wanted to dance all round the tree, but Lina would not permit them to come on her side.

Now Curdie liked the birds, and did not altogether *like* Lina. But neither, nor both together, made a *reason* for driving away the princess's creature. Doubtless she *had been* a goblins' creature, but the last time he saw her was in the king's house and the dove-tower, and at the old princess's feet. So he left her to do as she would, and the dance of the birds continued only a semicircle, troubled at the edges, and returning upon itself. But their song and their motions, nevertheless, and the waving of their wings, began at length to make him very sleepy. All the time he had kept doubting every now and then whether they could really be birds, and the sleepier he got, the more he imagined them something else, but he suspected no harm. Suddenly, just as he was sinking beneath the waves of slumber, he awoke in fierce pain. The birds were upon him—all over him—and had begun to tear him with beaks and claws. He had but time, however, to feel that he could not move under their weight, when they set up a hideous screaming, and scattered like a cloud. Lina was amongst them, snapping and striking with her paws, while her tail knocked them over and over. But they flew up, gathered, and descended on her in a swarm, perching upon every part of her body, so that he could see only a huge misshapen mass, which seemed to go rolling away into the darkness. He got up and tried to follow, but could see nothing, and after wandering about hither and thither for some time, found himself again beside the hawthorn. He feared greatly that the birds had been too much for Lina, and had torn her to pieces. In a little while, however, she came limping back, and lay down in her old place. Curdie also lay down, but, from the pain of her wounds, there was no sleep for him. When the light came he found his clothes a good deal torn and his skin as well, but gladly wondered why the wicked birds had not at once attacked his eyes. Then he turned looking for Lina. She rose and crept to him. But she was in far worse plight than he—plucked and gashed and torn with the beaks and claws of the birds, especially about the bare part of her neck, so that she was pitiful to see. And those worst wounds she could not reach to lick.

"Poor Lina!" said Curdie; "you got all those helping me."

She wagged her tail, and make it clear she understood him. Then it flashed upon Curdie's mind that perhaps this was the companion the princess had promised him. For the princess did so many things differently from what anybody looked for! Lina was no beauty certainly, but already, the first night, she had saved his life.

"Come along, Lina," he said; "we want water."

She put her nose to the earth, and after snuffing for a moment, darted off in a straight line. Curdie followed. The ground was so uneven, that after losing sight of her many times, at last he seemed to have lost her altogether. In a few minutes, however, he came upon her waiting for him. Instantly she darted off again. After he had lost and found her again many times, he found her the last time lying beside a great stone. As soon as he came up she began scratching at it with her paws. When he had raised it an inch or two, she shoved in first her nose and then her teeth, and lifted with all the might of her strong neck.

When at length between them they got it up, there was a beautiful little well. He filled his cap with the clearest and sweetest water, and drank. Then he gave to Lina, and she drank plentifully. Next he washed her wounds very carefully. And as he did so, he noted how much the bareness of her neck added to the strange repulsiveness of her appearance. Then he bethought him of the goat-skin wallet his mother had given him, and taking it from his shoulders, tried whether it would do to make a collar of for the poor animal. He found there was just enough, and the hair so similar in colour to Lina's, that no one could suspect it of having grown somewhere else. He took his knife, ripped up the seams of the wallet, and began trying the skin to her neck. It was plain she understood perfectly what he wished, for she endeavoured to hold her neck conveniently, turning it this way and that while he contrived, with his rather scanty material, to make the collar fit. As his mother had taken care to provide him with needles and thread, he soon had a nice gorget ready for her. He laced it on with one of his boot-laces, which its long hair covered. Poor Lina looked much better in it. Nor could any one have called it a piece of finery. If ever green eyes with a yellow light in them looked grateful, hers did.

As they had no longer any bag to carry them in, Curdie and Lina now ate what was left of the provisions. Then they set out again upon their journey. For seven days it lasted. They met with various adventures, and in all of them Lina proved so helpful, and so ready to risk her life for the sake of her companion, that Curdie grew not merely very fond but very trustful of her, and her ugliness, which at first only moved his pity, now actually increased his affection for her. One day, looking at her stretched on the grass before him, he said,—

"Oh, Lina! if the princess would but burn you in her fire of roses!"

She looked up at him, gave a mournful whine like a dog, and laid her head on his feet. What or how much he could not tell, but clearly she had gathered something from his words.

Chapter 12

More Creatures

One day from morning till night they had been passing through a forest. As soon as the sun was down Curdie began to be aware that there were more in it than themselves. First he saw only the swift rush of a figure across the trees at some distance. Then he saw another and then another at shorter intervals. Then he saw others both further off and nearer. At last, missing Lina and looking about after her, he saw an appearance almost as marvellous as herself steal up to her, and begin conversing with her after some beast fashion which evidently she understood.

Presently what seemed a quarrel arose between them, and stranger noises followed, mingled with growling. At length it came to a fight, which had not lasted long, however, before the creature of the wood threw itself upon its back, and held up its paws to Lina. She instantly walked on, and the creature got up and followed her. They had not gone far before another strange animal appeared, approaching Lina, when precisely the same thing was repeated, the vanquished animal rising and following with the former. Again, and yet again and again, a fresh animal came up, seemed to be reasoned and certainly was fought with and overcome by Lina, until at last, before they were out of the wood, she was followed by forty-nine of the most grotesquely ugly, the most extravagantly abnormal animals imagination can conceive. To describe them were a hopeless task. I knew a boy who used to make animals out of heather roots. Wherever he could find four legs, he was pretty sure to find a head and a tail. His beasts were a most comic menagerie, and right fruitful of laughter. But they were not so grotesque and extravagant as Lina and her followers. One of

85

them, for instance, was like a boa constrictor walking on four little stumpy legs near its tail. About the same distance from its head were two little wings, which it was for ever fluttering as if trying to fly with them. Curdie thought it fancied it did fly with them, when it was merely plodding on busily with its four little stumps. How it managed to keep up he could not think, till once when he missed it from the group: the same moment he caught sight of something at a distance plunging at an awful serpentine rate through the trees, and presently, from behind a huge ash, this same creature fell again into the group, quietly waddling along on its four stumps. Watching it after this, he saw that, when it was not able to keep up any longer, and they had all got a little space ahead, it shot into the wood away from the route, and made a great round, serpenting along in huge billows of motion, devouring the ground, undulating awfully, galloping as if it were all legs together, and its four stumps nowhere. In this mad fashion it shot ahead, and, a few minutes after, toddled in again amongst the rest, walking peacefully and somewhat painfully on its few fours.

From the time it takes to describe one of them it will be readily seen that it would hardly do to attempt a description of each of the forty-nine. They were not a goodly company, but well worth contemplating nevertheless; and Curdie had been too long used to the goblins' creatures in the mines and on the mountain, to feel the least uncomfortable at being followed by such a herd. On the contrary the marvellous vagaries of shape they manifested amused him greatly, and shortened the journey much. Before they were all gathered, however, it had got so dark that he could see some of them only a part at a time, and every now and then, as the company wandered on, he would be startled by some extraordinary limb or feature, undreamed of by him before, thrusting itself out of the darkness into the range of his ken. Probably there were some of his old acquaintances among them, although such had been the conditions of semi-darkness in which alone he had ever seen any of them, that it was not likely he would be able to identify any of them.

On they marched solemnly, almost in silence, for either with feet or voice the creatures seldom made any noise. By the time they reached the outside of the wood it was morning twilight. Into the open trooped the strange torrent of deformity, each one following Lina. Suddenly she stopped, turned towards them, and said something which they understood, although to Curdie's ear the sounds she made seemed to have no articulation. Instantly they all turned, and vanished in the forest, and Lina alone came trotting lithely and clumsily after her master.

Chapter 13

The Baker's Wife

They were now passing through a lovely country of hill and dale and rushing stream. The hills were abrupt, with broken chasms for water-courses, and deep little valleys full of trees. But now and then they came to a larger valley, with a fine river, whose level banks and the adjacent meadows were dotted all over with red and white kine, while on the fields above, that sloped a little to the foot of the hills, grew oats and barley and wheat, and on the sides of the hills themselves vines hung and chestnuts rose. They came at last to a broad, beautiful river, up which they must go to arrive at the city of Gwyntystorm, where the king had his court. As they went the valley narrowed, and then the river, but still it was wide enough for large boats. After this, while the river kept its size, the banks narrowed, until there was only room for a road between the river and the great cliffs that overhung it. At last river and road took a sudden turn, and lo! a great rock in the river, which dividing flowed around it, and on the top of the rock the city, with lofty walls and towers and battlements, and above the city the palace of the king, built like a strong castle. But the fortifications had long been neglected, for the whole country was now under one king, and all men said there was no more need for weapons or walls. No man pretended to love his neighbour, but every one said he knew that peace and quiet behaviour was the best thing for himself, and that, he said, was quite as useful, and a great deal more reasonable. The city was prosperous and rich, and if anybody was not comfortable, everybody else said he ought to be.

When Curdie got up opposite the mighty rock, which sparkled all over with crystals, he found a narrow bridge, defended by gates and portcullis and towers with loopholes. But the gates stood wide open, and were dropping from their great hinges; the portcullis was eaten away with rust, and clung to the grooves evidently immovable; while the loopholed towers had neither floor nor roof, and their tops were fast filling up their interiors. Curdie thought it a pity, if only for their old story, that they should be thus neglected. But everybody in the city regarded these signs of decay as the best proof of the prosperity of the place. Commerce and self-interest, they said, had got the better of violence, and the troubles of the past were whelmed in the riches that flowed in at their open gates. Indeed there was once sect of philosophers in it which taught that it would be better to forget all the past history of the city, were it not that its former imperfections taught its present inhabitants how superior they and their times were, and enabled them to glory over their ancestors. There were even certain quacks in the city who advertised pills for enabling people to think well of themselves, and some few bought of them, but most laughed, and said, with evident truth, that they did not require them. Indeed, the general theme of discourse when they met was, how much wiser they were than their fathers.

Curdie crossed the river, and began to ascend the winding road that led up to the city. They met a good many idlers, and all stared at them. It was no wonder they should stare, but there was an unfriendliness in their looks which Curdie did not like. No one, however, offered them any molestation: Lina did not invite liberties. After a long ascent, they reached the principal gate of the city and entered.

The street was very steep, ascending towards the palace, which rose in great strength above all the houses. Just as they entered, a baker, whose shop was a few doors inside the gate, came out in his white apron, and ran to the shop of his friend the barber on the opposite side of the way. But as he ran he stumbled and fell heavily. Curdie hastened to help him up, and found he had bruised his forehead badly. He swore grievously at the stone for tripping him up, declaring it was the third time he had fallen over it within the last month; and saying what was the king about that he allowed such a stone to stick up for ever on the main street of his royal residence of Gwyntystorm! What was a king for if he would not take care of his people's heads! And he stroked his forehead tenderly.

"Was it your head or your feet that ought to bear the blame of your fall?" asked Curdie.

"Why, you booby of a miner! my feet, of course," answered the baker.

"Nay, then," said Curdie, "the king can't be to blame."

"Oh, I see!" said the baker. "You're laying a trap for me. Of course, if you come to that, it was my head that ought to have looked after my feet. But it is the king's part to look after us all, and have his streets smooth."

"Well, I don't see," said Curdie, "why the king should take care of the baker, when the baker's head won't take care of the baker's feet."

"Who are you to make game of the king's baker?" cried the man in a rage.

But, instead of answering, Curdie went up to the bump on the street which had repeated itself on the baker's head, and turning the hammer end of his mattock, struck it such a blow that it flew wide in pieces. Blow after blow he struck, until he had levelled it with the street.

But out flew the barber upon him in a rage.

"What do you break my window for, you rascal, with your pickaxe?"

"I am very sorry," said Curdie. "It must have been a bit of stone that flew from my mattock. I couldn't help it, you know."

"Couldn't help it! A fine story! What do you go breaking the rock for—the very rock upon which the city stands?"

"Look at your friend's forehead," said Curdie. "See what a lump he has got on it with falling over that same stone."

"What's that to my window?" cried the barber. "His forehead can mend itself; my poor window can't."

"But he's the king's baker," said Curdie, more and more surprised at the man's anger.

"What's that to me? This is a free city. Every man here takes care of himself, and the king takes care of us all. I'll have the price of my window out of you, or the exchequer shall pay for it."

Something caught Curdie's eye. He stooped, picked up a piece of the stone he had just broken, and put it in his pocket.

"I suppose you are going to break another of my windows with that stone!" said the barber.

"Oh no," said Curdie. "I didn't mean to break your window, and I certainly won't break another."

"Give me that stone," said the barber.

Curdie gave it to him, and the barber threw it over the city wall.

"I thought you wanted the stone," said Curdie.

"No, you fool!" answered the barber. "What should I want with a stone?"

Curdie stooped and picked up another.

"Give me that stone," said the barber.

"No," answered Curdie. "You have just told me you don't want a stone, and I do."

The barber took Curdie by the collar.

"Come, now! you pay me for that window."

"How much?" asked Curdie.

The barber said, "A crown." But the baker, annoyed at the heartlessness of the barber, in thinking more of his broken window than the bump on his friend's forehead, interfered.

"No, no," he said to Curdie; "don't you pay any such sum. A little pane like that cost only a quarter."

"Well, to be certain," said Curdie, "I'll give him a half." For he doubted the baker as well as the barber. "Perhaps one day, if he find he has asked too much, he will bring me the difference."

"Ha! ha!" laughed the barber. "A fool and his money are soon parted."

But as he took the coin from Curdie's hand he grasped it in affected reconciliation and real satisfaction. In Curdie's, his was the cold smooth leathery palm of a monkey. He looked up, almost expecting to see him pop the money in his cheek; but he had not yet got so far as that, though he was well on the road to it: then he would have no other pocket.

"I'm glad that stone is gone, anyhow," said the baker. "It was the bane of my life. I had no idea how easy it was to remove it. Give me your pickaxe, young miner, and I will show you how a baker can make the stones fly."

He caught the tool out of Curdie's hand, and flew at one of the foundation stones of the gateway. But he jarred his arm terribly, scarcely chipped the stone, dropped the mattock with a cry of pain, and ran into his own shop. Curdie picked up the implement, and looking after the baker, saw bread in the window, and followed him in. But the baker, ashamed of himself, and thinking he was coming to laugh at him, popped out of the back door, and when Curdie entered, the baker's wife came from the bakehouse to serve him. Curdie requested to know the price of a certain good-sized loaf.

Now the baker's wife had been watching what had passed since first her husband ran out of the shop, and she liked the look of Curdie. Also she was more honest than her husband. Casting a glance to the back door, she replied,—

"That is not the best bread. I will sell you a loaf of what we bake for ourselves." And when she had spoken she laid a finger on her lips. "Take care of yourself in this place, my son," she added. "They do not love strangers. I was once a stranger here, and I know what I say." Then fancying she heard her husband,—"That is a strange animal you have," she said, in a louder voice.

"Yes," answered Curdie. "She is no beauty, but she is very good, and we love each other. Don't we, Lina?"

Lina looked up and whined. Curdie threw her the half of his loaf, which she ate while her master and the baker's wife talked a little. Then the baker's wife gave them some water, and Curdie having paid for his loaf, he and Lina went up the street together.

Chapter 14

The Dogs of Gwyntystorm

The steep street led them straight up to a large market-place, with butchers' shops, about which were many dogs. The moment they caught sight of Lina, one and all they came rushing down upon her, giving her no chance of explaining herself. When Curdie saw the dogs coming he heaved up his mattock over his shoulder, and was ready, if they would have it so. Seeing him thus prepared to defend his follower, a great ugly bull-dog flew at him. With the first blow Curdie struck him through the brain, and the brute fell dead at his feet. But he would not at once recover his weapon, which stuck in the skull of his foe, and a huge mastiff, seeing him thus hampered, flew at him next. Now Lina, who had shown herself so brave upon the road thither, had grown shy upon entering the city, and kept always at Curdie's heel. But it was her turn now. The moment she saw her master in danger she seemed to go mad with rage. As the mastiff jumped at Curdie's throat, Lina flew at his, seized him with her tremendous jaws, gave one roaring grind, and he lay beside the bull-dog with his neck broken. They were the best dogs in the market, after the judgment of the butchers of Gwyntystorm. Down came their masters, knife in hand.

Curdie drew himself up fearlessly, mattock on shoulder, and awaited their coming, while at his heel his awful attendant showed not only her outside fringe of icicle-teeth, but a double row of right serviceable fangs she wore inside her mouth, and her green eyes flashed yellow as gold. The butchers not liking the look of either of them or of the dogs at their feet, drew back, and began to remonstrate in the manner of outraged men.

"Stranger," said the first, "that bull-dog is mine."

"Take him, then," said Curdie, indignant.

"You've killed him!"

"Yes—else he would have killed me."

"That's no business of mine."

"No?"

"No."

"That makes it the more mine, then."

"This sort of thing won't do, you know," said the other butcher.

"That's true," said Curdie.

"That's my mastiff," said the butcher.

"And as he ought to be," said Curdie.

"Your brute shall be burnt alive for it," said the butcher.

"Not yet," answered Curdie. "We have done no wrong. We were walking quietly up your street, when your dogs flew at us. If you don't teach your dogs how to treat strangers, you must take the consequences."

"They treat them quite properly," said the butcher. "What right has any one to bring an abomination like that into our city? The horror is enough to make an idiot of every child in the place."

"We are both subjects of the king, and my poor animal can't help her looks. How would you like to be served like that because you were ugly? She's not a bit fonder of her looks than you are—only what can she do to change them?"

"I'll do to change them," said the fellow.

Thereupon the butchers brandished their long knives and advanced, keeping their eyes upon Lina.

"Don't be afraid, Lina," cried Curdie. "I'll kill one—you kill the other."

Lina gave a howl that might have terrified an army, and crouched ready to spring. The butchers turned and ran.

By this time a great crowd had gathered behind the butchers, and in it a number of boys returning from school, who began to stone the strangers. It was a way they had with man or beast they did not expect to make anything by. One of the stones struck Lina; she caught it in her teeth and crunched it that it fell in gravel from her mouth. Some of the foremost of the crowd saw this, and it terrified them. They drew back; the rest took fright from their retreat; the panic spread; and at last the crowd scattered in all directions. They ran, and cried out, and said the devil and his dam were come to Gwyntystorm. So Curdie and Lina were left standing unmolested in the market-place. But the terror of them spread throughout the city, and everybody began to shut and lock his door, so that by the time the setting sun shone down the street, there was not a shop left open, for fear of the devil and his horrible dam. But all the upper windows within sight of them were crowded with heads watching them where they stood lonely in the deserted market-place.

Curdie looked carefully all round, but could not see one open door. He caught sight of the sign of an inn however, and laying down his mattock, and telling Lina to take care of it, walked up to the door of it and knocked. But the people in the house, instead of opening the door, threw things at him from the windows. They would not listen to a word he said, but sent him back to Lina with the blood running down his face. When Lina saw that, she leaped up in a fury and was rushing at the house, into which she would certainly have broken; but Curdie called her, and made her lie down beside him while he bethought him what next he should do.

"Lina," he said, "the people keep their gates open, but their houses and their hearts shut."

As if she knew it was her presence that had brought this trouble upon him she rose, and went round and round him, purring like a tigress, and rubbing herself against his legs.

Now there was one little thatched house that stood squeezed in between two tall gables, and the sides of the two great houses shot out projecting windows that nearly met across the roof of the little one, so that it lay in the street like a doll's house. In this house lived a poor old woman, with a grandchild. And because she never gossiped or quarreled, or chaffered in the market, but went without what she could not afford, the people called her a witch, and would have done her many an ill turn if they had not been afraid of her. Now while Curdie was looking in another direction the door opened, and out came a little dark-haired, black-eyed, gipsy-looking child, and toddled across the market-place towards the outcasts. The moment they saw her coming, Lina lay down flat on the road, and with her two huge forepaws covered her mouth, while Curdie went to meet her, holding out his arms. The little one came straight to him, and held up her mouth to be kissed. Then she took him by the hand, and drew him towards the house, and Curdie yielded to the silent invitation. But when Lina rose to follow, the child shrunk from her, frightened a little. Curdie took her up, and holding her on one arm, patted Lina with the other hand. Then the child wanted also to pat doggy, as she called her by a right bountiful stretch of courtesy, and having once patted her, nothing would serve but Curdie must let her have a ride on doggy. So he set her on Lina's back, holding her hand, and she rode home in merry triumph, all unconscious of the hundreds of eyes staring at her foolhardiness from the windows about the market-place, or the murmur of deep disapproval that rose from as many lips. At the door stood the grandmother to receive them. She caught the child to her bosom with delight at her courage, welcomed Curdie, and showed no dread of Lina. Many were the significant nods exchanged, and many a one said to another that the devil and the witch were old friends. But the woman was only a wise woman, who having seen how Curdie and Lina behaved to each other, judged from that what sort they were, and so made them welcome to her house. She was not like her fellow-townspeople, for that they were strangers recommended them to her.

The moment the door was shut, the other doors began to open, and soon there appeared little groups about here and there a threshold, while a few of the more courageous ventured out upon the square—all ready to make for their houses again, however, upon the least sign of movement in the little thatched one.

The baker and the barber had joined one of these groups, and were busily wagging their tongues against Curdie and his horrible beast.

"He can't be honest," said the barber; "for he paid me double the worth of the pane he broke in my window."

And then he told them how Curdie broke his window by breaking a stone in the street with his hammer. There the baker struck in.

"Now that was the stone," said he, "over which I had fallen three times within the last month: could it be by fair means he broke that to pieces at the first blow? Just to make up my mind on that point I tried his own hammer against a stone in the gate; it nearly broke both my arms, and loosened half the teeth in my head!"

Chapter 15

Derba and Barbara

Meantime the wanderers were hospitably entertained by the old woman and her grandchild, and they were all very comfortable and happy together. Little Barbara sat upon Curdie's knee, and he told her stories about the mines and his adventures in them. But he never mentioned the king or the princess, for all that story was hard to believe. And he told her about his mother and father, and how good they were. And Derba sat and listened. At last little Barbara fell asleep in Curdie's arms, and her grandmother carried her to bed.

It was a poor little house, and Derba gave up her own room to Curdie, because he was honest and talked wisely. Curdie saw how it was, and begged her to allow him to lie on the floor, but she would not hear of it.

In the night he was waked by Lina pulling at him. As soon as he spoke to her she ceased, and Curdie, listening, thought he heard some one trying to get in. He rose, took his mattock, and went about the house, listening and watching; but although he heard noises now at one place, now at another, he could not think what they meant, for no one appeared. Certainly, considering how she had frightened them all in the day, it was not likely any one would attack Lina at night. By-and-by the noises ceased, and Curdie went back to his bed, and slept undisturbed.

In the morning, however, Derba came to him in great agitation, and said they had fastened up the door, so that she could not get out. Curdie rose immediately and went with her: they found that not only the door, but every window in the house was so secured on the outside that it was impossible to open one of them without using great force. Poor Derba looked anxiously in Curdie's face. He broke out laughing.

"They are much mistaken," he said, "if they fancy they could keep Lina and a miner in any house in Gwyntystorm—even if they built up doors and windows."

With that he shouldered his mattock. But Derba begged him not to make a hole in her house just yet. She had plenty for breakfast, she said, and before it was time for dinner they would know what the people meant by it.

And indeed they did. For within an hour appeared one of the chief magistrates of the city, accompanied by a score of soldiers with drawn swords, and followed by a great multitude of the people, requiring the miner and his brute to yield themselves, the one that he might be tried for the disturbance he had occasioned and the injury he had committed, the other that she might be roasted alive for her part in killing two valuable and harmless animals belonging to worthy citizens. The summons was preceded and followed by flourish of trumpet, and was read with every formality by the city marshal himself.

The moment he ended, Lina ran into the little passage, and stood opposite the door.

"I surrender," cried Curdie.

"Then tie up your brute, and give her here."

"No, no," cried Curdie through the door. "I surrender; but I'm not going to do your hangman's work. If you want my dog, you must take her."

"Then we shall set the house on fire, and burn witch and all."

"It will go hard with us but we shall kill a few dozen of you first," cried Curdie. "We're not the least afraid of you."

With that Curdie turned to Derba, and said:—

"Don't be frightened. I have a strong feeling that all will be well. Surely no trouble will come to you for being good to strangers."

"But the poor dog!" said Derba.

Now Curdie and Lina understood each other more than a little by this time, and not only had he seen that she understood the proclamation, but when she looked up at him after it was read, it was with such a grin, and such a yellow flash, that he saw also she was determined to take care of herself.

"The dog will probably give you reason to think a little more of her ere long," he answered. "But now," he went on, "I fear I must hurt your house a little. I have great confidence, however, that I shall be able to make up to you for it one day."

"Never mind the house, if only you can get safe off," she answered. "I don't think they will hurt this precious lamb," she added, clasping little Barbara to her bosom. "For myself, it is all one; I am ready for anything."

"It is but a little hole for Lina I want to make," said Curdie. "She can creep through a much smaller one than you would think."

Again he took his mattock, and went to the back wall.

"They won't burn the house," he said to himself. "There is too good a one on each side of it."

The tumult had kept increasing every moment, and the city marshal had been shouting, but Curdie had not listened to him. When now they heard the blows of his mattock, there went up a great cry, and the people taunted the soldiers that they were afraid of a dog and his miner. The soldiers therefore made a rush at the door, and cut its fastenings.

The moment they opened it, out leaped Lina, with a roar so unnaturally horrible that the sword-arms of the soldiers dropped by their sides, paralysed with the terror of that cry; the crowd fled in every direction, shrieking and yelling with mortal dismay; and without even knocking down with her tail, not to say biting a man of them with her pulverizing jaws, Lina vanished—no one knew whither, for not one of the crowd had had courage to look upon her.

The moment she was gone, Curdie advanced and gave himself up. The soldiers were so filled with fear, shame, and chagrin, that they were ready to kill him on the spot. But he stood quietly facing them, with his mattock on his shoulder; and the magistrate wishing to examine him, and the people to see him made an example of, the soldiers had to content themselves with taking him. Partly for derision, partly to hurt him, they laid his mattock against his back, and tied his arms to it.

They led him up a very steep street, and up another still, all the crowd following. The king's palace-castle rose towering above them; but they stopped before they reached it, at a low-browed door in a great, dull, heavy-looking building.

The city marshal opened it with a key which hung at his girdle, and ordered Curdie to enter. The place within was dark as night, and while he was feeling his way with his feet, the marshal gave him a rough push. He fell, and rolled once or twice over, unable to help himself because his hands were tied behind him.

It was the hour of the magistrate's second and more important breakfast, and until that was over he never found himself capable of attending to a case with concentration sufficient to the distinguishing of the side upon which his own advantage lay; and hence was this respite for Curdie, with time to collect his thoughts. But indeed he had very few to collect, for all he had to do, so far as he could see, was to wait for what would come next. Neither had he much power to collect them, for he was a good deal shaken.

In a few minutes he discovered, to his great relief, that, from the projection of the pick-end of his mattock beyond his body, the fall had loosened the ropes tied round it. He got one hand disengaged, and then the other; and presently stood free, with his good mattock once more in right serviceable relation to his arms and legs.

Chapter 16

The Mattock

While the magistrate reinvigorated his selfishness with a greedy breakfast, Curdie found doing nothing in the dark rather wearisome work. It was useless attempting to think what he should do next, seeing the circumstances in which he was presently to find himself were altogether unknown to him. So he began to think about his father and mother in their little cottage home, high in the clear air of the open mountain-side, and the thought, instead of making his dungeon gloomier by the contrast, make a light in his soul that destroyed the power of darkness and captivity. But he was at length startled from his waking dream by a swell in the noise outside. All the time there had been a few of the more idle of the inhabitants about the door, but they had been rather quiet. Now, however, the sounds of feet and voices began to grow, and grew so rapidly that it was plain a multitude was gathering. For the people of Gwyntystorm always gave themselves an hour of pleasure after their second breakfast, and what greater pleasure could they have than to see a stranger abused by the officers of justice? The noise grew till it was like the roaring of the sea, and that roaring went on a long time, for the magistrate, being a great man, liked to know that he was waited for: it added to the enjoyment of his breakfast, and, indeed, enabled him to eat a little more after he had thought his powers exhausted. But at length, in the waves of the human noises rose a bigger wave, and by the running and shouting and outcry, Curdie learned that the magistrate was approaching.

Presently came the sound of the great rusty key in the lock, which yielded with groaning reluctance; the door was thrown back, the light rushed in, and with it came the voice of the city marshal, calling upon

Curdie, by many legal epithets opprobrious, to come forth and be tried for his life, inasmuch as he had raised a tumult in his majesty's city of Gwyntystorm, troubled the hearts of the king's baker and barber, and slain the faithful dogs of his majesty's well-beloved butchers.

He was still reading, and Curdie was still seated in the brown twilight of the vault, not listening, but pondering with himself how this king the city marshal talked of could be the same with the majesty he had seen ride away on his grand white horse, with the Princess Irene on a cushion before him, when a scream of agonized terror arose on the farthest skirt of the crowd, and, swifter than flood or flame, the horror spread shrieking. In a moment the air was filled with hideous howling, cries of unspeakable dismay, and the multitudinous noise of running feet. The next moment, in at the door of the vault bounded Lina, her two green eyes flaming yellow as sunflowers, and seeming to light up the dungeon. With one spring she threw herself at Curdie's feet, and laid her head upon them panting. Then came a rush of two or three soldiers darkening the doorway, but it was only to lay hold of the key, pull the door to, and lock it; so that once more Curdie and Lina were prisoners together.

For a few moments Lina lay panting hard: it is breathless work leaping and roaring both at once, and that in a way to scatter thousands of people. Then she jumped up, and began snuffing about all over the place; and Curdie saw what he had never seen before—two faint spots of light cast from her eyes upon the ground, one on each side of her snuffing nose. He got out his tinder-box—a miner is never without one—and lighted a precious bit of candle he carried in a division of it—just for a moment, for he must not waste it.

The light revealed a vault without any window or other opening than the door. It was very old and much neglected. The mortar had vanished from between the stones, and it was half filled with a heap of all sorts of rubbish, beaten down in the middle, but looser at the sides; it sloped from the door to the foot of the opposite wall; evidently for a long time the vault had been left open, and every sort of refuse thrown into it. A single minute served for the survey, so little was there to note.

Meantime, down in the angle between the back wall and the base of the heap Lina was scratching furiously with all the eighteen great strong claws of her mighty feet.

"Ah, ha!" said Curdie to himself, catching sight of her, "if only they will leave us long enough to ourselves!"

With that he ran to the door, to see if there was any fastening on the inside. There was none: in all its long history it never had had one. But a few blows of the right sort, now from the one, now from the other end of his mattock, were as good as any bolt, for they so ruined the lock that no key would ever turn in it again. Those who heard them fancied he was trying to get out, and laughed spitefully. As soon as he had done, he extinguished his candle, and went down to Lina.

She had reached the hard rock which formed the floor of the dungeon, and was now clearing away the earth a little wider. Presently she looked up in his face and whined, as much to say, "My paws are not hard enough to get any further."

"Then get out of my way, Lina," said Curdie, "and mind you keep your eyes shining, for fear I should hit you."

So saying, he heaved his mattock, and assailed with the hammer end of it the spot she had cleared.

The rock was very hard, but when it did break it broke in good-sized pieces. Now with hammer, now with pick, he worked till he was weary, then rested, and then set to again. He could not tell how the day went, as he had no light but the lamping of Lina's eyes. The darkness hampered him greatly, for he would not let Lina come close enough to give him all the light she could, lest he should strike her. So he had, every now and then, to feel with his hands to know how he was getting on, and to discover in what direction to strike: the exact spot was a mere imagination.

He was getting very tired and hungry, and beginning to lose heart a little, when out of the ground, as if he had struck a spring of it, burst a dull, gleamy, lead-coloured light, and the next moment he heard a hollow splash and echo. A piece of rock had fallen out of the floor, and dropped into water beneath. Already Lina, who had been lying a few yards off all the time he worked, was on her feet and peering through the hole. Curdie got down on his hands and knees, and looked. They were over what seemed a natural cave in the rock, to which apparently the river had access, for, at a great distance below, a faint light was gleaming upon water. If they could but reach it, they might get out; but even if it was deep enough, the height was very dangerous. The first thing, whatever might follow, was to make the hole larger. It was comparatively easy to break away the sides of it, and in the course of another hour he had it large enough to get through.

And now he must reconnoitre. He took the rope they had tied him with—for Curdie's hindrances were always his furtherance—and fastened one end of it by a slip-knot round the handle of his pickaxe, then dropped the other end through, and laid the pickaxe so that, when he was through himself, and hanging on to the edge, he could place it across the hole to support him on the rope. This done, he took the rope in his hands, and, beginning to descend, found himself in a narrow cleft widening into a cave. His rope was not very long, and would not do much to lessen the force of his fall—he thought with himself—if he should have to drop into the water; but he was not more than a couple of yards below the dungeon when he spied an opening on the opposite side of the cleft: it might be but a shallow hole, or it might lead them out. He dropped himself a little below its level, gave the rope a swing by pushing his feet against the side of the cleft, and so penduled himself into it. Then he laid a stone on the end of the rope that it should not forsake him, called to Lina, whose yellow eyes were gleaming over the mattock-grating above, to watch there till he returned, and went cautiously in.

It proved a passage, level for some distance, then sloping gently up. He advanced carefully, feeling his way as he went. At length he was stopped by a door—a small door, studded with iron. But the wood was in places so much decayed that some of the bolts had dropped out, and he felt sure of being able to open it. He returned, therefore, to fetch Lina and his mattock. Arrived at the cleft, his strong miner arms bore him swiftly up along the rope and through the hole into the dungeon. There he undid the rope from his mattock, and making Lina take the end of it in her teeth, and get through the hole, he lowered her—it was all he could do, she was so heavy. When she came opposite the passage, with a slight push of her tail she shot herself into it, and let go the rope, which Curdie drew up. Then he lighted his candle and searching in the rubbish found a bit of iron to take the place of his pickaxe across the hole. Then he searched again in the rubbish, and found half an old shutter. This he propped up leaning a little over the hole, with a bit of stick, and heaped against the back of it a quantity of the loosened earth. Next he tied his mattock to the end of the rope, dropped it, and let it hang. Last, he got through the hole himself, and pulled away the propping stick, so that the shutter fell over the hole with a quantity of earth on top of it. A few motions of hand over hand, and he swung himself and his mattock into the passage beside Lina. There he secured the end of the rope, and they went on together to the door.

Chapter 17

The Wine-Cellar

He lighted his candle and examined it. Decayed and broken as it was, it was strongly secured in its place by hinges on the one side, and either lock or bolt, he could not tell which, on the other. A brief use of his pocket-knife was enough to make room for his hand and arm to get through, and then he found a great iron bolt—but so rusty that he could not move it. Lina whimpered. He took his knife again, made the hole bigger, and stood back. In she shot her small head and long neck, seized the bolt with her teeth, and dragged it grating and complaining back. A push then opened the door. It was at the foot of a short flight of steps. They ascended, and at the top Curdie found himself in a space which, from the echo to his stamp, appeared of some size, though of what sort he could not at first tell, for his hands, feeling about, came upon nothing. Presently, however, they fell on a great thing: it was a wine-cask. He was just setting out to explore the place by a thorough palpation, when he heard steps coming down a stair. He stood still, not knowing whether the door would open an inch from his nose or twenty yards behind his back. It did neither. He heard the key turn in the lock, and a stream of light shot in, ruining the darkness, about fifteen yards away on his right.

A man carrying a candle in one hand and a large silver flagon in the other, entered, and came towards him. The light revealed a row of huge wine-casks, that stretched away into the darkness of the other end of the long vault. Curdie retreated into the recess of the stair, and peeping round the corner of it, watched him, thinking what he could do to prevent him from locking them in. He came on and on, until Curdie feared he would pass the recess and see them. He was just preparing to rush out, and master him before he should give alarm, not in the least knowing what he should do next, when, to his relief, the man stopped at the third cask from where he stood. He set down his light on the top of it, removed what seemed a large vent-peg, and poured into the cask a quantity of something from the flagon. Then he turned to the next cask, drew some wine, rinsed the flagon, threw the wine away, drew and rinsed and threw away again, then drew and drank, draining to the bottom. Last of all, he filled the flagon from the cask he had first visited, replaced then the vent-peg, took up his candle, and turned towards the door.

"There is something wrong here!" thought Curdie.

"Speak to him, Lina," he whispered.

The sudden howl she gave made Curdie himself start and tremble for a moment. As to the man, he answered Lina's with another horrible howl, forced from him by the convulsive shudder of every muscle of his body, then reeled gasping to and fro, and dropped his candle. But just as Curdie expected to see him fall dead he recovered himself, and flew to the door, through which he darted, leaving it open behind him. The moment he ran, Curdie stepped out, picked up the candle still alight, sped after him to the door, drew out the key, and then returned to the stair and waited. In a few minutes he heard the sound of many feet and voices. Instantly he turned the tap of the cask from which the man had been drinking, set the candle beside it on the floor, went down the steps and out of the little door, followed by Lina, and closed it behind them.

Through the hole in it he could see a little, and hear all. He could see how the light of many candles filled the place, and could hear how some two dozen feet ran hither and thither through the echoing cellar; he could hear the clash of iron, probably spits and pokers, now and then; and at last heard how, finding nothing remarkable except the best wine running to waste, they all turned on the butler, and accused him of having fooled them with a drunken dream. He did his best to defend himself, appealing to the evidence of their own senses that he was as sober as they were. They replied that a fright was no less a fright that the cause was imaginary, and a dream no less a dream that the fright had waked him from it. When he discovered, and triumphantly adduced as corroboration, that the key was gone from the door, they said it merely showed how drunk he had been—either that or how frightened, for he had certainly dropped it. In vain he protested that he had never taken it out of the lock—that he never did when he went in, and certainly had not this time stopped to do so when he came out; they asked him why he had to go to the cellar at such a time of the day, and said it was because he had already drunk all the wine that was left from dinner. He said if he had dropped the key, the key was to be found, and they must help him to find it. They told him they wouldn't move a peg for him. He declared, with much language, he would have them all turned out of the king's service. They said they would swear he was drunk. And so positive were they about it, that as last the butler himself began to think whether it was possible they could be in the right. For he knew that sometimes when he had been drunk he fancied things had taken place which he found afterwards could not have happened. Certain of his fellow-servants, however, had all the time a doubt whether the cellar goblin had not appeared to him, or at least roared at him, to protect the wine. In any case nobody wanted to find the key for him; nothing could please them better than that the door of the wine-cellar should never more be locked. By degrees the hubbub died away, and they departed, not even pulling to the door, for there was neither handle nor latch to it.

As soon as they were gone, Curdie returned, knowing now that they were in the wine-cellar of the palace, as, indeed, he had suspected. Finding a pool of wine in a hollow of the floor, Lina lapped it up eagerly: she had had no breakfast, and was now very thirsty as well as hungry. Her master was in a similar plight, for he had but just begun to eat when the magistrate arrived with the soldiers. If only they were all in bed, he thought, that he might find his way to the larder! For he said to himself that, as he was sent there by the young princess's great-great-grand-mother to serve her or her father in some way, surely he must have a right to his food in the palace, without which he could do nothing. He would go at once and reconnoitre.

So he crept up the stair that led from the cellar. At the top was a door, opening on a long passage, dimly lighted by a lamp. He told Lina to lie down upon the stair while he went on. At the end of the passage he found a door ajar, and, peeping through, saw right into a great stone hall, where a huge fire was blazing, and through which men in the king's livery were constantly coming and going. Some also in the same livery were lounging about the fire. He noted that their colours were the same with those he himself, as king's miner, wore; but from what he had seen and heard of the habits of the place, he could not hope they would treat him the better for that.

The one interesting thing at the moment, however, was the plentiful supper with which the table was spread. It was something at least to stand in sight of food, and he was unwilling to turn his back on the prospect so long as a share in it was not absolutely hopeless. Peeping thus, he soon made up his mind that if at any moment the hall should be empty, he would at that moment rush in and attempt to carry off a dish. That he might lose no time by indecision, he selected a large pie upon which to pounce instantaneously. But after he had watched for some minutes, it did not seem at all likely the chance would arrive before supper-time, and he was just about to turn away and rejoin Lina, when he saw that there was not a person in the place. Curdie never made up his mind and then hesitated. He darted in, seized the pie, and bore it, swiftly and noiselessly, to the cellar stair.

Chapter 18

The King's Kitchen

Back to the cellar Curdie and Lina sped with their booty, where, seated on the steps, Curdie lighted his bit of candle for a moment. A very little bit it was now, but they did not waste much of it in examination of the pie; that they effected by a more summary process. Curdie thought it the nicest food he had ever tasted, and between them they soon ate it up. Then Curdie would have thrown the dish along with the bones into the water, that there might be no traces of them; but he thought of his mother, and hid it instead; and the very next minute they wanted it to draw some wine into. He was careful it should be from the cask of which he had seen the butler drink. Then they sat down again upon the steps, and waited until the house should be quiet. For he was there to do something, and if it did not come to him in the cellar, he must go to meet it in other places. Therefore, lest he should fall asleep, he set the end of the helve of his mattock on the ground, and seated himself on the cross part, leaning against the wall, so that as long as he kept awake he should rest, but the moment he began to fall asleep he must fall awake instead. He quite expected some of the servants would visit the cellar again that night, but whether it was that they were afraid of each other, or believed more of the butler's story than they had chosen to allow, not one of them appeared.

When at length he thought he might venture, he shouldered his mattock and crept up the stair. The lamp was out in the passage, but he could not miss his way to the servants' hall. Trusting to Lina's quickness in concealing herself, he took her with him.

When they reached the hall they found it quiet and nearly dark. The last of the great fire was glowing red, but giving little light. Curdie stood and warmed himself for a few moments: miner as he was, he had found the cellar cold to sit in doing nothing; and standing thus he thought of looking if there were any bits of candle about. There were many candlesticks on the supper-table, but to his disappointment and indignation their candles seemed to have been all left to burn out, and some of them, indeed, he found still hot in the neck.

Presently, one after another, he came upon seven men fast asleep, most of them upon tables, one in a chair, and one on the floor. They seemed, from their shape and colour, to have eaten and drunk so much that they might be burned alive without waking. He grasped the hand of each in succession, and found two ox-hoofs, three pig-hoofs, one concerning which he could not be sure whether it was the hoof of a donkey or a pony, and one dog's paw. "A nice set of people to be about a king!" thought Curdie to himself, and turned again to his candle hunt. He did at last find two or three little pieces, and stowed them away in his pockets.

They now left the hall by another door, and entered a short passage, which led them to the huge kitchen, vaulted, and black with smoke. There too the fire was still burning, so that he was able to see a little of the state of things in this quarter also. The place was dirty and disorderly. In a recess, on a heap of brushwood, lay a kitchenmaid, with a table-cover around her, and a skillet in her hand: evidently she too had been drinking. In another corner lay a page, and Curdie noted how like his dress was to his own. In the cinders before the hearth were huddled three dogs and five cats, all fast asleep, while the rats were running about the floor. Curdie's heart ached to think of the lovely child-princess living over such a sty. The mine was a paradise to a palace with such servants in it.

Leaving the kitchen, he got into the region of the sculleries. There horrible smells were wandering about, like evil spirits that come forth with the darkness. He lighted a candle—but only to see ugly sights. Everywhere was filth and disorder. Mangy turn-spit dogs were lying about, and gray rats were gnawing at refuse in the sinks. It was like a hideous dream. He felt as if he should never get out of it, and longed for one glimpse of his mother's poor little kitchen, so clean and bright and airy. Turning from it at last in miserable disgust, he almost ran back through the kitchen, re-entered the hall, and crossed it to another door.

It opened upon a wider passage, leading to an arch in a stately corridor, all its length lighted by lamps in niches. At the end of it was a large and beautiful hall, with great pillars. There sat three men in the royal livery, fast asleep, each in a great arm-chair, with his feet on a huge footstool. They looked like fools dreaming themselves kings; and Lina looked as if she longed to throttle them. At one side of the hall was the grand staircase, and they went up.

Everything that now met Curdie's eyes was rich—not glorious like the splendours of the mountain cavern, but rich and soft—except where, now and then, some rough old rib of the ancient fortress came through, hard and discoloured. Now some dark bare arch of stone, now some rugged and blackened pillar, now some huge beam, brown with the smoke and dust of centuries, looked like a thistle in the midst of daisies, or a rock in a smooth lawn.

They wandered about a good while, again and again finding themselves where they had been before. Gradually, however, Curdie was gaining some idea of the place. By-and-by Lina began to look frightened, and as they went on Curdie saw that she looked more and more frightened. Now, by this time he had come to understand that what made her look frightened was always the fear of frightening, and he therefore concluded they must be drawing nigh to somebody. At last, in a gorgeously-painted gallery, he saw a curtain of crimson, and on the curtain a royal crown wrought in silks and stones. He felt sure this must be the king's chamber, and it was here he was wanted; or, if it was not the place he was bound for, something would meet him and turn him aside; for he had come to think that so long as a man wants to do right he may go where he can: when he can go no further, then it is not the way. "Only," said his father, in assenting to the theory, "he must really want to do right, and not merely fancy he does. He must want it with his heart and will, and not with his rag of a tongue."

So he gently lifted the corner of the curtain, and there behind it was a half-open door. He entered, and the moment he was in, Lina stretched herself along the threshold between the curtain and the door.

Chapter 19

The King's Chamber

He found himself in a large room, dimly lighted by a silver lamp that hung from the ceiling. Far at the other end was a great bed, surrounded with dark heavy curtains. He went softly towards it, his heart beating fast. It was a dreadful thing to be alone in the king's chamber at the dead of night. To gain courage he had to remind himself of the beautiful princess who had sent him. But when he was about half-way to the bed, a figure appeared from the farther side of it, and came towards him, with a hand raised warningly. He stood still. The light was dim, and he could distinguish little more than the outline of a young girl. But though the form he saw was much taller than the princess he remembered, he never doubted it was she. For one thing, he knew that most girls would have been frightened to see him there in the dead of the night, but like a true princess, and the princess he used to know, she walked straight on to meet him. As she came she lowered the hand she had lifted, and laid the forefinger of it upon her lips. Nearer and nearer, quite near, close up to him she came, then stopped, and stood a moment looking at him.

"You are Curdie," she said.

"And you are the Princess Irene," he returned.

"Then we know each other still," she said, with a sad smile of pleasure. "You will help me."

"That I will," answered Curdie. He did not say, "If I can;" for he knew that what he was sent to do, that he could do. "May I kiss your hand, little princess?"

She was only between nine and ten, though indeed she looked several years older, and her eyes almost those of a grown woman, for she had had terrible trouble of late.

She held out her hand.

"I am not the *little* princess any more. I have grown up since I saw you last, Mr. Miner."

The smile which accompanied the words had in it a strange mixture of playfulness and sadness.

"So I see, Miss Princess," returned Curdie; "and therefore, being more of a princess, you are the more my princess. Here I am, sent by your great-great-grandmother, to be your servant.—May I ask why you are up so late, princess?"

"Because my father wakes *so* frightened, and I don't know what he *would* do if he didn't find me by his bedside. There! he's waking now."

She darted off to the side of the bed she had come from. Curdie stood where he was.

A voice altogether unlike what he remembered of the mighty, noble king on his white horse came from the bed, thin, feeble, hollow, and husky, and in tone like that of a petulant child:—

"I will not, I will not. I am a king, and I *will* be a king. I hate you and despise you, and you shall not torture me!"

"Never mind them, father dear," said the princess. "I am here, and they shan't touch you. They dare not, you know, so long as you defy them."

"They want my crown, darling; and I can't give them my crown, can I? for what is a king without his crown?"

"They shall never have your crown, my king," said Irene. "Here it is—all safe, you see. I am watching it for you."

Curdie drew near the bed on the other side. There lay the grand old king—he looked grand still, and twenty years older. His body was pillowed high; his beard descended long and white over the crimson coverlid; and his crown, its diamonds and emeralds gleaming in the twilight of the curtains, lay in front of him, his long, thin old hands folded round the rigol, and the ends of his beard straying among the lovely stones. His face was like that of a man who had died fighting nobly; but one thing made it dreadful: his eyes, while they moved about as if searching in this direction and in that, looked more dead than his face. He saw neither his daughter nor his crown: it was the voice of the one and the touch of the other that comforted him. He kept murmuring what seemed words, but was unintelligible to Curdie, although, to judge from the look of Irene's face, she learned and concluded from it.

By degrees his voice sank away and the murmuring ceased, although still his lips moved. Thus lay the old king on his bed, slumbering with his crown between his hands; on one side of him stood a lovely little maiden, with blue eyes, and brown hair going a little back from her temples, as if blown by a wind that no one felt but herself; and on the other a stalwart young miner, with his mattock over his shoulder. Stranger sight still was Lina lying along the threshold—only nobody saw her just then.

A moment more and the king's lips ceased to move. His breathing had grown regular and quiet. The princess gave a sigh of relief, and came round to Curdie.

"We can talk a little now," she said, leading him towards the middle of the room. "My father will sleep now till the doctor wakes him to give him his medicine. It is not really medicine, though, but wine. Nothing but that, the doctor says, could have kept him so long alive. He always comes in the middle of the night to give it him with his own hands. But it makes me cry to see him waked up when so nicely asleep."

"What sort of man is your doctor?" asked Curdie.

"Oh, such a dear, good, kind gentleman!" replied the princess. "He speaks so softly, and is so sorry for his dear king! He will be here presently, and you shall see for yourself. You will like him very much."

"Has your king-father been long ill?" asked Curdie.

"A whole year now," she replied. "Did you not know? That's how your mother never got the red petticoat my father promised her. The lord chancellor told me that not only Gwyntystorm but the whole land was mourning over the illness of the good man."

Now Curdie himself had not heard a word of his majesty's illness, and had no ground for believing that a single soul in any place he had visited on his journey had heard of it. Moreover, although mention had been made of his majesty again and again in his hearing since he came to Gwyntystorm, never once had he heard an allusion to the state of his health. And now it dawned upon him also that he had never heard the least expression of love to him. But just for the time he thought it better to say nothing on either point.

"Does the king wander like this every night?" he asked.

"Every night," answered Irene, shaking her head mournfully. "That is why I never go to bed at night. He is better during the day—a little, and then I sleep—in the dressing-room there, to be with him in a moment if he should call me. It is so sad he should have only me and not my mamma! A princess is nothing to a queen!"

"I wish he would like me," said Curdie, "for then I might watch by him at night, and let you go to bed, princess."

"Don't you know then," returned Irene, in wonder. "How was it you came?—Ah! you said my grandmother sent you. But I thought you knew that he wanted you."

And again she opened wide her blue stars.

"Not I," said Curdie, also bewildered, but very glad.

"He used to be constantly saying—he was not so ill then as he is now—that he wished he had you about him."

"And I never to know it!" said Curdie, with displeasure.

"The master of the horse told papa's own secretary that he had written to the miner-general to find you and send you up; but the miner-general wrote back to the master of the horse, and he told the secretary, and the secretary told my father, that they had searched every mine in the kingdom and could hear nothing of you. My father gave a great sigh, and said he feared the goblins had got you after all, and your father and mother were dead of grief. And he has never mentioned you since, except when wandering. I cried very much. But one of my grandmother's pigeons with its white wing flashed a message to me through the window one day, and then I knew that my Curdie wasn't eaten by the goblins, for my grandmother wouldn't have taken care of him one time to let him be eaten the next. Where were you, Curdie, that they couldn't find you?"

"We will talk about that another time, when we are not expecting the doctor," said Curdie.

As he spoke, his eyes fell upon something shining on the table under the lamp. His heart gave a great throb, and he went nearer.—Yes, there could be no doubt;—it was the same flagon that the butler had filled in the wine-cellar.

"It looks worse and worse!" he said to himself, and went back to Irene, where she stood half dreaming.

"When will the doctor be here?" he asked once more—this time hurriedly.

The question was answered—not by the princess, but by something which that instant tumbled heavily into the room. Curdie flew towards it in vague terror about Lina.

On the floor lay a little round man, puffing and blowing, and uttering incoherent language. Curdie thought of his mattock, and ran laid it aside.

"Oh, dear Dr. Kelman!" cried the princess, running up and taking hold of his arm; "I am *so* sorry!" She pulled and pulled, but might almost as well have tried to set up a cannon-ball. "I hope you have not hurt yourself?"

"Not at all, not at all," said the doctor, trying to smile and to rise both at once, but finding it impossible to do either.

"If he slept on the floor he would be late for breakfast," said Curdie to himself, and held out his hand to help him.

But when he took hold of it, Curdie very nearly let him fall again, for what he held was not even a foot: it was the belly of a creeping thing. He managed, however, to hold both his peace and his grasp, and pulled the doctor roughly on his legs—such as they were.

"Your royal highness has rather a thick mat at the door," said the doctor, patting his palms together. "I hope my awkwardness may not have startled his majesty."

While he talked Curdie went to the door: Lina was not there.

The doctor approached the bed.

"And how has my beloved king slept to-night?" he asked.

"No better," answered Irene, with a mournful shake of her head.

"Ah, that is very well!" returned the doctor, his fall seeming to have muddled either his words or his meaning. "We must give him his wine, and then he will be better still."

Curdie darted at the flagon, and lifted it high, as if he had expected to find it full, but had found it empty.

"That stupid butler! I heard them say he was drunk!" he cried in a loud whisper, and was gliding from the room.

"Come here with that flagon, you! page!" cried the doctor.

Curdie came a few steps towards him with the flagon dangling from his hand, heedless of the gushes that fell noiseless on the thick carpet.

"Are you aware, young man," said the doctor, "that it is not every wine can do his majesty the benefit I intend he should derive from my prescription?"

"Quite aware, sir," answered Curdie. "The wine for his majesty's use is in the third cask from the corner."

"Fly, then," said the doctor, looking satisfied.

Curdie stopped outside the curtain and blew an audible breath—no more: up came Lina noiseless as a shadow. He showed her the flagon.

"The cellar, Lina: go," he said.

She galloped away on her soft feet, and Curdie had indeed to fly to keep up with her. Not once did she make even a dubious turn. From the king's gorgeous chamber to the cold cellar they shot. Curdie dashed the wine down the back stair, rinsed the flagon out as he had seen the butler do, filled it from the cask of which he had seen the butler drink, and hastened with it up again to the king's room.

The little doctor took it, poured out a full glass, smelt, but did not taste it, and set it down. Then he leaned over the bed, shouted in the king's ear, blew upon his eyes, and pinched his arm: Curdie thought he saw him run something bright into it. As last the king half woke. The doctor seized the glass, raised his head, poured the wine down his throat, and let his head fall back on the pillow again. Tenderly wiping his beard, and bidding the princess good-night in paternal tones, he then took his leave. Curdie would gladly have driven his pick into his head, but that was not in his commission, and he let him go.

The little round man looked very carefully to his feet as he crossed the threshold.

"That attentive fellow of a page has removed the mat," he said to himself, as he walked along the corridor. "I must remember him."

Chapter 20

Counter-Plotting

C urdie was already sufficiently enlightened as to how things were going, to see that he must have the princess of one mind with him, and they must work together. It was clear that amongst those about the king there was a plot against him: for one thing, they had agreed in a lie concerning himself; and it was plain also that the doctor was working out a design against the health and reason of his majesty, rendering the question of his life a matter of little moment. It was in itself sufficient to justify the worst fears, that the people outside the palace were ignorant of his majesty's condition: he believed those inside it also—the butler excepted—were ignorant of it as well. Doubtless his majesty's councillors desired to alienate the hearts of his subjects from their sovereign. Curdie's idea was that they intended to kill the king, marry the princess to one of themselves, and found a new dynasty; but whatever their purpose, there was treason in the palace of the worst sort: they were making and keeping the king incapable, in order to effect that purpose. The first thing to be seen to therefore was, that his majesty should neither eat morsel nor drink drop of anything prepared for him in the palace. Could this have been managed without the princess, Curdie would have preferred leaving her in ignorance of the horrors from which he sought to deliver her. He feared also the danger of her knowledge betraying itself to the evil eyes about her; but it must be risked—and she had always been a wise child.

Another thing was clear to him—that with such traitors no terms of honour were either binding or possible, and that, short of lying, he might use any means to foil them. And he could not doubt that the old princess had sent him expressly to frustrate their plans.

While he stood thinking thus with himself, the princess was earnestly watching the king, with looks of childish love and womanly tenderness that went to Curdie's heart. Now and then with a great fan of peacock feathers she would fan him very softly; now and then, seeing a cloud begin to gather upon the sky of his sleeping face, she would climb upon the bed, and bending to his ear whisper into it, then draw back and watch again—generally to see the cloud disperse. In his deepest slumber, the soul of the king lay open to the voice of his child, and that voice had power either to change the aspect of his visions, or, which was better still, to breathe hope into his heart, and courage to endure them.

Curdie came near, and softly called her.

"I can't leave papa just yet," she returned, in a low voice.

"I will wait," said Curdie; "but I want very much to say something."

In a few minutes she came to him where he stood under the lamp.

"Well, Curdie, what is it?" she said.

"Princess," he replied, "I want to tell you that I have found why your grandmother sent me."

"Come this way, then," she answered, "where I can see the face of my king."

Curdie placed a chair for her in the spot she chose, where she would be near enough to mark any slightest change on her father's countenance, yet where their low-voiced talk would not disturb him. There he sat down beside her and told her all the story—how her grandmother had sent her good pigeon for him, and how she had instructed him, and sent him there without telling him what he had to do. Then he told her what he had discovered of the state of things generally in Gwyntystorm, and specially what he had heard and seen in the palace that night.

"Things are in a bad state enough," he said in conclusion;—"lying and selfishness and inhospitality and dishonesty everywhere; and to crown all, they speak with disrespect of the good king, and not a man of them knows he is ill."

"You frighten me dreadfully," said Irene, trembling.

"You must be brave for your king's sake," said Curdie.

"Indeed I will," she replied, and turned a long loving look upon the beautiful face of her father. "But what *is* to be done? And how *am* I to believe such horrible things of Dr. Kelman?"

"My dear princess," replied Curdie, "you know nothing of him but his face and his tongue, and they are both false. Either you must beware of him, or you must doubt your grandmother and me; for I tell you, by the gift she gave me of testing hands, that this man is a snake. That round body he shows is but the case of a serpent. Perhaps the creature lies there, as in its nest, coiled round and round inside."

"Horrible!" said Irene.

"Horrible indeed; but we must not try to get rid of horrible things by refusing to look at them, and saying they are not there. Is not your beautiful father sleeping better since he had the wine?"

"Yes."

"Does he always sleep better after having it?"

She reflected an instant.

"No; always worse—till to-night," she answered.

"Then remember that was the wine I got him—not what the butler drew. Nothing that passes through any hand in the house except yours or mine must henceforth, till he is well, reach his majesty's lips."

"But how, dear Curdie?" said the princess, almost crying.

"That we must contrive," answered Curdie. "I know how to take care of the wine; but for his food—now we must think."

"He takes hardly any," said the princess, with a pathetic shake of her little head which Curdie had almost learned to look for.

"The more need," he replied, "there should be no poison in it." Irene shuddered. "As soon as he has honest food he will begin to grow better. And you must be just as careful with yourself, princess," Curdie went on, "for you don't know when they may begin to poison you too."

"There's no fear of me; don't talk about me," said Irene. "The good food!—how are we to get it, Curdie? That is the whole question."

"I am thinking hard," answered Curdie. "The good food? Let me see—let me see!—Such servants as I saw below are sure to have the best of everything for themselves: I will go and see what I can find on their supper-table."

"The chancellor sleeps in the house, and he and the master of the king's horse always have their supper together in a room off the great hall, to the right as you go down the stair," said Irene. "I would go with you, but I dare not leave my father. Alas! he scarcely ever takes more than a mouthful. I can't think how he lives! And the very thing he would like, and often asks for—a bit of bread—I can hardly ever get for him: Dr. Kelman has forbidden it, and says it is nothing less than poison to him."

"Bread at least he *shall* have," said Curdie; "and that, with the honest wine, will do as well as anything, I do believe. I will go at once and look for some. But I want you to see Lina first, and know her, lest, coming upon her by accident at any time, you should be frightened."

"I should like very much to see her," said the princess.

Warning her not to be startled by her ugliness, he went to the door and called her.

She entered, creeping with downcast head, and dragging her tail over the floor behind her. Curdie watched the princess as the frightful creature came nearer and nearer. One shudder went from head to foot of her, and next instant she stepped to meet her. Lina dropped flat on the floor, and covered her face with her two big paws. It went to the heart of the princess: in a moment she was on her knees beside her, stroking her ugly head, and patting her all over.

"Good dog! Dear ugly dog!" she said.

Lina whimpered.

"I believe," said Curdie, "from what your grandmother told me, that Lina is a woman, and that she was naughty, but is now growing good."

Lina had lifted her head while Irene was caressing her; now she dropped it again between her paws; but the princess took it in her hands, and kissed the forehead betwixt the gold-green eyes.

"Shall I take her with me or leave her?" asked Curdie.

"Leave her, poor dear," said Irene, and Curdie, knowing the way now, went without her.

He took his way first to the room the princess had spoken of, and there also were the remains of supper; but neither there nor in the kitchen could he find a scrap of plain wholesome-looking bread. So he returned and told her that as soon as it was light he would go into the city for some, and asked her for a handkerchief to tie it in. If he could not bring it himself, he would send it by Lina, who could keep out of sight better than he, and as soon as all was quiet at night he would come to her again. He also asked her to tell the king that he was in the house.

His hope lay in the fact that bakers everywhere go to work early. But it was yet much too early. So he persuaded the princess to lie down, promising to call her if the king should stir.

Chapter 21

The Loaf

His majesty slept very quietly. The dawn had grown almost day, and still Curdie lingered, unwilling to disturb the princess. At last, however, he called her, and she was in the room in a moment. She had slept, she said, and felt quite fresh. Delighted to find her father still asleep, and so peacefully, she pushed her chair close to the bed, and sat down with her hands in her lap.

Curdie got his mattock from where he had hidden it behind a great mirror, and went to the cellar, followed by Lina. They took some breakfast with them as they passed through the hall, and as soon as they had eaten it went out the back way.

At the mouth of the passage Curdie seized the rope, drew himself up, pushed away the shutter, and entered the dungeon. Then he swung the end of the rope to Lina, and she caught it in her teeth. When her master said, "Now, Lina!" she gave a great spring, and he ran away with the end of the rope as fast as ever he could. And such a spring had she made, that by the time he had to bear her weight she was within a few feet of the hole. The instant she got a paw through, she was all through.

Apparently their enemies were waiting till hunger should have cowed them, for there was no sign of any attempt having been made to open the door. A blow or two of Curdie's mattock drove the shattered lock clean from it, and telling Lina to wait there till he came back, and let no one in, he walked out into the silent street, and drew the door to behind him. He could hardly believe it was not yet a whole day since he had been thrown in there with his hands tied at his back.

Down the town he went, walking in the middle of the street, that, if any one saw him, he might see he was not afraid, and hesitate to rouse an attack on him. As to the dogs, ever since the death of their two companions, a shadow that looked like a mattock was enough to make them scamper. As soon as he reached the archway of the city gate he turned to reconnoitre the baker's shop, and perceiving no sign of movement, waited there watching for the first.

After about an hour, the door opened, and the baker's man appeared with a pail in his hand. He went to a pump that stood in the street, and having filled his pail returned with it into the shop. Curdie stole after him, found the door on the latch, opened it very gently, peeped in, saw nobody, and entered. Remembering perfectly from what shelf the baker's wife had taken the loaf she said was the best, and seeing just one upon it, he seized it, laid the price of it on the counter, and sped softly out, and up the street. Once more in the dungeon beside Lina, his first thought was to fasten up the door again, which would have been easy, so many iron fragments of all sorts and sizes lay about; but he bethought himself that if he left it as it was, and they came to find him, they would conclude at once that they had made their escape by it, and would look no farther so as to discover the hole. He therefore merely pushed the door close and left it. Then once more carefully arranging the earth behind the shutter, so that it should again fall with it, he returned to the cellar.

And now he had to convey the loaf to the princess. If he could venture to take it himself, well; if not, he would send Lina. He crept to the door of the servants' hall, and found the sleepers beginning to stir. One said it was time to go to bed; another, that he would go to the cellar instead, and have a mug of wine to waken him up; while a third challenged a fourth to give him his revenge at some game or other.

"Oh, hang your losses!" answered his companion; "you'll soon pick up twice as much about the house, if you but keep your eyes open."

Perceiving there would be risk in attempting to pass through, and reflecting that the porters in the great hall would probably be awake also, Curdie went back to the cellar, took Irene's handkerchief with the loaf in it, tied it round Lina's neck, and told her to take it to the princess.

Using every shadow and every shelter, Lina slid through the servants like a shapeless terror through a guilty mind, and so, by corridor and great hall, up the stair to the king's chamber.

Irene trembled a little when she saw her glide soundless in across the silent dusk of the morning, that filtered through the heavy drapery of the windows, but she recovered herself at once when she saw the bundle about her neck, for it both assured her of Curdie's safety, and gave her hope of her father's. She untied it with joy, and Lina stole away, silent as she had come. Her joy was the greater that the king had woke up a little while before, and expressed a desire for food—not that he felt exactly hungry, he said, and yet he wanted something. If only he might have a piece of nice fresh bread! Irene had no knife, but with eager hands she broke a great piece from the loaf, and poured out a full glass of wine. The king ate and drank, enjoyed the bread and the wine much, and instantly fell asleep again.

It was hours before the lazy people brought their breakfast. When it came, Irene crumbled a little about, threw some into the fire-place, and managed to make the tray look just as usual.

In the meantime, down below in the cellar, Curdie was lying in the hollow between the upper sides of two of the great casks, the warmest place he could find. Lina was watching. She lay at his feet, across the two casks, and did her best so to arrange her huge tail that it should be a warm coverlid for her master.

By-and-by Dr. Kelman called to see his patient; and now that Irene's eyes were opened, she saw clearly enough that he was both annoyed and puzzled at finding his majesty rather better. He pretended however to congratulate him, saying he believed he was quite fit to see the lord chamberlain: he wanted his signature to something important; only he must not strain his mind to understand it, whatever it might be: if his majesty did, he would not be answerable for the consequences. The king said he would see the lord chamberlain, and the doctor went. Then Irene gave him more bread and wine, and the king ate and drank, and smiled a feeble smile, the first real one she had seen for many a day. He said he felt much better, and would soon be able to take matters into his own hands again. He had a strange miserable feeling, he said, that things were going terribly wrong, although he could not tell how. Then the princess told him that Curdie was come, and that at night, when all was quiet, for nobody in the palace must know, he would pay his majesty a visit. Her great-great-grandmother had sent him, she said. The king looked strangely upon her, but, the strange look passed into a smile clearer than the first, and Irene's heart throbbed with delight.

Chapter 22

The Lord Chamberlain

At noon the lord chamberlain appeared. With a long, low bow, and paper in hand, he stepped softly into the room. Greeting his majesty with every appearance of the profoundest respect, and congratulating him on the evident progress he had made, he declared himself sorry to trouble him, but there were certain papers, he said, which required his signature—and therewith drew nearer to the king, who lay looking at him doubtfully. He was a lean, long, yellow man, with a small head, bald over the top, and tufted at the back and about the ears. He had a very thin, prominent, hooked nose, and a quantity of loose skin under his chin and about the throat, which came craning up out of his neckcloth. His eyes were very small, sharp, and glittering, and looked black as jet. He had hardly enough of a mouth to make a smile with. His left hand held the paper, and the long, skinny fingers of his right a pen just dipped in ink.

But the king, who for weeks had scarcely known what he did, was to-day so much himself as to be aware that he was not quite himself; and the moment he saw the paper, he resolved that he would not sign without understanding and approving of it. He requested the lord chamberlain therefore to read it. His lordship commenced at once but the difficulties he seemed to encounter, and the fits of stammering that seized him, roused the king's suspicion tenfold. He called the princess.

"I trouble his lordship too much," he said to her: "you can read print well, my child—let me hear how you can read writing. Take that paper from his lordship's hand, and read it to me from beginning to end, while my lord drinks a glass of my favourite wine, and watches for your blunders."

"Pardon me, your majesty," said the lord chamberlain, with as much of a smile as he was able to extemporize, "but it were a thousand pities to put the attainments of her royal highness to a test altogether too severe. Your majesty can scarcely with justice expect the very organs of her speech to prove capable of compassing words so long, and to her so unintelligible."

"I think much of my little princess and her capabilities," returned the king, more and more aroused, "Pray, my lord, permit her to try."

"Consider, your majesty: the thing would be altogether without precedent. It would be to make sport of statecraft," said the lord chamberlain.

"Perhaps you are right, my lord," answered the king with more meaning than he intended should be manifest while to his growing joy he felt new life and power throbbing in heart and brain. "So this morning we shall read no farther. I am indeed ill able for business of such weight."

"Will your majesty please sign your royal name here?" said the lord chamberlain, preferring the request as a matter of course, and approaching with the feather end of the pen pointed to a spot where was a great red seal.

"Not to-day, my lord," replied the king.

"It is of the greatest importance, your majesty," softly insisted the other.

"I descried no such importance in it," said the king.

"Your majesty heard but a part."

"And I can hear no more to-day."

"I trust your majesty had ground enough, in a case of necessity like the present, to sign upon the representation of his loyal subject and chamberlain?—Or shall I call the lord chancellor?" he added, rising.

"There is no need. I have the very highest opinion of your judgement, my lord," answered the king; "—that is, with respect to means: we *might* differ as to ends."

The lord chamberlain made yet further attempts at persuasion; but they grew feebler and feebler, and he was at last compelled to retire without having gained his object. And well might his annoyance be keen! For that paper was the king's will, drawn up by the attorney-general; nor until they had the king's signature to it was there much use in venturing farther. But his worst sense of discomfiture arose from finding the king with so much capacity left, for the doctor had pledged himself so to weaken his brain that he should be as a child in their hands, incapable of refusing anything requested of him: his lordship began to doubt the doctor's fidelity to the conspiracy.

The princess was in high delight. She had not for weeks heard so many words, not to say words of such strength and reason, from her father's lips: day by day he had been growing weaker and more lethargic. He was so much exhausted however after this effort, that he asked for another piece of bread and more wine, and fell fast asleep the moment he had taken them in.

The lord chamberlain sent in a rage for Dr. Kelman. He came, and while professing himself unable to understand the symptoms described by his lordship, yet pledged himself again that on the morrow the king should do whatever was required of him.

The day went on. When his majesty was awake, the princess read to him—one story-book after another; and whatever she read, the king listened as if he had never heard anything so good before, making out in it the wisest meanings. Every now and then he asked for a piece of bread and a little wine, and every time he ate and drank he slept, and every time he woke he seemed better than the last time. The princess bearing her part, the loaf was eaten up and the flagon emptied before night. The butler took the flagon away, and brought it back filled to the brim, but both were thirsty as well as hungry when Curdie came again.

Meanwhile he and Lina, watching and waking alternately, had plenty of sleep. In the afternoon, peeping from the recess, they saw several of the servants enter hurriedly, one after the other, draw wine, drink it, and steal out; but their business was to take care of the king, not of his cellar, and they let them drink. Also, when the butler came to fill the flagon, they restrained themselves, for the villain's fate was not yet ready for him. He looked terribly frightened, and had brought with him a large candle and a small terrier—which latter indeed threatened to be troublesome, for he went roving and sniffing about until he came to the recess where they were. But as soon as he showed himself, Lina opened her jaws so wide, and glared at him so horribly, that, without even uttering a whimper, he tucked his tail between his legs and ran to his master. He was drawing the wicked wine at the moment, and did not see him, else he would doubtless have run too.

When supper-time approached, Curdie took his place at the door into the servants' hall; but after a long hour's vain watch, he began to fear he should get nothing: there was so much idling about, as well as coming and going. It was hard to bear—chiefly from the attractions of a splendid loaf, just fresh out of the oven, which he longed to secure for the king and princess. At length his chance did arrive: he pounced upon the loaf and carried it away, and soon after got hold of a pie.

This time however, both loaf and pie were missed. The cook was called. He declared he had provided both. One of themselves, he said, must have carried them away for some friend outside the palace. Then a housemaid, who had not long been one of them, said she had seen some one like a page running in the direction of the cellar with something in his hands. Instantly all turned upon the pages, accusing them, one after another. All denied, but nobody believed one of them: where there is no truth there can be no faith.

To the cellar they all set out to look for the missing pie and loaf. Lina heard them coming, as well she might, for they were talking and quarrelling loud, and gave her master warning. They snatched up everything, and got all signs of their presence out at the back door before the servants entered. When they found nothing, they all turned on the chambermaid, and accused her, not only of lying against the pages, but of having taken the things herself. Their language and behaviour so disgusted Curdie, who could hear a great part of what passed, and he saw the danger of discovery now so much increased, that he began to devise how best at once to rid the palace of the whole pack of them. That however, would be small gain so long as the treacherous officers of state continued in it. They must be first dealt with. A thought came to him, and the longer he looked at it the better he liked it.

As soon as the servants were gone, quarrelling and accusing all the way, they returned and finished their supper. Then Curdie, who had long been satisfied that Lina understood almost every word he said, communicated his plan to her, and knew by the wagging of her tail and the flashing of her eyes that she comprehended it. Until they had the king safe through the worst part of the night, however, nothing could be done.

They had now merely to go on waiting where they were till the household should be asleep. This waiting and waiting was much the hardest thing Curdie had to do in the whole affair. He took his mattock, and going again into the long passage, lighted a candle-end, and proceeded to examine the rock on all sides. But this was not merely to pass the time: he had a reason for it. When he broke the stone in the street, over which the baker fell, its appearance led him to pocket a fragment for further examination; and since then he had satisfied himself that it was the kind of stone in which gold is found, and that the yellow particles in it were pure metal. If such stone existed here in any plenty, he could soon make the king rich, and independent of his ill-conditioned subjects. He was therefore now bent on an examination of the rock; nor had he been at it long before he was persuaded that there were large quantities of gold in the half-crystalline white stone, with its veins of opaque white and of green, of which the rock, so far as he had been able to inspect it, seemed almost entirely to consist. Every piece he broke was spotted with particles and little lumps of a lovely greenish yellow—and that was gold. Hitherto he had worked only in silver, but he had read, and heard talk, and knew therefore about gold. As soon as he had got the king free of rogues and villains, he would have all the best and most honest miners, with his father at the head of them, to work this rock for the king.

It was a great delight to him to use his mattock once more. The time went quickly, and when he left the passage to go to the king's chamber, he had already a good heap of fragments behind the broken door.

Chapter 23

Dr. Kelman

As soon as he had reason to hope the way was clear, Curdie ventured softly into the hall, with Lina behind him. There was no one asleep on the bench or floor, but by the fading fire sat a girl weeping. It was the same who had seen him carrying off the food, and had been so hardly used for saying so. She opened her eyes when he appeared, but did not seem frightened at him.

"I know why you weep," said Curdie; "and I am sorry for you."

"It *is* hard not to be believed just *because* one speaks the truth," said the girl, "but that seems reason enough with some people. My mother taught me to speak the truth, and took such pains with me that I should find it hard to tell a lie, though I could invent many a story these servants would believe at once; for the truth is a strange thing here, and they don't know it when they see it. Show it to them, and they all stare as if it were a wicked lie, and that with the lie yet warm that has just left their own mouths!—You are a stranger," she said, and burst out weeping afresh, "but the stranger you are to such a place and such people the better!"

"I am the person," said Curdie, "whom you saw carrying the things from the supper-table." He showed her the loaf. "If you can trust, as well as speak the truth, I will trust you.—Can you trust me?"

She looked at him steadily for a moment.

"I can," she answered.

"One thing more," said Curdie: "have you courage as well as faith?"

"I think so."

"Look my dog in the face and don't cry out.—Come here, Lina."

Lina obeyed. The girl looked at her, and laid her hand on her head.

137

"Now I know you are a true woman," said Curdie. "—I am come to set things right in this house. Not one of the servants know I am here. Will you tell them to-morrow morning, that, if they do not alter their ways, and give over drinking, and lying, and stealing, and unkindness, they shall every one of them be driven from the palace?"

"They will not believe me."

"Most likely; but will you give them the chance?"

"I will."

"Then I will be your friend. Wait here till I come again."

She looked him once more in the face, and sat down.

When he reached the royal chamber, he found his majesty awake, and very anxiously expecting him. He received him with the utmost kindness, and at once as it were put himself in his hands by telling him all he knew concerning the state he was in. His voice was feeble, but his eye was clear, and although now and then his words and thoughts seemed to wander, Curdie could not be certain that the cause of their not being intelligible to him did not lie in himself. The king told him that for some years, ever since his queen's death, he had been losing heart over the wickedness of his people. He had tried hard to make them good, but they got worse and worse. Evil teachers, unknown to him, had crept into the schools; there was a general decay of truth and right principle at least in the city; and as that set the example to the nation, it must spread. The main cause of his illness was the despondency with which the degeneration of his people affected him. He could not sleep, and had terrible dreams; while, to his unspeakable shame and distress, he doubted almost everybody. He had striven against his suspicion, but in vain, and his heart was sore, for his courtiers and councillors were really kind; only he could not think why none of their ladies came near his princess. The whole country was discontented, he heard, and there were signs of gathering storm outside as well as inside his borders. The master of the horse gave him sad news of the insubordination of the army; and his great white horse was dead, they told him; and his sword had lost its temper: it bent double the last time he tried it!—only perhaps that was in a dream; and they could not find his shield; and one of his spurs had lost the rowel. Thus the poor king went wandering in a maze of sorrows, some of which were purely imaginary, while others were truer than he understood. He told how thieves came at night and tried to take his crown, so that he never dared let it out of his hands even when he slept; and how, every night, an evil demon in the shape of his physician came and poured poison down his throat. He knew it to be poison, he said, somehow, although it tasted like wine.

Here he stopped, faint with the unusual exertion of talking. Curdie seized the flagon, and ran to the wine-cellar.

In the servants' hall the girl still sat by the fire, waiting for him. As he returned he told her to follow him, and left her at the chamber door till he should rejoin her. When the king had had a little wine, he informed him that he had already discovered certain of his majesty's enemies, and one of the worst of them was the doctor, for it was no other demon than the doctor himself who had been coming every night, and giving him a slow poison.

"So!" said the king. "Then I have not been suspicious enough, for I thought it was but a dream! Is it possible Kelman can be such a wretch? Who then am I to trust?"

"Not one in the house, except the princess and myself," said Curdie.

"I will not go to sleep," said the king.

"That would be as bad as taking the poison," said Curdie. "No, no, sire; you must show your confidence by leaving all the watching to me, and doing all the sleeping your majesty can."

The king smiled a contented smile, turned on his side, and was presently fast asleep. Then Curdie persuaded the princess also to go to sleep, and telling Lina to watch, went to the housemaid. He asked her if she could inform him which of the council slept in the palace, and show him their rooms. She knew every one of them, she said, and took him the round of all their doors, telling him which slept in each room. He then dismissed her, and returning to the king's chamber, seated himself behind the curtain at the head of the bed, on the side farthest from the king. He told Lina to get under the bed, and make no noise.

About one o'clock the doctor came stealing in. He looked round for the princess, and seeing no one, smiled with satisfaction as he approached the wine where it stood under the lamp. Having partly filled a glass, he took from his pocket a small phial, and filled up the glass from it. The light fell upon his face from above, and Curdie saw the snake in it plainly visible. He had never beheld such an evil countenance: the man hated the king, and delighted in doing him wrong.

With the glass in his hand, he drew near the bed, set it down, and began his usual rude rousing of his majesty. Not at once succeeding, he took a lancet from his pocket, and was parting its cover with an involuntary hiss of hate between his closed teeth, when Curdie stooped and whispered to Lina, "Take him by the leg, Lina." She darted noiselessly upon him. With a face of horrible consternation, he gave his leg one tug to free it; the next instant Curdie heard the one scrunch with which she crushed the bone like a stick of celery. He tumbled on the floor with a yell.

"Drag him out, Lina," said Curdie.

Lina took him by the collar, and dragged him out. Her master followed to direct her, and they left him lying across the lord chamberlain's door, where he gave another horrible yell, and fainted.

The king had waked at his first cry, and by the time Curdie re-entered he had got at his sword where it hung from the centre of the tester, had drawn it, and was trying to get out of bed. But when Curdie told him all was well, he lay down again as quietly as a child comforted by his mother from a troubled dream. Curdie went to the door to watch.

The doctor's yells had roused many, but not one had yet ventured to appear. Bells were rung violently, but none were answered; and in a minute or two Curdie had what he was watching for. The door of the lord chamberlain's room opened, and, pale with hideous terror, his lordship peeped out. Seeing no one, he advanced to step into the corridor, and tumbled over the doctor. Curdie ran up, and held out his hand. He received in it the claw of a bird of prey—vulture or eagle, he could not tell which.

His lordship, as soon as he was on his legs, taking him for one of the pages, abused him heartily for not coming sooner, and threatened him with dismissal from the king's service for cowardice and neglect. He began indeed what bade fair to be a sermon on the duties of a page, but catching sight of the man who lay at his door, and seeing it was the doctor, he fell out upon Curdie afresh for standing there doing nothing, and ordered him to fetch immediate assistance. Curdie left him, but slipped into the king's chamber, closed and locked the door, and left the rascals to look after each other. Ere long he heard hurrying footsteps, and for a few minutes there was a great muffled tumult of scuffling feet, low voices, and deep groanings; then all was still again.

Irene slept through the whole—so confidently did she rest, knowing Curdie was in her father's room watching over him.

Chapter 24

The Prophecy

Curdie sat and watched every motion of the sleeping king. All the night, to his ear, the palace lay as quiet as the nursery of healthful children. At sunrise he called the princess.

"How has his Majesty slept?" were her first words as she entered the room.

"Quite quietly," answered Curdie; "that is, since the doctor was got rid of."

"How did you manage that?" inquired Irene; and Curdie had to tell all about it.

"How terrible!" she said. "Did it not startle the king dreadfully?"

"It did rather. I found him getting out of bed, sword in hand."

"The brave old man!" cried the princess.

"Not so old!" said Curdie, "—as you will soon see. He went off again in a minute or so; but for a little while he was restless, and once when he lifted his hand it came down on the spikes of his crown, and he half waked."

"But where *is* the crown?" cried Irene, in sudden terror.

"I stroked his hands," answered Curdie, "and took the crown from them; and ever since he has slept quietly, and again and again smiled in his sleep."

"I have never seen him do that," said the princess. "But what have you done with the crown, Curdie?"

"Look," said Curdie, moving away from the bedside.

Irene followed him—and there, in the middle of the floor, she saw a strange sight. Lina lay at full length, fast asleep, her tail stretched out straight behind her and her fore-legs before her: between the two paws meeting in front of it, her nose just touching it behind, glowed and flashed the crown, like a nest for the humming-birds of heaven.

Irene gazed, and looked up with a smile.

"But what if the thief were to come, and she not to wake?" she said. "Shall I try her?" And as she spoke she stooped towards the crown.

"No, no, no!" cried Curdie, terrified. "She would frighten you out of your wits. I would do it to show you, but she would wake your father. You have no conception with what a roar she would spring at my throat. But you shall see how lightly she wakes the moment I speak to her.—Lina!"

She was on her feet the same instant, with her great tail sticking out straight behind her, just as it had been lying.

"Good dog!" said the princess, and patted her head. Lina wagged her tail solemnly, like the boom of an anchored sloop. Irene took the crown, and laid it where the king would see it when he woke.

"Now, princess," said Curdie, "I must leave you for a few minutes. You must bolt the door, please, and not open it to any one."

Away to the cellar he went with Lina, taking care, as they passed through the servants' hall, to get her a good breakfast. In about one minute she had eaten what he gave her, and looked up in his face: it was not more she wanted, but work. So out of the cellar they went through the passage, and Curdie into the dungeon, where he pulled up Lina, opened the door, let her out, and shut it again behind her. As he reached the door of the king's chamber, Lina was flying out of the gate of Gwyntystorm as fast as her mighty legs could carry her.

"What's come to the wench?" growled the men-servants one to another, when the chambermaid appeared among them the next morning. There was something in her face which they could not understand, and did not like.

"Are we all dirt?" they said. "What are you thinking about? Have you seen yourself in the glass this morning, miss?"

She made no answer.

"Do you want to be treated as you deserve, or will you speak, you hussy?" said the first woman-cook. "I would fain know what right *you* have to put on a face like that!"

"You won't believe me," said the girl.

"Of course not. What is it?"

"I must tell you, whether you believe me or not," she said.

"Of course you must."

"It is this, then: if you do not repent of your bad ways, you are all going to be punished—all turned out of the palace together."

"A mighty punishment!" said the butler. "A good riddance, say I, of the trouble of keeping minxes like you in order! And why, pray, should we be turned out? What have I to repent of now, your holiness?"

"That you know best yourself," said the girl.

"A pretty piece of insolence! How should *I* know, forsooth, what a menial like you had got against me! There *are* people in this house—oh! I'm not blind to their ways! but every one for himself, say I!—Pray, Miss Judgment, who gave you such an impertinent message to his majesty's household?"

"One who is come to set things right in the king's house."

"Right, indeed!" cried the butler; but that moment the thought came back to him of the roar he had heard in the cellar, and he turned pale and was silent.

The steward took it up next.

"And pray, pretty prophetess," he said, attempting to chuck her under the chin, "what have *I* got to repent of?"

"That you know best yourself," said the girl. "You have but to look into your books or your heart."

"Can you tell *me,* then, what I have to repent of?" said the groom of the chambers.

"That you know best yourself," said the girl once more. "The person who told me to tell you said the servants of this house had to repent of thieving, and lying, and unkindness, and drinking; and they will be made to repent of them one way, if they don't do it of themselves another."

Then arose a great hubbub; for by this time all the servants in the house were gathered about her, and all talked together, in towering indignation.

"Thieving, indeed!" cried one. "A pretty word in a house where everything is left lying about in a shameless way, tempting poor innocent girls!—a house where nobody cares for anything, or has the least respect to the value of property!"

"I suppose you envy me this brooch of mine," said another. "There was just a half-sheet of note-paper about it, not a scrap more, in a drawer that's always open in the writing-table in the study! What sort of place is that for a jewel? Can you call it stealing to take a thing from such a place as that? Nobody cared a straw about it. It might as well have been in the dust-hole! If it had been locked up—then, to be sure!"

"Drinking!" said the chief porter, with a husky laugh. "And who wouldn't drink when he had a chance? Or who would repent it, except that the drink was gone? Tell me that, Miss Innocence."

"Lying!" said a great, coarse footman. "I suppose you mean when I told you yesterday you were a pretty girl when you didn't pout? Lying, indeed! Tell us something worth repenting of! Lying is the way of Gwyntystorm. You should have heard Jabez lying to the cook last night! He wanted a sweetbread for his pup, and pretended it was for the princess! Ha! ha! ha!"

"Unkindness! I wonder who's unkind! Going and listening to any stranger against her fellow-servants, and then bringing back his wicked words to trouble them!" said the oldest and worst of the housemaids. "—One of ourselves, too!—Come, you hypocrite! this is all an invention of yours and your young man's, to take your revenge of us because we found you out in a lie last night. Tell true now:—wasn't it the same that stole the loaf and the pie that sent you with the impudent message?"

As she said this, she stepped up to the housemaid and gave her, instead of time to answer, a box on the ear that almost threw her down; and whoever could get at her began to push and hustle and pinch and punch her.

"You invite your fate," she said quietly.

They fell furiously upon her, drove her from the hall with kicks and blows, hustled her along the passage, and threw her down the stair to the wine-cellar, then locked the door at the top of it, and went back to their breakfast.

In the meantime the king and the princess had had their bread and wine, and the princess, with Curdie's help, had made the room as tidy as she could—they were terribly neglected by the servants. And now Curdie set himself to interest and amuse the king, and prevent him from thinking too much, in order that he might the sooner think the better. Presently, at his majesty's request, he began from the beginning, and told everything he could recall of his life, about his father and mother and their cottage on the mountain, of the inside of the mountain and the work there, about the goblins and his adventures with them. When he came to finding the princess and her nurse overtaken by the twilight on the mountain, Irene took up her share of the tale, and told all about herself to that point, and then Curdie took it up again; and so they went on, each fitting in the part that the other did not know, thus keeping the hoop of the story running straight; and the king listened with wondering and delighted ears, astonished to find what he could so ill comprehend, yet fitting so well together from the lips of two narrators. At last, with the mission given him by the wonderful princess and his consequent adventures, Curdie brought up the whole tale to the present moment. Then a silence fell, and Irene and Curdie thought the king was asleep. But he was far from it; he was thinking about many things. After a long pause he said:—

"Now at last, my children, I am compelled to believe many things I could not and do not yet understand—things I used to hear, and sometimes see, as often as I visited my mother's home. Once, for instance, I heard my mother say to her father—speaking of me—'He is a good, honest boy, but he will be an old man before he understands;' and my grandfather answered, 'Keep up your heart, child: my mother will look after him.' I thought often of their words, and the many strange things besides I both heard and saw in that house; but by degrees, because I could not understand them, I gave up thinking of them. And indeed I had almost forgotten them, when you, my child, talking that day about the Queen Irene and her pigeons, and what you had seen in her garret, brought them all back to my mind in a vague mass. But now they keep coming back to me, one by one, every one for itself; and I shall just hold my peace, and lie here quite still, and think about them all till I get well again."

What he meant they could not quite understand, but they saw plainly that already he was better.

"Put away my crown," he said. "I am tired of seeing it, and have no more any fear of its safety."

They put it away together, withdrew from the bedside, and left him in peace.

Chapter 25

The Avenger

There was nothing now to be dreaded from Dr. Kelman, but it made Curdie anxious, as the evening drew near, to think that not a soul belonging to the court had been to visit the king, or ask how he did, that day. He feared, in some shape or other, a more determined assault. He had provided himself a place in the room, to which he might retreat upon approach, and whence he could watch; but not once had he had to betake himself to it.

Toward night the king fell asleep. Curdie thought more and more uneasily of the moment when he must again leave them for a little while. Deeper and deeper fell the shadows. No one came to light the lamp. The princess drew her chair close to Curdie: she would rather it were not so dark, she said. She was afraid of something—she could not tell what; nor could she give any reason for her fear but that all was so dreadfully still. When it had been dark about an hour, Curdie thought Lina might be returned; and reflected that the sooner he went the less danger was there of any assault while he was away. There was more risk of his own presence being discovered, no doubt, but things were now drawing to a crisis, and it must be run. So, telling the princess to lock all the doors of the bedchamber, and let no one in, he took his mattock, and with here a run, and there a halt under cover, gained the door at the head of the cellar-stair in safety. To his surprise he found it locked, and the key was gone. There was no time for deliberation. He felt where the lock was, and dealt it a tremendous blow with his mattock. It needed but a second to dash the door open. Some one laid a hand on his arm.

"Who is it?" said Curdie.

147

"I told you they wouldn't believe me, sir," said the housemaid. "I have been here all day."

He took her hand, and said, "You are a good, brave girl. Now come with me, lest your enemies imprison you again."

He took her to the cellar, locked the door, lighted a bit of candle, gave her a little wine, told her to wait there till he came, and went out the back way.

Swiftly he swung himself up into the dungeon. Lina had done her part. The place was swarming with creatures—animal forms wilder and more grotesque than ever ramped in nightmare dream. Close by the hole, waiting his coming, her green eyes piercing the gulf below, Lina had but just laid herself down when he appeared. All about the vault and up the slope of the rubbish-heap lay and stood and squatted the forty-nine whose friendship Lina had conquered in the wood. They all came crowding about Curdie.

He must get them into the cellar as quickly as ever he could. But when he looked at the size of some of them, he feared it would be a long business to enlarge the hole sufficiently to let them through. At it he rushed, hitting vigorously at its edge with his mattock. At the very first blow came a splash from the water beneath, but ere he could heave a third, a creature like a tapir, only that the grasping point of its proboscis was hard as the steel of Curdie's hammer, pushed him gently aside, making room for another creature, with a head like a great club, which it began banging upon the floor with terrible force and noise. After about a minute of this battery, the tapir came up again, shoved Clubhead aside, and putting its own head into the hole began gnawing at the sides of it with the finger of its nose, in such a fashion that the fragments fell in a continuous gravelly shower into the water. In a few minutes the opening was large enough for the biggest creature amongst them to get through it.

Next came the difficulty of letting them down: some were quite light, but the half of them were too heavy for the rope, not to say for his arms. The creatures themselves seemed to be puzzling where or how they were to go. One after another of them came up, looked down through the hole, and drew back. Curdie thought if he let Lina down, perhaps that would suggest something; possibly they did not see the opening on the other side. He did so, and Lina stood lighting up the entrance of the passage with her gleaming eyes. One by one the creatures looked down again, and one by one they drew back, each standing aside to glance at the next, as if to say, *Now you have a look.* At last it came to the turn of the serpent with the long body, the four short legs behind, and the little wings before. No sooner had he poked his head through than he poked it farther through—and farther, and farther yet, until there was little more than his legs left in the dungeon. By that time he had got his head and neck well into the passage beside Lina. Then his legs gave a great waddle and spring, and he tumbled himself, far as there was betwixt them, heels over head into the passage.

"That is all very well for you, Mr. Legserpent!" thought Curdie to himself; "but what is to be done with the rest?"

He had hardly time to think it however, before the creature's head appeared again through the floor. He caught hold of the bar of iron to which Curdie's rope was tied, and settling it securely across the narrowest part of the irregular opening, held fast to it with his teeth. It was plain to Curdie, from the universal hardness amongst them, that they must all, at one time or another, have been creatures of the mines.

He saw at once what this one was after. He had planted his feet firmly upon the floor of the passage, and stretched his long body up and across the chasm to serve as a bridge for the rest. He mounted instantly upon his neck, threw his arms round him as far as they would go, and slid down in ease and safety, the bridge just bending a little as his weight glided over it. But he thought some of the creatures would try his teeth.

One by one the oddities followed, and slid down in safety. When they seemed to be all landed, he counted them: there were but forty-eight. Up the rope again he went, and found one which had been afraid to trust himself to the bridge, and no wonder! for he had neither legs nor head nor arms nor tail: he was just a round thing, about a foot in diameter, with a nose and mouth and eyes on one side of the ball. He had made his journey by rolling as swiftly as the fleetest of them could run. The back of the legserpent not being flat, he could not quite trust himself to roll straight and not drop into the gulf. Curdie took him in his arms, and the moment he looked down through the hole, the bridge made itself again, and he slid into the passage in safety, with Ballbody in his bosom.

He ran first to the cellar, to warn the girl not to be frightened at the avengers of wickedness. Then he called to Lina to bring in her friends.

One after another they came trooping in, till the cellar seemed full of them. The housemaid regarded them without fear.

"Sir," she said, "there is one of the pages I don't take to be a bad fellow."

"Then keep him near you," said Curdie. "And now can you show me a way to the king's chamber not through the servants' hall?"

"There is a way through the chamber of the colonel of the guard," she answered, "but he is ill, and in bed."

"Take me that way," said Curdie.

By many ups and downs and windings and turnings she brought him to a dimly-lighted room, where lay an elderly man asleep. His arm was outside the coverlid, and Curdie gave his hand a hurried grasp as he went by. His heart beat for joy, for he had found a good, honest human hand.

"I suppose that is why he is ill," he said to himself.

It was now close upon supper-time, and when the girl stopped at the door of the king's chamber, he told her to go and give the servants one warning more.

"Say the messenger sent you," he said. "I will be with you very soon."

The king was still asleep. Curdie talked to the princess for a few minutes, told her not to be frightened whatever noises she heard, only to keep her door locked till he came, and left her.

Chapter 26

The Vengeance

By the time the girl reached the servants' hall they were seated at supper. A loud, confused exclamation arose when she entered. No one made room for her; all stared with unfriendly eyes. A page, who entered the next minute by another door, came to her side.

"Where do *you* come from, hussy?" shouted the butler, and knocked his fist on the table with a loud clang.

He had gone to fetch wine, had found the stair door broken open and the cellar-door locked, and had turned and fled. Amongst his fellows, however, he had now regained what courage could be called his.

"From the cellar," she replied. "The messenger broke open the door, and sent me to you again."

"The messenger! Pooh! What messenger?"

"The same who sent me before to tell you to repent."

"What! will you go fooling it still? Haven't you had enough of it?" cried the butler in a rage, and starting to his feet, drew near threateningly.

"I must do as I am told," said the girl.

"Then why *don't* you do as *I* tell you, and hold your tongue?" said the butler. "Who wants your preachments? If anybody here has anything to repent of, isn't that enough—and more than enough for him—but you must come bothering about, and stirring up, till not a drop of quiet will settle inside him? You come along with me, young woman; we'll see if we can't find a lock somewhere in the house that'll hold you in!"

"Hands off, Mr. Butler!" said the page, and stepped between.

"Oh, ho!" cried the butler, and pointed his fat finger at him. "That's you, is it, my fine fellow? So it's you that's up to her tricks, is it?"

The youth did not answer, only stood with flashing eyes fixed on him, until, growing angrier and angrier, but not daring a step nearer, he burst out with rude but quavering authority,—

"Leave the house, both of you! Be off, or I'll have Mr. Steward to talk to you. Threaten your masters, indeed! Out of the house with you, and show us the way you tell us of!"

Two or three of the footmen got up and ranged themselves behind the butler.

"Don't say *I* threaten you, Mr. Butler," expostulated the girl from behind the page. "The messenger said I was to tell you again, and give you one chance more."

"Did the *messenger* mention me in particular?" asked the butler, looking the page unsteadily in the face.

"No, sir," answered the girl.

"I thought not! I should like to hear him!"

"Then hear him now," said Curdie, who that moment entered at the opposite corner of the hall. "I speak of the butler in particular when I say that I know more evil of him than of any of the rest. He will not let either his own conscience or my messenger speak to him: I therefore now speak myself. I proclaim him a villain, and a traitor to his majesty the king.— But what better is any one of you who cares only for himself, eats, drinks, takes good money, and gives vile service in return, stealing and wasting the king's property, and making of the palace, which ought to be an example of order and sobriety, a disgrace to the country?"

For a moment all stood astonished into silence by this bold speech from a stranger. True, they saw by his mattock over his shoulder that he was nothing but a miner boy, yet for a moment the truth told notwithstanding. Then a great roaring laugh burst from the biggest of the footmen as he came shouldering his way through the crowd towards Curdie.

"Yes, I'm right," he cried; "I thought as much! This *messenger,* forsooth, is nothing but a gallows-bird—a fellow the city marshal was going to hang, but unfortunately put it off till he should be starved enough to save rope and be throttled with a pack-thread. He broke prison, and here he is preaching!"

As he spoke, he stretched out his great hand to lay hold of him. Curdie caught it in his left hand, and heaved his mattock with the other. Finding, however, nothing worse than an ox-hoof, he restrained himself, stepped back a pace or two, shifted his mattock to his left hand, and struck him a little smart blow on the shoulder. His arm dropped by his side, he gave a roar, and drew back.

His fellows came crowding upon Curdie. Some called to the dogs; others swore; the women screamed; the footmen and pages got round him in a half-circle, which he kept from closing by swinging his mattock, and here and there threatening a blow.

"Whoever confesses to having done anything wrong in this house, however small, however great, and means to do better, let him come to this corner of the room," he cried.

None moved but the page, who went towards him skirting the wall. When they caught sight of him, the crowd broke into a hiss of derision.

"There! see! Look at the sinner! He confesses! actually confesses! Come, what is it you stole? The barefaced hypocrite! There's your sort to set up for reproving other people! Where's the other now?"

But the maid had left the room, and they let the page pass, for he looked dangerous to stop. Curdie had just put him betwixt him and the wall, behind the door, when in rushed the butler with the huge kitchen poker, the point of which he had blown red-hot in the fire, followed by the cook with his longest spit. Through the crowd, which scattered right and left before them, they came down upon Curdie. Uttering a shrill whistle, he caught the poker a blow with his mattock, knocking the point to the ground, while the page behind him started forward, and seizing the point of the spit, held on to it with both hands, the cook kicking him furiously.

Ere the butler could raise the poker again, or the cook recover the spit, with a roar to terrify the dead, Lina dashed into the room, her eyes flaming like candles. She went straight at the butler. He was down in a moment, and she on top of him, wagging her tail over him like a lioness.

"Don't kill him, Lina," said Curdie.

"Oh, Mr. Miner!" cried the butler.

"Put your foot on his mouth, Lina," said Curdie. "The truth Fear tells is not much better than her lies."

The rest of the creatures now came stalking, rolling, leaping, gliding, hobbling into the room, and each as he came took the next place along the wall, until, solemn and grotesque, all stood ranged, awaiting orders.

And now some of the culprits were stealing to the doors nearest them. Curdie whispered to the two creatures next to him. Off went

Ballbody, rolling and bounding through the crowd like a spent cannon shot, and when the foremost reached the door to the corridor, there he lay at the foot of it grinning; to the other door scuttled a scorpion, as big as a huge crab. The rest stood so still that some began to think they were only boys dressed up to look awful; they persuaded themselves they were only another part of the housemaid and page's vengeful contrivance, and their evil spirits began to rise again. Meantime Curdie had, with a second sharp blow from the hammer of his mattock, disabled the cook, so that he yielded the spit with a groan. He now turned to the avengers.

"Go at them," he said.

The whole nine-and-forty obeyed at once, each for himself, and after his own fashion. A scene of confusion and terror followed. The crowd scattered like a dance of flies. The creatures had been instructed not to hurt much, but to hunt incessantly, until every one had rushed from the house. The women shrieked, and ran hither and thither through the hall, pursued each by her own horror, and snapped at by every other in passing. If one threw herself down in hysterical despair, she was instantly poked or clawed or nibbled up again. Though they were quite as frightened at first, the men did not run so fast; and by-and-by some of them, finding they were only glared at, and followed, and pushed, began to summon up courage once more, and with courage came impudence. The tapir had the big footman in charge: the fellow stood stock-still, and let the beast come up to him, then put out his finger and playfully patted his nose. The tapir gave the nose a little twist, and the finger lay on the floor. Then indeed the footman ran, and did more than run, but nobody heeded his cries. Gradually the avengers grew more severe, and the terrors of the imagination were fast yielding to those of sensuous experience, when a page, perceiving one of the doors no longer guarded, sprang at it, and ran out. Another and another followed. Not a beast went after, until, one by one, they were every one gone from the hall, and the whole menie in the kitchen. There they were beginning to congratulate themselves that all was over, when in came the creatures trooping after them, and the second act of their terror and pain began. They were flung about in all directions; their clothes were torn from them; they were pinched and scratched any and everywhere; Ballbody kept rolling up them and over them, confining his attentions to no one in particular; the scorpion kept grabbing at their legs with his huge pincers; a three-foot centipede kept screwing up their bodies, nipping as he went; varied as numerous were their woes. Nor was it long before the last of them had fled from the kitchen to the sculleries. But thither also they were followed, and there again they were hunted about. They were bespattered with the dirt of their own neglect; they were soused in the stinking water that had boiled green; they were smeared with rancid dripping; their faces were rubbed in maggots: I dare not tell all that was done to them. At last they got the door into a back-yard open, and rushed out. Then first they knew that the wind was howling and the rain falling in sheets. But there was no rest for them even there. Thither also were they followed by the inexorable avengers, and the only door here was a door out of the palace: out every soul of them was driven, and left, some standing, some lying, some crawling, to the farther buffeting of the waterspouts and whirlwinds ranging every street of the city. The door was flung to behind them, and they heard it locked and bolted and barred against them.

Chapter 27

More Vengeance

As soon as they were gone, Curdie brought the creatures back to the servants' hall, and told them to eat up everything on the table. It *was* a sight to see them all standing round it—except such as had to get upon it—eating and drinking, each after its fashion, without a smile, or a word, or a glance of fellowship in the act. A very few moments served to make everything eatable vanish, and then Curdie requested them to clean the house, and the page who stood by to assist them.

Every one set about it except Ballbody: he could do nothing at cleaning, for the more he rolled, the more he spread the dirt. Curdie was curious to know what he had been, and how he had come to be such as he was; but he could only conjecture that he was a gluttonous alderman whom nature had treated homœopathically.

And now there was such a cleaning and clearing out of neglected places, such a burying and burning of refuse, such a rinsing of jugs, such a swilling of sinks, and such a flushing of drains, as would have delighted the eyes of all true housekeepers and lovers of cleanliness generally.

Curdie meantime was with the king, telling him all he had done. They had heard a little noise, but not much, for he had told the avengers to repress outcry as much as possible; and they had seen to it that the more any one cried out the more he had to cry out upon, while the patient ones they scarcely hurt at all.

Having promised his majesty and her royal highness a good breakfast, Curdie now went to finish the business. The courtiers must be dealt with. A few who were the worst, and the leaders of the rest, must be made examples of; the others should be driven from their beds to the street.

He found the chiefs of the conspiracy holding a final consultation in the smaller room off the hall. These were the lord chamberlain, the attorney-general, the master of the horse, and the king's private secretary: the lord chancellor and the rest, as foolish as faithless, were but the tools of these.

The housemaid had shown him a little closet, opening from a passage behind, where he could overhear all that passed in that room; and now Curdie heard enough to understand that they had determined, in the dead of that night, rather in the deepest dark before the morning, to bring a certain company of soldiers into the palace, make away with the king, secure the princess, announce the sudden death of his majesty, read as his the will they had drawn up, and proceed to govern the country at their ease, and with results: they would at once levy severer taxes, and pick a quarrel with the most powerful of their neighbors. Everything settled, they agreed to retire, and have a few hours' quiet sleep first—all but the secretary, who was to sit up and call them at the proper moment. Curdie stole away, allowed them half an hour to get to bed, and then set about completing his purgation of the palace.

First he called Lina, and opened the door of the room where the secretary sat. She crept in, and laid herself down against it. When the secretary, rising to stretch his legs, caught sight of her eyes, he stood frozen with terror. She made neither motion nor sound. Gathering courage, and taking the thing for a spectral illusion, he made a step forward. She showed her other teeth, with a growl neither more than audible or less than horrible. The secretary sank fainting into a chair. He was not a brave man, and besides, his conscience had gone over to the enemy, and was sitting against the door by Lina.

To the lord chamberlain's door next, Curdie conducted the legserpent, and let him in.

Now his lordship had had a bedstead made for himself, sweetly fashioned of rods of silver gilt: upon it the legserpent found him asleep, and under it he crept. But out he came on the other side, and crept over it next, and again under it, and so over it, under it, over it, five or six times, every time leaving a coil of himself behind him, until he had softly folded all his length about the lord chamberlain and his bed. This done, he set up his head, looking down with curved neck right over his lordship's, and began to hiss in his face. He woke in terror unspeakable, and would have started up; but the moment he moved, the legserpent drew his coils closer, and closer still, and drew and drew until the quaking traitor heard the joints of his bedstead grinding and gnarring. Presently he persuaded himself that it was only a horrid nightmare, and began to struggle with all his strength to throw it off. Thereupon the legserpent gave his hooked nose such a bite, that his teeth met through it—but it was hardly thicker than the bowl of a spoon; and then the vulture knew that he was in the grasp of his enemy the snake, and yielded. As soon as he was quiet the legserpent began to untwist and retwist, to uncoil and recoil himself, swinging and swaying, knotting and relaxing himself with strangest curves and convolutions, always, however, leaving at least one coil around his victim. At last he undid himself entirely, and crept from the bed. Then first the lord chamberlain discovered that his tormentor had bent and twisted the bedstead, legs and canopy and all, so about him, that he was shut in a silver cage out of which it was impossible for him to find a way. Once more, thinking his enemy was gone, he began to shout for help. But the instant he opened his mouth his keeper darted at him and bit him, and after three or four such essays, with like result, he lay still.

The master of the horse Curdie gave in charge to the tapir. When the soldier saw him enter—for he was not yet asleep—he sprang from his bed, and flew at him with his sword. But the creature's hide was invulnerable to his blows, and he pecked at his legs with his proboscis until he jumped into bed again, groaning, and covered himself up; after which the tapir contented himself with now and then paying a visit to his toes.

For the attorney-general, Curdie led to his door a huge spider, about two feet long in the body, which, having made an excellent supper, was full of webbing. The attorney-general had not gone to bed, but sat in a chair asleep before a great mirror. He had been trying the effect of a diamond star which he had that morning taken from the jewel-room. When he woke he fancied himself paralysed; every limb, every finger even, was motionless: coils and coils of broad spider ribbon bandaged his members to his body, and all to the chair. In the glass he saw himself wound about, under and over and around, with slavery infinite. On a footstool a yard off sat the spider glaring at him.

Clubhead had mounted guard over the butler, where he lay tied hand and foot under the third cask. From that cask he had seen the wine run into a great bath, and therein he expected to be drowned. The doctor, with his crushed leg, needed no one to guard him.

And now Curdie proceeded to the expulsion of the rest. Great men or underlings, he treated them all alike. From room to room over the house he went, and sleeping or waking took the man by the hand. Such was the state to which a year of wicked rule had reduced the moral condition of the court, that in it all he found but three with human hands. The possessors of these he allowed to dress themselves and depart in peace. When they perceived his mission, and how he was backed, they yielded without dispute.

Then commenced a general hunt, to clear the house of the vermin. Out of their beds in their night-clothing, out of their rooms, gorgeous chambers or garret nooks, the creatures hunted them. Not one was allowed to escape. Tumult and noise there was little, for the fear was too deadly for outcry. Ferreting them out everywhere, following them upstairs and downstairs, yielding no instant of repose except upon the way out, the avengers persecuted the miscreants, until the last of them was shivering outside the palace gates, with hardly sense enough left to know where to turn.

When they set out to look for shelter, they found every inn full of the servants expelled before them, and not one would yield his place to a superior suddenly levelled with himself. Most houses refused to admit them on the ground of the wickedness that must have drawn on them such a punishment; and not a few would have been left in the streets all night, had not Derba, roused by the vain entreaties at the doors on each side of her cottage, opened hers, and given up everything to them. The lord chancellor was only too glad to share a mattress with a stable-boy, and steal his bare feet under his jacket.

In the morning Curdie appeared, and the outcasts were in terror, thinking he had come after them again. But he took no notice of them: his object was to request Derba to go to the palace: the king required her services. She needed take no trouble about her cottage, he said; the palace was henceforward her home: she was the king's chastelaine over men and maidens of his household. And this very morning she must cook his majesty a nice breakfast.

Chapter 28

The Preacher

Various reports went undulating through the city as to the nature of what had taken place in the palace. The people gathered, and stared at the house, eyeing it as if it had sprung up in the night. But it looked sedate enough, remaining closed and silent, like a house that was dead. They saw no one come out or go in. Smoke rose from a chimney or two; there was hardly another sign of life. It was not for some little time generally understood that the highest officers of the crown as well as the lowest menials of the palace had been dismissed in disgrace: for who was to recognise a lord chancellor in his night-shirt? and what lord chancellor would, so attired in the street, proclaim his rank and office aloud? Before it was day most of the courtiers crept down to the river, hired boats, and betook themselves to their homes or their friends in the country. It was assumed in the city that the domestics had been discharged upon a sudden discovery of general and unpardonable peculation; for, almost everybody being guilty of it himself, petty dishonesty was the crime most easily credited and least easily passed over in Gwyntystorm.

Now that same day was Religion day, and not a few of the clergy, always glad to seize on any passing event to give interest to the dull and monotonic grind of their intellectual machines, made this remarkable one the ground of discourse to their congregations. More especially than the rest, the first priest of the great temple where was the royal pew, judged himself, from his relation to the palace, called upon to "improve the occasion,"—for they talked ever about improvement at Gwyntystorm, all the time they were going downhill with a rush.

The book which had, of late years, come to be considered the most sacred, was called The Book of Nations, and consisted of proverbs, and history traced through custom: from it the first priest chose his text; and his text was, *Honesty is the best Policy*. He was considered a very eloquent man, but I can offer only a few of the larger bones of his sermon. The main proof of the verity of their religion, he said, was, that things always went well with those who professed it; and its first fundamental principle, grounded in inborn invariable instinct, was, that every One should take care of that One. This was the first duty of Man. If every one would but obey this law, number one, then would every one be perfectly cared for—one being always equal to one. But the faculty of care was in excess of need, and all that overflowed, and would otherwise run to waste, ought to be gently turned in the direction of one's neighbour, seeing that this also wrought for the fulfilling of the law, inasmuch as the reaction of excess so directed was upon the director of the same, to the comfort, that is, and well-being of the original self. To be just and friendly was to build the warmest and safest of all nests, and to be kind and loving was to line it with the softest of all furs and feathers, for the one precious, comfort-loving self there to lie, revelling in downiest bliss. One of the laws therefore most binding upon men because of its relation to the first and greatest of all duties, was embodied in the Proverb he had just read; and what stronger proof of its wisdom and truth could they desire than the sudden and complete vengeance which had fallen upon those worse than ordinary sinners who had offended against the king's majesty by forgetting that *Honesty is the best Policy!*

At this point of the discourse the head of the legserpent rose from the floor of the temple, towering above the pulpit, above the priest, then curving downwards, with open mouth slowly descended upon him. Horror froze the sermon-pump. He stared upwards aghast. The great teeth of the animal closed upon a mouthful of the sacred vestments, and slowly he lifted the preacher from the pulpit, like a handful of linen from a wash-tub, and, on his four solemn stumps, bore him out of the temple, dangling aloft from his jaws. At the back of it he dropped him into the dust-hole amongst the remnants of a library whose age had destroyed its value in the eyes of the chapter. They found him burrowing in it, a lunatic henceforth—whose madness presented the peculiar feature, that in its paroxysms he jabbered sense.

Bone-freezing horror pervaded Gwyntystorm. If their best and wisest were treated with such contempt, what might not the rest of them look for? Alas for their city! their grandly respectable city! their loftily reasonable city! Where it was all to end, the Convenient alone could tell!

But something must be done. Hastily assembling, the priest chose a new first priest, and in full conclave unanimously declared and accepted, that the king in his retirement had, through the practice of the blackest magic, turned the palace into a nest of demons in the midst of them. A grand exorcism was therefore indispensable.

In the meantime the fact came out that the greater part of the courtiers had been dismissed as well as the servants, and this fact swelled the hope of the Party of Decency, as they called themselves. Upon it they proceeded to act, and strengthened themselves on all sides.

The action of the king's body-guard remained for a time uncertain. But when at length its officers were satisfied that both the master of the horse and their colonel were missing, they placed themselves under the orders of the first priest.

Everyone dated the culmination of the evil from the visit of the miner and his mongrel; and the butchers vowed, if they could but get hold of them again, they would roast both of them alive. At once they formed themselves into a regiment, and put their dogs in training for attack.

Incessant was the talk, innumerable were the suggestions, and great was the deliberation. The general consent, however, was that as soon as the priests should have expelled the demons, they would depose the king, and, attired in all his regal insignia, shut him in a cage for public show; then choose governors, with the lord chancellor at their head, whose first duty should be to remit every possible tax; and the magistrates, by the mouth of the city marshal, required all able-bodied citizens, in order to do their part towards the carrying out of these and a multitude of other reforms, to be ready to take arms at the first summons.

Things needful were prepared as speedily as possible, and a mighty ceremony, in the temple, in the market-place, and in front of the palace, was performed for the expulsion of the demons. This over, the leaders retired to arrange an attack upon the palace.

But that night events occurred which, proving the failure of their first, induced the abandonment of their second intent. Certain of the prowling order of the community, whose numbers had of late been steadily on the increase, reported frightful things. Demons of indescribable ugliness had been espied careening through the midnight streets and courts. A citizen—some said in the very act of house-breaking, but no one cared to look into trifles at such a crisis—had been seized from behind, he could not see by what, and soused in the river. A well-known receiver of stolen goods had had his shop broken open, and when he came down in the morning had found everything in ruin on the pavement. The wooden image of justice over the door of the city marshal had had the arm that held the sword *bitten* off. The gluttonous magistrate had been pulled from his bed in the dark, by beings of which he could see nothing but the flaming eyes, and treated to a bath of the turtle soup that had been left simmering by the side of the kitchen fire. Having poured it over him, they put him again into his bed, where he soon learned how a mummy must feel in its cerements. Worst of all, in the market-place was fixed up a paper, with the king's own signature, to the effect that whoever henceforth should show inhospitality to strangers, and should be convicted of the same, should be instantly expelled the city; while a second, in the butchers' quarter, ordained that any dog which henceforward should attack a stranger should be immediately destroyed. It was plain, said the butchers, that the clergy were of no use; *they* could not exorcise demons! That afternoon, catching sight of a poor old fellow in rags and tatters, quietly walking up the street, they hounded their dogs upon him, and had it not been that the door of Derba's cottage was standing open, and was near enough for him to dart in and shut it ere they reached him, he would have been torn in pieces.

And thus things went on for some days.

Chapter 29

Barbara

In the meantime, with Derba to minister to his wants, with Curdie to protect him, and Irene to nurse him, the king was getting rapidly stronger. Good food was what he most wanted, and of that, at least of certain kinds of it, there was plentiful store in the palace. Everywhere since the cleansing of the lower regions of it, the air was clean and sweet, and under the honest hands of the one housemaid the king's chamber became a pleasure to his eyes. With such changes it was no wonder if his heart grew lighter as well as his brain clearer.

But still evil dreams came and troubled him, the lingering results of the wicked medicines the doctor had given him. Every night, sometimes twice or thrice, he would wake up in terror, and it would be minutes ere he could come to himself. The consequence was that he was always worse in the morning, and had loss to make up during the day. This retarded his recovery greatly. While he slept, Irene or Curdie, one or the other, must still be always by his side.

One night, when it was Curdie's turn with the king, he heard a cry somewhere in the house, and as there was no other child, concluded, notwithstanding the distance of her grandmother's room, that it must be Barbara. Fearing something might be wrong, and noting the king's sleep more quiet than usual, he ran to see. He found the child in the middle of the floor, weeping bitterly, and Derba slumbering peacefully in bed. The instant she saw him the night-lost thing ceased her crying, smiled, and stretched out her arms to him. Unwilling to wake the old woman, who had been working hard all day, he took the child, and carried her with him. She clung to him so, pressing her tear-wet radiant face against his, that her little arms threatened to choke him. When he re-entered the chamber, he found the king sitting up in bed, fighting the phantoms of some hideous dream. Generally upon such occasions, although he saw his watcher, he could not dissociate him from the dream, and went raving on. But the moment his eyes fell upon little Barbara, whom he had never seen before, his soul came into them with a rush, and a smile like the dawn of an eternal day overspread his countenance: the dream was nowhere, and the child was in his heart. He stretched out his arms to her, the child stretched out hers to him, and in five minutes they were both asleep, each in the other's embrace. From that night Barbara had a crib in the king's chamber, and as often as he woke, Irene or Curdie, whichever was watching, took the sleeping child and laid her in his arms, upon which, invariably and instantly, the dream would vanish. A great part of the day too she would be playing on or about the king's bed; and it was a delight to the heart of the princess to see her amusing herself with the crown, now sitting upon it, now rolling it hither and thither about the room like a hoop. Her grandmother entering once while she was pretending to make porridge in it, held up her hands in horror-struck amazement; but the king would not allow her to interfere, for the king was now Barbara's playmate, and his crown their plaything.

The colonel of the guard also was growing better. Curdie went often to see him. They were soon friends, for the best people understand each other the easiest, and the grim old warrior loved the miner boy as if he were at once his son and his angel. He was very anxious about his regiment. He said the officers were mostly honest men, he believed, but how they might be doing without him, or what they might resolve, in ignorance of the real state of affairs, and exposed to every misrepresentation, who could tell? Curdie proposed that he should send for the major, offering to be the messenger. The colonel agreed, and Curdie went—not without his mattock, because of the dogs.

But the officers had been told by the master of the horse that their colonel was dead, and although they were amazed he should be buried without the attendance of his regiment, they never doubted the information. The handwriting itself of their colonel was insufficient, counteracted by the fresh reports daily current, to destroy the lie. The major regarded the letter as a trap for the next officer in command, and sent his orderly to arrest the messenger. But Curdie had had the wisdom not to wait for an answer.

The king's enemies said that he had first poisoned the good colonel of the guard, and then murdered the master of the horse, and other faithful councillors; and that his oldest and most attached domestics had but escaped from the palace with their lives—nor all of them, for the butler was missing. Mad or wicked, he was not only unfit to rule any longer, but worse than unfit to have in his power and under his influence the young princess, only hope to Gwyntystorm and the kingdom.

The moment the lord chancellor reached his house in the country and had got himself clothed, he began to devise how yet to destroy his master; and the very next morning set out for the neighbouring kingdom of Borsagrass, to invite invasion, and offer a compact with its monarch.

Chapter 30

Peter

At the cottage on the mountain everything for a time went on just as before. It was indeed dull without Curdie, but as often as they looked at the emerald it was gloriously green, and with nothing to fear or regret, and everything to hope, they required little comforting. One morning, however, at last, Peter, who had been consulting the gem, rather now from habit than anxiety, as a farmer his barometer in undoubtful weather, turned suddenly to his wife, the stone in his hand, and held it up with a look of ghastly dismay.

"Why, that's never the emerald!" said Joan.

"It is," answered Peter; "but it were small blame to any one that took it for a bit of bottle glass!"

For, all save one spot right in the centre, of intensest and most brilliant green, it looked as if the colour had been burnt out of it.

"Run, run, Peter!" cried his wife. "Run and tell the old princess. It may not be too late. The boy must be lying at death's door."

Without a word Peter caught up his mattock, darted from the cottage, and was at the bottom of the hill in less time than he usually took to get halfway.

The door of the king's house stood open; he rushed in and up the stair. But after wandering about in vain for an hour, opening door after door, and finding no way farther up, the heart of the old man had well-nigh failed him. Empty rooms, empty rooms!—desertion and desolation everywhere.

At last he did come upon the door to the tower-stair. Up he darted. Arrived at the top, he found three doors, and, one after the other, knocked at them all. But there was neither voice nor hearing. Urged by his faith and his dread, slowly, hesitatingly, he opened one. It revealed a bare garret-room, nothing in it but one chair and one spinning-wheel. He closed it, and opened the next—to start back in terror, for he saw nothing but a great gulf, a moonless night, full of stars, and, for all the stars, dark, dark!—a fathomless abyss. He opened the third door, and a rush like the tide of a living sea invaded his ears. Multitudinous wings flapped and flashed in the sun, and, like the ascending column from a volcano, white birds innumerable shot into the air, darkening the day with the shadow of their cloud, and then, with a sharp sweep, as if bent sideways by a sudden wind, flew northward, swiftly away, and vanished. The place felt like a tomb. There seemed no breath of life left in it. Despair laid hold upon him; he rushed down thundering with heavy feet. Out upon him darted the housekeeper like an ogress-spider, and after her came her men; but Peter rushed past them, heedless and careless—for had not the princess mocked him?—and sped along the road to Gwyntystorm. What help lay in a miner's mattock, a man's arm, a father's heart, he would bear to his boy.

Joan sat up all night waiting his return, hoping and hoping. The mountain was very still, and the sky was clear; but all night long the miner sped northwards, and the heart of his wife was troubled.

Chapter 31

The Sacrifice

Things in the palace were in a strange condition: the king playing with a child and dreaming wise dreams, waited upon by a little princess with the heart of a queen, and a youth from the mines, who went nowhere, not even into the king's chamber, without his mattock on his shoulder and a horrible animal at his heels; in a room near by the colonel of his guard, also in bed, without a soldier to obey him; in six other rooms, far apart, six miscreants, each watched by a beast-gaoler; ministers to them all, an old woman, a young woman, and a page; and in the wine-cellar, forty-three animals, creatures more grotesque than ever brain of man invented. None dared approach its gates, and seldom one issued from them.

All the dwellers in the city were united in enmity to the palace. It swarmed with evil spirits, they said whereas the evil spirits were in the city, unsuspected. One consequence of their presence was that, when the rumour came that a great army was on the march against Gwyntystorm, instead of rushing to their defences, to make new gates, free portcullises and drawbridges, and bar the river, each and all flew first to their treasures, burying them in their cellars and gardens, and hiding them behind stones in their chimneys; and, next to rebellion, signing an invitation to his majesty of Borsagrass to enter at their open gates, destroy their king, and annex their country to his own.

The straits of isolation were soon found in the palace: its invalids were requiring stronger food, and what was to be done? for if the butchers sent meat to the palace, was it not likely enough to be poisoned? Curdie said to Derba he would think of some plan before morning.

But that same night, as soon as it was dark, Lina came to her master, and let him understand she wanted to go out. He unlocked a little private postern for her, left it so that she could push it open when she returned, and told the crocodile to stretch himself across it inside. Before midnight she came back with a young deer.

Early the next morning the legserpent crept out of the wine-cellar, through the broken door behind, shot into the river, and soon appeared in the kitchen with a splendid sturgeon. Every night Lina went out hunting, and every morning Legserpent went out fishing, and both invalids and household had plenty to eat. As to news, the page, in plain clothes, would now and then venture out into the market-place and gather some.

One night he came back with the report that the army of the king of Borsagrass had crossed the border. Two days after, he brought the news that the enemy was now but twenty miles from Gwyntystorm.

The colonel of the guard rose, and began furbishing his armour—but gave it over to the page, and staggered across to the barracks, which were in the next street. The sentry took him for a ghost or worse, ran into the guard-room, bolted the door, and stopped his ears. The poor colonel, who was yet hardly able to stand, crawled back despairing.

For Curdie, he had already, as soon as the first rumour reached him, resolved, if no other instructions came, and the king continued unable to give orders, to call Lina and the creatures, and march to meet the enemy. If he died, he died for the right, and there was a right end of it. He had no preparations to make, except a good sleep.

He asked the king to let the housemaid take his place by his majesty that night, and went and lay down on the floor of the corridor, no farther off than a whisper would reach from the door of the chamber. There, with an old mantle of the king's thrown over him, he was soon fast asleep.

Somewhere about the middle of the night, he woke suddenly, started to his feet, and rubbed his eyes. He could not tell what had waked him. But could he be awake, or was he not dreaming? The curtain of the king's door, a dull red ever before, was glowing a gorgeous, a radiant purple; and the crown wrought upon it in silks and gems was flashing as if it burned! What could it mean? Was the king's chamber on fire? He darted to the door and lifted the curtain. Glorious terrible sight!

A long and broad marble table, that stood at one end of the room, had been drawn into the middle of it, and thereon burned a great fire, of a sort that Curdie knew—a fire of glowing, flaming roses, red and white. In the midst of the roses lay the king, moaning, but motionless. Every rose that fell from the table to the floor, some one, whom Curdie could not plainly see for the brightness, lifted and laid burning upon the king's face, until at length his face too was covered with the live roses, and he lay all within the fire, moaning still, with now and then a shuddering sob. And the shape that Curdie saw and could not see, wept over the king as he lay in the fire, and often she hid her face in handfuls of her shadowy hair, and from her hair the water of her weeping dropped like sunset rain in the light of the roses. At last she lifted a great armful of her hair, and shook it over the fire, and the drops fell from it in showers, and they did not hiss in the flames, but there arose instead as it were the sound of running brooks. And the glow of the red fire died away, and the glow of the white fire grew gray, and the light was gone, and on the table all was black—except the face of the king, which shone from under the burnt roses like a diamond in the ashes of a furnace.

Then Curdie, no longer dazzled, saw and knew the old princess. The room was lighted with the splendour of her face, of her blue eyes, of her sapphire crown. Her golden hair went streaming out from her through the air till it went off in mist and light. She was large and strong as a Titaness. She stooped over the table-altar, put her mighty arms under the living sacrifice, lifted the king, as if he were but a little child, to her bosom, walked with him up the floor, and laid him in his bed. Then darkness fell.

The miner-boy turned silent away, and laid himself down again in the corridor. An absolute joy filled his heart, his bosom, his head, his whole body. All was safe; all was well. With the helve of his mattock tight in his grasp, he sank into a dreamless sleep.

Chapter 32

The King's Army

He woke like a giant refreshed with wine.

When he went into the king's chamber, the housemaid sat where he had left her, and everything in the room was as it had been the night before, save that a heavenly odour of roses filled the air of it. He went up to the bed. The king opened his eyes, and the soul of perfect health shone out of them. Nor was Curdie amazed in his delight.

"Is it not time to rise, Curdie?" said the king.

"It is, your majesty. To-day we must be doing," answered Curdie.

"What must we be doing to-day, Curdie?"

"Fighting, sire."

"Then fetch me my armour—that of plated steel, in the chest there. You will find the underclothing with it."

As he spoke, he reached out his hand for his sword, which hung in the bed before him, drew it, and examined the blade.

"A little rusty!" he said, "but the edge is there. We shall polish it ourselves to-day—not on the wheel. Curdie, my son, I wake from a troubled dream. A glorious torture has ended it, and I live. I know not well how things are, but thou shalt explain them to me as I get on my armour.—No, I need no bath. I am clean.—Call the colonel of the guard."

In complete steel the old man stepped into the chamber. He knew it not, but the old princess had passed through his room in the night.

"Why, Sir Bronzebeard!" said the king, "you are dressed before me! Thou needest no valet, old man, when there is battle in the wind!"

"Battle, sire!" returned the colonel. "—Where then are our soldiers?"

"Why, there, and here," answered the king, pointing to the colonel first, and then to himself. "Where else, man?—The enemy will be upon us ere sunset, if we be not upon him ere noon. What other thing was in thy brave brain when thou didst don thine armour, friend?"

"Your majesty's orders, sire," answered Sir Bronzebeard.

The king smiled and turned to Curdie.

"And what was in thine, Curdie—for thy first word was of battle?"

"See, your majesty," answered Curdie; "I have polished my mattock. If your majesty had not taken the command, I would have met the enemy at the head of my beasts, and died in comfort, or done better."

"Brave boy!" said the king. "He who takes his life in his hand is the only soldier. Thou shalt head thy beasts to-day.—Sir Bronzebeard, wilt thou die with me if need be?"

"Seven times, my king," said the colonel.

"Then shall we win this battle!" said the king. "—Curdie, go and bind securely the six, that we lose not their guards.—Canst thou find us a horse, think'st thou, Sir Bronzebeard? Alas! they told us our white charger was dead."

"I will go and fright the varletry with my presence, and secure, I trust, a horse for your majesty, and one for myself."

"And look you, brother!" said the king; "bring one for my miner boy too, and a sober old charger for the princess, for she too must go to the battle, and conquer with us."

"Pardon me, sire," said Curdie; "a miner can fight best on foot. I might smite my horse dead under me with a missed blow. And besides, I must be near my beasts."

"As you will," said the king. "—Three horses then, Sir Bronzebeard."

The colonel departed, doubting sorely in his heart how to accoutre and lead from the barrack stables three horses, in the teeth of his revolted regiment.

In the hall he met the housemaid.

"Can you lead a horse?" he asked.

"Yes, sir."

"Are you willing to die for the king?"

"Yes, sir."

"Can you do as you are bid?"

"I can keep on trying, sir."

"Come, then. Were I not a man I would be a woman such as thou."

When they entered the barrack-yard, the soldiers scattered like autumn leaves before a blast of winter. They went into the stable unchallenged—and lo! in a stall, before the colonel's eyes, stood the king's white charger, with the royal saddle and bridle hung high beside him!

"Traitorous thieves!" muttered the old man in his beard, and went along the stalls, looking for his own black charger. Having found him, he returned to saddle first the king's. But the maid had already the saddle upon him, and so girt that the colonel could thrust no finger-tip between girth and skin. He left her to finish what she had so well begun, and went and graithed his own. He then chose for the princess a great red horse, twenty years old, which he knew to possess every equine virtue. This and his own he led to the palace, and the maid led the king's.

The king and Curdie stood in the court, the king in full armour of silvered steel, with a circlet of rubies and diamonds round his helmet. He almost leaped for joy when he saw his great white charger come in, gentle as a child to the hand of the housemaid. But when the horse saw his master in his armour, he reared and bounded in jubilation, yet did not break from the hand that held him. Then out came the princess attired and ready, with a hunting-knife her father had given her by her side. They brought her mother's saddle, splendent with gems and gold, set it on the great red horse, and lifted her to it. But the saddle was so big, and the horse so tall, that the child found no comfort in them.

"Please, king papa," she said, "can I not have my white pony?"

"I did not think of him, little one," said the king. "Where is he?"

"In the stable," answered the maid. "I found him half-starved, the only horse within the gates, the day after the servants were driven out. He has been well fed since."

"Go and fetch him," said the king.

As the maid appeared with the pony, from a side door came Lina and the forty-nine, following Curdie.

"I will go with Curdie and the Uglies," cried the princess; and as soon as she was mounted she got into the middle of the pack.

So out they set, the strangest force that ever went against an enemy. The king in silver armour sat stately on his white steed, with the stones flashing on his helmet; beside him the grim old colonel, armed in steel, rode his black charger; behind the king, a little to the right, Curdie walked afoot, his mattock shining in the sun; Lina followed at his heel; behind her came the wonderful company of Uglies; in the midst of them rode the gracious little Irene, dressed in blue, and mounted on the prettiest of white ponies; behind the colonel, a little to the left, walked the page, armed in a breastplate, headpiece, and trooper's sword he had found in the palace, all much too big for him, and carrying a huge brass trumpet which he did his best to blow; and the king smiled and seemed pleased with his music, although it was but the grunt of a brazen unrest. Alongside of the beasts walked Derba carrying Barbara—their refuge the mountains, should the cause of the king be lost; as soon as they were over the river they turned aside to ascend the cliff, and there awaited the forging of the day's history. Then first Curdie saw that the housemaid, whom they had all forgotten, was following, mounted on the great red horse, and seated in the royal saddle.

Many were the eyes unfriendly of women that had stared at them from door and window as they passed through the city; and low laughter and mockery and evil words from the lips of children had rippled about their ears; but the men were all gone to welcome the enemy, the butchers the first, the king's guard the last. And now on the heels of the king's army rushed out the women and children also, to gather flowers and branches, wherewith to welcome their conquerors.

About a mile down the river, Curdie, happening to look behind him, saw the maid, whom he had supposed gone with Derba, still following on the great red horse. The same moment the king, a few paces in front of him, caught sight of the enemy's tents, pitched where, the cliffs receding, the bank of the river widened to a little plain.

Chapter 33

The Battle

He commanded the page to blow his trumpet; and, in the strength of the moment, the youth uttered a right war-like defiance.

But the butchers and the guard, who had gone over armed to the enemy, thinking that the king had come to make his peace also, and that it might thereafter go hard with them, rushed at once to make short work with them, and both secure and commend themselves. The butchers came on first—for the guards had slackened their saddle-girths—brandishing their knives, and talking to their dogs. Curdie and the page, with Lina and her pack, bounded to meet them. Curdie struck down the foremost with his mattock. The page, finding his sword too much for him, threw it away and seized the butcher's knife, which as he rose he plunged into the foremost dog. Lina rushed raging and gnashing amongst them. She would not look at a dog so long as there was a butcher on his legs, and she never stopped to kill a butcher, only with one grind of her jaws crushed a leg of him. When they were all down, then indeed she flashed amongst the dogs.

Meantime the king and the colonel had spurred towards the advancing guard. The king clove the major through the skull and collar-bone, and the colonel stabbed the captain in the throat. Then a fierce combat commenced—two against many. But the butchers and their dogs quickly disposed of, up came Curdie and his beasts. The horses of the guard, struck with terror, turned in spite of the spur, and fled in confusion.

Thereupon the forces of Borsagrass, which could see little of the affair, but correctly imagined a small determined body in front of them, hastened to the attack. No sooner did their first advancing wave appear through the foam of the retreating one, than the king and the colonel and the page, Curdie and the beasts, went charging upon them. Their attack, especially the rush of the Uglies, threw the first line into great confusion, but the second came up quickly; the beasts could not be everywhere, there were thousands to one against them, and the king and his three companions were in the greatest possible danger.

A dense cloud came over the sun, and sank rapidly towards the earth. The cloud moved "all together," and yet the thousands of white flakes of which it was made up moved each for itself in ceaseless and rapid motion: those flakes were the wings of pigeons. Down swooped the birds upon the invaders; right in the face of man and horse they flew with swift-beating wings, blinding eyes and confounding brain. Horses reared and plunged and wheeled. All was at once in confusion. The men made frantic efforts to seize their tormentors, but not one could they touch; and they outdoubled them in numbers. Between every wild clutch came a peck of beak and a buffet of pinion in the face. Generally the bird would, with sharp-clapping wings, dart its whole body, with the swiftness of an arrow, against its singled mark, yet so as to glance aloft the same instant, and descent skimming; much as the thin stone, shot with horizontal cast of arm, having touched and torn the surface of the lake, ascends to skim, touch, and tear again. So mingled the feathered multitude in the grim game of war. It was a storm in which the wind was birds, and the sea men. And ever as each bird arrived at the rear of the enemy, it turned, ascended, and sped to the front of charge again.

The moment the battle began, the princess's pony took fright, and turned and fled. But the maid wheeled her horse across the road and stopped him; and they waited together the result of the battle.

And as they waited, it seemed to the princess right strange that the pigeons, every one as it came to the rear, and fetched a compass to gather force for the re-attack, should make the head of her attendant on the red horse the goal around which it turned; so that about them was an unintermittent flapping and flashing of wings, and a curving, sweeping torrent of the side-poised wheeling bodies of birds. Strange also it seemed that the maid should be constantly waving her arm towards the battle. And the time of the motion of her arm so fitted with the rushes of birds, that it looked as if the birds obeyed her gesture, and she were casting living javelins by the thousand against the enemy. The moment a pigeon had rounded her head, it went off straight as bolt from bow, and with trebled velocity.

But of these strange things, other besides the princess had taken not. From a rising ground whence they watched the battle in growing dismay, the leaders of the enemy saw the maid and her motions, and, concluding her an enchantress, whose were the airy legions humiliating them, set spurs to their horses, made a circuit, outflanked the king, and came down upon her. But suddenly by her side stood a stalwart old man in the garb of a miner, who, as the general rode at her, sword in hand, heaved his swift mattock, and brought it down with such force on the forehead of his charger, that he fell to the ground like a log. His rider shot over his head and lay stunned. Had not the great red horse reared and wheeled, he would have fallen beneath that of the general.

With lifted sabre, one of his attendant officers rode at the miner. But a mass of pigeons darted in the faces of him and his horse, and the next moment he lay beside his commander. The rest of them turned and fled, pursued by the birds.

"Ah, friend Peter!" said the maid; "thou hast come as I told thee! Welcome and thanks!"

By this time the battle was over. The rout was general. The enemy stormed back upon their own camp, with the beasts roaring in the midst of them, and the king and his army, now reinforced by one, pursuing. But presently the king drew rein.

"Call off your hounds, Curdie, and let the pigeons do the rest," he shouted, and turned to see what had become of the princess.

In full panic fled the invaders, sweeping down their tents, stumbling over their baggage, trampling on their dead and wounded, ceaselessly pursued and buffeted by the white-winged army of heaven. Homeward they rushed the road they had come, straight for the borders, many dropping from pure fatigue, and lying where they fell. And still the pigeons were in their necks as they ran. At length to the eyes of the king and his army nothing was visible save a dust-cloud below, and a bird-cloud above.

Before night the bird-cloud came back, flying high over Gwyntystorm. Sinking swiftly, it disappeared among the ancient roofs of the palace.

Chapter 34

Judgment

The king and his army returned, bringing with them one prisoner only, the lord chancellor. Curdie had dragged him from under a fallen tent, not by the hand of a man, but by the foot of a mule.

When they entered the city, it was still as the grave. The citizens had fled home. "We must submit," they cried, "or the king and his demons will destroy us." The king rode through the streets in silence, ill-pleased with his people. But he stopped his horse in the midst of the market-place, and called, in a voice loud and clear as the cry of a silver trumpet, "Go and find your own. Bury your dead, and bring home your wounded." Then he turned him gloomily to the palace.

Just as they reached the gates, Peter, who, as they went, had been telling his tale to Curdie, ended it with the words,—

"And so there I was, in the nick of time to save the two princesses!"

"The *two* princesses, father! The one on the great red horse was the housemaid," said Curdie, and ran to open the gates for the king.

They found Derba returned before them, and already busy preparing them food. The king put up his charger with his own hands, rubbed him down, and fed him.

When they had washed, and eaten and drunk, he called the colonel, and told Curdie and the page to bring out the traitors and the beasts, and attend him to the market-place.

By this time the people were crowding back into the city, bearing their dead and wounded. And there was lamentation in Gwyntystorm, for no one could comfort himself, and no one had any to comfort him. The nation was victorious, but the people were conquered.

The king stood in the centre of the market-place, upon the steps of the ancient cross. He had laid aside his helmet and put on his crown, but he stood all armed beside, with his sword in his hand. He called the people to him, and, for all the terror of the beasts, they dared not disobey him. Those even, who were carrying their wounded laid them down, and drew near trembling.

Then the king said to Curdie and the page,—

"Set the evil men before me."

He looked upon them for a moment in mingled anger and pity, then turned to the people and said,—

"Behold your trust! Ye slaves, behold your leaders! I would have freed you, but ye would not be free. Now shall ye be ruled with a rod of iron, that ye may learn what freedom is, and love it and seek it. These wretches I will send where they shall mislead you no longer."

He made a sign to Curdie, who immediately brought up the leg serpent. To the body of the animal they bound the lord chamberlain, speechless with horror. The butler began to shriek and pray, but they bound him on the back of Clubhead. One after another, upon the largest of the creatures they bound the whole seven, each through the unveiling terror looking the villain he was. Then said the king,—

"I thank you, my good beasts; and I hope to visit you ere long. Take these evil men with you, and go to your place."

Like a whirlwind they were in the crowd, scattering it like dust. Like hounds they rushed from the city, their burdens howling and raving.

What became of them I have never heard.

Then the king turned once more to the people and said, "Go to your houses;" nor vouchsafed them another word. They crept home like chidden hounds.

The king returned to the palace. He made the colonel a duke, and the page a knight, and Peter he appointed general of all the mines. But to Curdie he said,—

"You are my own boy, Curdie. My child cannot choose but love you, and when you are both grown up—if you both will—you shall marry each other, and be king and queen when I am gone. Till then be the king's Curdie."

Irene held out her arms to Curdie. He raised her in his, and she kissed him.

"And my Curdie too!" she said.

Thereafter the people called him Prince Conrad; but the king always called him either just *Curdie,* or *My miner-boy.*

They sat down to supper, and Derba and the knight and the housemaid waited, and Barbara sat on the king's left hand. The housemaid poured out the wine; and as she poured out for Curdie red wine that foamed in the cup, as if glad to see the light whence it had been banished so long, she looked him in the eyes. And Curdie started, and sprang from his seat, and dropped on his knees, and burst into tears. And the maid said with a smile, such as none but one could smile,—

"Did I not tell you, Curdie, that it might be you would not know me when next you saw me?"

Then she went from the room, and in a moment returned in royal purple, with a crown of diamonds and rubies, from under which her hair went flowing to the floor, all about her ruby-slippered feet. Her face was radiant with joy, the joy overshadowed by a faint mist as of unfulfilment. The king rose and kneeled on one knee before her. All kneeled in like homage. Then the king would have yielded her his royal chair. But she made them all sit down, and with her own hands placed at the table seats for Derba and the page. Then in ruby crown and royal purple she served them all.

Chapter 35

The End

The king sent Curdie out into his dominions to search for men and women that had human hands. And many such he found, honest and true, and brought them to his master. So a new and upright government, a new and upright court, was formed, and strength returned to the nation.

But the exchequer was almost empty, for the evil men had squandered everything, and the king hated taxes unwillingly paid. Then came Curdie and said to the king that the city stood upon gold. And the king sent for men wise in the ways of the earth, and they built smelting furnaces, and Peter brought miners, and they mined the gold, and smelted it, and the king coined it into money, and therewith established things well in the land.

The same day on which he found his boy, Peter set out to go home. When he told the good news to Joan his wife, she rose from her chair and said, "Let us go." And they left the cottage, and repaired to Gwyntystorm. And on a mountain above the city they built themselves a warm house for their old age, high in the clear air.

As Peter mined one day by himself, at the back of the king's wine-cellar, he broke into a cavern all crusted with gems, and much wealth flowed therefrom, and the king used it wisely.

Queen Irene—that was the right name of the old princess—was thereafter seldom long absent from the palace. Once or twice when she was missing, Barbara, who seemed to know of her sometimes when nobody else had a notion whither she had gone, said she was with the dear old Uglies in the wood. Curdie thought that perhaps her business might be with others there as well. All the uppermost rooms in the palace were left to her use, and when any one was in need of her help, up thither he must go. But even when she was there, he did not always succeed in finding her. She, however, always knew that such a one had been looking for her.

Curdie went to find her one day. As he ascended the last stair, to meet him came the well-known scent of her roses; and when he opened her door, lo! there was the same gorgeous room in which his touch had been glorified by her fire! And there burned the fire—a huge heap of red and white roses. Before the hearth stood the princess, an old gray-haired woman, with Lina a little behind her, slowly wagging her tail, and looking like a beast of prey that can hardly so long restrain itself from springing as to be sure of its victim. The queen was casting roses, more and more roses, upon the fire. At last she turned and said, "Now, Lina!"—and Lina dashed burrowing into the fire. There went up a black smoke and a dust, and Lina was never more seen in the palace.

Irene and Curdie were married. The old king died, and they were king and queen. As long as they lived Gwyntystorm was a better city, and good people grew in it. But they had no children, and when they died the people chose a king. And the new king went mining and mining in the rock under the city, and grew more and more eager after the gold, and paid less and less heed to his people. Rapidly they sunk towards their old wickedness. But still the king went on mining, and coining gold by the pailful, until the people were worse even than in the old time. And so greedy was the king after gold, that when at last the ore began to fail, he caused the miners to reduce the pillars which Peter and they that followed him had left standing to bear the city. And from the girth of an oak of a thousand years, they chipped them down to that of a fir tree of fifty.

One day at noon, when life was at its highest, the whole city fell with a roaring crash. The cries of men and the shrieks of women went up with its dust, and then there was a great silence.

Where the mighty rock once towered, crowded with homes and crowned with a palace, now rushes and raves a stone-obstructed rapid of the river. All around spreads a wilderness of wild deer, and the very name of Gwyntystorm has ceased from the lips of men.

THE GOLDEN KEY

There was a boy who used to sit in the twilight and listen to his great-aunt's stories.

She told him that if he could reach the place where the end of the rainbow stands he would find there a golden key.

"And what is the key for?" the boy would ask. "What is the key of? What will it open?"

"That nobody knows," his aunt would reply. "He has to find that out."

"I suppose, being gold," the boy once said, thoughtfully, "that I could get a good deal of money for it if I sold it."

"Better never find it than sell it," returned his aunt.

And then the boy went to bed and dreamed about the golden key.

Now all that his great-aunt told the boy about the golden key would have been nonsense, had it not been that their little house stood on the borders of Fairyland. For it is perfectly well known that out of Fairyland nobody ever can find where the rainbow stands. The creature takes such good care of its golden key, always flitting from place to place, lest any one should find it! But in Fairyland it is quite different. Things that look real in this country look very thin indeed in Fairyland, while some of the things that here cannot stand still for a moment, will not move there. So it was not in the least absurd of the old lady to tell her nephew such things about the golden key.

"Did you ever know anybody find it?" he asked, one evening.

"Yes. Your father, I believe, found it."

"And what did he do with it, can you tell me?"

"He never told me."

"What was it like?"

"He never showed it to me."

"How does a new key come there always?"

"I don't know. There it is."

"Perhaps it is the rainbow's egg."

"Perhaps it is. You will be a happy boy if you find the nest."

"Perhaps it comes tumbling down the rainbow from the sky."

"Perhaps it does."

One evening, in summer, he went into his own room, and stood at the lattice-window, and gazed into the forest which fringed the outskirts of Fairyland. It came close up to his great-aunt's garden, and, indeed, sent some straggling trees into it. The forest lay to the east, and the sun, which was setting behind the cottage, looked straight into the dark wood with his level red eye. The trees were all old, and had few branches below, so that the sun could see a great way into the forest; and the boy, being keen-sighted, could see almost as far as the sun. The trunks stood like rows of red columns in the shine of the red sun, and he could see down aisle after aisle in the vanishing distance. And as he gazed into the forest he began to feel as if the trees were all waiting for him, and had something they could not go on with till he came to them. But he was hungry, and wanted his supper. So he lingered.

Suddenly, far among the trees, as far as the sun could shine, he saw a glorious thing. It was the end of a rainbow, large and brilliant. He could count all the seven colours, and could see shade after shade beyond the violet; while before the red stood a colour more gorgeous and mysterious still. It was a colour he had never seen before. Only the spring of the rainbow-arch was visible. He could see nothing of it above the trees.

"The golden key!" he said to himself, and darted out of the house, and into the wood.

He had not gone far before the sun set. But the rainbow only glowed the brighter. For the rainbow of Fairyland is not dependent upon the sun as ours is. The trees welcomed him. The bushes made way for him. The rainbow grew larger and brighter; and at length he found himself within two trees of it.

It was a grand sight, burning away there in silence, with its gorgeous, its lovely, its delicate colours, each distinct, all combining. He could now see a great deal more of it. It rose high into the blue heavens, but bent so little that he could not tell how high the crown of the arch must reach. It was still only a small portion of a huge bow.

He stood gazing at it till he forgot himself with delight—even forgot the key which he had come to seek. And as he stood it grew more wonderful still. For in each of the colours, which was as large as the column of a church, he could faintly see beautiful forms slowly ascending as if by the steps of a winding stair. The forms appeared irregularly—now one, now many, now several, now none—men and women and children— all different, all beautiful.

He drew nearer to the rainbow. It vanished. He started back a step in dismay. It was there again, as beautiful as ever. So he contented himself with standing as near it as he might, and watching the forms that ascended the glorious colours towards the unknown height of the arch, which did not end abruptly, but faded away in the blue air, so gradually that he could not say where it ceased.

When the thought of the golden key returned, the boy very wisely proceeded to mark out in his mind the space covered by the foundation of the rainbow, in order that he might know where to search, should the rainbow disappear. It was based chiefly upon a bed of moss.

Meantime it had grown quite dark in the wood. The rainbow alone was visible by its own light. But the moment the moon rose the rainbow vanished. Nor could any change of place restore the vision to the boy's eyes. So he threw himself down upon the mossy bed, to wait till the sunlight would give him a chance of finding the key. There he fell fast asleep.

When he woke in the morning the sun was looking straight into his eyes. He turned away from it, and the same moment saw a brilliant little thing lying on the moss within a foot of his face. It was the golden key. The pipe of it was of plain gold, as bright as gold could be. The handle was curiously wrought and set with sapphires. In a terror of delight he put out his hand and took it, and had it.

He lay for a while, turning it over and over, and feeding his eyes upon its beauty. Then he jumped to his feet, remembering that the pretty thing was of no use to him yet. Where was the lock to which the key belonged? It must be somewhere, for how could anybody be so silly as make a key for which there was no lock? Where should he go to look for it? He gazed about him, up into the air, down to the earth, but saw no keyhole in the clouds, in the grass, or in the trees.

Just as he began to grow disconsolate, however, he saw something glimmering in the wood. It was a mere glimmer that he saw, but he took it for a glimmer of rainbow, and went towards it.—And now I will go back to the borders of the forest.

Not far from the house where the boy had lived, there was another house, the owner of which was a merchant, who was much away from home. He had lost his wife some years before, and had only one child, a little girl, whom he left to the charge of two servants, who were very idle and careless. So she was neglected and left untidy, and was sometimes ill-used besides.

Now it is well known that the little creatures commonly called fairies, though there are many different kinds of fairies in Fairyland, have an exceeding dislike to untidiness. Indeed, they are quite spiteful to slovenly people. Being used to all the lovely ways of the trees and flowers, and to the neatness of the birds and all woodland creatures, it makes them feel miserable, even in their deep woods and on their grassy carpets, to think that within the same moonlight lies a dirty, uncomfortable, slovenly house. And this makes them angry with the people that live in it, and they would gladly drive them out of the world if they could. They want the whole earth nice and clean. So they pinch the maids black and blue, and play them all manner of uncomfortable tricks.

But this house was quite a shame, and the fairies in the forest could not endure it. They tried everything on the maids without effect, and at last resolved upon making a clean riddance, beginning with the child. They ought to have known that it was not her fault, but they have little principle and much mischief in them, and they thought that if they got rid of her the maids would be sure to be turned away.

So one evening, the poor girl having been put to bed early, before the sun was down, the servants went off to the village, locking the door behind them. The child did not know she was alone, and lay contentedly looking out of her window towards the forest, of which, however, she could not see much, because of the ivy and other creeping plants which had straggled across her window. All at once she saw an ape making faces at her out of the mirror, and the heads carved upon a great old wardrobe grinning fearfully. Then two old spider-legged chairs came forward into the middle of the room, and began to dance a queer, old-fashioned dance. This set her laughing, and she forgot the ape and the grinning heads. So the fairies saw they had made a mistake, and sent the chairs back to their places. But they knew that she had been reading the story of Silverhair all day. So the next moment she heard the voices of the three bears upon the stair, big voice, middle voice, and little voice, and she heard their soft, heavy tread, as if they had had stockings over their boots, coming nearer and nearer to the door of her room, till she could bear it no longer. She did just as Silverhair did, and as the fairies wanted her to do: she darted to the window, pulled it open, got upon the ivy, and so scrambled to the ground. She then fled to the forest as fast as she could run.

Now, although she did not know it, this was the very best way she could have gone; for nothing is ever so mischievous in its own place as it is out of it; and, besides, these mischievous creatures were only the children of Fairyland, as it were, and there are many other beings there as well; and if a wanderer gets in among them, the good ones will always help him more than the evil ones will be able to hurt him.

The sun was now set, and the darkness coming on, but the child thought of no danger but the bears behind her. If she had looked round, however, she would have seen that she was followed by a very different creature from a bear. It was a curious creature, made like a fish, but covered, instead of scales, with feathers of all colours, sparkling like those of a humming-bird. It had fins, not wings, and swam through the air as a fish does through the water. Its head was like the head of a small owl.

After running a long way, and as the last of the light was disappearing, she passed under a tree with drooping branches. It dropped its branches to the ground all about her, and caught her as in a trap. She struggled to get out, but the branches pressed her closer and closer to the trunk. She was in great terror and distress, when the air-fish, swimming into the thicket of branches, began tearing them with its beak. They loosened their hold at once, and the creature went on attacking them, till at length they let the child go. Then the air-fish came from behind her, and swam on in front, glittering and sparkling all lovely colours; and she followed.

It led her gently along till all at once it swam in at a cottage-door. The child followed still. There was a bright fire in the middle of the floor, upon which stood a pot without a lid, full of water that boiled and bubbled furiously. The air-fish swam straight to the pot and into the boiling water, where it lay quiet. A beautiful woman rose from the opposite side of the fire and came to meet the girl. She took her up in her arms, and said,—

"Ah, you are come at last! I have been looking for you a long time."

She sat down with her on her lap, and there the girl sat staring at her. She had never seen anything so beautiful. She was tall and strong, with white arms and neck, and a delicate flush on her face. The child could not tell what was the colour of her hair, but could not help thinking it had a tinge of dark green. She had not one ornament upon her, but she looked as if she had just put off quantities of diamonds and emeralds. Yet here she was in the simplest, poorest little cottage, where she was evidently at home. She was dressed in shining green.

The girl looked at the lady, and the lady looked at the girl.

"What is your name?" asked the lady.

"The servants always called me Tangle."

"Ah, that was because your hair was so untidy. But that was their fault, the naughty women! Still it is a pretty name, and I will call you Tangle too. You must not mind my asking you questions, for you may ask me the same questions, every one of them, and any others that you like. How old are you?"

"Ten," answered Tangle.

"You don't look like it," said the lady.

"How old are you, please?" returned Tangle.

"Thousands of years old," answered the lady.

"You don't look like it," said Tangle.

"Don't I? I think I do. Don't you see how beautiful I am?"

And her great blue eyes looked down on the little Tangle, as if all the stars in the sky were melted in them to make their brightness.

"Ah! but," said Tangle, "when people live long they grow old. At least I always thought so."

"I have no time to grow old," said the lady. "I am too busy for that. It is very idle to grow old.—But I cannot have my little girl so untidy. Do you know I can't find a clean spot on your face to kiss?"

"Perhaps," suggested Tangle, feeling ashamed, but not too much so to say a word for herself—"perhaps that is because the tree made me cry so."

"My poor darling!" said the lady, looking now as if the moon were melted in her eyes, and kissing her little face, dirty as it was, "the naughty tree must suffer for making a girl cry."

"And what is your name, please?" asked Tangle.

"Grandmother," answered the lady.

"Is it really?"

"Yes, indeed. I never tell stories, even in fun."

"How good of you!"

"I couldn't if I tried. It would come true if I said it, and then I should be punished enough."

And she smiled like the sun through a summer-shower.

"But now," she went on, "I must get you washed and dressed, and then we shall have some supper."

"Oh! I had supper long ago," said Tangle.

"Yes, indeed you had," answered the lady—"three years ago. You don't know that it is three years since you ran away from the bears. You are thirteen and more now."

Tangle could only stare. She felt quite sure it was true.

"You will not be afraid of anything I do with you—will you?" said the lady.

"I will try very hard not to be; but I can't be certain, you know," replied Tangle.

"I like your saying so, and I shall be quite satisfied," answered the lady.

She took off the girl's night-gown, rose with her in her arms, and going to the wall of the cottage, opened a door. Then Tangle saw a deep tank, the sides of which were filled with green plants, which had flowers of all colours. There was a roof over it like the roof of the cottage. It was filled with beautiful clear water, in which swam a multitude of such fishes as the one that had led her to the cottage. It was the light their colours gave that showed the place in which they were.

The lady spoke some words Tangle could not understand, and threw her into the tank.

The fishes came crowding about her. Two or three of them got under her head and kept it up. The rest of them rubbed themselves all over her, and with their wet feathers washed her quite clean. Then the lady, who had been looking on all the time, spoke again; whereupon some thirty or forty of the fishes rose out of the water underneath Tangle, and so bore her up to the arms the lady held out to take her. She carried her back to the fire, and, having dried her well, opened a chest, and taking out the finest linen garments, smelling of grass and lavender, put them upon her, and over all a green dress, just like her own, shining like hers, and soft like hers, and going into just such lovely folds from the waist, where it was tied with a brown cord, to her bare feet.

"Won't you give me a pair of shoes too, grandmother?" said Tangle.

"No, my dear; no shoes. Look here. I wear no shoes."

So saying she lifted her dress a little, and there were the loveliest white feet, but no shoes. Then Tangle was content to go without shoes too. And the lady sat down with her again, and combed her hair, and brushed it, and then left it to dry while she got the supper.

First she got bread out of one hole in the wall; then milk out of another; then several kinds of fruit out of a third; and then she went to the pot on the fire, and took out the fish, now nicely cooked, and, as soon as she had pulled off its feathered skin, ready to be eaten.

"But," exclaimed Tangle. And she stared at the fish, and could say no more.

"I know what you mean," returned the lady. "You do not like to eat the messenger that brought you home. But it is the kindest return you can make. The creature was afraid to go until it saw me put the pot on, and heard me promise it should be boiled the moment it returned with you. Then it darted out of the door at once. You saw it go into the pot of itself the moment it entered, did you not?"

"I did," answered Tangle, "and I thought it very strange; but then I saw you, and forgot all about the fish."

"In Fairyland," resumed the lady, as they sat down to the table, "the ambition of the animals is to be eaten by the people; for that is their highest end in that condition. But they are not therefore destroyed. Out of that pot comes something more than the dead fish, you will see."

Tangle now remarked that the lid was on the pot. But the lady took no further notice of it till they had eaten the fish, which Tangle found nicer than any fish she had ever tasted before. It was as white as snow, and as delicate as cream. And the moment she had swallowed a mouthful of it, a change she could not describe began to take place in her. She heard a murmuring all about her, which became more and more articulate, and at length, as she went on eating, grew intelligible. By the time she had finished her share, the sounds of all the animals in the forest came crowding through the door to her ears; for the door still stood wide open, though it was pitch-dark outside; and they were no longer sounds only; they were speech, and speech that she could understand. She could tell what the insects in the cottage were saying to each other too. She had even a suspicion that the trees and flowers all about the cottage were holding midnight communications with each other; but what they said she could not hear.

As soon as the fish was eaten, the lady went to the fire and took the lid off the pot. A lovely little creature in human shape, with large white wings, rose out of it, and flew round and round the roof of the cottage; then dropped, fluttering, and nestled in the lap of the lady. She spoke to it some strange words, carried it to the door, and threw it out into the darkness. Tangle heard the flapping of its wings die away in the distance.

"Now have we done the fish any harm?" she said, returning.

"No," answered Tangle, "I do not think we have. I should not mind eating one every day."

"They must wait their time, like you and me too, my little Tangle."

And she smiled a smile which the sadness in it made more lovely.

"But," she continued, "I think we may have one for supper to-morrow."

So saying she went to the door of the tank, and spoke; and now Tangle understood her perfectly.

"I want one of you," she said,—"the wisest."

Thereupon the fishes got together in the middle of the tank, with their heads forming a circle above the water, and their tails a larger circle beneath it. They were holding a council, in which their relative wisdom should be determined. At length one of them flew up into the lady's hand, looking lively and ready.

"You know where the rainbow stands?" she asked.

"Yes, mother, quite well," answered the fish.

"Bring home a young man you will find there, who does not know where to go."

The fish was out of the door in a moment. Then the lady told Tangle it was time to go to bed; and, opening another door in the side of the cottage, showed her a little arbour, cool and green, with a bed of purple heath growing in it, upon which she threw a large wrapper made of the feathered skins of the wise fishes, shining gorgeous in the firelight. Tangle was soon lost in the strangest, loveliest dreams. And the beautiful lady was in every one of her dreams.

In the morning she woke to the rustling of leaves over her head, and the sound of running water. But, to her surprise, she could find no door—nothing but the moss-grown wall of the cottage. So she crept through an opening in the arbour, and stood in the forest. Then she bathed in a stream that ran merrily through the trees, and felt happier; for having once been in her grandmother's pond, she must be clean and tidy ever after; and, having put on her green dress, felt like a lady.

She spent that day in the wood, listening to the birds and beasts and creeping things. She understood all that they said, though she could not repeat a word of it; and every kind had a different language, while there was a common though more limited understanding between all the inhabitants of the forest. She saw nothing of the beautiful lady, but she felt that she was near her all the time; and she took care not to go out of sight of the cottage. It was round, like a snow-hut or a wigwam; and she could see neither door nor window in it. The fact was, it had no windows; and though it was full of doors, they all opened from the inside, and could not even be seen from the outside.

She was standing at the foot of a tree in the twilight, listening to a quarrel between a mole and a squirrel, in which the mole told the squirrel that the tail was the best of him, and the squirrel call the mole Spade-fists, when, the darkness having deepened around her, she became aware of something shining in her face, and looking round, saw that the door of the cottage was open, and the red light of the fire flowing from it like a river through the darkness. She left Mole and Squirrel to settle matters as they might, and darted off to the cottage. Entering, she found the pot boiling on the fire, and the grand, lovely lady sitting on the other side of it.

"I've been watching you all day," said the lady. "You shall have something to eat by-and-by, but we must wait till our supper comes home."

She took Tangle on her knee, and began to sing to her—such songs as made her wish she could listen to them for ever. But at length in rushed the shining fish, and snuggled down in the pot. It was followed by a youth who had outgrown his worn garments. His face was ruddy with health, and in his hand he carried a little jewel, which sparkled in the firelight.

The first words the lady said were,—

"What is that in your hand, Mossy?"

Now Mossy was the name his companions had given him, because he had a favourite stone covered with moss, on which he used to sit whole days reading; and they said the moss had begun to grow upon him too.

Mossy held out his hand. The moment the lady saw that it was the golden key, she rose from her chair, kissed Mossy on the forehead, made him sit down on her seat, and stood before him like a servant. Mossy could not bear this, and rose at once. But the lady begged him, with tears in her beautiful eyes, to sit, and let her wait on him.

"But you are a great, splendid, beautiful lady," said Mossy.

"Yes, I am. But I work all day long—that is my pleasure; and you will have to leave me so soon!"

"How do you know that, if you please, madam?" asked Mossy.

"Because you have got the golden key."

"But I don't know what it is for. I can't find the key-hole. Will you tell me what to do?"

"You must look for the key-hole. That is your work. I cannot help you. I can only tell you that if you look for it you will find it."

"What kind of box will it open? What is there inside?"

"I do not know. I dream about it, but I know nothing."

"Must I go at once?"

"You may stop here to-night, and have some of my supper. But you must go in the morning. All I can do for you is to give you clothes. Here is a girl called Tangle, whom you must take with you."

"That *will* be nice," said Mossy.

"No, no!" said Tangle. "I don't want to leave you, please, grand-mother."

"You must go with him, Tangle. I am sorry to lose you, but it will be the best thing for you. Even the fishes, you see, have to go into the pot, and then out into the dark. If you fall in with the Old Man of the Sea, mind you ask him whether he has not got some more fishes ready for me. My tank is getting thin."

So saying, she took the fish from the pot, and put the lid on as before. They sat down and ate the fish, and then the winged creature rose from the pot, circled the roof, and settled on the lady's lap. She talked to it, carried it to the door, and threw it out into the dark. They heard the flap of its wings die away in the distance.

The lady then showed Mossy into just such another chamber as that of Tangle; and in the morning he found a suit of clothes laid beside him. He looked very handsome in them. But the wearer of Grandmother's clothes never thinks about how he or she looks, but thinks always how handsome other people are.

Tangle was very unwilling to go.

"Why should I leave you? I don't know the young man," she said to the lady.

"I am never allowed to keep my children long. You need not go with him except you please, but you must go some day; and I should like you to go with him, for he has the golden key. No girl need be afraid to go with a youth that has the golden key. You will take care of her, Mossy, will you not?"

"That I will," said Mossy.

And Tangle cast a glance at him, and thought she should like to go with him.

"And," said the lady, "if you should lose each other as you go through the—the—I never can remember the name of that country,—do not be afraid, but go on and on."

She kissed Tangle on the mouth and Mossy on the forehead, led them to the door, and waved her hand eastward. Mossy and Tangle took each other's hand and walked away into the depth of the forest. In his right hand Mossy held the golden key.

They wandered thus a long way, with endless amusement from the talk of the animals. They soon learned enough of their language to ask them necessary questions. The squirrels were always friendly, and gave them nuts out of their own hoards; but the bees were selfish and rude, justifying themselves on the ground that Tangle and Mossy were not subjects of their queen, and charity must begin at home, though indeed they had not one drone in their poorhouse at the time. Even the blinking moles would fetch them an earth-nut or a truffle now and then, talking as if their mouths, as well as their eyes and ears, were full of cotton wool, or their own velvety fur. By the time they got out of the forest they were very fond of each other, and Tangle was not in the least sorry that her grandmother had sent her away with Mossy.

At length the trees grew smaller, and stood farther apart, and the ground began to rise, and it got more and more steep, till the trees were all left behind, and the two were climbing a narrow path with rocks on each side. Suddenly they came upon a rude doorway, by which they entered a narrow gallery cut in the rock. It grew darker and darker, till it was pitch-dark, and they had to feel their way. At length the light began to return, and at last they came out upon a narrow path on the face of a lofty precipice. This path went winding down the rock to a wide plain, circular in shape, and surrounded on all sides by mountains. Those opposite to them were a great way off, and towered to an awful height, shooting up sharp, blue, ice-enamelled pinnacles. An utter silence reigned where they stood. Not even the sound of water reached them.

Looking down, they could not tell whether the valley below was a grassy plain or a great still lake. They had never seen any space look like it. The way to it was difficult and dangerous, but down the narrow path they went, and reached the bottom in safety. They found it composed of smooth, light-coloured sandstone, undulating in parts, but mostly level. It was no wonder to them now that they had not been able to tell what it was, for this surface was everywhere crowded with shadows. It was a sea of shadows. The mass was chiefly made up of the shadows of leaves innumerable, of all lovely and imaginative forms, waving to and fro, floating and quivering in the breath of a breeze whose motion was unfelt, whose sound was unheard. No forests clothed the mountain-sides, no trees were anywhere to be seen, and yet the shadows of the leaves, branches, and stems of all various trees covered the valley as far as their eyes could reach. They soon spied the shadows of flowers mingled with those of the leaves, and now and then the shadow of a bird with open beak, and throat distended with song. At times would appear the forms of strange, graceful creatures, running up and down the shadow-boles and along the branches, to disappear in the wind-tossed foliage. As they walked they waded knee-deep in the lovely lake. For the shadows were not merely lying on the surface of the ground, but heaped up above it like substantial forms of darkness, as if they had been cast upon a thousand different planes of the air. Tangle and Mossy often lifted their heads and gazed upwards to descry whence the shadows came; but they could see nothing more than a bright mist spread above them, higher than the tops of the mountains, which stood clear against it. No forests, no leaves, no birds were visible.

After a while, they reached more open spaces, where the shadows were thinner; and came even to portions over which shadows only flitted, leaving them clear for such as might follow. Now a wonderful form, half bird-like half human, would float across on outspread sailing pinions. Anon an exquisite shadow group of gambolling children would be followed by the loveliest female form, and that again by the grand stride of

201

a Titanic shape, each disappearing in the surrounding press of shadowy foliage. Sometimes a profile of unspeakable beauty or grandeur would appear for a moment and vanish. Sometimes they seemed lovers that passed linked arm in arm, sometimes father and son, sometimes brothers in loving contest, sometimes sisters entwined in gracefullest community of complex form. Sometimes wild horses would tear across, free, or bestrode by noble shadows of ruling men. But some of the things which pleased them most they never knew how to describe.

About the middle of the plain they sat down to rest in the heart of a heap of shadows. After sitting for a while, each, looking up, saw the other in tears: they were each longing after the country whence the shadows fell.

"We *must* find the country from which the shadows come," said Mossy.

"We must, dear Mossy," responded Tangle. "What if your golden key should be the key to *it?*"

"Ah! that would be grand," returned Mossy.—"But we must rest here for a little, and then we shall be able to cross the plain before night."

So he lay down on the ground, and about him on every side, and over his head, was the constant play of the wonderful shadows. He could look through them, and see the one behind the other, till they mixed in a mass of darkness. Tangle, too, lay admiring, and wondering, and longing after the country whence the shadows came. When they were rested they rose and pursued their journey.

How long they were in crossing this plain I cannot tell: but before night Mossy's hair was streaked with grey, and Tangle had got wrinkles on her forehead.

As evening drew on, the shadows fell deeper and rose higher. At length they reached a place where they rose above their heads, and made all dark around them. Then they took hold of each other's hand, and walked on in silence and in some dismay. They felt the gathering darkness, and something strangely solemn besides, and the beauty of the shadows ceased to delight them. All at once Tangle found that she had not a hold of Mossy's hand, though when she lost it she could not tell.

"Mossy, Mossy!" she cried aloud in terror.

But no Mossy replied.

A moment after, the shadows sank to her feet, and down under her feet, and the mountains rose before her. She turned towards the gloomy region she had left, and called once more upon Mossy. There the gloom lay tossing and heaving, a dark, stormy, foamless sea of shadows, but no Mossy rose out of it, or came climbing up the hill on which she stood. She threw herself down and wept in despair.

Suddenly she remembered that the beautiful lady had told them, if they lost each other in a country of which she could not remember the name, they were not to be afraid, but to go straight on.

"And besides," she said to herself, "Mossy has the golden key, and so no harm will come to him, I do believe."

She rose from the ground, and went on.

Before long she arrived at a precipice, in the face of which a stair was cut. When she had ascended half-way, the stair ceased, and the path led straight into the mountain. She was afraid to enter, and turning again towards the stair, grew giddy at sight of the depth beneath her, and was forced to throw herself down in the mouth of the cave.

When she opened her eyes, she saw a beautiful little creature with wings standing beside her, waiting.

"I know you," said Tangle. "You are my fish."

"Yes. But I am a fish no longer. I am an aëranth now."

"What is that?" asked Tangle.

"What you see I am," answered the shape. "And I am come to lead you through the mountain."

"Oh! thank you, dear fish—aëranth, I mean," returned Tangle, rising.

Thereupon the aëranth took to his wings, and flew on through the long, narrow passage, reminding Tangle very much of the way he had swum on before her when he was a fish. And the moment his white wings moved, they began to throw off a continuous shower of sparks of all colours, which lighted up the passage before them.—All at once he vanished, and Tangle heard a low, sweet sound, quite different from the rush and crackle of his wings. Before her was an open arch, and through it came light, mixed with the sound of sea-waves.

She hurried out, and fell, tired and happy, upon the yellow sand of the shore. There she lay, half asleep with weariness and rest, listening to the low plash and retreat of the tiny waves, which seemed ever enticing the land to leave off being land, and become sea. And as she lay, her eyes were fixed upon the foot of a great rainbow standing far away against the sky on the other side of the sea. At length she fell fast asleep.

When she awoke, she saw an old man with long white hair down to his shoulders, leaning upon a stick covered with green buds, and so bending over her.

"What do you want here, beautiful woman?" he said.

"Am I beautiful? I am so glad!" answered Tangle, rising. "My grandmother is beautiful."

"Yes. But what do you want?" he repeated, kindly.

"I think I want you. Are you not the Old Man of the Sea?"

"I am."

"Then grandmother says, have you any more fishes ready for her?"

"We will go and see, my dear," answered the old man, speaking yet more kindly than before. "And I can do something for you, can I not?"

"Yes—show me the way up to the country from which the shadows fall," said Tangle.

For there she hoped to find Mossy again.

"Ah! indeed, that would be worth doing," said the old man. "But I cannot, for I do not know the way myself. But I will send you to the Old Man of the Earth. Perhaps he can tell you. He is much older than I am."

Leaning on his staff, he conducted her along the shore to a steep rock, that looked like a petrified ship turned upside down. The door of it was the rudder of a great vessel, ages ago at the bottom of the sea. Immediately within the door was a stair in the rock, down which the old man went, and Tangle followed. At the bottom the old man had his house, and there he lived.

As soon as she entered it, Tangle heard a strange noise, unlike anything she had ever heard before. She soon found that it was the fishes talking. She tried to understand what they said; but their speech was so old-fashioned, and rude, and undefined, that she could not make much of it.

"I will go and see about those fishes for my daughter," said the Old Man of the Sea.

And moving a slide in the wall of his house, he first looked out, and then tapped upon a thick piece of crystal that filled the round opening. Tangle came up behind him, and peeping through the window into the heart of the great deep green ocean, saw the most curious creatures, some very ugly, all very odd, and with especially queer mouths, swimming about everywhere, above and below, but all coming towards the window in answer to the tap of the Old Man of the Sea. Only a few could get their mouths against the glass; but those who were floating miles away yet turned their heads towards it. The Old Man looked through the whole flock carefully for some minutes, and then turning to Tangle, said,—

"I am sorry I have not got one ready yet. I want more time than she does. But I will send some as soon as I can."

He then shut the slide.

Presently a great noise arose in the sea. The old man opened the slide again, and tapped on the glass, whereupon the fishes were all as still as sleep.

"They were only talking about you," he said. "And they do speak such nonsense!—To-morrow," he continued, "I must show you the way to the Old Man of the Earth. He lives a long way from here."

"Do let me go at once," said Tangle.

"No. That is not possible. You must come this way first."

He led her to a hole in the wall, which she had not observed before. It was covered with the green leaves and white blossoms of a creeping plant.

"Only white-blossoming plants can grow under the sea," said the old man. "In there you will find a bath, in which you must lie till I call you."

Tangle went in, and found a smaller room or cave, in the further corner of which was a great basin hollowed out of a rock, and half-full of the clearest sea-water. Little streams were constantly running into it from cracks in the wall of the cavern. It was polished quite smooth inside, and had a carpet of yellow sand in the bottom of it. Large green leaves and white flowers of various plants crowded up and over it, draping and covering it almost entirely.

No sooner was she undressed and lying in the bath, than she began to feel as if the water were sinking into her, and she were receiving all the good of sleep without undergoing its forgetfulness. She felt the good coming all the time. And she grew happier and more hopeful than she had been since she lost Mossy. But she could not help thinking how very sad it was for a poor old man to live there all alone, and have to take care of a whole seaful of stupid and riotous fishes.

After about an hour, as she thought, she heard his voice calling her, and rose out of the bath. All the fatigue and aching of her long journey had vanished. She was as whole, and strong, and well as if she had slept for seven days.

Returning to the opening that led into the other part of the house, she started back with amazement, for through it she saw the form of a grand man, with a majestic and beautiful face, waiting for her.

"Come," he said; "I see you are ready."

She entered with reverence.

"Where is the Old Man of the Sea?" she asked, humbly.

"There is no one here but me," he answered, smiling. Some people call me the Old Man of the Sea. Others have another name for me, and are terribly frightened when they meet me taking a walk by the shore. Therefore I avoid being seen by them, for they are so afraid, that they never see what I really am. You see me now.—But I must show you the way to the Old Man of the Earth."

He led her into the cave where the bath was, and there she saw, in the opposite corner, a second opening in the rock.

"Go down that stair, and it will bring you to him," said the Old Man of the Sea.

With humble thanks Tangle took her leave. She went down the winding-stair, till she began to fear there was no end to it. Still down and down it went, rough and broken, with springs of water bursting out of the rocks and running down the steps beside her. It was quite dark about her, and yet she could see. For after being in that bath, people's eyes always give out a light they can see by. There were no creeping things in the way. All was safe and pleasant though so dark and damp and deep.

At last there was not one step more, and she found herself in a glimmering cave. On a stone in the middle of it sat a figure with its back towards her—the figure of an old man bent double with age. From behind she could see his white beard spread out on the rocky floor in front of him. He did not move as she entered, so she passed round that she might stand before him and speak to him. The moment she looked in his face, she saw that he was a youth of marvellous beauty. He sat entranced with the delight of what he beheld in a mirror of something like silver, which lay on the floor at his feet, and which from behind she had taken for his white beard. He sat on, heedless of her presence, pale with the joy of his vision. She stood and watched him. At length, all trembling, she spoke. But her voice made no sound. Yet the youth lifted up his head. He showed no surprise, however, at seeing her—only smiled a welcome.

"Are you the Old Man of the Earth?" Tangle had said.

And the youth answered, and Tangle heard him, though not with her ears:—

"I am. What can I do for you?"

"Tell me the way to the country whence the shadows fall."

"Ah! that I do not know. I only dream about it myself. I see its shadows sometimes in my mirror: the way to it I do not know. But I think the Old Man of the Fire must know. He is much older than I am. He is the oldest man of all."

"Where does he live?"

"I will show you the way to his place. I never saw him myself."

So saying, the young man rose, and then stood for a while gazing at Tangle.

"I wish I could see that country too," he said. "But I must mind my work."

He led her to the side of the cave, and told her to lay her ear against the wall.

"What do you hear?" he asked.

"I hear," answered Tangle, "the sound of a great water running inside the rock."

"That river runs down to the dwelling of the oldest man of all—the Old Man of the Fire. I wish I could go to see him. But I must mind my work. That river is the only way to him."

Then the Old Man of the Earth stooped over the floor of the cave, raised a huge stone from it, and left it leaning. It disclosed a great hole that went plumb-down.

"That is the way," he said.

"But there are no stairs."

"You must throw yourself in. There is no other way."

She turned and looked him full in the face—stood so for a whole minute, as she thought: it was a whole year—then threw herself headlong into the hole.

When she came to herself, she found herself gliding down fast and deep. Her head was under water, but that did not signify, for, when she thought about it, she could not remember that she had breathed once since her bath in the cave of the Old Man of the Sea. When she lifted up her head a sudden and fierce heat struck her, and she sank it again instantly, and went sweeping on.

Gradually the stream grew shallower. At length she could hardly keep her head under. Then the water could carry her no farther. She rose from the channel, and went step for step down the burning descent. The water ceased altogether. The heat was terrible. She felt scorched to the bone, but it did not touch her strength. It grew hotter and hotter. She said, "I can bear it no longer." Yet she went on.

At the long last, the stair ended at a rude archway in an all but glowing rock. Through this archway Tangle fell exhausted into a cool mossy cave. The floor and walls were covered with moss—green, soft, and damp. A little stream spouted from a rent in the rock and fell into a basin of moss. She plunged her face into it and drank. Then she lifted her head and looked around. Then she rose and looked again. She saw no one in the cave. But the moment she stood upright she had a marvellous sense that she was in the secret of the earth and all its ways. Everything she had seen, or learned from books; all that her grandmother had said or sung to her; all the talk of the beasts, birds, and fishes; all that had happened to her on her journey with Mossy, and since then in the heart of the earth with the Old man and the Older man—all was plain: she understood it all, and saw that everything meant the same thing, though she could not have put it into words again.

The next moment she descried, in a corner of the cave, a little naked child, sitting on the moss. He was playing with balls of various colours and sizes, which he disposed in strange figures upon the floor beside him. And now Tangle felt that there was something in her knowledge which was not in her understanding. For she knew there must be an infinite meaning in the change and sequence and individual forms of the figures into which the child arranged the balls, as well as in the varied harmonies of their colours, but what it all meant she could not tell.* He went on busily, tirelessly, playing his solitary game, without looking up, or seeming to know that there was a stranger in his deep-withdrawn cell. Diligently as a lace-maker shifts her bobbins, he shifted and arranged his balls. Flashes of meaning would now pass from them to Tangle, and now again all would be not merely obscure, but utterly dark. She stood looking for a long time, for there was fascination in the sight; and the longer she looked the more an indescribable vague intelligence went on rousing itself in her mind. For seven years she had stood there watching

* I think I must be indebted to Novalis for these geometrical figures.

the naked child with his coloured balls, and it seemed to her like seven hours, when all at once the shape the balls took, she knew not why, reminded her of the Valley of Shadows, and she spoke:—

"Where is the Old Man of the Fire?" she said.

"Here I am," answered the child, rising and leaving his balls on the moss. "What can I do for you?"

There was such an awfulness of absolute repose on the face of the child that Tangle stood dumb before him. He had no smile, but the love in his large grey eyes was deep as the centre. And with the repose there lay on his face a shimmer as of moonlight, which seemed as if any moment it might break into such a ravishing smile as would cause the beholder to weep himself to death. But the smile never came, and the moonlight lay there unbroken. For the heart of the child was too deep for any smile to reach from it to his face.

"Are you the oldest man of all?" Tangle at length, although filled with awe, ventured to ask.

"Yes, I am. I am very, very old. I am able to help you, I know. I can help everybody."

And the child drew near and looked up in her face so that she burst into tears.

"Can you tell me the way to the country the shadows fall from?" she sobbed.

"Yes. I know the way quite well. I go there myself sometimes. But you could not go my way; you are not old enough. I will show you how you can go."

"Do not send me out into the great heat again," prayed Tangle.

"I will not," answered the child.

And he reached up, and put his little cool hand on her heart.

"Now," he said, "you can go. The fire will not burn you. Come."

He led her from the cave, and following him through another archway, she found herself in a vast desert of sand and rock. The sky of it was of rock, lowering over them like solid thunderclouds; and the whole place was so hot that she saw, in bright rivulets, the yellow gold and white silver and red copper trickling molten from the rocks. But the heat never came near her.

When they had gone some distance, the child turned up a great stone, and took something like an egg from under it. He next drew a long curved line in the sand with his finger, and laid the egg in it. He then spoke something Tangle could not understand. The egg broke, a small snake came out, and, lying in the line in the sand, grew and grew till he filled it. The moment he was thus full-grown, he began to glide away, undulating like a sea-wave.

"Follow that serpent," said the child. " He will lead you the right way."

Tangle followed the serpent. But she could not go far without looking back at the marvellous Child. He stood alone in the midst of the glowing desert, beside a fountain of red flame that had burst forth at his feet, his naked whiteness glimmering a pale rosy red in the torrid fire. There he stood, looking after her, till, from the lengthening distance, she could see him no more. The serpent went straight on, turning neither to the right nor left.

Meantime Mossy had got out of the lake of shadows, and, following his mournful, lonely way, had reached the sea-shore. It was a dark, stormy evening. The sun had set. The wind was blowing from the sea. The waves had surrounded the rock within which lay the Old Man's house. A deep water rolled between it and the shore, upon which a majestic figure was walking alone.

Mossy went up to him and said,—

"Will you tell me where to find the Old Man of the Sea?"

"I am the Old Man of the Sea," the figure answered.

"I see a strong kingly man of middle age," returned Mossy.

Then the Old Man looked at him more intently, and said,—

"Your sight, young man, is better than that of most who take this way. The night is stormy: come to my house and tell me what I can do for you."

Mossy followed him. The waves flew from before the footsteps of the Old Man of the Sea, and Mossy followed upon dry sand.

When they had reached the cave, they sat down and gazed at each other.

Now Mossy was an old man by this time. He looked much older than the Old Man of the Sea, and his feet were very weary.

After looking at him for a moment, the Old Man took him by the hand and led him into his inner cave. There he helped him to undress, and laid him in the bath. And he saw that one of his hands Mossy did not open.

"What have you in that hand?" he asked.

Mossy opened his hand, and there lay the golden key.

"Ah!" said the Old Man, "that accounts for your knowing me. And I know the way you have to go."

"I want to find the country whence the shadows fall," said Mossy.

"I dare say you do. So do I. But meantime, one thing is certain.— What is that key for, do you think?"

"For a keyhole somewhere. But I don't know why I keep it. I never could find the keyhole. And I have lived a good while, I believe," said Mossy, sadly. "I'm not sure that I'm not old. I know my feet ache."

"Do they?" said the Old Man, as if he really meant to ask the question; and Mossy, who was still lying in the bath, watched his feet for a moment before he replied,

"No, they do not," he answered. "Perhaps I am not old either."

"Get up and look at yourself in the water."

He rose and looked at himself in the water, and there was not a grey hair on his head or a wrinkle on his skin.

"You have tasted of death now," said the Old Man. "Is it good?"

"It is good," said Mossy. "It is better than life."

"No," said the Old Man: "it is only more life.—Your feet will make no holes in the water now."

"What do you mean?"

"I will show you that presently."

They returned to the outer cave, and sat and talked together for a long time. At length the Old Man of the Sea rose, and said to Mossy,—

"Follow me."

He led him up the stair again, and opened another door. They stood on the level of the raging sea, looking towards the east. Across the waste of waters, against the bosom of a fierce black cloud, stood the foot of a rainbow, glowing in the dark.

"This indeed is my way," said Mossy, as soon as he saw the rainbow, and stepped out upon the sea. His feet made no holes in the water. He fought the wind, and clomb the waves, and went on towards the rainbow.

The storm died away. A lovely day and a lovelier night followed. A cool wind blew over the wide plain of the quiet ocean. And still Mossy journeyed eastward. But the rainbow had vanished with the storm.

Day after day he held on, and he thought he had no guide. He did not see how a shining fish under the waters directed his steps. He crossed the sea, and came to a great precipice of rock, up which he could discover but one path. Nor did this lead him farther than half-way up the rock, where it ended on a platform. Here he stood and pondered.—It could not be that the way stopped here, else what was the path for? It was a rough

211

path, not very plain, yet certainly a path.—He examined the face of the rock. It was smooth as glass. But as his eyes kept roving hopelessly over it, something glittered, and he caught sight of a row of small sapphires. They bordered a little hole in the rock.

"The keyhole!" he cried.

He tried the key. It fitted. It turned. A great clang and clash, as of iron bolts on huge brazen caldrons, echoed thunderously within. He drew out the key. The rock in front of him began to fall. He retreated from it as far as the breadth of the platform would allow. A great slab fell at his feet. In front was still the solid rock, with this one slab fallen forward out of it. But the moment he stepped upon it, a second fell, just short of the edge of the first, making the next step of a stair, which thus kept dropping itself before him as he ascended into the heart of the precipice. It led him into a hall fit for such an approach—irregular and rude in formation, but floor, sides, pillars, and vaulted roof, all one mass of shining stones of every colour that light can show. In the centre stood seven columns, ranged from red to violet. And on the pedestal of one of them sat a woman, motionless, with her face bowed upon her knees. Seven years had she sat there waiting. She lifted her head as Mossy drew near. It was Tangle. Her hair had grown to her feet, and was rippled like the windless sea on broad sands. Her face was beautiful, like her grandmother's, and as still and peaceful as that of the Old Man of the Fire. Her form was tall and noble. Yet Mossy knew her at once.

"How beautiful you are, Tangle!" he said, in delight and astonishment.

"Am I?" she returned. "Oh, I have waited for you so long! But you, you are like the Old Man of the Sea. No. You are like the Old Man of the Earth. No, no. You are like the oldest man of all. You are like them all. And yet you are my own old Mossy! How did you come here? What did you do after I lost you? Did you find the key-hole? Have you got the key still?"

She had a hundred questions to ask him, and he a hundred more to ask her. They told each other all their adventures, and were as happy as man and woman could be. For they were younger and better, and stronger and wiser, than they had ever been before.

It began to grow dark. And they wanted to more than ever to reach the country whence the shadows fall. So they looked about them for a way out of the cave. The door by which Mossy entered had closed again, and there was half a mile of rock between them and the sea. Neither could

Tangle find the opening in the floor by which the serpent had led her thither. They searched till it grew so dark that they could see nothing, and gave it up.

After a while, however, the cave began to glimmer again. The light came from the moon, but it did not look like moonlight, for it gleamed through those seven pillars in the middle, and filled the place with all colours. And now Mossy saw that there was a pillar beside the red one, which he had not observed before. And it was of the same new colour that he had seen in the rainbow when he saw it first in the fairy forest. And on it he saw a sparkle of blue. It was the sapphires round the keyhole.

He took the key. It turned in the lock to the sounds of Æolian music. A door opened upon slow hinges, and disclosed a winding stair within. The key vanished from his fingers. Tangle went up. Mossy followed. The door closed behind them. They climbed out of the earth; and, still climbing, rose above it. They were in the rainbow. Far abroad, over ocean and land, they could see through its transparent walls the earth beneath their feet. Stairs beside stairs wound up together, and beautiful beings of all ages climbed along with them.

They knew that they were going up to the country whence the shadows fall.

And by this time I think they must have got there.

Poetry

INTRODUCTION

From very early in his life, George MacDonald aspired above all things to be a poet. He loved language and was deeply convinced that the spirit of song was one with the spirit of virtue. Thoughts—which were from God—skillfully and beautifully expressed in their purest form were prime vehicles of truth.

His complete poems, which he collected and published in 1893, fill two rather large volumes. While they are of interest to the avid MacDonald reader, they tend to be obscure and syntactically difficult. Occasional lines rivet one's attention, such as those from "Death and Birth" that present compellingly his understanding of the manner in which the Holy Spirit can direct individuals:

> Find the secret—follow and find!
> All forget that lies behind;
> Me, the schools, yourselves, forsake;
> In your souls a silence make;
> Hearken till a whisper come,
> Listen, follow, and be dumb.

His *A Book of Strife in the form of the diary of an old soul* remains as the highest expression of his poetic talent. First published in 1885, it was probably composed over an extended period of time, but much of it appears to be prompted by his desperate inner struggle to come to terms with his grief over the deaths of his children Mary and Maurice.

It consists of a separate seven-line stanza for each possible day of the year. In presenting himself as meditating on his own perplexities and grapplings with doubt, he avoids an air of devotional preachiness. His humility, his constant soul-searching and sense of need, his spirit of utter dependence upon God, and the vibrancy of his hope are among the aspects of his spiritual life that find moving expression in these stanzas.

Selections from
A BOOK OF STRIFE

January 4

Death, like high faith, levelling, lifteth all.
When I awake, my daughter and my son,
Grown sister and brother, in my arms shall fall,
Tenfold my girl and boy. Sure every one
Of all the brood to the old wings will run.
Whole-hearted is my worship of the man
From whom my earthly history began.

January 9

If to myself—"God sometimes interferes"—
I said, my faith at once would be struck blind.
I see him all in all, the lifing mind,
Or nowhere in the vacant miles and years.
A love he is that watches and that hears,
Or but a mist fumed up from minds of men,
Whose fear and hope reach out beyond their ken.

February 1

I to myself have neither power nor worth,
Patience nor love, nor anything right good;
My soul is a poor land, plenteous in dearth—

Here blades of grass, there a small herb for food—
A nothing that would be something if it could,
But if obedience, Lord, in me do grow,
I shall one day be better than I know.

February 2

The worst power of an evil mood is this—
It makes the bastard self seem in the right,
Self, self the end, the goal of human bliss,
But if the Christ-self in us be the might
Of saving God, why should I spend my force
With a dark thing to reason of the light
Not push it rough aside, and hold obedient course?

February 4

My Lord, I find that nothing else will do,
But follow where thou goest, sit at thy feet,
And where I have thee not, still run to meet.
Roses are scentless, hopeless are the morns,
Rest is but weakness, laughter crackling thorns,
If thou, the Truth, do not make them the true;
Thou art my life, O Christ, and nothing else will do.

February 17

Lord, I have fallen again—a human clod!
Selfish I was, and heedless to offend;
Stood on my rights. Thy own child would not send
Away his shreds of nothing for the whole God!
Wretched, to thee who savest, low I bend:
Give me the power to let my rag-rights go
In the great wind that from thy gulf doth blow.

February 23

I cannot see, my God, a reason why
From morn to night I go not gladsome, free;
For, if thou art what my soul thinketh thee,
There is no burden but should lightly lie,
No duty but a joy at heart must be:
Love's perfect will can be nor sore nor small,
For God is light—in him no darkness is at all.

March 6

This day be with me, Lord, when I go forth,
Be nearer to me than I am able to ask.
In merriment, in converse, or in task,
Walking the street, listening to men of worth,
Or greeting such as only talk and bask,
Be thy thought still my waiting soul around,
And if He come, I shall be watching found.

April 2

Some things wilt thou not one day turn to dreams?
Some dreams wilt thou not one day turn to fact?
The thing that painful, more than should be, seems,
Shall not thy sliding years with them retract—
Shall fair realities not counteract?
The thing that was well dreamed of bliss and joy—
Wilt thou not breathe thy life into the toy?

April 5

What has been shall not only be, but is.
The hues of dreamland, strange and sweet and tender,
Are but hint-shadows of full many a splendour
Which the high Parent-love will yet unroll

Before his child's obedient, humble soul.
Ah, me, my God! in thee lies every bliss,
Whose shadow men go hunting wearily amiss.

May 2

Even when their foolish words they turned on him
He did not his disciples send away;
He knew their hearts were foolish, eyes were dim,
And therefore by his side needs must they stay.
Thou wilt not, Lord, send me away from thee.
When I am foolish, make thy cock crow grim;
If that is not enough, turn, Lord, and look on me.

May 11

Haste to me, Lord, when this fool-heart of mine
Begins to gnaw itself with selfish craving;
Or, like a foul thing scarcely worth the saving,
Swoln up with wrath, desireth vengeance fine.
Haste, Lord, to help, when reason favors wrong;
Haste when thy soul, the high-born thing divine,
Is torn by passion's raving, maniac throng.

May 13

Even thou canst give me neither thought nor thing,
Were it the priceless pearl hid in the land,
Which, if I fix thereon a greedy gaze,
Becomes not poison that doth burn and cling;
Their own bad look my foolish eyes doth daze,
They see the gift, see not the giving hand—
From the living root the apple dead I wring.

May 15

Afresh I seek thee. Lead me—once more I pray—
Even should it be against my will, thy way.

Let me not feel thee foreign any hour,
Or shrink from thee as an estranged power.
Through doubt, through faith, through bliss,
   through stark dismay,
Through sunshine, wind, or snow, or fog, or shower,
Draw me to thee who art my only day.

May 16

I would go near thee—but I cannot press
Into thy presence—it helps not to presume.
Thy doors are deeds; the handles are their doing.
He whose day-life is obedient righteousness,
Who, after failure, or a poor success,
Rises up, stronger effort yet renewing—
He finds thee, Lord, at length, in his own common room.

May 19

O Christ, my life, possess me utterly.
Take me and make a little Christ of me.
If I am anything but thy father's son,
'Tis something not yet from the darkness won.
Oh, give me light to live with open eyes.
Oh, give me life to hope above all skies.
Give me thy spirit to haunt the Father with my cries.

May 20

'Tis hard for man to rouse his spirit up—
It is the human creative agony,
Though but to hold the heart an empty cup,
Or tighten on the team the rigid rein,
Many will rather lie among the slain
Than creep through narrow ways the light to gain—
Than wake the will, and be born bitterly.

May 21

But he who would be born again indeed,
Must wake his soul unnumbered times a day,
And urge himself to life with holy greed;
Now ope his bosom to the wind's free play;
And now, with patience forceful, hard, lie still,
Submiss and ready to the making will,
Athirst and empty, for God's breath to fill.

May 27

So bound in selfishness am I, so chained,
I know it must be glorious to be free
But know not what, full-fraught, the word doth mean.
By loss on loss I have severely gained
Wisdom enough my slavery to see;
But liberty, pure, absolute, serene,
No freest-visioned slave has ever seen.

May 29

Yet hints come to me from the realm unknown;
Airs drift across the twilight border land,
Odored with life; and as from some far strand
Sea-murmured, whispers to my heart are blown
That fill me with a joy I cannot speak,
Yea, from whose shadow words drop faint and weak:
Thee, God, I shadow in that region grand.

May 30

O Christ, who didst appear in Judah land,
Thence by the cross go back to God's right hand,
Plain history, and things our sense beyond,
In thee together come and correspond:
How rulest thou from the undiscovered bourn

The world-wise world that laughs thee still to scorn?
Please, Lord, let thy disciple understand.

May 31

'Tis heart on heart thou rulest. Thou art the same
At God's right hand as here expose to shame.
And therefore workest now as thou didst then—
Feeding the faint divine in humble men,
Through all thy realms from thee goes out heart-power,
Working the holy, satisfying hour,
When all shall love, and all be love again.

June 15

Who sets himself not sternly to be good,
Is but a fool, who judgments of true things
Has none, however oft the claim renewed.
And he who thinks, in his great plentitude,
To right himself, and set his spirit free
Without the might of higher communings,
Is foolish also—save he willed himself to be!

June 16

How many helps thou giv'st to those would learn!
To some sore pain, to others a sinking heart;
To some a weariness worse than any smart;
To some a haunting, fearing, blind concern;
Madness to some; to some the shaking dart
Of hideous death still following as they turn;
To some a hunger that will not depart.

June 19

Me thou hast given an infinite unrest,
A hunger—not at first after known good,
But something vague I knew not, and yet would—

The veiled Isis, thy will not understood;
A conscience tossing ever in my breast;
And something deeper, that will not be expressed
Save as the Spirit thinking in the Spirit's brood.

June 20

But now the Spirit and I are one in this—
My hunger now is after righteousness;
My spirit hopes in God to set me free
From the low self loathed of the higher me.
Great elder brother of my second birth,
Dear o'er all names but one, in heaven or earth,
Teach me all day to love eternally.

July 17

I cannot tell why this day I am ill;
But I am well because it is thy will—
Which is to make me pure and right like thee.
Not yet I need escape—'tis bearable
Because thou knowest. And when harder things
Shall rise and gather, and overshadow me,
I shall have comfort in thy strengthenings.

July 28

Oh, let me live in thy realities,
Nor substitute my notions for thy facts,
Notion with notion making leagues and pacts;
They are to truth but as dream-deeds to acts,
And questioned, make me doubt of everything.—
"O Lord, my God" my heart gets up and cries,
"Come thy own self, and with thee my faith bring."

August 7

In holy things may be unholy greed.
Thou giv'st a glimpse of many a lovely thing
Not to be stored for use in any mind,
But only for the present spiritual need.
The holiest bread, if hoarded, soon will breed
The mammon-moth, the having-pride, I find.
'Tis momently thy heart gives out heart-quickening.

August 30

But why should it be possible to mistrust—
Nor possible only, but its opposite hard?
Why should not man believe because he must—
By sight's compulsion? Why should he be scarred
With conflict? worn with doubting fine and long?—
No man is fit for heaven's musician throng
Who has not tuned an instrument all shook and jarred.

August 31

Therefore, O Lord, when all things common seem,
When all is dust, and self the centre clod,
When grandeur is a hopeless, foolish dream,
And anxious care more reasonable than God,—
Out of Job's ashes I will call to thee—
In spite of dead distrust call earnestly:—
Oh thou who livest, call, then answer dying me.

September 1

We are a shadow and a shining, we!
One moment nothing seems but what we see,
Or aught to rule but common Circumstance—
Nought is to seek but praise, to shun but chance;
A moment more, and God is all in all,

And not a sparrow from its nest can fall
But from the ground its chirp goes up into his hall.

September 2

I know at least which is the better mood.
When on a heap of cares I sit and brood,
Like Job upon his ashes, sorely vext,
I feel a lower thing than when I stood
The world's true heir, fearless as, on its stalk,
A lily meeting Jesus in his walk:
I am not *all* mood—I can judge betwixt.

September 25

Lord, loosen in me the hold of visible things;
Help me to walk by faith and not by sight;
I would, through thickest veils and coverings,
See into the chambers of the living light.
Lord, in the land of things that swell and seem,
Help me to walk by the other light supreme
Which shows thy facts behind man's vaguely hinting dream.

October 2

But thou art making me, I thank thee, sire.
What thou hast done and doest thou know'st well,
And I will help thee:—gently in thy fire
I will lie burning; on thy potter's-wheel
I will whirl patient, though my brain should reel:
Thy grace shall be enough the grief to quell,
And growing strength perfect through weakness dire.

October 3

I have not knowledge, wisdom, insight, thought,
Or understanding, fit to justify

Thee in thy work, O Perfect. Thou hast brought
Me up to this—and lo! what thou hast wrought,
I cannot call it good. But I can cry—
"O enemy, the maker hath not done:
One day thou shalt behold, and from the sight wilt run."

November 23

How oft I say the same things in these lines!
Even as a man, buried in during dark,
Turns ever where the edge of twilight shines,
Prays ever toward the vague eternal mark;
Or as the sleeper, having dreamed he drinks,
Back straightway into thirstful dreaming sinks,
So turns my will to thee, for thee still longs, still pines.

December 3

This weariness of mine, may it not come
From something that doth need no setting right?
Shall fruit be blamed if it hang wearily
A day before it perfected drop plumb
To the sad earth from off its nursing tree?
Ripeness must always come with loss of might
The weary evening fall before the resting night.

December 9

For then thou wilt be able, then at last,
To glad me as thou hungerest to do;
Then shall thy life my heart all open find,
A thoroughfare to thy great spirit-wind;
Then shall I rest within thy hold Vast,
One with the bliss of the eternal mind;
And all creation rise in me created new.

December 25

Thou hast not made, or taught me, Lord, to care
For times and seasons—but this one glad day
Is the blue sapphire clasping all the lights
That flash in the girdle of the year so fair
When thou wast born a man—because alway
Thou wast and art a man through all the flights
Of thought, and time, and thousandfold creation's play.

Novels

INTRODUCTION

While MacDonald most aspired to be a poet and took most delight in writing fantasies, he soon discovered his contemporaries had a limited interest in both. If he was to have a writing ministry, he had to write what the public would read. When his publisher urged upon him the writing of novels, he hesitated, feeling inadequate for the task, then set himself earnestly to try. After many unsuccessful attempts, a publisher finally agreed to bring out *David Elginbrod* in 1863. Its success established him in the public eye as a talented novelist and determined the course of his career for the following thirty-five years.

Central to his romance novels are their strong theological interests. He could construct and unfold a story with sufficient skill to maintain the interest of his readers, but his work is not remarkable for his narrative plots. His novels would not be in the demand they are today if it were not for the manner in which they ponder so earnestly the relation between Christian theology and human behavior. MacDonald's vision is most basically characterized by two elements: a vivid and compelling vision of the beauty of ideal goodness incarnate in individual lives, and a deep understanding of the nature of the human struggle simply to be good. He can arouse within his reader the aspiration after goodness as effectively as any writer.

The selections that follow illustrate, among other of his ideas, his view of the ideal person, how the grace of God is working in human experience, the spiritual dangers inherent in material possessions, the role of conscience and of hope in Christian motivation, and the implications of divine love in human experience.

A Sunday with Falconer

From

DAVID ELGINBROD

Book III, Chapter 13

It was not often that Falconer went to church; but he seemed to have some design in going oftener than usual at present. The Sunday after the one last mentioned, he went as well, though not to the same church, and calling for Hugh took him with him. What they found there, and the conversation following thereupon, I will try to relate, because, although they do not immediately affect my outward story, they greatly influenced Hugh's real history.

They heard the Morning Service and the Litany read in an ordinary manner, though somewhat more devoutly than usual. Then, from the communion-table, rose a voice vibrating with solemn emotion, like the voice of Abraham pleading for Sodom. It thrilled through Hugh's heart. The sermon which followed affected him no less, although, when he came out, he confessed to Falconer that he had only caught flying glimpses of its meaning, scope, and drift.

"I seldom go to church," said Falconer; "but when I do, I come here: and always feel that I am in the presence of one of the holy servants of God's great temple not made with hands. I heartily trust that man. He is what he seems to be."

"They say he is awfully heterodox."

"They do."

"How then can he remain in the church, if he is as honest as you say?"

"In this way, as I humbly venture to think," Falconer answered. "He looks upon the formulae of the church as utterances of *living* truth—vital embodiments—to be regarded as one ought to regard human faces. In these human faces, others may see this or that inferior expression, may find out the mean and the small and the incomplete: he looks for and finds the ideal; the grand, sacred, God-meant meaning; and by that he holds as *the* meaning of the human countenances, for it is the meaning of him who made them. So with the confession of the Church of England: he believes that not man only, but God also, and God first and chief, had to do with the making of it; and therefore he looks in it for the Eternal and the Divine, and he finds what he seeks. And as no words can avoid bearing in them the possibility of a variety of interpretations, he would exclude whatever the words might mean, or, regarded merely as words, do mean, in a narrow exposition: he thinks it would be dishonest to take the low meaning as *the* meaning. To return to the faces: he passes by moods and tempers, and beholds the main character—that on whose surface the temporal and transient floats. Both in faces and in formulae he loves the divine substance, with his true, manly, brave heart; and as for the faults in both—for man, too, has his share in both—I believe he is ready to die by them, if only in so doing he might die for them.—I had a vision of him this morning as I sat and listened to his voice, which always seems to me to come immediately from his heart, as if his heart spoke with lips of its own. Shall I tell you my vision?—

"I saw a crowd—priests and laymen—speeding, hurrying, darting away, up a steep, crumbling height. Mitres, hoods, and hats rolled behind them to the bottom. Every one for himself, with hands and feet they scramble and flee, to save their souls from the fires of hell which come rolling in along the hollow below with the forward 'pointing spires' of billowy flame. But beneath, right in the course of the fire, stands one man upon a little rock which goes down to the centre of the great world, and faces the approaching flames. He stands bareheaded, his eyes bright with faith in God, and the mighty mouth that utters his truth, fixed in holy defiance. His denial comes from no fear, or weak dislike to that which is painful. On neither side will he tell lies for peace. He is ready to be lost for his fellow-men. In the name of God he rebukes the flames of hell. The fugitives pause on the top, look back, call him *lying prophet,* and shout evil opprobrious names at the man who counts not his own life dear to him, who has forgotten his own soul in his sacred devotion to men, who fills up what is left behind of the sufferings of Christ, for his body's sake—for the human race, of which he is the head. Be sure that, come what may of the rest, let the flames of hell ebb or flow, that man is safe, for he is delivered already from the only devil that can make hell itself a torture, the devil of selfishness—the only one that can *possess* a man and make himself his own living hell. He is out of all that region of things, and already dwelling in the secret place of the Almighty."

"Go on, go on."

"He trusts in God so absolutely, that he leaves his salvation to him—utterly, fearlessly; and, forgetting it, as being no concern of his, sets himself to do the work that God has given him to do, even as his Lord did before him, counting that alone worthy of his care. Let God's will be done, and all is well. If God's will be done, he cannot fare ill. To him, God is all in all. If it be possible to separate such things, it is the glory of God, even more than the salvation of men, that he seeks. He will not have it that his Father in heaven is not perfect. He believes entirely that God loves, yea, *is* love; and, therefore, that hell itself must be subservient to that love, and but an embodiment of it; that the grand work of Justice is to make way for a Love which will give to every man that which is right and ten times more, even if it should be by means of awful suffering—a suffering which the Love of the Father will not shun, either for himself or his children, but will eagerly meet for their sakes, that he may give them all that is in his heart."

"Surely you speak your own opinions in describing thus warmly the faith of the preacher."

"I do. He is accountable for nothing I say. All I assert is, that this is how I seem to myself to succeed in understanding him."

"How is it that so many good people call him heterodox!"

"I do not mind that. I am annoyed only when good-hearted people, with small natures and cultivated intellects, patronise him, and talk forgivingly of his warm heart and unsound judgment. To these, theology must be like a map—with plenty of lines in it. They cannot trust their house on the high table-land of his theology, because they cannot see the outlines bounding the said table-land. It is not small enough for them. They cannot take it in. Such can hardly be satisfied with the creation, one would think, seeing there is no line of division anywhere in it. They would take care there should be no mistake."

"Does God draw no lines, then?"

"When he does, there are pure lines, without breadth, and consequently invisible to mortal eyes; not Chinese walls of separation, such as these definers would construct. Such minds are *à priori* incapable of theorising upon his theories. Or, to alter the figure, they will discover a thousand faults in his drawing, but they can never behold the figure constructed by his lines, and containing the faults which they believe they discover."

"But can those theories in religion be correct which are so hard to see?"

"They are only hard to certain natures."

"But those natures are above the average."

"Yes, in intellect and its cultivation—nothing more."

"You have granted them heart."

"Not much; but what there is, good."

"That is allowing a great deal, though. Is it not hard then to say that such cannot understand him?"

"Why? They will get to heaven, which is all they want. And they will understand him one day, which is more than they pray for. Till they have done being anxious about their own salvation, we must forgive them that they can contemplate with calmness the damnation of a universe, and believe that God is yet more indifferent than they."

"But do they not bring the charge likewise against you, of being unable to understand them?"

"Yes. And so it must remain, till the Spirit of God decide the matter, which I presume must take place by slow degrees. For this decision can only consist in the enlightenment of souls to see the truth; and therefore has to do with individuals only. There is no triumph for the Truth but that. She knows no glorying over the vanquished, for in her victory the vanquished is already of the vanquishers. Till then, the Right must be content to be called the Wrong, and—which is far harder—to seem the Wrong. There is no spiritual victory gained by a verbal conquest; or by any kind of torture, even should the rack employed be that of the purest logic. Nay more: so long as the wicked themselves remain impenitent, there is mourning in heaven; and when there is no longer any hope over one last remaining sinner, heaven itself must confess its defeat, heap upon that sinner what plagues you will."

Hugh pondered, and continued pondering till they reached Falconer's chambers. At the door Hugh paused.

"Will you not come in?"

"I fear I shall become troublesome."

"No fear of that. I promise to get rid of you as soon as I find you so."

"Thank you. Just let me know when you have had enough of me."

They entered. Mrs. Ashton, who, unlike her class, was never missing when wanted, got them some bread and cheese; and Falconer's Fortunatus-purse of a cellar—the bottom of his cupboard—supplied its usual bottle of port; to which fare the friends sat down.

My Own Acquaintance

From

ROBERT FALCONER

Part III, Chapter 8

Bewildered with the rapid sequence of events, I was following in the crowd. Falconer looked about till he saw me, and gave me a nod which meant *come along*. Before we reached Bow Street, however, the offending policeman, who had been walking a little behind in conversation with one of the others, advanced to Falconer, touched his hat, and said something, to which Falconer replied.

"Remember, I have my eye upon you," was all I heard, however, as he left the crowd and rejoined me. We turned and walked eastward again.

The storm kept on intermittently, but the streets were rather more crowded than usual notwithstanding.

"Look at that man in the woolen jacket," said Falconer. "What a beautiful outline of face! There must be something noble in that man."

"I did not see him," I answered, "I was taken up with a woman's face, like that of a beautiful corpse. It's eyes were bright. There was gin in its brain."

The streets swarmed with human faces gleaming past. It was a night of ghosts.

There stood a man who had lost one arm, earnestly pumping bilge-music out of an accordion with the other, holding it to his body with the stump. There was a woman, pale with hunger and gin, three matchboxes in one extended hand, and the other holding a baby to her breast.

As we looked, the poor baby let go its hold, turned its little head, and smiled a wan, shrivelled, old-fashioned smile in our faces.

"Another happy baby, you see, Mr. Gordon," said Falconer. "A child, fresh from God, finds its heaven where no one else would. The devil could drive woman out of Paradise; but the devil himself cannot drive the Paradise out of a woman."

"What can be done for them?" I said, and at the moment, my eye fell upon a row of little children, from two to five years of age, seated upon the curb-stone.

They were chattering fast, and apparently carrying on some game, as happy as if they had been in the fields.

"Wouldn't you like to take all those little grubby things, and put them in a great tub and wash them clean?" I said.

"They'd fight like spiders," rejoined Falconer.

"They're not fighting now."

"Then don't make them. It would be all useless. The probability is that you would only change the forms of the various evils, and possibly for worse. You would buy all that man's glue-lizards, and that man's three-foot rules, and that man's dog-collars and chains, at three times their value, that they might get more drink than usual, and do nothing at all for their living to-morrow.—What a happy London you would make if you were Sultan Haroun!" he added, laughing. "You would put an end to poverty altogether, would you not?"

I did not reply at once.

"But I beg your pardon," he resumed; "I am very rude."

"Not at all," I returned. "I was only thinking how to answer you. They would be no worse after all than those who inherit property and lead idle lives."

"True; but they would be no better. Would you be content that your quondam poor should be no better off than the rich? What would be gained thereby? Is there no truth in the words 'Blessed are the poor'? A deeper truth than most Christians dare to see.—Did you ever observe that there is not one word about the vices of the poor in the Bible—from beginning to end?"

"But they have their vices."

"Indubitably. I am only stating a fact. The Bible is full enough of the vices of the rich. I make no comment."

"But don't you care for their sufferings?"

"They are of secondary importance quite. But if you had been as much amongst them as I, perhaps you would be of my opinion, that the poor are not, cannot possibly feel so wretched as they seem to us. They live in a climate, as it were, which is their own, by natural law comply with it, and find it not altogether unfriendly. The Laplander will prefer his wastes to the rich fields of England, not merely from ignorance, but for the sake of certain blessings amongst which he has been born and brought up. The blessedness of life depends far more on its interest than upon its comfort. The need of exertion and the doubt of success, renders life much more interesting to the poor than it is to those who, unblessed with anxiety for the bread that perisheth, waste their poor hearts about rank and reputation."

"I thought such anxiety was represented as an evil in the New Testament."

"Yes. But it is a still greater evil to lose it any other way than by faith in God. You would remove the anxiety by destroying its cause: God would remove it by lifting them above it, by teaching them to trust in him, and thus making them partakers of the divine nature. Poverty is a blessing when it makes a man look up."

"But you cannot say it does so always."

"I cannot determine when, where, and how much; but I am sure it does. And I am confident that to free those hearts from it by any deed of yours would be to do them the greatest injury you could. Probably their want of foresight would prove the natural remedy, speedily reducing them to their former condition—not however without serious loss."

"But will not this theory prove at last an anaesthetic rather than an anodyne? I mean that, although you may adopt it at first for refuge from the misery the sight of their condition occasions you, there is surely a danger of its rendering you at last indifferent to it."

"Am I indifferent? But you do not know me yet. Pardon my egotism. There may be such danger. Every truth has its own danger or shadow. Assuredly I would have no less labour spent upon them. But there can be no *true* labour done, save in as far as we are fellow-labourers with God. We must work with him, not *against* him. Every one who works without believing that God is doing the best, the absolute good for them, is, must be, more or less, thwarting God. He would take the poor out of God's hands. For others, as for ourselves, we must trust him. If we could thoroughly understand anything, that would be enough to prove it undivine; and that which is but one step beyond our understanding must be in some of its relations as mysterious as if it were a hundred. But through all this darkness about the poor, at least I can see wonderful veins and fields of light, and with the help of this partial vision, I trust for the rest. The only and the greatest thing man is capable of is Trust in God."

"What then is a man to do for the poor? How is he to work with God?" I asked.

"He must be a man amongst them—a man breathing the air of a higher life, and therefore in all natural ways fulfilling his endless human relations to them. Whatever you do for them, let your own being, that is you in relation to them, be the background, that so you may be a link between them and God, or rather I should say, between them and the knowledge of God."

While Falconer spoke, his face grew grander and grander, till at last it absolutely shone. I felt that I walked with a man whose faith was his genius.

"Of one thing I am pretty sure," he resumed, "that the same recipe Goethe gave for the enjoyment of life, applies equally to all work: 'Do the thing that lies next you.' That is all our business. Hurried results are worse than none. We must force nothing, but be partakers of the divine patience. How long it took to make the cradle! and we fret that the baby Humanity is not reading Euclid and Plato, even that it is not understanding the Gospel of St. John! If there is one thing evident in the world's history, it is that God hasteneth not. All haste implies weakness. Time is as cheap as space and matter. What they call the church militant is only at drill yet, and a good many of the officers too not out of the awkward squad. I am sure I, for a private, am not. In the drill a man has to conquer himself, and move with the rest by individual attention to his own duty: to what mighty battlefields the recruit may yet be led, he does not know. Meantime he has nearly enough to do with his goose-step, while there is plenty of single combat, skirmish, and light cavalry work generally, to get him ready for whatever is to follow. I beg your pardon: I am preaching."

"Eloquently," I answered.

Of some of the places into which Falconer led me that night I will attempt no description—places blazing with lights and mirrors, crowded with dancers, billowing with music, close and hot, and full of the saddest of all sights, the uninteresting faces of commonplace women.

"There is passion," I said, as we came out of one of these dreadful places, "that lingers about the heart like the odour of violets, like a glimmering twilight on the borders of moonrise; and there is a passion that wraps itself in the vapours of patchouli and coffins, and streams from the eyes like gaslight from a tavern. And yet the line is ill to draw between them. It is very dreadful. These are women."

"They are in God's hands," answered Falconer. "He hasn't done with them yet. Shall it take less time to make a woman than to make a world? Is not the woman the greater? She may have her ages of chaos, her centuries of crawling slime, yet rise a woman at last."

"How much alike all those women were!"

"A family likeness, alas! which always strikes you first."

"Some of them looked quite modest."

"There are great differences. I do not know anything more touching than to see how a woman will sometimes wrap around her the last remnants of a soiled and ragged modesty. It has moved me almost to tears to see such a one hanging her head in shame during the singing of a detestable song. That poor thing's shame was precious in the eyes of the Master, surely."

"Could nothing be done for her?"

"I contrived to let her know where she would find a friend if she wanted to be good: that is all you can do in such cases. If the horrors of their life do not drive them out at such an open door, you can do nothing else, I fear—for the time."

The Curate and the Doctor

From

THOMAS WINGFOLD, CURATE

Chapter LXXIII

There is something strange about that young man's illness," said Faber, as soon as they had left the house. "I fancy you know more than you can tell; and if so, then I have committed no indiscretion in saying as much."

"Perhaps it might be an indiscretion to acknowledge as much, however," said the curate, with a smile.

"You are right. I have not been long in the place," returned Faber, "and you have had no opportunity of testing me. But I am indifferent honest as well as you, though I don't go with you in every thing."

"People would have me believe you don't go with me in any thing."

"They say as much, do they?" returned Faber, with some annoyance. "I thought I had been careful not to trespass on your preserves."

"As for preserves, I don't know of any," answered the curate. "There is no true bird in the grounds that won't manage somehow to escape the snare of the fowler."

"Well," said the doctor, "I know nothing about God and all that kind of thing, but, though I don't think I'm a coward exactly either, I know I should like to have your pluck."

"I haven't got any pluck," said the curate.

"Tell that to the marines," said Faber. "I daren't go and say what I think or don't think even in the bedroom of my least orthodox patient—at least, if I do, I instantly repent it—while you go on saying what you really believe Sunday after Sunday! How you can believe it I don't know, and it's no business of mine."

"Oh! yes it is!" returned Wingfold. "But as to the pluck, it may be a man's duty to say in the pulpit what he would be just as wrong to say by a sick-bed."

"That has nothing to do with the pluck! That's all I care about."

"It has every thing to do with what you take for pluck. My pluck is only Don Worm."

"I don't know what you mean by that."

"It's Benedick's name, in *Much Ado about Nothing* for the conscience. *My* pluck is nothing but my conscience."

"It's a damned fine thing to have anyhow, whatever name you put upon it!" said Faber.

"Excuse me if I find your epithet more amusing than apt," said Wingfold, laughing.

"You are quite right," said Faber. "I apologize."

"As to the pluck again," Wingfold resumed, "if you think of this one fact: that my whole desire is to believe in God, and that the only thing I can be sure of sometimes is that, if there be a God, none but an honest man will ever find him: you will not then say there is much pluck in my speaking the truth?"

"I don't see that that makes it a hair easier, in the face of such a set of gaping noodles as—"

"I beg your pardon: there is more lack of conscience than of brains in the Abbey of a Sunday, I fear."

"Well, all I have to say is, I can't for the life of me see what you want to believe in a God for! It seems to me the world would go on rather better without any such fancy. Look here, now: there is young Spenser—out there at Horwood—a patient of mine. His wife died yesterday—one of the loveliest young creatures you ever saw. The poor fellow is as bad about it as fellow can be. Well, he's one of your sort, and said to me the other day, just as you would have him, 'It's the will of God,' he said, 'and we must hold our peace.' 'Don't talk to me about God,' I said, for I couldn't stand it. 'Do you mean to tell me that if there was a God, he would have taken such a lovely creature as that away from her husband and her helpless infant at the age of two-and-twenty? I scorn to believe it.'"

"What did he say to that?"

"He turned as white as death, and said never a word."

"Ah! you forgot that you were taking from him his only hope of seeing her again!"

"I certainly did not think of that," said Faber.

"Even then," resumed Wingfold, "I should not say you were wrong, if you were prepared to add that you had searched every possible region of existence, and had found no God; or that you had tried every theory man had invented, or even that you were able to invent yourself, and had found none of them consistent with the being of a God. I do not say that then you would be right in your judgment, for another man of equal weight, might have had a different experience. I only say I would not then blame you. But you must allow it a very serious thing to assert as a conviction, without such grounds as the assertor has pretty fully satisfied himself concerning, what *could* only drive the sting of death ten times deeper."

The doctor was silent.

"I doubt not you spoke in a burst of indignation; but it seems to me the indignation of a man unaccustomed to ponder the things concerning which he expresses such a positive conviction."

"You are wrong there," returned Faber; "for I was brought up in the straitest sect of the Pharisees, and know what I am saying."

"The straitest sect of the Pharisees can hardly be the school in which to gather any such idea of a God as one could wish to be a reality."

"They profess to know."

"Is that any argument of weight, they and their opinions being what they are? If there be a God, do you imagine he would choose any strait sect under the sun to be his interpreters?"

"But the question is not of the idea of a God, but of the existence of any, seeing, if he exists, he must be such as the human heart could never accept as God, inasmuch as he at least permits, if not himself enacts, cruelty. My argument to poor Spenser remains—however unwise or indeed cruel it may have been."

"I grant it a certain amount of force—as much exactly as had gone to satisfy the children whom I heard the other day agreeing that Dr. Faber was a very cruel man, for he pulled out nurse's tooth, and gave poor little baby such a nasty, nasty powder!"

"Is that a fair parallel? I must look at it."

"I think it is. What you do is often unpleasant, sometimes most painful, but it does not follow that you are a cruel man, and a hurter instead of a healer of men."

"I think there is a fault in the analogy," said Faber. "For here am I nothing but a slave to laws already existing, and compelled to work according to them. It is not my fault, therefore, that the remedies I have to use are unpleasant. But if there be a God, he has the matter in his own hands."

"There is weight and justice in your argument, which may well make the analogy appear at first sight false. But is there no theory possible that should make it perfect?"

"I do not see how there should be any. For, if you say that God is under any such compulsion as I am under, then surely the house is divided against itself, and God is not God any more."

"For my part," said the curate, "I think I *could* believe in a God who did but his imperfect best: in one all power, and not all goodness, I could not believe. But suppose that the design of God involved the perfecting of men as the *children of God—'I said ye are gods'*—that he would have them partakers of his own blessedness in kind—be as himself:—suppose his grand idea could not be contented with creatures perfect *only* by his gift, so far as that should reach, and having no willing causal share in the perfection—that is, partaking not at all of God's individuality and free-will and choice of good;—then suppose that suffering were the only way through which the individual soul could be set, in separate and self-individuality, so far apart from God that it might *will,* and so become a partaker of his singleness and freedom; and suppose that this suffering must be and had been initiated by God's taking his share, and that the infinitely greater share; suppose, next, that God saw the germ of a pure affection, say in your friend and his wife, but saw also that it was a germ so imperfect and weak that it could not encounter the coming frosts and winds of the world without loss and decay, while, if they were parted now for a few years, it would grow and strengthen and expand to the certainty of an infinitely higher and deeper and keener love through the endless ages to follow—so that by suffering should come, in place of contented decline, abortion, and death, a troubled birth of joyous result in health and immortality;—suppose all this, and what then?"

Faber was silent a moment, and then answered,

"Your theory has but one fault: it is too good to be true."

"My theory leaves plenty of difficulty, but has no such fault as that. Why, what sort of a God would content you, Mr. Faber? The one idea is too bad, the other is too good, to be true. Must you expand and pare until you get one exactly to the measure of yourself ere you can accept it as thinkable or possible? Why, a less God than that would not rest your soul a week. The only possibility of believing in a God seems to me to lie in finding an idea of a God large enough, grand enough, pure enough, lovely enough to be fit to believe in."

"And have you found such, may I ask?"

"I think I am finding such."

"Where?"

"In the man of the New Testament. I have thought a little more about these things, I fancy, than you have, Mr. Faber: I may come to be sure of something; I don't see how a man can ever be sure of *nothing*."

"Don't suppose me quite dumbfoundered, thought I can't answer you off-hand," said Mr. Faber, as they reached his door. "Come in with me, and I will make up the medicine myself; it will save time. There are a thousand difficulties," he resumed in the surgery, "some of them springing from peculiar points that come before one of my profession, which I doubt if you would be able to meet so readily. But about this poor fellow Lingard: know Glaston gossip says he is out of his mind."

"If I were you, Mr. Faber, I would not take pains to contradict it. He is not out of his mind, but has such trouble in it as might well drive him out. Don't you even hint at that, though."

"I understand," said Faber.

"If doctor and minister did understand each other and work together," said Wingfold, "I fancy a good deal more might be done."

"I don't doubt it. What sort of fellow is that cousin of theirs—Bascombe is his name, I believe?"

"A man to suit you, I should think," said the curate; "a man with a most tremendous power of believing in nothing."

"Come, come!" returned the doctor, "you don't know half enough about me to tell what sort of man I should like or dislike."

"Well, all I will say more of Bascombe is that if he were not conceited, he would be honest; and if he were as honest as he believes himself, he would not be so ready to judge every one dishonest who does not agree with him."

"I hope we may have another talk soon," said the doctor, searching for a cork. "Some day I may tell you a few things that may stagger you."

"Likely enough: I am only learning to walk yet," said Wingfold. "But a man may stagger and not fall, and I am ready to hear any thing you choose to tell me."

Faber handed him the bottle, and he took his leave.

Down the Hill

From

WEIGHED AND WANTING

Chapter XXIII

When Franks, the acrobat, and his family left Mrs. Baldwin's garret
to go to another yet poorer lodging, it was with heavy hearts: they
crept silent away, to go down yet a step of the world's stair. I have read
somewhere in Jean Paul of a curiously contrived stair, on which while
you thought you were going down you were really ascending: I think it
was so with the Frankses and the stair they were upon. But to many the
world is but a treadmill, on which while they seem to be going up and up,
they are only serving to keep things going round and round.

I think God has more to do with the fortunes of the poor a thousand
fold than with those of the rich. In the fortunes of the poor there are many
more changes, and they are of greater import as coming closer to the heart
of their condition. To careless and purblind eyes these fortunes appear
on an almost dead level of toil and privation; but they have more
variations of weather, more chequers of sunshine and shade, more storms
and calms, than lives passed on airier slopes. Who could think of God as
a God like Christ—and other than such he were not God—and imagine
he would not care as much for the family of John Franks as for the family
of Gerald Raymount? It is impossible to believe that he loves such as
Cornelius or Vavasor as he loves a Christopher. There must be a difference! The God of truth cannot love the unlovely in the same way as he
loves the lovely. The one he loves for what he is and what he has begun
to be; the other he loves because he sorely needs love—as sorely as the

other, and must begin to grow lovely one day. Nor dare we forget that the celestial human thing is in itself lovely as made by God, and pitiably lovely as spoiled by man. That is the Christ-thing which is the root of every man, created in his image—that which, when he enters the men, he possesses. The true earthly father must always love those children more who are obedient and loving—but he will not neglect one bad one for twenty good ones. "The Father himself loveth you because ye have loved me;" but "There is more joy in heaven over one sinner that repenteth than over ninety and nine that need no repentance." The great joy is the first rush of love in the new-opened channel for its issue and entrance.

The Frankses were on the down-going side of the hill Difficulty, and down they must go, unable to help themselves. They had found a cheaper lodging, but entered it with misgiving; their gains had been very moderate since their arrival in London, and their expenses greater than in the country. Also Franks was beginning to feel or to fancy his strength and elasticity not quite what they had been. The first suspicion of the approach of old age and the beginning of that weakness whose end is sure, may well be a startling one. The man has begun to be a nobody in the world's race—is henceforth himself but the course of the race between age and death—a race in which the victor is known ere the start. Life with its self-discipline withdraws itself thenceforth more to the inside, and goes on with greater vigor. The man has now to trust and yield constantly. He is coming to know the fact that he was never his own strength, had never the smallest power in himself at his strongest. But he is learning also that he is as safe as ever in the time when he gloried in his might—yea, as safe as then he imagined himself on his false foundation. He lays hold of the true strength, makes it his by laying hold of it. He trusts in the unchangeable thing at the root of all his strength, which gave it all the truth it had—a truth far deeper than he knew, a reality unfathomable, though not of the nature he then fancied. Strength has ever to be made perfect in weakness, and old age is one of the weaknesses in which it is perfected.

Poor Franks had not got so far yet as to see this, and the feeling of the approach of old age helped to relax the springs of his hopefulness. Also his wife had not yet got over her last confinement. The baby, too, was sickly. And there was not much popular receptivity for acrobatics in the streets; coppers came in slowly; the outlay was heavy; and the outlook altogether was of the gray without the gold. But his wife's words were always cheerful, though the tone of them had not a little of the mournful. Their tone came of temperament, the words themselves of love and its courage. The daughter of a gamekeeper, the neighbors regarded her as throwing herself away when she married Franks; but she had got an honest and brave husband, and never when life was hardest repented giving herself to him.

For a few weeks they did pretty well in their new lodging. They managed to pay their way, and had food enough—though not quite so good as husband and wife wished each for the other, and both for their children. The boys had a good enough time of it. They had not yet in London exhausted their own wonder. The constant changes around made of their lives a continuous novel—nay, a romance, and being happy they could eat anything and thrive on it.

The lives of the father and mother over-vault the lives of the children, shutting out all care if not all sorrow, and every change is welcomed as a new delight. Their parents, where positive cruelty has not installed fear and cast out love, are the divinities of even the most neglected. They feel towards them much the same, I fancy, as the children of ordinary parents in the middle class—love them more than children given over to nurses and governesses love theirs. Nor do I feel certain that the position of the children of the poor, in all its oppression, is not more favorable to the development of the higher qualities of the human mind, such as make the least show, than many of those more pleasant places for which some religious moralists would have us give the thanks of the specially favored. I suspect, for instance, that imagination, fancy, perception, insight into character, the faculty of fitting means to ends, the sense of adventure, and many other powers and feelings are more likely to be active in the children of the poor, to the greater joy of their existence, than in others. These Frankses, too, had a strict rule over them, and that increases much the capacity for enjoyment. The father, according to his lights, was, as we have seen, a careful and conscientious parent, and his boys were strongly attached to him, never thought of shirking their work, and endured a good deal of hardness and fatigue without grumbling: their mother had opened their eyes to the fact that their father took his full share in all he required of them, and did his best for them. They were greatly proud of their father one and all believing him not only the first man in his profession, but the best man that ever was in the world; and to believe so of one's parent is a stronger aid to righteousness than all things else whatever, until the day-star of the knowledge of the great Father goes up in the heart, to know whom, in like but better fashion, as the best more than man and the perfect Father of men, is the only thing to redeem us from misery and wrong, and lift us into the glorious liberty of the sons and daughters of God.

They were now reduced to one room, and the boys slept on the floor. This was no hardship, now that summer was nigh, only the parents found it interfered a little with their freedom of speech. Nor did it mend the matter to send them early to bed, for the earlier they went the longer were they in going to sleep. At the same time they had few things to talk of which they minded their hearing, and to the mother at least it was a pleasure to have all her chickens in the nest with her.

One evening after the boys were in bed, the father and mother sat talking. They had a pint of beer on the table between them, of which the woman tasted now and then that the man might imagine himself sharing it with her. Silence had lasted for some time. The mother was busy rough-patching a garment of Moxy's. The man's work for the day was over, but not the woman's!

"Well, I dunnow!" he said at last, and there ceased.

"What don ye know, John?" asked his wife, in a tone she would have tried to make cheerful had she but suspected it half as mournful as it was.

"There's that Mr. Christopher as was such a friend!" he said: "—you don't disremember what he used to say about the Almighty and that? You remember as how he used to say a man could no more get out o' the sight o' them eyes o' hisn than a child could get out o' sight o' the eyes on his mother as was a watchin' of him!"

"Yes, John, I do remember all that very well, and a great comfort it was to me at the time to hear him say so, an' has been many's the time since, when I had no other—leastways none but you an' the children. I often think over what he said to you an' me then when I was down, an' not able to hold my head up, nor feelin' as if I should ever lift it no more!"

"Well, I dunnow!" said Franks, and paused again. But this time he resumed, "What troubles me is this:—if that there mother as was a lookin' arter her child, was to see him doin' no better 'n you an' me, an' day by day gettin' furder on the wrong way, I should say she wan't much of a mother to let us go on in that 'ere way as I speak on."

There are, or there used to be when I was a boy, who, in their reverence for the name of the Most High, would have shown horror at the idea that he could not do anything or everything in a moment as it pleased him, but would not have been shocked at all at the idea that he might not please to give this or that man any help. In their eyes power was a grander thing than love, though it is nowhere said in the Book that God is omnipotence. Such, because they are told that he is omnipotent, call him Omnipotence; when told that he is Love, do not care to argue that he must then be loving? But as to doing what he wills with a word—see what it cost him to redeem the world! He did not find that easy, or to be done in a moment without pain or toil. Yea, awfully omnipotent is God. For he wills, effects and perfects the thing which, because of the bad in us, he has to carry out in suffering and sorrow, his own and his Son's. Evil is a hard thing for God himself to overcome. Yet thoroughly and altogether and triumphantly will he overcome it; and that not by crushing it underfoot—any god of man's idea could do that!—but by conquest of heart over heart, of life in life, of life over death. Nothing shall be too hard for the God that fears not pain, but will deliver and make true and blessed at his own severest cost.

For a time, then, the Frankses went on, with food to eat and money to pay their way, but going slowly down the hill, and finding it harder and harder to keep their footing. By and by the baby grew worse, pining visibly. They sought help at the hospital, but saw no Mr. Christopher, and the baby did not improve. Still they kept on, and every day the husband brought home a little money. Several times they seemed on the point of an engagement, but as often something came between, until at length Franks almost ceased to hope, and grew more and more silent, until at last he might well have appeared morose. The wonder to me is that any such as do not hope in a Power loving to perfection, should escape moroseness. Under the poisonous influences of anxiety, a loving man may become unkind, even cruel to the very persons for whose sake he is anxious. In good sooth what we too often count righteous care, but our Lord calls the care of the world, consumes the life of the heart as surely as the love of money. At the root they are the same. Yet evil thing as anxiety is, it were a more evil thing to be delivered from it by anything but the faith of the Son of God—that is faith in his Father and our Father; it would be but another and worse, because more comfortable form of the same slavery.

251

Poor Franks, however, with but a little philosophy, had much affection, which is indeed the present God in a man—and so did not go far in the evil direction. The worse sign of his degenerating temper was the more frequently muttered oath of impatience with his boys—never with his wife; and not one of them was a moment uneasy in consequence—only when the *gov'nor* wasn't jolly, neither were they.

The mind of Franks, so it appears to me, was mainly a slow sullen stream of subthought, a something neither thought nor feeling but partaking of the character of both, a something more than either, namely, the substance of which both are formed—the undeveloped elemental life, risen a little way, and but a little way, towards consciousness. The swifter flow of this stream is passion, the gleams of it where it ripples into the light, are thoughts. This sort of nature can endure much without being unhappy. What would crush a swift-thinking man is upborne by the denser tide. Its conditions are gloomier, and it consorts more easily with gloom. But light and motion and a grand future are waiting for such as he. All their sluggish half-slumberous being will be roused and wrought into conscious life—nor the unconscious whence it arises be therein exhausted, for that will be ever supplied and upheld by the indwelling Deity. In his own way Franks was in conflict with the problems of life; neither was he very able to encounter them; but on the other hand he was one to whom wonders might safely be shown, for he would use them not speculatively but practically. "Nothing almost sees miracles but misery," perhaps because to misery alone, save it be to the great unselfish joy, is it safe to show miracles. Those who must see ere they will believe, may have to be brought to the verge of the infinite grave that a condition fit for seeing may be effected in them. "Blessed are they who have not seen and yet have believed."

Drama

INTRODUCTION

MacDonald was interested all his life in the theater and aspired himself to be a dramatist. His first long poem, *Within and Without,* is a closet drama, and very early in his career he composed a four-act drama for the stage entitled *If I Had a Father.* He was, however, never successful in attracting professional interest in it, and he finally published it in his collection *The Gifts of the Child Christ, and other tales* in 1882.

His primary interest in writing drama was to present the theater-going public with fare that would provoke their thought concerning their own spiritual needs. His desire was fulfilled in an unexpected way in 1876 when Louisa, desparately attempting to supplement the family budget, undertook to have her talented family present dramas to the public for a modest charge. It quickly became a highly successful family undertaking.

Their most successful performance was their adaptation of the Second Part of *Pilgrim's Progress.* The following is their script of John Bunyan's classic, adapted by Louisa. As a family acting troup, they presented it in churches and rented public halls for some ten years throughout England and also in Italy. MacDonald would play the part of Greatheart, Lilia Christiana. Their work was consistently highly acclaimed, so that it became an important aspect of their unique ministry.

The script is complete with the words for seven accompanying songs. It was published by Oxford University Press in 1925, has not been published since, and is quite rare. As with any dramatic script, it must be acted to be fully appreciated, but reading it gives added and very helpful insight into the life and ministry of the family. It also underscores MacDonald's own concerns in his vision of the nature of the Christian life.

Dramatic Illustrations
of Passages
from the Second Part of

THE PILGRIM'S PROGRESS

by John Bunyan

Arranged in the year 1877 by
Mrs. George MacDonald

Oxford University Press
LONDON: HUMPHREY MILFORD
1925

PREFACE

These scenes from the Second Part of Bunyan's *Pilgrim's Progress* were arranged by my mother, Mrs. George MacDonald, nearly fifty years ago. They were intended to be played only by her family and were so played many times in the years 1877 to 1887. Though not written for publication, they are now printed in response to requests from persons anxious to give a dramatic rendering of Bunyan's work.

The most important point in performing these scenes is to act with simplicity and sincerity and without attempt at theatrical effect. Except in the second scene, where a wicket-gate and paling are needed, no scenery was used: the stage was hung with curtains of appropriate colour and design to each scene.

The men and women were dressed in the costume of Bunyan's period. The allegorical and celestial persons wore simple Greek garments. Greatheart appeared in shining armour with a large red cross on the front of his white tabard.

The music at the beginning and between the scenes was from Handel's *Messiah* and other classical works: only a piano was used. In most of the scenes there was a good deal of movement, but except in one or two places I have not attempted to add to the few stage directions found in the acting copy.

Winifred Troup
December, 1924

CHARACTERS

CHRISTIANA

MATTHEW

SAMUEL

JAMES

JOSEPH

her four sons

MERCY

GREATHEART

PRUDENCE

PIETY

CHARITY

MISTRESS BATS-EYES

MADAM TIMOROUS

MASTER FEEBLEMIND

MISTRESS MUCHAFRAID

MR. BRISK

MR. HONEST

SECRET, a heavenly messenger

THE KEEPER OF THE WICKET-GATE

A SHEPHERD'S BOY

Dramatic Illustrations
from
the Second Part of

THE PILGRIM'S PROGRESS
by John Bunyan

Scene I

Room in CHRISTIANA'S *house. Table in centre, four chairs, sticks, and kerchiefs.* CHRISTIANA *at table, L., weeping* JOSEPH *at her knee.* MATTHEW *behind her chair,* SAMUEL *and* JAMES, R.

JOSEPH.   Mother, mother, why do you weep?

JAMES.   Why do you weep, mother?

CHRISTIANA.   Sons, I had a dream last night, by the which I perceive we are all undone. I have sinned away Christian, your father. He went the pilgrim's journey to the Celestial City; he has now gone over the river. He would have had us with him, but I would not go myself; I also have hindered you of life.

MATTHEW.   Oh, mother, mother! *(Weeping.)* Let us after our father. Oh, that it had been our lot to go with him! It would have fared well with us, beyond what 'tis like to do now.

CHRISTIANA.   Oh, that I had not hardened my heart against all his entreaties; his restless groans, his brinish tears, and his loving persuasions. How the remembrance of my unkind, unnatural and ungodly carriages to him clogs my conscience now. There was not anything that Christian either said to me or did before me all the while that his burden did hang upon his back, but it returns upon me now as in flashes of lightning, till I feel the caul of my heart rent in sunder.

CHILDREN.   Oh, mother, mother! *(Weeping.)*

CHRISTIANA.   'Specially that bitter outcry of his: "What shall I do to be saved?" It rings in my ears most dolefully.

SAMUEL.   Let us go after him.

MATTHEW.   Lord have mercy on our mother.

CHRISTIANA.   I foolishly imagined concerning his troubles that he was overrun with melancholy humours; yet now 'twill not out of my mind but that they sprang from another cause—to wit, for that the light of Light was given him, by the help of which—as I perceived last night in my dream—he has escaped the snares of death.

CHILDREN.   Oh, woe!

MATTHEW.   Woe worth the day!

CHRISTIANA.   Lord, have mercy on me! have mercy on me, a sinner.

They sing "O Lamb of God."

Knocking at the door.

CHRISTIANA.   If thou comest in God's name, come in.

VOICE OUTSIDE.   Amen!

Enter Messenger.

MESSENGER.   Peace be to this house.

CHRISTIANA.   And to thy spirit.

CHILDREN.   And to thy spirit.

MESSENGER.   Knowest thou wherefore I am come?

CHRISTIANA.   Tell me whence art thou come; and what is thy errand here? *(Trembling.)*

MESSENGER.   Christiana, my name is Secret; I dwell with those that are high. It is talked of where I dwell as if thou hadst a desire to go thither. The Merciful One has sent me to tell thee that he is a God ready to forgive, and that he taketh delight to multiply the pardon of offences. He knows that thou are aware of the evil thou didst formerly do to thy husband, in hardening thy heart against his way and in keeping his babes in ignorance; but he would have thee know that he inviteth thee now to come into his presence, to his table, and he will feed thee with the best of his house.

MATTHEW.   Mother, hear him; let us go.

MESSENGER.   There is Christian, thy husband that was, with legions more, his companions, ever beholding that face that doth minister life to beholders, and they will all be glad when they shall hear the sound of thy feet step over thy Father's threshold.

CHRISTIANA *(greatly abashed, bows her head to the ground and groans).*   Oh, my Lord, my Lord!

MESSENGER.   Christiana, here is also a letter from thy husband's King which I have brought thee. *(Holds out parchment roll written on in letters of gold.)*

CHRISTIANA.   For me! *(Takes parchment, reads thereon.)* How great an honour! from the King himself!

MESSENGER.   He would have thee do as did Christian, thy husband, for that was the way to come to his city, to dwell in his presence with joy for evermore.

CHRISTIANA.   Oh, sir! how good! Sir, will you carry me and my children with you, that we also may go and worship this King?

MESSENGER.   Christiana, the bitter is before the sweet. Thou must through troubles, as did he that went before thee, enter this Celestial City. Wherefore I advise thee to do as did Christian thy husband. Go to the wicket gate yonder, over the plain, for that stands in the head of the way up which thou must go, and I wish thee all good speed. Also, I advise that thou put this letter in thy bosom; that thou read therein to thyself, and to thy children, until you have got it by rote of heart, for it is one of thy songs that thou must sing while thou art in this house of thy pilgrimage; also this thou must deliver in at the further gate.

CHRISTIANA *(greatly affected).*   Come, my children, let us pack up and begone to the gate that leads to the Celestial Country, that we may see your father, and be with him and his companions in peace, according to the laws of that land.

MATTHEW.   Gladly, mother, we will help you.

JOSEPH and JAMES.   Oh, joy! joy! that we are going to follow our father.

MESSENGER *(at the door).*   Then fare ye well; and do ye follow him.

CHRISTIANA.   Blessings be upon you, sir.

CHILDREN.   Blessings be upon you, sir.

Exit Messenger, R. *A knock.*

MATTHEW *(at the door).*   Mother, here come Mistress Bats-eyes and Madam Timorous, and our friend Mercy.

CHRISTIANA.   If you come in God's name, come in.

Enter Mistress Bats-eyes, Madam Timorous, *and* Mercy, R.

Christiana *is preparing to go away.*

MISTRESS BATS-EYES.   "In God's name come in!" Who would look for such language from thee? Such jargon! Christiana, I thought you had more sense. What! Packing? Neighbour, pray what is your meaning by this?

CHRISTIANA.   I am preparing for a journey, Mistress Bats-eyes.

MADAM TIMOROUS.   For *what* journey, I pray you?

CHRISTIANA. *(crosses to* Timorous).   Even to go after my good husband, Madam Timorous. *(Weeps.)*

MADAM T.   I hope not so, good neighbour; pray, for your poor children's sakes, do not so unwomanly cast away yourself.

CHRISTIANA.   Nay, my children shall go with me; not one of them is willing to stay behind.

MADAM T.   I wonder in my very heart what, or who, has brought you into this mind.

CHRISTIANA.   Oh, neighbours, knew you but as much as I do, I doubt not but that you would go with me.

MISTRESS B.   Prythee, what new knowledge hast thou got, that so worketh off thy mind from thy friends, and that tempteth thee to go nobody knows whither?

CHRISTIANA.   I have been sorely afflicted since my husband's departure from me: but that which troubleth me most, is my churlish carriages to him, when he was under his distress. Besides, I am now as he was then: nothing will serve me but going on pilgrimage.

MADAM T.   Oh, the madness that has possessed thee and thy husband, to run yourselves upon such difficulties! You have heard, I am sure, what your husband did meet with, even—in a manner—at the first step he took on his way.

MISTRESS B.   We also heard, over and above, how he met with the lions, and Apollyon and the Shadow of Death, and many other things. Nor is the danger that he met with at Vanity Fair to be forgotten by thee;

for if he, though a man, was so hard put to't, what canst thou, being but a poor woman, do?

CHRISTIANA. Tempt me not, my neighbour. I have now a price put into my hand to get gain, and I should be a fool of the greatest size, if I should have no heart to strike in with the opportunity. And for that you tell me of all these troubles that I am like to meet with in the way, they are so far off from being to me a discouragement that they show I am in the right. "The bitter must come before the sweet," and that also will make the sweet the sweeter. Wherefore since you came not to my house in God's name, as I said, I pray you to be gone, and not disquiet me further.

MADAM T. Come, neighbour Mercy, let us leave her in her own hands since she scorns our counsel and company.

MERCY. Neighbour, I did indeed come with you to see Christiana this morning; and since she is, as you see, a-taking of her last farewell of her country, I think to walk, this sunshine morning, a little way with her to help her on the way.

MADAM T. Well, I see you have a mind to go a-fooling too! but take heed in time, and be wise.

MISTRESS B. Go, lass, waste thy youth in looking for that thou never wilt see; yet bethink thee, while we are out of danger we are out, but when we are in we are in. So I'm back to my old place without you. Come along, Madam Timorous, you were never foolhardy.

MADAM T. I thank my stars, never.

Exeunt Mistress Bats-eyes *and* Madam Timorous, R.

CHRISTIANA. Now, boys, we will start: and, Mercy, I take this as an unexpected favour, that thou shouldst set foot out of doors with me, to accompany me a little in my way.

MERCY. If I thought it would be to purpose to go with you, I would never go near the town any more.

CHRISTIANA. Well, Mercy, cast in thy lot with me; I well know what will be the end of our pilgrimage. My husband is where he would not but be for all the gold in the Spanish mines. Nor shalt thou be rejected, though thou goest but upon my invitation. The King who hath sent for me and my children is one that delighteth in mercy. Besides, if thou wilt, I will hire thee, and thou shalt go along with me as my servant; yet we will have all things in common betwixt thee and me; only, go along with me.

MERCY. But how shall I be ascertained that I also shall be entertained? Had I this hope but from one that can tell, I would make no stick at all, but would go, being helped by him that can help, though the way was never so tedious.

CHRISTIANA. Well, loving Mercy, I will tell thee what thou shalt do. Go with me to the wicket-gate, and there I will further enquire for thee; and if there thou shalt not meet with encouragement, I will be content that thou shalt return to thy place.

MERCY. Then will I go thither, and will take what shall follow; and the Lord grant that my lot may there fall, even as the King of Heaven shall have his heart upon me.

CHRISTIANA. I am glad at my heart not only that I have a companion but that thou my poor maid art prevailed to fall in love with thy own salvation. (Mercy *weeps.*) Why weepeth my sister so?

MERCY. Alas! who can but lament, that shall but rightly consider what a state and condition my poor relations are in that yet remain in our sinful town—and that which makes my grief the more heavy is because they have no instructor, nor any to tell them what is to come.

CHRISTIANA. Compassion becometh pilgrims; and thou mournest for thy friends as my good Christian did for me when he left me; but his Lord and ours did gather up his tears, and put them into his bottle; and now both thou and I and my sweet babes are reaping the fruit and benefit of them. I hope, Mercy, these tears of thine will not be lost; for the Truth hath said, that "They that sow in tears, shall reap in joy"—in singing. And "he that goeth forth and weepeth bearing precious seed, shall doubtless come again with rejoicing bringing his sheaves with him."

[Song: "Let the Most Blessed"]

Let the most Blessed be my guide,
    If't be his blessed will,
Unto his gate, into his fold,
    Up to his Holy Hill.

And let him never suffer me
  To swarve or turn aside
From his free grace and holy ways,
  Whate'er shall me betide.

And let him gather them of mine,
  That I have left behind;
Lord, make them pray they may be thine,
  With all their heart and mind.

Exeunt, L, singing.

Re-enter Mistress Bats-eyes *and* Madam Timorous, R.

MISTRESS B.   And so, and so, they are gone! *(Nodding her head.)*

MADAM T.   Ay, go they would, whatever come on't; and methinks I know it by this; for that which was the great argument to persuade her to stay at home (to wit, the troubles she was like to meet with in the way) was one great argument with her to put her forward on her journey. For she told us, in so many words, "the bitter goes before the sweet, yea, and for as much as it so doth, it makes the sweet the sweeter."

MISTRESS B.   Oh, this blind and foolish woman! Would she but have taken warning by her husband's afflictions! for my part, I see, if he were here again he would rest him content in a whole skin, and never run so many hazards for nothing.

MADAM T. *(crossing).*   Away with such fantastical fools from the town; a good riddance, for my part, I say, of her. Should she stay where she dwells and retain this her mind, who could live quietly by her? for she would either be dumpish or unneighbourly, or talk of such matters as no wise body can abide; wherefore, for my part, I shall never be sorry for her departure.

MISTRESS B.   Let her go, and let better come in her room; 'twas never a good world since these whimsical fools dwelt in it.

Exeunt.
CURTAIN.

Scene II

Before the Wicket Gate.

Enter (L.) MATTHEW *and* SAMUEL, MERCY *and* JOSEPH, CHRISTIANA *and* JAMES.

MATTHEW.   We are well through the Slough of Despond at last.

JOSEPH.   I thought I should never get out, the mud was so thick.

JAMES.   Mother, I nearly lost my shoe in the mud; indeed, we had to look well to our steps.

SAMUEL.   And then only made shift to get staggeringly through.

MERCY.   We had indeed to be wary.

Soft music from the end of "And the Glory of the Lord"—piano only.

CHRISTIANA.   I had like to 'a' been in, and that not once nor twice, but hark! *(They listen.)*

KEEPER OF THE GATE *(outside).*   Blessed is she that believeth, for there shall be a performance of those things which were told her from the Lord.

Music ends here with last four bars.

MERCY *(to* Christiana).   Had I as good ground to hope for a loving reception at the wicket-gate as you, I think no Slough of Despond would discourage me.

CHRISTIANA.   Well, you know your sore, and I know mine; and good friend, we shall all have enough evil before we come at our journey's end. But how must we manage our calling at this wicket-gate?

MERCY.   You see what is writ over the doorway? "Knock, and it shall be opened."

MATTHEW.   You are our mother; knock thereat for us.

CHRISTIANA.   I fear to venture into his presence. Mercy, knock thou for us.

MERCY.   I! who am not invited as you were. I have no credentials: you had a letter from the King. *I* am full of fear.

CHRISTIANA *(reading her parchment).*   "Ask, and it shall be given you. Seek, and ye shall find. Knock, and it shall be opened." His own

266

words! yes, I will. *(Goes up to the gate—knocks.)* No answer! who am I to knock at this gate? *(She knocks—pause.)* No one opens.

JAMES.   Mother, knock once more.

CHRISTIANA.   Yes, child. *(She knocks again.)*

MATTHEW.   I think I hear a dog come barking upon us.

SAMUEL.   Yea, indeed! Mother, look there! it is a large mastiff. How he shows his teeth.

JOSEPH *(running up to* Christiana).   Pray, pray, let us go back! I am so frightened. 'Tis the largest dog I ever set eyes on.

JAMES.   Let us go back, mother.

CHRISTIANA.   Nay, what will the King feel, if he see us turn our backs on him, having once knocked? We must not faint at sound of alien dogs.

MERCY.   Knock then again, Christiana. I will stand by thee.

MATTHEW.   I will brave and hold the dog, mother, if thou wilt knock for us.

SAMUEL.   Oh, knock, knock, mother! The keeper of the gate will espy us, and think us cowards. We will not fear what man or dogs can do unto us.

MATTHEW.   I will stand by thee, sweet mother. Knock, and that vehemently.

Christiana *knocks loud and strong.*

KEEPER *(without).*   Who is there? *(Opens the gate.)*

CHRISTIANA.   Christiana!

KEEPER.   Is she alone?

MATTHEW.   Matthew, her son, is here too.

KEEPER.   And any other one?

JAMES.   Also her son James.

KEEPER.   And be there no other?

SAMUEL.   Here I am, my lord, my name is Samuel.

KEEPER.   Hath not Christiana four sons?

JOSEPH.   The fourth is little Joseph. I am here with mother. We want to come in and journey on our father Christian's road.

Keeper *leaves the wicket-gate and comes down to* Christiana—*pats*
Joseph *on the head.*

CHRISTIANA *(bowing low).* Let not our Lord be offended with his handmaidens, for that we have knocked at his princely gate.

KEEPER. Whence come ye? and what is that you would have?

CHRISTIANA. We are come from whence Christian did come, and upon the same errand as he—to wit, to be, if it shall please you, graciously admitted by this gate into the way that leads to the Celestial City. And I answer, my lord, in the next place, that I am Christiana, once the wife of Christian, that now is gotten above.

KEEPER. What! is she now become a pilgrim, that but a while ago abhorred that life?

CHRISTIANA. Yes; and so are these my sweet babes also.

KEEPER *(taking her hand).* Peace be unto thee. Come in, then. *(Lets her in with* Joseph.*)* For he says "Suffer the little children to come unto me, and forbid them not." *(Places his hands on the children's heads. Lets them in. To trumpeter above.)* Entertain Christiana with shouting, and sound of trumpets for joy. *(Goes in and shuts the gate.)*

> Music *(a few bars from the "Hallelujah Chorus").* Christiana, her babes, *and* Keeper *behind the paling on the left of the gate.* Mercy, *in agitation, outside, on the right.*

CHRISTIANA. My lord, I have a companion of mine that stands yet without, that is come hither upon the same account as myself; one that is much dejected in her mind, for that she comes, as she thinks, without sending for, (Mercy *knocks)* whereas I was sent to by my husband's King to come.

> Mercy *knocks again so loud that she makes* Christiana *to start.*

KEEPER. Who is there?

CHRISTIANA. It is my friend—her name is Mercy.

> Keeper *opens the gate.* Mercy *falls down in a swoon.*

KEEPER. Damsel, in the name of the King, I bid thee rise up. He bids me admit you. "To him that knocketh it shall be opened."

MERCY. Oh, sir, I am faint; there is scarce life left in me.

KEEPER. There was one once said, "When my soul fainted within me, I remembered the Lord; and my prayer came in unto thee—into thine holy temple." Fear not, but stand upon thy feet, and tell me wherefore thou art come.

MERCY *(kneeling).* I am come for that unto which I was never invited, as my friend Christiana was. Hers was from the King, and mine was but from her. Wherefore, I fear I presume.

KEEPER. Did she desire thee to come with her to this place?

MERCY. Yes; and, as my lord sees, I am come. And if there is any grace or forgiveness of sins to spare, I beseech that I, thy poor handmaid, may be partaker thereof.

KEEPER *(to those inside).* Fetch a bundle of myrrh and give it to Mercy to smell on, thereby to stay her fainting. (Matthew *bringeth a bunch of herbs.* Keeper *gives it to* Mercy. *He crosseth his arms, looks up.)* He has said, "I pray for all them that believe on me by what means soever they come unto me."

MERCY *(reviving).* We are sorry for our sins.

ALL. We beg of our Lord his pardon.

KEEPER. He sends you his forgiveness, in sign of which receive ye this kiss. *(He kisseth her on the forehead.* Mercy *rises from her knees, and he leadeth her gently in behind the paling.* Keeper *stands between* Christiana *and* Mercy.) And now remain together awhile until I send a manservant of the King's to conduct you on your way. Go now into our Lord's summer parlour; and there while you wait, you shall be greatly gladded; for you shall there be shown by what deed you were saved, and that sight you shall have again and again, as you travel on, to your great comfort.

MERCY. Righteous is my lord when I plead with him, yet let me talk with him of his judgments. Wherefore does he keep so cruel a dog in his yard at the sight of which such women and children as we are ready to fly from thy gates for fear?

KEEPER. That dog has another owner. He has frighted many an honest pilgrim from worse to better by the great voice of his roarings. But what, my purchased one, I trow, hadst thou known never so little beforehand, thou wouldst not have been afraid of a dog?

[Song: "Blest be the Day"]

Blest be the day that I began
A pilgrim for to be;

And blessed also be that man
    That thereto moved me.

'Tis true, 'twas long ere I began
    To seek to live for ever;
But now I run fast as I can,
    'Tis better late than never.

Our tears to joy, our fears to faith,
    Are turned, as we see;
Thus our beginning (as one saith)
    Shows what our end will be.

CURTAIN.

Scene III

At the door of the House Beautiful.

PIETY. *(Knocking heard.)* Who is there?

GREATHEART *(outside).*   It is I. *(He enters.)* Ah, Piety.

PIETY.   Welcome, Master Greatheart. I well knew that voice! But what brings you here so late to-night? The sun is set.

GREATHEART.   I have brought some pilgrims hither where by my Lord's commandment they must lodge. I had been here some time ago, had I not been opposed by the giant that did use to back the lions, but after a tedious combat with him, I have cut him off, and have brought the pilgrims hither in safety.

PIETY.   Whence come they?

GREATHEART.   They are Christiana's company; besides them I have brought two others of weaker faith, one Master Feeblemind and his kinswoman Mistress Muchafraid.

PIETY.   Bid them welcome in.

GREATHEART.   Here is Mistress Muchafraid, poor woman, and Master Feeblemind.

Enter Muchafraid *and* Feeblemind.

PIETY. Come in, good friends; be not afraid. We will receive you and rest you.

FEEBLEMIND. Master Greatheart has been our deliverer from the caves of Giant Slaygood.

PIETY. You are welcome here. Our Lord to whom we go hath for the feeble as well as for the strong; but will you not tell me something of your history?

MUCHAFRAID. I will, but may I first go in? My legs are weary; I can scarce stand.

PIETY. Go in then, good woman. You will find a place preparing for you.

MUCHAFRAID. The King give you his blessing.

Exit Mistress Muchafraid.

PIETY. Pray, Master Feeblemind, how comes it that you are a pilgrim?

FEEBLEMIND. I am a sickly man, as you see, and because Death did usually once a day knock at my door, I thought I would never be well at home, so I took myself to a pilgrim's life.

GREATHEART. He is, as you see, a man of scarce any strength of body.

FEEBLEMIND. Nor yet of mind. But now I will, if I can but crawl, spend my life in the pilgrim's way.

PIETY. And when you came to the gate at the head of the way, did not the Lord receive thee?

FEEBLEMIND. Ay, that he did! and entertained me freely; neither objected he against my feeble looks. And when I came to the Hill Difficulty, it was judged too hard for me, so I was carried up by one of his servants.

PIETY. Was it not Master Greatheart who carried you?

FEEBLEMIND. Verily it was he!

PIETY. And have you not met with others who have proved themselves friends by the way?

FEEBLEMIND. Verily, I have found much relief of many pilgrims, though none were willing to go so softly as I am forced to go; yet still as they came on they gave me good cheer.

GREATHEART. Was it not in Fearing Lane that Giant Slaygood took you and dragged you to his prison house?

Piety *and* Feeblemind *cross.*

FEEBLEMIND.   It was in that very lane. But I conceited he should not kill me, since I went not willingly into his den. I believed all the while I should come out again.

PIETY.   I am glad that is so, for I have heard that not any pilgrim is taken captive by violent hands, if he keep heart-whole towards his master.

FEEBLEMIND.   Yea, mistress, cast down I was, but not destroyed. Robbed I looked to be, and robbed to be sure I am; but I have escaped with my life; for the which I thank my King as author, and you, Master Greatheart, as the means.

GREATHEART.   To them that have no might he increaseth strength.

FEEBLEMIND.   It is so. Other brunts I also look for—but on this I have resolved: to wit, to *run* when I can, to *go* when I cannot run, and to *creep* when I cannot go.

GREATHEART.   Our Lord is of very tender compassion, especially to them that are afraid.

PIETY.   He carries it wonderful lovingly to the weaker ones of us.

FEEBLEMIND.   As to the main, I thank him who loves me, and that gave himself for me, I am fixed. My way is before me; my mind is beyond the river that has no bridge, though I am as you see but of a feeble mind.

PIETY.   Will you go in now and a good night to you. I shall meet you again. (*Exit* Feeblemind.) And, Master Greatheart, will you not go in and stay till morning?

GREATHEART.   No, I will return to my Lord to-night, but I must first bring in Christiana, her companion Mercy, and her four boys. They, too, are travel worn.

Enter Christiana, *her four boys from behind*
half advancing.

CHRISTIANA.   Oh, sir, I know not how to be willing you should leave us in our pilgrimage. You have been so faithful and so loving to us. You a have fought so stoutly for us, you have been so hearty in counselling of us, that I shall never forget your favour towards us. (*Enter* Mercy.)

MERCY.   Oh, that we might have thy company to our journey's end! How can such poor women as we hold out in a way so full of troubles as this way is, without a friend and defender?

SAMUEL. Pray sir, be persuaded to go with us, because we are so weak, and the way is so dangerous as it is.

GREATHEART. I am at my Lord's commandment. If he shall allot me to be your guide quite through, I will willingly wait upon you; but here you failed at first; for when he bid me come thus far with you, then you should have begged me of him to have gone quite through with you, and he would have granted your request. However, at present, I must withdraw; and so, good Christiana, Mercy and my brave boys, adieu! *Exit.*

PIETY *(to* Christiana). And whence comest thou, good woman, and who are thy kinsfolk?

CHRISTIANA. I am a widow woman. I come from the City of Destruction. My husband's name was Christian, the pilgrim.

PIETY. How! Was he your husband?

CHRISTIANA. Yes, and these are his children, and this *(taking* Mercy *by the hand)* is one of my townswomen, Mercy by name.

PIETY. I will tell it within that Christiana and her children are come on pilgrimage. *(Turning to go in.)* Ah, what a noise for gladness will there be when I do but drop that word out of my mouth.

Joyful music. Exit Piety. *Pilgrims linger at left side. Enter* Prudence *with open hands.* Piety *and* Charity *right upper.*

PRUDENCE. Come in, Christiana, come in, thou wife of that good man, come in thou blessed woman! Come in with all that are with thee.

All advance. Charity *receives them all with a kiss.*

CHARITY. Welcome, ye vessels of the grace of God. Welcome to us your friends.

PIETY. We welcome you in the name of our King, who is such a lover of poor pilgrims that the like is not to be found from the East to the West. Come and sit down.

CHARITY. You must be an-hungered; come and eat. You are sadly worn.

PRUDENCE. And as it is somewhat late, you shall go soon to rest, but first refresh yourselves with a morsel of meat.

PIETY.   Let us give thanks.

For why? The Lord our God is good,
   His mercy is forever sure,
His truth at all times firmly stood
   And shall from age to age endure.

They sing ["Table Song"].

Gracious Father, O Lord, hear us when we call on thy name.
Accept our gratitude for favours now bestowed.
Bounteous Father, O Lord hear us.

CHARITY.   Eat now my children. *(Giving them food.)*

PRUDENCE.   And you Christiana, eat. You and Mercy have much before you. So take to yourselves what the Lord giveth.

CURTAIN.

Scene IV

In the House Beautiful. CHARITY, PRUDENCE, *and* PIETY.

CHARITY.   Hast thou seen our new guests this morning, Prudence?

PRUDENCE.   Yea, Charity, I saw them as they went through the gardens after their bath.

PIETY.   The King's messenger sent to me, saying, "Wash them, make them clean from the soil they have gathered in travelling."

CHARITY.   And they came out of the bath not only sweet and clean, but also much enlivened and strengthened in their joints.

PRUDENCE.   So when they came in again they looked fairer a deal than when they went out to the washing; and as they passed our Lord's messenger he looked on them and said "Fair as the moon." Then he sent for white raiment, and commanded them to put it on.

CHARITY.   Yea, it was fine linen, white and clean. And did you hear them when they were thus adorned? They seemed to be a terror one to another.

PIETY. Verily, they could not see that glory each one had in herself, for the glory they could see in each other.

PRUDENCE. For, "you are fairer than I am," said one, and "you are more comely than I am," said another.

PIETY. Also the little children stood amazed to see into what fashion they were brought.

PRUDENCE. Verily they were a weary company when they came in yesternight. But they tell me that Master Greatheart had gave them each some pomegranate to eat and a piece of an honeycombe, as he said, a little to sweeten their mouths as they rested their legs by the way: to Christiana also he gave a little bottle of spirits.

PIETY. She will need them the journey through, for without strength from the King himself, they cannot walk that road.

CHARITY. And Mercy, hath she eaten well too, and is she rested?

PIETY. Yea, Charity, her youth is renewed like the eagle's. She will now run and not be weary, she will walk and not faint.

PRUDENCE. Her faintness came only from fear that her King had not invited her. She is full of joy now that he has bidden her come in.

Enter Christiana *with* Samuel *and* Joseph.

CHARITY. How is it that Master Greatheart has left them?

PRUDENCE. He had orders from the King to let them travel on alone for a while. They were at the outset so taken with their present blessings, that dangers to come were forgotten by them.

CHRISTIANA. We wondered since our Lord knew it was to our profit to have a conductor that he sent him not with us all the way.

PIETY. He thinketh it not always necessary to grant things not asked for, lest by so doing they become of little esteem.

PRUDENCE. He will be enquired of by them to do it for them, and it is a poor thing that is not worth the asking for.

CHRISTIANA. Shall we then go back to our Lord, confess our folly, and ask for Master Greatheart again?

PRUDENCE. To go back again you need not. Your confession of your folly is enough. At every of our Lord's lodgings that you shall come to, you shall find no want at all. *(Enter* Mercy *with* Matthew *and* James. *Exit* Piety.) Come, my pretty boys, what think you now of going on pilgrimage?

JAMES.   Lady, I was almost beat out of heart agoing up the Hill Difficulty, but good Master Greatheart did lend me a helping hand at my need.

MATTHEW.   Yea, my mother too began to pant, but I did call to her mind what she herself had taught me, namely, that the way to Heaven is as a ladder, and the way to Hell is down a hill.

CHRISTIANA.   And my boys, I'm glad to say, had rather go up the ladder to Life, than down the hill to Death.

MERCY.   But the proverb is, To go down the hill is easy.

SAMUEL.   The day is coming in my opinion when going down the hill will be the hardest of all.

CHARITY.   You spoke of dangers—tell us what evil did attend you?

CHRISTIANA.   We sat in the King's arbour, a lovely resting place indeed, where we refreshed ourselves and sang praises to the King; but after we had gotten on our road again, my bottle of wine sent me from the Lord himself was gone. So Mercy, who delights in making our way the way of peace, went back with my little boy for it.

MERCY *(sits)*.   And Master Greatheart told us it was in that same place that Christian, her husband, lost his roll. So I fear 'tis a losing place.

PRUDENCE.   I wonder what is the cause of this.

MATTHEW.   Our guide said the cause was sleep or forgetfulness.

CHRISTIANA.   He said that some sleep when they should keep awake.

MATTHEW.   And that this is the very cause why some pilgrims, in some things, come off losers.

CHARITY.   Yea, under the greatest enjoyments let us watch and remember what we have already received.

MERCY.   For want of doing so, Greatheart said, ofttimes the pilgrims' rejoicing ends in tears and their sunshine in a cloud.

CHARITY *(to the boys)*.   And how did you fare in going through the country of the lions?

Samuel *and* Joseph *go up to* Charity—

James *to* Prudence.

MATTHEW.   Though we heard them roar, we went along bravely till we came within sight of them.

JAMES. But Master Greatheart was a strong man, so he was not afraid of a lion.

JOSEPH. But we were all so little—we were all afraid of them, and we cringed behind.

JAMES. Yes, we were very much afraid of the lions—they made so much roar. So we stopped and stayed behind.

MERCY. At which our guide smiled and said, "How now, my boys, do you love to go before when no danger doth approach, and to come behind as soon as the lions appear?"

PRUDENCE. But, Matthew, did you not have to encounter Giant Grim?

MATTHEW. Yes, Mistress Prudence, when Master Greatheart drew his sword with intent to make a way for us in spite of the lions, then up comes old Grim, who said he was going to back the lions.

JAMES. He said to Master Greatheart, "Why do you come here?"

SAMUEL. And then Master Greatheart told him that we had all come on pilgrimage, and he said to the giant, "This is the way they must go, and go it they shall, in spite of thee and thy lions."

JOSEPH. But old Grim roared out, "This is not your way, neither shall the pilgrims go therein. I am come forth to withstand them, and to that end I will back the lions."

MATTHEW. And then he fell to swearing. He swore by the lions that we should not have passage there, and he bade us turn aside. But then Master Greatheart made his first approach to Grim, and laid so heavily at him with his sword that he was forced to retreat.

JAMES. But have you forgot what the wicked Grim said then? He roared out, "Will you slay me on my own ground?"

CHARITY. Wicked Grim! It was the King's highway that you were in.

MATTHEW. So Master Greatheart told him. And, said he, "These women and children, though weak, shall hold on their way in spite of thee and thy lions"; and with that he gave him again a downright blow, and brought him on his knees. With this blow also he broke his helmet, and with the next he cut off an arm.

JOSEPH. And the giant roared so hideously that he frightened my mother and Mercy. And yet we were all glad to see him sprawling upon the ground.

CHARITY. And what did the lions then?

SAMUEL.   Oh, they were chained! And so of themselves they could do nothing.

MATTHEW.   Wherefore when old Grim, that intended to back them, was dead, Master Greatheart said to us, "Come now and follow me, and no hurt shall happen to you from these chained lions."

MERCY.   So we went on and passed them; but trembling much—they look so fierce.

JOSEPH.   I was very frightened and—

JAMES.   And we all felt as if we should die, but we got by without further hurt.

CHRISTIANA.   Oh, but we were right sorry to lose Greatheart. *(Sighs.)*

MERCY.   Oh that we might have had his company all the road. How can we hold out without a friend and defender?

CHARITY.   Sisters, if you will be persuaded to stay here awhile, you shall have what the house will afford.

PIETY.   Yea, and that with a very good will.

CHRISTIANA.   We thank you for your hospitality and willingly accept your proffer: and Prudence, will you catechize my boys?

PRUDENCE.   I have already asked them many questions, and I find, Christiana, that you have trained them well. Boys, you must still hearken to your mother, for she can teach you more. You must also observe diligently, and that with carefulness, what the heavens and the earth do teach you. But especially be much in the meditation of that book that was the cause of your father becoming a pilgrim. I, for my part, my children, will teach you what I am able while you are here, and shall be glad if you will ask me questions that tend to a godly edifying.

Exeunt all but Christiana *and* Mercy. *They embrace.*

MERCY.   I am the willinger to stay awhile here to grow better acquainted with these maids. Methinks Prudence, Piety, and Charity have very comely and sober countenances.

CHRISTIANA.   We shall see what they will do, and for lodging I think we have spent already one of the best nights that ever we had in our lives. But what was the matter that you did laugh in your sleep? I suppose you was in a dream.

MERCY. So I was, and a sweet dream it was, but are you sure I laughed?

CHRISTIANA. Yes, you laughed heartily; but prithee, Mercy, tell me thy dream.

MERCY. It was such a dream as I cannot tell thee all. I was a-dreamed that I sat all alone in a solitary place, and was bemoaning the hardness of my heart; and as I bemoaned me I looked up and saw a shining one with wings and a wonderful innocent smile on his face coming towards me saying, "Mercy, what aileth thee?" Now when he had heard me make my complaint he said, "Peace be to thee." He also wiped mine eyes with his handkerchief and clad me in silver and gold. Then he took me by the hand and said, "Mercy, come after me." This, and much more I cannot tell thee of; so I woke from my dream. But did I laugh?

CHRISTIANA. Laugh! Ay and well you might to see yourself so well. For you must give me leave to tell you that I believe it was a good dream. "God speaketh once, yea, twice, yet man perceiveth it not. In a dream, in a vision of the night, when deep sleep falleth upon men, and slumberings upon the bed." We need not, when a-bed, lie awake to talk with God. He can visit us while we sleep, and cause us then to hear his voice.

MERCY. Well, I am glad of my dream; for I hope ere long to see it fulfilled, to the making of me laugh again.

CHRISTIANA. I think it is now high time that we should join our friends to know what we must do.

CURTAIN.

Scene V

The same. A week later. CHRISTIANA, MERCY, *and* MR. BRISK.

MR. BRISK. Christiana, I have been out for a run with thy boys round the King's garden.

CHRISTIANA. I thank you for noticing them, Mr. Brisk.

MR. BRISK. I have been chiding them also for that they did eat of the green plums that had fallen from the trees; and already Matthew has had a twinge of the gripes.

CHRISTIANA. They must suffer if they do that they are bidden not to do; but if they are ill, where shall I find a physician? You know all in these parts, Mr. Brisk—can you tell me?

MR. BRISK. There is one, Dr. Skill, whom I will send as I go by his house; or Mercy perchance will step out with me and see where he dwells. (*Exit* Christiana.)

MERCY. Mr. Brisk, I have work here to do which will not allow of my leaving the house. In a case of necessity the maid Prudence would accompany me.

MR. BRISK. How nimble your fingers are! They fly like the wind.

MERCY. I hope they are not as fitful as the wind. Were I to flit about as you would always have me be doing, Mr. Brisk, my works would never be perfected.

MR. BRISK. In those words you imply a reproof. I take it from thee, fair Mercy, but I would have you know I would do so from no other.

MERCY. The heart knoweth its own weakness, and if need there be for reproof, none so well as itself can apply a word offered in season. But I did not presume to counsel thee.

MR. BRISK. Mercy, I confess when I am near thee that my too great desire to be on the stir has a very wholesome check. You are not like those maidens who are lovers of and seekers after pleasure.

MERCY. It is only that I find my pleasure in more lasting enjoyments. I am as desirous of happiness as they, but I dare not seek it first. In so doing it always flies ahead of my desires.

MR. BRISK. You mean, you seek duty first.

MERCY. I wish I could say I always do; but duty wears so oft the garb of pleasure, that I fear to err sometimes in an excess of its performance.

MR. BRISK. Oh! I do not so. I thank Heaven I am not as other men. I am religious, I fast twice a week, I pay tithes of all I possess and am fervent in business.

MERCY. But withal there may be one thing wanting.

MR. BRISK. If there be you will not hear of it from my neighbours. All the world speaks well of me.

MERCY. Was there not One who said, "Woe unto you when all men shall speak well of you."

MR. BRISK. Mercy, you seem to love judgment rather than mercy.

MERCY.   "My song shall be of mercy and of judgment." The one cannot stand without the other.

MR. BRISK.   Verily! Then keep thou to mercy and I will personate judgment. So, hand in hand *(taking her hand)* we will as pilgrims walk on together man and wife.

MERCY.   Not so quickly, sir. I am not sure enough of my own discernment. Your courtesy and good opinion of me as a woman, are flattering and kindly, but I must speak with our friends on this matter ere I answer thee. I am but young and need assistance from my elders, Piety and Prudence.

MR. BRISK.   Christiana and Charity always look on me with favour.

MERCY.   Perchance it may be so, but I am not advised as yet of their opinion. Prithee, gentle sir, away for a while. I am timid and must get help from my King. He promised it when he let me in at the wicket-gate.

MR. BRISK.   I will. I will go and apprize Dr. Skill of Christiana's need of him.

MERCY.   Go not to him until she ask thee.

MR. BRISK.   Oh, but I well know there is no time to lose. I take time by the forelock! *(Enter* Piety *and* Prudence. *To* Prudence.) I have been watching your guest at her work. How deftly she plies her needle! A pretty income she must make with such skill in her handicraft! (Mercy *moves away.)* I find her very attractive. If she speak to thee of me stand my friend.

PRUDENCE.   Oh, is't so, Mr. Brisk? She must also, and before me, consult Piety.

Enter Charity *and* Christiana.

MR. BRISK.   But here is my friend Charity. *(To* Mercy.) Remember, Mercy, the greatest of these is Charity. *(Kneels and kisses her hand. Exit.)*

PRUDENCE.   What meaneth this, Mercy?

MERCY.   Mr. Brisk has more than once addressed me in terms of admiration, and being gentle in manner and fair to look upon, my inclination was at first to listen to him.

PIETY.   But has he offered you his love?

MERCY.   He said that we two would do well to go on pilgrimage together; that his wisdom and judgment would join well with my gentleness. Something of this kind, I think, he said.

PIETY.   Seek ye first the kingdom of God and his righteousness.

MERCY.   Yea, Piety, and I am not clear in my mind that that kingdom is the first object of his search; and being very ignorant, I come to you for information.

CHARITY.   Do you love him, child?

MERCY.   My heart yearns towards him with compassion, but if he be a traitor to my King, I could not bear him company.

PRUDENCE.   To be a true helpmate to a man you should have more than compassion in your heart for him. You should so reverence him as a guide to your steps.

CHARITY.   If you love not the same things, your hearts will be divided; and where division is there is no strength. Without oneness of purpose, love will not endure.

PRUDENCE.   He is given to speech, but his works are no true handmaids to his words. He is most zealous for religion when Religion has on her silver slippers. He loves then to walk abroad with her, if the sun shine and the people applaud her. But he strives not against wind and tide.

MERCY.   He says he fasts twice a week: and old Master Talkative, his kinsman, says he makes long prayers. Is that a sign of religion in the heart?

CHARITY.   Judge not, that ye be not judged; yet I fear me his fellowship with Master Talkative shows that Mercy would do well to set limits to her intimacy with Mr. Brisk.

CHRISTIANA.   Is that the same Talkative Christian my husband did meet with?

PIETY.   The same. He is the son of one Saywell, of Prating Row, but notwithstanding his fine tongue, he is but a sorry fellow.

MERCY.   I saw him but once. He seemed to me a very pretty man.

CHARITY.   That is to them that have not a thorough acquaintance with him, for he is best abroad: near home he is ugly enough.

PRUDENCE.   You see Charity begins at home. But your saying that he is a pretty man brings to my mind what I have observed in the work of some painters whose pictures show best at a distance, but very near more unpleasing. Alas! the common people say of him, "A saint abroad, a churl at home."

CHARITY. Verily—Prudence—

PIETY. His poor family find it so. He is such a railer at and so unreasonable with his servants that they neither know how to do for nor to speak to him.

PRUDENCE. We must beware of false prophets. Though this Master Talkative speaks much of his experience and his clearness of doctrine, yet I must tell you his house is as empty of religion as the white of an egg is of savour!

Exeunt Piety *and* Charity.

MERCY. I am bound to believe you because, like Christians, you make your reports of men. You speak of these things not of ill will, but because it is even as you say. But Mr. Brisk is not like this, I hope—I will prove him when he comes again.

PRUDENCE. That is well: we have advice to try the spirits.

Enter Piety.

PIETY. Christiana, will you go to Dr. Skill; he has come with Mr. Brisk to see your boys, believing them to be terrible ill, and lo! they are at play, hearty and well.

MERCY. I did beg of him not to weary this good doctor by coming. I see Mr. Brisk is officious.

CHRISTIANA. He meant it kindly, Mercy. I will go and speak with him.

Exeunt Christiana *and* Piety (L.).

PRUDENCE *(rises, seats herself near* Mercy). Mercy, I think thee had better pen a letter to Mr. Brisk.

MERCY. I am but a poor scribe; I would rather speak with him. Prudence, would you think it well to go for me to him, and ask him to stop here awhile?

PRUDENCE. That I will do for thee; and forget not, the wisdom of the serpent has the same source as the harmlessness of the dove. The Lord direct thee, Mercy.

> Prudence *kisseth* Mercy *and exit.* Mercy *separates her work, ties robes and break up together in a bundle. Enter* Mr. Brisk.

MR. BRISK. I could not stop long away from this chamber; there is something here I get nowhere else. What! always at it! Such industry! Yet I would see your eyes a little oftener, if I might. I am jealous of that work you gaze on. There is a desire in women to go neat and fine, and in truth it is a comely thing to see such robes as these. But need you them all at once?

MERCY. Not for myself do I make them. Thought you that these were all for *my* poor body when many go naked and cold?

MR. BRISK. Thou art wise to sell such rare garments. Why, prithee, what dost earn in a day?

MERCY. *(Trembles and blushes. Aside.)* I do not sell my work.

MR. BRISK. What is't, sweetheart, that troubles thee?

MERCY. I cannot tell thee, but talk not that way to me.

MR. BRISK. May I not do something for thee? I would serve thee.

MERCY. Sir, you can if you will, serve me in one thing.

MR. BRISK. In a thousand—only command me.

MERCY. Carry this bundle for me to a house I will tell thee of in the next street out of the city.

MR. BRISK *(taking bundle in left hand).* I am glad thou art so frugal as to sell thy goods. I will give it to my servant to carry withal. He will bear the money back to you in safety. He is honest as the day.

MERCY. Mr. Brisk, I do not sell my work. My poor widow to whom this goes has no money at all—she is bedridden and has a sick daughter. This raiment is for them to wear. Also here is a bed cover for her. *(Hangs patchwork quilt over his extended arm holding the bundle.)*

MR. BRISK. And you would have me walk abroad with this pack on my arm? and meet my gay friends, my Lady this and my Lord t'other one, with this lump o' bread coming forth from the bundle! I trow not indeed! Art serious, Mercy?

MERCY.   Yea, verily, to visit the fatherless and the widow in their affliction and to keep himself unspotted from the world is what I would like best to see my husband—had I one—a-doing.

MR. BRISK.   The world would laugh at me in such a case. And I can see how with all your pretty face and manners you are a-fooling of me.

MERCY.   Nay. I thought I but put upon thee a great honour, in sending thee on such a message from the King; for, inasmuch as we do it unto the least of these his brethren, we do it unto him.

MR. BRISK.   If these be your conditions for serving you, I would have you know that it is not befitting a gentleman of my breeding to carry a bundle in the king's highway. I see thou wast not bred at court. I have wasted here my morning. A fair day to you. Commend me to the sisters and Christiana.

Exit Mr. Brisk.

Enter Prudence *and* Piety.

PRUDENCE.   And is he gone?

MERCY.   Yea. I will look no more on him, for I purpose never to have a clog to my soul.

PIETY.   His courage was soon cooled when he found your conditions were to work for the poor and wretched.

Enter Christiana.

CHRISTIANA.   Mr. Brisk tells me at the door, that Mercy is a pretty lass, but troubled with ill conditions.

PRUDENCE.   Did I not tell thee that Mr. Brisk would soon forsake thee? Yea, he will raise up an ill report of thee, for, notwithstanding his pretence to religion and his seeming love to Mercy, yet Mercy and he are of tempers so different that they never could have come together.

Mercy *weeps on* Prudence *shoulder*.

CURTAIN.

Scene VI

The Valley of Humiliation.

PRUDENCE, PIETY, MERCY, CHRISTIANA, *and her* SONS.

PIETY.   We are sent to the head of this Valley of Humiliation with you. Here we shall meet again with our friend Master Greatheart. He will be your guide and conductor.

PRUDENCE.   Here he is.

Enter Greatheart. *All bow low*.

GREATHEART.   Christiana, gladly I greet you all again. *(Takes their hands.)*

CHRISTIANA.   Not half so glad as we.

MERCY.   Thou hast come for our help.

GREATHEART.   Yea, the Lord of Hosts is with us.

PRUDENCE.   This is the place, Christiana, where your husband met with Apollyon, and where they had that terrible fight that they had.

PIETY.   But as you have Master Greatheart with you, we hope you will fare the better.

PRUDENCE.   For his God is your God for ever and ever. He will be your guide even unto death. Farewell.

PIETY.   Fare ye well.

PILGRIMS.   Fare ye well. *(They bow.)*

Exeunt Prudence *and* Piety.

GREATHEART.   'Tis true. We are now on the very spot of ground on which Christian stood and up there came Apollyon against him. And look! did I not tell you? here is some of your husband's blood on these stones to this day! Behold also how here, and there, are yet to be seen upon the place some of the shivers of Apollyon's broken darts. See also how they did beat the ground with their feet as they fought, to make good their places against each other: how also, with their by-blows, they did split the very stones in pieces.

MATTHEW.   How was it my father did have such a sore combat with Apollyon? he was so good a man.

GREATHEART.   That fray was the fruit of those slips that he got in going down the hill, for they that get slips there must look for combats here: and hence it is that this place has got so hard a name, for the common people when they hear that some frightful thing has befallen such an one in such a place, are of opinion that that place is haunted with some foul fiend or evil spirit, when, alas! it is for the fruit of their doing, that such things do befall them there.

MERCY.   Yea, Master Greatheart, I have heard that this Valley of Humiliation is of itself as fruitful as any the crow flies over.

CHRISTIANA.   And I am persuaded when we meet Christian he will give us an account of why he was so hardly beset in this place. Poor man! well, he is at rest and he also had a brave victory over this enemy. Let Him grant that dwelleth above, that we fare no worse when we come to be tried than he.

GREATHEART.   I know this Valley of Humiliation well. It is the best and most fruitful piece of ground in all these parts. It is fat ground, and, as you see, consisteth much in meadows. And if a man was to come here in the summer time, and if he knew not anything before thereof, he might see that which would be delightful to him.

MATTHEW.   Behold how green this valley is! also, how beautiful with lilies! When I was brought low he helped me.

Christiana crosses.

CHRISTIANA.   I have heard of many labouring men, ay, and many labouring women, that have gotten goodly estates in this Valley of Humiliation.

MERCY.   In that, God resisteth the proud and giveth grace to the humble; for indeed it is a very fruitful soil, and doth bring forth by handfuls.

CHRISTIANA.   Some also have wished that the next way to their Father's house were here, that they might be troubled no more with either hills or mountains to go over; but the way is the way, and there's an end!

MERCY.   Christiana, the end is our Father's house.

Shepherd-Boy, *within, sings ["Shepherd's Boy's Song"].*

He that is down needs fear no fall,
    He that is low no pride;
He that is humble ever shall
    Have God to be his guide.

Enter Shepherd-Boy.

GREATHEART.   Hark to what the shepherd-boy saith.

SHEPHERD-BOY *(singing)*.

I am content with what I have,
    Little be it or much;
And Lord, contentment still I crave,
    Because thou savest such.
Fulness to such a burden is,
    That go on pilgrimage;
Here little and hereafter bliss
    Is best from age to age.

CHRISTIANA.   How sweet he sings.

MERCY.   His voice is full of content.

SHEPHERD-BOY.   My father's sheep are folded for the night.

GREATHEART.   Do you hear him?

MATTHEW.   Yes, And see how poorly he is clad!

GREATHEART.   And yet I will dare to say that boy lives a merrier life, and wears more of that herb you see in his bosom than many that are dressed in silk and velvet.

CHRISTIANA.   What is the name of that beautiful herb?

GREATHEART.   Ask him; he knows it full well.

CHRISTIANA.   Boy, what is that flower thou wearest in thy bosom?

SHEPHERD-BOY.   It is the heartsease; a bunch of it comes fresh from the King every morning to those who dwell in this valley. Wilt have a sprig, lady? *(Offers it to* Christiana *and* Mercy.)

MERCY.   We must not rob thee.

SHEPHERD-BOY.   It increaseth by the giving of it to others. *(Gives to all.)*

GREATHEART.   He speaks the truth. Our Lord had formerly a country house in this valley; did'st know him, boy?

SHEPHERD-BOY.   Right well. He loved much to be here. He loved also to walk these meadows, for he found the air was pleasant.

GREATHEART.   Here a man can be free from the noise and from the hurryings of life.

CHRISTIANA.   All states are full of noise and confusion; only the Valley of Humiliation is that empty and solitary place, it seemeth to me.

GREATHEART.   Here a man shall not be so let and hindered in his contemplation as in other places he is apt to be. In this still waste a man, losing all things else, may find himself face to face with God, and hear from him that which no man can utter again in words.

SHEPHERD-BOY.   In this valley nobody walks who does not love a pilgrim's life; and though Christian, as you may know, had the hard hap to meet here with Apollyon, and to enter with him into a brisk encounter, yet I must tell you that in former times men have met with angels here, and have found pearls here, and have also in this place found the words of life.

SAMUEL.   Is there any name to the spot where my father and Apollyon had their fight?

SHEPHERD-BOY.   Ay, indeed, there is; it is called Forgetful Green, and it is the most dangerous in all these parts.

GREATHEART.   Yea, for if at any time pilgrims meet with any brunt, it is when they forget what favours they have received, and how unworthy they are of them. But verily, Christian did here play the man, and did show himself as stout as Hercules could, had he been here, even he himself.

SHEPHERD-BOY.   And I must add, the Lord not only walked here in former days, but he meets his pilgrims here even now, by sending his Comforter to walk and to talk with those who love to trace here his grounds.

MERCY.   I think I am as well in this valley as I have been anywhere else in all our journey. The place, methinks, suits with my spirit. I love to be in such places, where there is no rattling of coaches nor rumbling with wheels.

CHRISTIANA. Methinks one may here, without molestation, be thinking what he is, whence he came, what he has done, and to what the King has called.

MERCY. Yes, here one may think, and break at heart, and melt in one's spirit. until one's eyes become as the rivers of the King.

MATTHEW. Oh, mother! Prudence told me that they that go wisely through this valley of Baca, make it a well, the rain also filleth the pools.

SAMUEL. This valley is that from whence the King will give to his own their vineyards; and they that go through it shall sing, as did our father, for all he met with Apollyon.

GREATHEART. 'Tis true. I have gone through this valley many a time, and never was better than when here. I have been conductor to several pilgrims, and they have confessed the same.

SHEPHERD-BOY. "To this man will I look," saith the King," even to him that is poor, and of a contrite spirit, and that trembleth at my word." *Exit.*

GREATHEART. But now we must move forward to the next valley, which is the Valley of the Shadow of Death, a place strangely haunted with evil things.

CHRISTIANA. Oh! this shadow makes me to quake. And Mercy, thou lookest pale with fear!

GREATHEART. Be of good comfort. Only look well to your feet, lest haply you be taken in some snare. And remember how the King gave his promise, "I will be with thee."

MATTHEW. Mother, his rod and his staff shall comfort you.

JAMES. And so we will fear no evil.

CHRISTIANA. Oh! but methinks, I see something yonder upon the road before us! A thing of a shape such as I have not seen! It comes with a great padding pace along!

JOSEPH. Mother! what is it?

CHRISTIANA. An ugly thing, child; an ugly thing.

MATTHEW. But, mother! what is it like?

CHRISTIANA. It is like I cannot tell what. And now! It is but a little way off!

SAMUEL. Where? Oh! where?

CHRISTIANA. It is nigh! *(Hides her head on Mercy's shoulder.)*

GREATHEART. Let them that are most afraid keep close to me. Let us meet it, and it will vanish. Fear not. Stand still, and see what an end will be put to this.

MERCY. Piety bid us resist the devil, and he would flee from us. So has it been now! for, Christiana, is it not gone?

CHRISTIANA *(looking up).* Yea? Of a truth!—Christian, poor man, went here all alone in the night; he had night almost quite through the way. Also these fiends were busy about him, as if they would have torn him in pieces. Many have spoken to me of this Shadow of Death, but none could tell me what it should mean. Verily, the heart knoweth its own bitterness, and a stranger intermeddleth not with its joy. To be here is a fearful thing.

GREATHEART. It is like doing business in great waters or like going down into the deep. This is like being in the heart of the sea, and like going down to the bottoms of the mountains. Now it seems as if the earth with its bars were about us for ever.

SAMUEL. Are we not yet at the end of this doleful place?

GREATHEART. We shall be out by and by. A light from above is our only light in this valley.

MERCY. Yea, let them that walk in darkness, and have no light, trust in the name of the Lord, and stay upon their God.

CHRISTIANA. He is the light of life.

GREATHEART. For my part, as I have told you already, I have gone through this valley and have been much harder put to it than now I am, and yet you see I am alive. I would not boast, for that I am not my own saviour, but I trust we shall have a good deliverance. Come, let us pray for light to Him that can lighten our darkness, and that can rebuke not only these, but all the Satans in hell.

MATTHEW. Master Greatheart, will you not draw your sword?

GREATHEART. In this valley, as Christian, your father, plainly learned, no weapon is of any avail, save the weapon called, "All Prayer."

Walks away, hands folded and lifted. All in like manner follow.

CURTAIN.

Scene VII

The Land of Beulah.

CHRISTIANA. MERCY.

CHRISTIANA.   Here we are come to the land of Beulah, where the sun shineth night and day.

MERCY.   We seem to need no sleep, and yet we all have as much refreshing as if we slept our sleep never so soundly.

Enter Matthew, *followed by the other boys.*

MATTHEW.   Mother, the whole country seems to be nothing but orchards and vineyards belonging to the King.

SAMUEL.   But there is a Town! Matthew, James, and I have been into it, and the bells are ringing, and the trumpets are sounding so melodiously!

JAMES.   And yet mother's and Mercy's heads would not ache with the noise.

MATTHEW.   Because they are all sounds and music, not noise.

JOSEPH.   No, not like the noise in Vanity Fair.

SAMUEL.   And all the people have such happy faces! As we came by, they cried out, "More pilgrims are come to town."

MATTHEW.   Some cried, "So many went over the water, and were let in at the Golden Gates to-day!"

CHRISTIANA. When we go over the water and enter the Golden Gates, then shall we finish our pilgrimage, and shall sit down to the marriage-supper of the Lamb.

Enter Greatheart.

JAMES.   Shall we see Christian, our father, there?

CHRISTIANA.   Indeed we shall. Good man! how joyful will he be when he shall see them that would not go with him, yet to enter after him into the gates of the Celestial City!

MERCY.   And our King will not stint his saints of gladness, I dare to say.

MATTHEW.   For my part, I see no reason why we should distrust our God any longer, since he has through all our journey, up the mountains and down the valleys, along the dark ways and into this light, given us such proofs of his love.

JAMES.   Master Greatheart, who is that comes here?

Enter Master Honest.

GREATHEART (advancing to Honest).   Friend, as we are so happily met, let me crave your name, and the name of the place you come from.

HONEST.   My name I cannot tell you—but I came from the town of Stupidity: it lieth about four degrees beyond the City of Destruction.

GREATHEART.   Oh! are you that countryman? Then I deem I have half a guess of you: your name is old Honesty—is it not?

HONEST.   Not *Honesty* in the abstract, but Honest is my name, and I wish that my nature may agree to what I am called. But, sir, how could you guess that I am such a man since I came from such a place?

GREATHEART.   I have heard of you before by my Master, for he knows all things that are done on the earth. But I have often wondered that any should come from your place, for your town is worse than the City of Destruction itself.

HONEST.   Yes; we lie more off from the sun, and so are more cold and senseless. But was a man in a mountain of ice, yet if the Sun of Righteousness will arise upon him, his frozen heart shall feel a thaw; and thus it hath been with me.

GREATHEART.   I believe it, father Honest! I believe it, for I know the thing is true.

CHRISTIANA *(to* Honest).   Are we far from the Delectable Mountains, sir?

HONEST.   They are on this side the river.

GREATHEART.   Only a day's journey from here.

CHRISTIANA.   It is on the banks of this river, at the foot of these mountains, I have heard, where the meadows are green, there are cotes and folds for the lambs of the Pilgrims' flocks.

MERCY.   Yes; I saw them as we passed by on the other side. There is a house built for the nourishing and bringing up of those lambs, the children of those that go on pilgrimage.

GREATHEART. There is one—a Man—who is entrusted with them—who can have compassion.

HONEST. 'Tis he that gathers these lambs with his arm, and carries them in his bosom.

MERCY. It is besides a very healthful neighbourhood. Here are delicate waters, pleasant meadows, and dainty flowers. Fine trees grow too beside the river, whose leaves, if taken inwardly, are good against all kinds of childish maladies.

CHRISTIANA. I will even commit my little ones to this Man, that by these waters they may be housed, harboured, succoured, and nourished, so that none of them may be lacking in time to come.

GREATHEART. Thou couldst not better. This Man, if any of them go astray or be lost, he will bring them again. He will also bind up that which is broken, and will strengthen them that are sick.

MERCY. I hear they will never be wanting for meat, drink, or clothing. They will be kept from thieves and robbers; for this Man, I hear tell, will die before one of those committed to his trust shall be lost.

CHRISTIANA. Here they shall be taught to walk in right paths, and that, you know, is a favour of no small account.

Enter Shepherd-Boy.

SHEPHERD-BOY. I will bear them thither for you; for all this is to be at the charge of your King: this house is an hospital for young children. Rest you here awhile with your friends—I will bear them to the King. You are both fatigued.

CHRISTIANA. Mayhap in body with walking so many steps, but not weary in spirit. *(Embraces three of her children.)* Go, my children. *(Embraces* Samuel.) You will love this good shepherd.

MERCY. The sheep hear his voice, and they follow him.

SAMUEL. Master Honest, will you go with us?

HONEST. That I will right gladly.

Exit Shepherd-Boy *with* children, *followed by* Honest.
Music: "He Shall Feed His Flock."

CHRISTIANA. We are glad to have got thus far. This Land of Beulah is a rich and fertile country.

MERCY.   'Tis full of promise and of comfort here to watch this river.

GREATHEART.   To some it has had its flowings, to others its ebbings, as they went over. It is here the pilgrims get news when they are to cross the river. And hark!—methinks even now I hear the sound of the Messenger's horn.

Horn. Enter Messenger *["Messenger's Horn"].*

MESSENGER.   Master Feeblemind! *(Enter* Master Feeblemind.) I have come to tell thee, Master Feeblemind, that thy Lord hath need of thee, and that in a very little time thou must behold his face in brightness. Take this as a token: Those that look out of the windows shall be darkened; and all the daughters of music shall be brought low. *Exit.*

FEEBLEMIND *(his hand to his eyes).*   Friends, I shall see your faces no more in this life; my windows are darkened. I go to him who is the light. I have nothing to leave but my feeble mind; wherefore, when I am gone, I desire that you, Master Greatheart, would bury it in a dunghill. *(Raises his hands.)*

GREATHEART.   I will.

FEEBLEMIND.   Hold out faith and patience.

Exit Feeblemind *with* Greatheart. *Re-enter* Greatheart, *and reads.*

GREATHEART.   He will swallow up death in victory; and the Lord God will wipe away tears from off all faces.

Horn. Enter Messenger.

MESSENGER.   Mistress Muchafraid! *(Enter* Mistress Muchafraid.) Thou trembling woman, this is to summon thee to be ready to go to thy King, to shout for joy for thy deliverance from all thy doubtings. And for a token: He has broken thy golden bowl, and loosed thy silver cord. *(Gives her a broken bowl and silver cord.)*

Exit Messenger.

MISTRESS MUCHAFRAID.   To shout for joy! My friends, do you hear his voice? I go after my kinsman. You know what I am and how troublesomely I have behaved myself in every company; my will is that my desponds and my slavish fears be by no man ever received from the day of my departure for ever. For I know that after my death they will offer themselves to others. For, to be plain with you, they are ghosts which my father and I entertained when first we began to be pilgrims, and could never shake them off after; and they will walk about and seek entertainment of the pilgrims, but for my sake, shut the doors upon them. Mercy, help me. *(Advances.)* Farewell, night! Welcome, day.

Exit, accompanied by Greatheart *and singing ["Table Song"]. Re-enter* Greatheart.

GREATHEART.   She went through the river singing, but none could understand what she said.

CHRISTIANA.   The tongue of the dumb shall sing.

Horn. Enter Messenger.

MESSENGER *(to* Christiana).   Hail, good woman! I bring thee tidings that the Master calleth for thee, and expecteth that thou shouldst stand in his presence in clothes of immortality. The King sends thee this token:—This arrow so pointed with love, let easily into thine heart, will by degrees work so effectually with you, that at the time appointed you must be gone. *(Gives her arrow.)*

Exit Messenger.

CHRISTIANA *(to* Greatheart).   See'st thou this? Knowest thou what this means?

GREATHEART.   Yea, verily! and heartily glad I am for thee! I would that my time were come! But my Master wills that I go back to help others to this place.

CHRISTIANA.   Wilt thou give advice how all things shall be prepared for my journey?

GREATHEART.   Yes, I will give all needful directions.

Exit.

CHRISTIANA. Mercy, say to my children, when next you meet them, that my blessing went with them in my latest breath, and that I shall look to see them follow me. Gladly shall I see they have kept their garments white.

MERCY. Of a surety they will follow thee and their father. To whom shall we give your possessions, Christiana?

CHRISTIANA. What little I have I bequeath to the poor. Mercy, you have in all places showed yourself true-hearted. *(Re-enter* Greatheart.) Be faithful unto death, and my King will give you a crown of life. I would also entreat you, Master Greatheart, to have an eye to my children, and if at any time you see them faint, speak comfortably to them.

GREATHEART. I will comfort them with the words of their Lord.

CHRISTIANA. That will be best of all. Mercy, my sweetheart, take this ring. *(Putting ring on her finger.)*

MERCY. Friend, I wish you a fair day when you set out for Mount Zion, and shall be glad to see that you go over the river dry-shod.

CHRISTIANA. Come wet, come dry, I long to be gone; for however the weather is in my journey, I shall have time enough, when I come there, to sit down, and rest me, and dry me.

GREATHEART. Hast thou no word for me, Christiana?

CHRISTIANA. Friend, thou hast helped me on my way. Thy travail has been sore for others, but he that loses his life shall find it; and thou shalt one day hear the words "Well done, good and faithful servant; enter thou into the joy of thy Lord." Give me thy aid. *(Faintly.)* Mercy, wilt come the other side, and help me away? He calleth me. I come, Lord, to be with the, and bless thee.

Song: "Jesu, Lover of My Soul."

Exit with Greatheart *and* Mercy.

Re-enter Mercy *and kneels. Re-enter* Greatheart.

GREATHEART. O Death, where is thy sting? O Death, where is thy victory?

Horn. Enter Messenger.

MESSENGER. Mercy, this is my token to thee: Thy pitcher is broken at the fountain. The fountain of life hath sent me: thou must prepare for a change of life, for thy Master is not willing that thou shouldst be so far from him any longer. *(Giving broken pitcher.) Exit.*

GREATHEART *(putting his hand on her head).* Mercy, hearest thou this word from thy Lord?

MERCY. Let him speak: his servant heareth. Master Greatheart, ever since it was my hap to be in your good company, you have been profitable to me. Let me entreat you that you send to my family who are still in the City of Destruction. Tell them how Christiana and I came to this place and whither we are gone.

GREATHEART. I will; I will.

MERCY. I have nothing to send them but my prayers and my tears. I see myself at the end of my journey. My toilsome days are ended, and I go now where I shall be with him in whose company I delight myself. His words I did use to gather for my food and for antidotes against my faintings. Wherever I have seen the print of his shoe in the earth, there have I coveted to set my foot also. He hath held me, and my steps hath he strengthened in his way. Take me, for I come unto thee.

GREATHEART. Lord, to thee I commend her spirit. Amen. *Exit with* Mercy.

Re-enter Greatheart.

GREATHEART *(With arms crossed.)* Thanks be unto God who giveth us the victory through our Lord Jesus Christ.

CURTAIN.

O Lamb of God.

O Lamb of God, . O Lamb of God, that

tak - est a - way . . the sins of the world, Have

mer - cy up - on us, Have mer - cy up -

- on us, Have mer - cy up - on us, Have

mer - cy up - on . . us.

Let the Most Blessed.

Music from *Popular Music of the Olden Time*, by W. CHAPPELL, F.S.A.
Published by Chappell & Company. London; 1859.

Let the most Bless - ed be my guide Ift
Un - to his gate, in - to his fold, Up

be his bless - ed will, . . }
to his ho - ly hill. . . } And let him ne - ver

suf - fer me To swarve or turn a - side From

his free grace and ho - ly ways, What-e'er shall me be -

tide, . . . And let him gath - er them of mine That

I have left be - hind; . . Lord, make them pray they

may be thine, With all their heart and mind. . .

Blest be the Day.

Music from *Popular Music of the Olden Time*, by W. CHAPPELL, F.S.A.

1. Blest be the day that I be-gan A pil-grim for to be; And bless-ed al-so be that man, That there-to mo-ved me.

2. 'Tis true, 'twas long ere I be-gan To seek to live for ever; But now I run fast as I can, 'Tis bet-ter late than never.

3. Our tears to joy, our fears to faith Are turn-ed, as we see; Thus our be-gin-ning, as one saith, Shews what our end will be.

Table Song.

BEETHOVEN.

Gra - cious Fa - ther, O Lord, hear us. When we call
on thy name, O Lord, hear us. Ac - cept our gra - ti - tude
for fa - vours now bestow'd. Boun - teous Fa - ther, O Lord,
hear us. Mer - ci - ful Fa - ther, O Lord, hear us.

Shepherd's Boy's Song.

p Andante.   MRS. GEORGE MACDONALD.

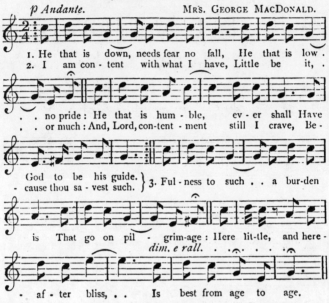

1. He that is down, needs fear no fall, He that is low .
2. I am con-tent with what I have, Little be it, .

. . no pride : He that is hum-ble, ev-er shall Have
. . or much : And, Lord, con-tent-ment still I crave, Be-

God to be his guide.
-cause thou sa-vest such. } 3. Ful-ness to such . . a bur-den

is That go on pil-grim-age : Here lit-tle, and here-
dim. e rall.

- af-ter bliss, . . Is best from age to age.

Messenger's Horn.

PIANOFORTE.

Jesu, Lover of my Soul.

Words by CHARLES WESLEY.

Music by C. POPHAM.

Je - su, lov - er of my soul, Let me to thy

bo - som fly, When the wa - ters near - er roll,

When temp - ta - tion's wave mounts high; Hide me, O my

Sa - viour, hide, Till the storm of life be past; Safe in - to the ha - ven guide, O re - ceive my soul at last.

rall. . . . .

Sermons

INTRODUCTION

George MacDonald once confessed that writing sermons was the most difficult writing that he did. At first, this may seem a surprising statement: if Christian truth is what mattered most to him over the entire span of his life, stating it should come easily. But, on second thought, perhaps the very importance to him of these convictions accounts for the difficulty he felt in expressing them.

If a person feels it is easy to tell the truth, MacDonald said, that person has never tried. Truth is elusive and paradoxical; to attempt to say precisely what one feels to be true requires one's best effort indeed. MacDonald gave his sermons his. One feels in his voice the passion of a man whose love of Scripture and whose vision of the beauty of Christ the Living Word compelled him to attempt with such evident earnestness to free his reader from mental bondage to all inferior theologies.

That the theological climate today is arguably quite different from that of MacDonald's does not diminish the compelling power of his vision of the nature and love of God, the joy of being rightly related to Him, and the beauty of righteousness. This section on his prose closes with two of his statements on the nature of the imagination.

Selections from
THE CREATION IN CHRIST

All things were made through Him, and
without Him was not anything made that
was made. In Him was life, and the life was
the light of men. John 1:3-4

The RSV gives as an alternate reading:
. . . was not anything made.
That which has been made
was life in Him.

Let us look at the passage as I think it ought to be translated, and after that, seek the meaning for the sake of which it was written. "All things were made through Him, and without Him was made not one thing. That which was made in Him was life, and the life was the light of men."

Note the antithesis of the *through* and the *in*.

In this grand assertion seems to me to lie, more than shadowed, the germ of creation and redemption—of all the divine in its relation to all the human.

I believe that Jesus Christ is the eternal Son of the eternal Father; that from the first of firstness Jesus is the Son, because God is the Father. I believe therefore that the Father is the greater, that if the Father had not been, the Son could not have been.

I will not apply logic to the thesis, nor would I state it now but for the sake of what is to follow. The true heart will remember the inadequacy of our speech, and our thought also, to the things that lie near the unknown roots of our existence. In saying what I do, I only say what Paul implies when he speaks of the Lord giving up the kingdom to His Father, that God may be all in all.

I worship the Son as the human God, the divine, the only Man, deriving His being and power from the Father, equal with Him as a son is the equal at once and the subject of his father—but *making Himself the equal of His Father in what is most precious in Godhead, namely, Love.*

The Father, in bringing out of the unseen the things that are seen, made essential use of the Son, so that all that exists was created *through* Him. What the difference between the part in creation of the Father and the part of the Son may be, who can understand? Perhaps we may one day come to see into it a little; for I dare hope that, through our willed sonship, we shall come far nearer ourselves to creating. The word *creation* applied to the loftiest success of human genius, seems to me a mockery of humanity, itself in process of creation.

Let us read the text again: "All things were made *through* Him, and without Him was made not one thing. That which was made *in* Him was life." You begin to see it? The power by which He created the worlds was given Him by His Father; He had in Himself a greater power than that by which He made the worlds. There was something made, not *through* but *in* Him; something brought into being by Himself. Here He creates in His grand way, in Himself, as did the Father. "That which was made *in* Him was *life.*"

What Is This Life?

What was that life, the thing made *in* the Son—made by Him inside Himself, not outside Him—made not *through* but *in* Him—the life that was His own, as God's is His own?

It was, I answer, that act in Him that corresponded in Him, as the Son, to the self-existence of His Father. Now what is the deepest in God? His power? No, for power could not make Him what we mean when we say *God.* Evil could, of course, never create one atom; but let us understand very plainly, that a being whose essence was only power would be such a negation of the divine that no righteous worship could be offered Him: His service must be fear, and fear only. Such a being, even were He righteous in judgment, yet could not be God.

The God Himself whom we love could not be righteous were He not something deeper and better still than we generally mean by the word— but, alas, how little can language say without seeming to say something wrong! In one word, God is Love. Love is the deepest depth, the essence of His nature, at the root of all His being. It is not merely that He could not be God, if He had made no creatures to whom to be God; but love is the heart and hand of His creation; it is His right to create, and His power to create as well. The love that foresees creation is itself the power to create.

Neither could He be righteous—that is, fair to His creatures—but that His love created them. His perfection is His love. All His divine rights rest upon His love. Ah, He is not the great monarch! The simplest peasant loving his cow, is more divine than any monarch whose monarchy is his glory. If God would not punish sin, or if He did it for anything but love, He would not be the Father of Jesus Christ, the God who works as Jesus wrought.

What then, I say once more, is in Christ correspondent to the creative power of God? It must be something that comes also of love; and in the Son the love must be to the already existent. Because of that eternal love which has no beginning, the Father must have the Son. God could not love, could not be love, without making things to love. Jesus has God to love, the love of the Son is responsive to the love of the Father.

The response to self-existent love is self-abnegating love. The refusal of Himself is that in Jesus which corresponds to the creation of God. His love takes action, creates, in self-abjuration, in the death of self as motive; in the drowning of self in the life of God, where it lives only as love.

The life of Christ is this—negatively, that He does nothing, cares for nothing for His own sake; positively, that He cares with His whole soul for the will, the pleasure of His Father. Because His Father is His father, therefore He will be His child. The truth in Jesus is His relation to His Father; the righteousness of Jesus is His fulfilment of that relation.

Meeting this relation, loving His Father with His whole being, He is not merely alive as born of God. Giving Himself with perfect will to God, choosing to die to Himself and live to God, He therein creates in

Himself a new and higher life. Standing upon Himself, He has gained
the power to awake life, the divine shadow of His own, in the hearts of
us His brothers and sisters, who have come from the same birthhome as
Himself, namely, the heart of His God and our God, His Father and our
Father, but who, without our Elder Brother to do it first, would never
have chosen that self-abjuration which is life, never have become alive
like Him. To will not from self, but with the Eternal, is to live.

There is no life for any man, other than the same kind that Jesus
has; His disciple must live by the same absolute devotion of his will to
the Father's; then is his life one with the life of the Father.

We Must Choose

Because we are come out of the divine nature, which chooses to be divine,
we must *choose* to be divine, to be of God, to be one with God, loving and
living as He loves and lives, and so be partakers of the divine nature, or
we perish. Man cannot originate this life; it must be shown him, and he
must choose it. God is the father of Jesus and of us—of every possibility
of our being; but while God is the father of His children, Jesus is the
father of their sonship. For in Him is made the life which is sonship to
the Father—the recognition, namely, in fact and life, that the Father has
His claim upon His sons and daughters.

We are not and cannot become true sons without our will willing
His will, our doing following His making. It was the will of Jesus to be
the thing God willed and meant Him, that made Him the true son of God.
He was not the son of God because He could not help it, but because He
willed to be in Himself the son that He was in the divine idea.

So with us: we must *be* the sons we are. We are not made to be what
we cannot help being; sons and daughters are not after such fashion! We
are sons and daughters in God's claim; we must be sons and daughters
in our will. And we can be sons and daughters, saved into the original
necessity and bliss of our being, only by choosing God for the father He
is, and doing His will—yielding ourselves true sons to the absolute
Father. Therein lies human bliss—only and essential. The working out
of this our salvation must be pain, and the handing of it down to them

that are below must ever be in pain; but the eternal form of the will of God in and for us, is intensity of bliss.

The Life Became Light

"And the life was the light of men."

The life of which I have now spoken became light to men in the appearing of Him in whom it came into being. The life became light that men might see it, and themselves live by choosing that life also, by choosing so to live, such to be.

There is always something deeper than anything said—a something of which all human, all divine words, figures, pictures, motion-forms, are but the outer laminar spheres through which the central reality shines more or less plainly. Light itself is but the poor outside form of a deeper, better thing, namely, life. The life is Christ. The light too is Christ, but only the body of Christ. The life is Christ Himself. The light is what we *see* and shall see in Him; the life is what me may *be* in Him.

Therefore the obedient human God appeared as the obedient divine man, doing the works of His Father—the things, that is, which His Father did—doing them humbly before unfriendly brethren. The Son of the Father must take His own form in the substance of flesh, that He may be seen of men, and so become the light of men—not that men may have light, but that men may have life. Seeing what they could not originate, they may, through the life that is in them, begin to hunger after the life of which they are capable, and which is essential to their being.

Let us not forget that the devotion of the Son could never have been but for the devotion of the Father, who never seeks His own glory one atom more than does the Son; who is devoted to the Son, and to all His sons and daughters, with a devotion perfect and eternal, with fathomless unselfishness. The bond of the universe, the fact at the root of every vision, revealing that "love is the only good in the world," and selfishness the one thing hateful, in the city of the living God unutterable, is the devotion of the Son to the Father. It is the life of the universe.

It is not the fact that God created all things, that makes the universe a whole; but that He through whom He created them loves Him perfectly, is eternally content in His Father, is satisfied to be because His Father is with Him. It is not the fact that God is all in all, that unites the universe; it is the love of the Son to the Father. For of no onehood comes unity; there can be no oneness where there is only one. For the very beginnings of unity there must be two.

Without Christ, therefore, there could be no universe. The reconciliation wrought by Jesus is not the primary source of unity, of safety to the world; that reconciliation was the necessary working out of the eternal antecedent fact, the fact making itself potent upon the rest of the family—that God and Christ are one, are father and son, the Father loving the Son as only the Father can love, the Son loving the Father as only the Son can love. The prayer of the Lord for unity between men and the Father and Himself, springs from the eternal need of love. The more I regard it, the more I am lost in the wonder and glory of the thing.

Life in Us

But light is not enough; light is for the sake of life. We too must have life in ourselves. We too must, like the Life Himself, live. We can live in no way but that in which Jesus lived, in which life was made in Him. That way is, to give up our life. This is the one supreme action of life possible to us for the making of life in ourselves. Christ did it of Himself, and so became light to us, that we might be able to do it in ourselves, after Him, and through His originating act.

We must do it ourselves, I say. The help that He has given and gives, the light and the spirit-working of the Lord, the Spirit, in our hearts, is all in order that we may, as we must, do it ourselves. Till then we are not alive; life is not made in us. The whole strife and labour and agony of the Son with every man, is to get him to die as He died. All preaching that aims not at this, is a building with wood and hay and stubble. If I say not with whole heart, "My Father, do with me as you will, only help me against myself and for you," then I have not yet laid hold upon that for which Christ had laid hold upon me.

The faith that a man must put in God reaches above earth and sky, stretches beyond the farthest outlying star of the creatable universe. The question is not at present, however, of removing mountains, a thing that will one day be simple to us, but of waking and rising from the dead *now*.

When a man truly and perfectly says with Jesus, and as Jesus said it, "Thy will be done," he closes the everlasting life-circle. The life of the Father and the Son flows through him. He is a part of the divine organism. Then is the prayer of the Lord in him fulfilled: "I in them and thou in me, that they may be made perfect in one."

Friends, those of you who know, or suspect, that these things are true, let us arise and live—arise even in the darkest moments of spiritual stupidity, when hope itself sees nothing to hope for. Let us not trouble ourselves about the cause of our earthliness, except we know it to be some unrighteousness in us, but go at once to the Life.

Let us comfort ourselves in the thought of the Father and the Son. So long as there dwells harmony, so long as the Son loves the Father with all the love the Father can welcome, all is well with the little ones. God is all right—why should we mind standing in the dark for a minute outside His window? Of course we miss the *inness*, but there is a bliss of its own in waiting.

What if the rain be falling, and the wind blowing? What if we stand alone, or, more painful still, have some dear one beside us, sharing our *outness*? What even if the window be not shining, because of the curtains of good inscrutable drawn across it? Let us think to ourselves, or say to our friend, "God is; Jesus is not dead. Nothing can be going wrong, however it may look so to hearts unfinished in childness."

Your will, O God, be done! Nought else is other than loss, than decay, than corruption. There is no life but that born of the life that the Word made in Himself by doing your will, which life is the light of men. Through that light is born the life of men—the same life in them that came first into being in Jesus. As He laid down His life, so must men lay down their lives, that as He lives they may live also. That which was made in Him was life, and the life is the light of men; and yet His own, to whom He was sent, did not believe Him.

THE KNOWING OF THE SON

*His voice you have never heard, His form
you have never seen; and you do not have
His word abiding in you, for you do not
believe Him whom He has sent.*
John 5:37b-38

If Jesus said these words, He meant more, not less, than lies on their surface. They cannot be mere assertion of what everybody knew; neither can their repetition of similar negations be tautological. They were not intended to inform the Jews of a fact they would not have dreamed of denying. Who among them would say he had ever heard God's voice, or seen His shape? John himself says "No man has ever seen God." What is the tone of the passage? It is reproach. Then He reproaches them that they had not seen God, when no man has seen God at any time, and Paul says no man can see Him! Is there here any paradox?

The word *see* is used in one sense in the one statement, and in another sense in the other. In the one it means *see with the eyes;* in the other, *with the soul.* The one statement is made of all men; the other is made to certain of the Jews of Jerusalem concerning themselves. It is true that no man has seen God, and true that some men ought to have seen Him. No man has seen Him with his bodily eyes: these Jews ought to have seen Him with their spiritual eyes.

The argument of the Lord was indeed of small weight with, and of little use to, those to whom it most applied, for the more it applied, the more incapable were they of seeing that it did apply; but it would be of great force upon some that stood listening, their minds more or less open to the truth, and their hearts drawn to the Man before them.

His argument was this: "If you had ever heard the Father's voice; if you had ever known His call; if you had ever imagined Him, or a God anything like Him; if you had cared for His will so that His word was at home in your hearts, you would have known me when you saw me— known that I must come from Him, that I must be His messenger, and would have listened to me. The least acquaintance with God, such as any true heart must have, would have made you recognize that I came from the God of whom you knew that something. You would have been capable of knowing me by the light of His word abiding in you; by the shape you had beheld however vaguely; by the likeness of my face and my voice to those of my Father. You would have seen my Father in me; you would have known me by the little you knew of Him. That you do not know me now, as I stand here speaking to you, is that you do not know your own Father, even my Father; that throughout your lives you have refused to do His will, and so have not heard His voice; that you have shut your eyes from seeing Him, and have thought of Him only as a partisan of your ambitions. If you had loved my Father, you would have known His Son."

The Same Is True Today

If the Lord were to appear this day as once in Palestine, He would not come in the halo of the painters. Neither would He probably come as carpenter, or mason, or gardener. He would come in such form and condition as might bear to the present [culture] a relation like that which the form and condition He then came in bore to the motley Judea, Samaria, and Gailiee. If He came thus, in form altogether unlooked for, who would they be that recognized and received Him?

The idea involves no absurdity. He is not far from us at any moment—if the old story be indeed more than the best and strongest of the fables that possess the world. He might at any moment appear. Who, I ask, would be the first to receive him? Now, as then, it would of course be the childlike in heart, the truest, the least selfish. They would not be the highest in the estimation of any church, for the childlike are not yet the many. It might not even be those that knew most about the former visit of the Master, that had pondered every word of the Greek Testament.

It would certainly, if any, be those who were likest the Master—those, namely, that did the will of their Father and His Father, that built their house on the rock by hearing and doing His sayings. But are there any enough like Him to know Him at once by the sound of His voice, by the look of His face? There are multitudes who would at once be taken by a false Christ fashioned after their fancy, and would at once reject the Lord as a poor impostor. One thing is certain: they who first recognized him would be those that most loved righteousness and hated iniquity.

To Receive Him Is to Become Like Him

"And we all, with unveiled face, beholding
the glory of the Lord, are being changed into
His likeness, from one degree of glory to
another; for this comes from the Lord who is
the Spirit." 2 Corinthians 3:18

Let us see then what Paul teaches us in this passage about the life which is the light of men. It is his form of bringing to bear upon men the truth announced by John.

When Moses came out from speaking with God, his face was radiant; its shining was a wonder to the people, and a power upon them. But the radiance began at once to diminish and die away, as was natural, for it was not indigenous in Moses. Therefore Moses put a veil upon his face that they might not see it fade. As to whether this was right or wise, opinion may differ: it is not my business to discuss the question. When he went again into the tabernacle, he took off his veil, talked with God with open face, and again put on the veil when he came out.

Paul says that the veil which obscured the face of Moses lies now upon the hearts of the Jews, so that they cannot understand him, but that when they turn to the Lord (go into the tabernacle with Moses) the veil shall be taken away, and they shall see God. Then will they understand that the glory is indeed faded upon the face of Moses, but by reason of the glory of Jesus that overshines it.

Paul says that the sight of the Lord will take that veil from their hearts. His light will burn it away. His presence gives liberty. Where He is, there is no more heaviness, no more bondage, no more wilderness or Mount Sinai. The Son makes free with sonship.

Paul's idea is, that when we take into our understanding, our heart, our conscience, our being, the glory of God—namely Jesus Christ as He shows himself to our eyes, our hearts, our consciences—He works upon us, and will keep working, till we are changed to the very likeness we have thus mirrored in us; for with His likeness He comes Himself, and dwells in us. He will work until the same likeness is wrought out and perfected in us, the image, namely, of the humanity of God, in which image we were made at first, but which could never be developed in us except by the indwelling of the perfect likeness. By the power of Christ thus received and at home in us, we are changed—the glory in Him becoming glory in us, His glory changing us to glory.

One with God

But let us note this, that the dwelling of Jesus in us is the power of the Spirit of God upon us; for "the Lord is the Spirit," and "this comes from the Lord who is the Spirit." When we think Christ, Christ comes; when we receive His image into our spiritual mirror, He enters with it.

When our hearts turn to Him, that is opening the door to Him, that is holding up our mirror to him; then He comes in, not by our thought only, not in our idea only, but He comes Himself, and of His own will. Thus the Lord, the Spirit, becomes the soul of our souls, becomes spiritually what He always was creatively; and as our spirit informs, gives shape to our bodies, in like manner His soul informs, gives shape to our souls.

In this there is nothing unnatural, nothing at conflict with our being. It is but that the deeper soul that willed and wills our souls, rises up, the infinite Life, into the Self we call *I* and *me*, makes the *I* and *me* more and more His, and Himself more and more ours; until at length the glory of our existence flashes upon us, we face full to the sun that enlightens what it sent forth, and know ourselves alive with an infinite life, even the life of the Father. Then indeed we *are;* then indeed we have life; the life of Jesus has, through light, become life in us; the glory of God in the face of Jesus, mirrored in our hearts, has made us alive; we are one with God for ever and ever.

What less than such a splendor of hope would be worthy the revelation of Jesus? Filled with the soul of their Father, men shall inherit the glory of their Father; filled with themselves, they cast Him out, and rot. No other saving can save them. They must receive the Son, and through the Son the Father.

What it cost the Son to get so near to us that we could say *Come in,* is the story of His life. He stands at the door and knocks, and when we open to Him He comes in, and dwells with us, and we are transformed to the same image of truth and purity and heavenly childhood. Where power dwells, there is no force; where the spirit-Lord is, there is liberty.

The Lord Jesus, by free, potent communion with their inmost being, will change His obedient brethren till in every thought and impulse they are good like Him, unselfish, neighborly, brotherly like Him, loving the Father perfectly like Him, ready to die for the truth like Him, caring like Him for nothing in the universe but the will of God, which is love, harmony, liberty, beauty, and joy.

I do not know if we may call this having life in ourselves; but it is the waking up, the perfecting in us of the divine life inherited from our Father in heaven, who made us in His own image, whose nature remains in us, and makes it the deepest reproach to a man that he has neither heard His voice at any time, nor seen His shape. He who would thus live must, as a mirror draws into its bosom an outward glory, receive into his "heart of hearts" the inward glory of Jesus Christ, the Truth.

Selections from

THE CHILD IN THE MIDST

Mark 9:33-37; cf. Matthew 18:1-5

These passages record a lesson our Lord gave His disciples against ambition, against emulation. It is not for the sake of setting forth this lesson that I write about these words of our Lord, but for the sake of a truth, a revelation about God, in which His great argument reaches its height.

He took a little child—possibly a child of Peter; for St. Mark says that the incident fell at Capernaum, and "in the house"—a child therefore with some of the characteristics of Peter, whose very faults were those of a childish nature. We might expect the child of such a father to possess the childlike countenance and bearing essential to the conveyance of the lesson which I now desire to set forth as contained in the passage.

For it must be confessed that there are children who are not childlike. One of the saddest and not least common sights in the world is the face of a child whose mind is so brimful of worldly wisdom that the human childishness has vanished from it, as well as the divine childlikeness. For the *childlike* is the divine.

If the disciples could have seen that the essential childhood was meant, and not a blurred and half-obliterated childhood, the most selfish child might have done as well, but could have done no better than the one we have supposed in whom the true childhood is more evident. But when the child was employed as a manifestation, utterance, and sign of the truth that lay in his childhood, in order that the eyes as well as the

323

ears should be channels to the heart, it was essential—not that the child should be beautiful but—that the child should be childlike.

What Childlikeness Reveals

That this lesson did lie, not in the humanity, but in the childhood of the child, let me now show more fully. The disciples had been disputing who should be the greatest, and the Lord wanted to show them that such a dispute had nothing whatever to do with the way things went in His kingdom. Therefore, as a specimen of His subjects, He took a child and set him before them. It was not to show the scope but the nature of the kingdom.

He told them they could not enter into the kingdom save by becoming little children—by humbling themselves. For the idea of ruling was excluded where childlikeness was the one essential quality. It was to be no more who should rule, but who should serve; no more who should look down upon his fellows from the conquered heights of authority—even of sacred authority, but who should look up honoring humanity, and ministering to it, so that humanity itself might at length be persuaded of its own honor as a temple of the living God. It was to impress this lesson upon them that He showed them the child; therefore, I repeat, the lesson lay in the childhood of the child.

But I now approach my especial object; for this lesson led to the enunciation of a yet higher truth, upon which it was founded, and from which indeed it sprung. Nothing is required of man that is not first in God. It is because God is perfect that we are required to be perfect. And it is for the revelation of God to all the human souls, that they may be saved by knowing Him, and so becoming like Him, that this child is thus chosen and set before them in the gospel. He who, in giving the cup of water or the embrace, comes into contact with the essential childhood of the child—that is, embraces the *childish* humanity of it, (not he who embraces it out of love to humanity, or even love to God as the Father of it)—is partaker of the meaning, that is, the blessing, of this passage. It is the recognition of the childhood as divine that will show the disciple how vain the strife after relative place of honor in the great kingdom.

For it is *in my name*. This means *as representing me;* and, therefore, *as being like me*. Our Lord could not commission any one to be received in His name who could not more or less represent Him. But a special sense, a lofty knowledge of blessedness, belongs to the act of embracing a child as the visible likeness of the Lord Himself. For the blessedness is the perceiving of the truth—the blessing is the truth itself—the God-known truth, that the Lord has the heart of a child. The man who perceives this knows in himself that he is blessed—blessed because that is true.

But the argument as to the meaning of our Lord's words, *in my name,* is incomplete, until we follow our Lord's enunciation to its second and higher stage: "Whoever receives me, receives not me but Him who sent me." It will be allowed that the connection between the first and second link of the chain will probably be the same as the connection between the second and third. How is it that he who receives the Son receives the Father? Because the Son is as the Father; and he whose heart can perceive the essential in Christ, has the essence of the Father—that is, sees and holds to it by that recognition, and is one therewith by recognition and worship.

What, then, next, is the connection between the first and second? I think the same. "He that sees the essential in this child, the pure childhood, sees that which is the essence of me," grace and truth—in a word, childlikeness. It follows not that the former is perfect as the latter, but it is the same in kind, and therefore manifest in the child; it reveals that which is in Jesus.

Then to receive a child in the name of Jesus is to receive Jesus; to receive Jesus is to receive God; therefore to receive the child is to receive God Himself.

To receive the child because God receives it, or for its humanity, is one thing; to receive it because it is like God, or for its childhood, is another. The former will do little to destroy ambition. Alone it might argue only a wider scope to it, because it admits all men to the arena of the strife. But the latter strikes at the very root of emulation. As soon as even service is done for the honor and not for the service sake, the doer is that moment outside the kingdom. But when we receive the child in the name of Christ, the very childhood that we receive to our arms is humanity. We love its humanity in its childhood, for childhood is the deepest heart of humanity—its divine heart; and so in the name of the child we receive all humanity.

The Childlikeness of God

But to advance now to the highest point of this teaching of our Lord: "Whoever receives me, receives not me but Him who sent me." To receive a child in the name of God is to receive God Himself. How to receive Him? As alone He can be received—by knowing Him as He is. To know Him is to have Him in us. And that we may know Him, let us now receive this revelation of him, in the words of our Lord Himself. Here is the argument of highest import founded upon the teaching of our Master in the utterance before us.

God is represented in Jesus, for that God is like Jesus: Jesus is represented in the child, for that Jesus is like the child. Therefore God is represented in the child, for that He is like the child. God is child-like. In the true vision of this fact lies the receiving of God in the child.

Let me ask, do you believe in the Incarnation? And if you do, let me ask further, was Jesus ever less divine than God? I answer for you, Never. God is man, and infinitely more. Our Lord became flesh, but did not *become* man. He took on Him the form of man: He was man already. And He was, is, and ever shall be divinely childlike. He could never have been a child if He would ever have ceased to be a child, for in Him the transient found nothing. Childhood belongs to the divine nature. Obedience, then, is as divine as Will, Service as divine as Rule. How? Because they are one in their nature; they are both a doing of the truth. The love in them is the same. The Fatherhood and the Sonship are one, save that the Fatherhood looks down lovingly, and the Sonship looks up lovingly. Love is all. And God is all in all. He is ever seeking to get down to us—to be the divine man to us. And we are ever saying, "That be far from you, Lord!" We are careful, in our unbelief, over the divine dignity, of which He is too grand to think.

Let us dare, then, to climb the height of divine truth to which this utterance of our Lord would lead us. Does it not lead us up higher: that the devotion of God to His creatures is perfect? that He does not think about Himself but about them? that He wants nothing for Himself, but finds His blessedness in the outgoing of blessedness?

In this, then, is God like the child: that He is simply and altogether our friend, our father—our more than friend, father, and mother—our infinite love-perfect God. Grand and strong beyond all that human imagination can conceive of poet-thinking and kingly action, He is delicate beyond all that human tenderness can conceive of husband and wife, homely beyond all that human heart can conceive of father or mother.

He has not two thoughts about us. With Him all is simplicity of purpose and meaning and effort and end—namely, that we should be as He is, think the same thoughts, mean the same things, possess the same blessedness. It is so plain that any one may see it, every one ought to see it, every one shall see it. It must be so. He is utterly true and good to us, nor shall anything withstand His will.

How terribly, then, have the theologians misrepresented God! Nearly all of them represent Him as the great King on a grand throne, thinking how grand He is, and making it the business of His being and the end of His universe to keep up His glory, wielding the bolts of a Jupiter against them that take His name in vain. They would not allow this, but follow out what they say, and it comes much to this.

Brothers, have you found our king? There He is, kissing little children and saying they are like God. There He is at table with the head of a fisherman lying on His bosom, and somewhat heavy at heart that even he, the beloved disciple, cannot yet understand Him well. The simplest peasant who loves his children and his sheep were—no, not a truer, for the other is false, but—a true type of our God beside that monstrosity of a monarch.

The God who is ever uttering himself in the changeful profusions of nature; who takes millions of years to form a soul that shall understand Him and be blessed; who never needs to be, and never is, in haste; who welcomes the simplest thought of truth or beauty as the return for seed He has sown upon the old fallows of eternity; who rejoices in the response of a faltering moment to the age-long cry of His wisdom in the streets; the God of music, of painting, of building, the Lord of Hosts, the God of mountains and oceans; whose laws go forth from one unseen point of wisdom, and thither return without an atom of loss; the God of history working in time unto Christianity; this God is the God of little children, and He alone can be perfectly abandonedly simple and devoted. The deepest, purest love of a woman has its well-spring in Him. Our longing desires can no more exhaust the fulness of the treasures of the Godhead, than our imagination can touch their measure. Of Him not a thought, not a joy, not a hope of one of His creatures can pass unseen; and while one of them remains unsatisfied, He is not Lord over all.

Therefore, with angels and with archangels, with the spirits of the just made perfect, with the little children of the kingdom, yea, with the Lord Himself, and for all them that know Him not, we praise and magnify and laud His name in itself, saying *Our Father*. We do not draw back for that we are unworthy, nor even for that we are hard-hearted and care not for the good. For it is His childlikeness that makes Him our God and Father. The perfection of his relation to us swallows up all our imperfections, all our defects, all our evils; for our childhood is born of His fatherhood. That man is perfect in faith who can come to God in the utter dearth of his feelings and his desires, without a glow or an aspiration, with the weight of low thoughts, failures, neglects, and wandering forgetfulness, and say to Him, "You are my refuge, because you are my home."

Such a faith will not lead to presumption. The man who can pray such a prayer will know better than another, that God is not mocked; that He is not a man that He should repent; that tears and entreaties will not work on him to the breach of one of His laws; that for God to give a man because he asked for it that which was not in harmony with His laws of truth and right, would be to damn him—to cast him into the outer darkness. And He knows that out of that prison the childlike, imperturbable God will let no man come till he has "paid the last penny."

And if he should forget this, the God to whom he belongs does not forget it, does not forget him. Life is no series of chances with a few providences sprinkled between to keep up a justly failing belief, but one providence of God; and the man shall not live long before life itself shall remind him, it may be in agony of soul, of that which he has forgotten. When he prays for comfort, the answer may come in dismay and terror and the turning aside of the Father's countenance; for love itself will, for love's sake, turn the countenance away from that which is not lovely; and he will have to read, written upon the dark wall of his imprisoned conscience, the words, awful and glorious, *Our God is a consuming fire.*

Selections from

LIGHT

This is the message we have heard from Him
and proclaim to you, that God is light and
in Him is no darkness at all. 1 John 1:5

And this is the judgment, that the light has
come into the world, and men loved
darkness rather than light, because their
deeds were evil. John 3:19

W e call the story of Jesus, told so differently, yet to my mind so consistently, by four narrators, *the gospel.* What makes this tale *the good news?* Is everything in the story of Christ's life on earth good news? Is it good news that the one only good man was served by his fellow-men as Jesus was served—cast out of the world in torture and shame? Is it good news that He came to his own, and His own received Him not? What makes it fit, I repeat, to call the tale *good news?*

If we asked this or that theologian, we should, in so far as he was a true man, and answered from his own heart and not from the tradition of the elders, understand what he saw in it that made it good news to him, though it might involve what would be anything but good news to some of us. The deliverance it might seem to this or that man to bring, might be founded on such notions of God as to not a few of us contain as little of good as of news.

To share in the deliverance which some men find in what they call the gospel—for all do not apply the word to the tale itself, but to certain deductions made from the epistles and their own consciousness of evil—we should have to believe such things of God as would be the opposite of an evangel to us—yea, a message from hell itself. We must first believe in an unjust God, from whom we have to seek refuge. True, they call Him just, but say He does that which seems to the best in me the essence of injustice. They will tell me I judge after the flesh: I answer, Is it then to the flesh the Lord appeals when He says, "Why do you not judge for yourselves what is right?" Is He not the light that lights every man that comes into the world?

They tell me I was born in sin, and I know it to be true; they tell me also that I am judged with the same severity as if I had been born in righteousness, and that I know to be false. They make it a consequence of the purity and justice of God that He will judge us, born in evil, for which birth we were not accountable, by our sinfulness, instead of by our guilt. They tell me, or at least give me to understand, that every wrong thing I have done makes me subject to be treated as if I had done that thing with the free will of one who had in him no taint of evil—when, perhaps, I did not at the time recognize the thing as evil, or recognized it only in the vaguest fashion.

Is there any gospel in telling me that God is unjust, but that there is a way of deliverance from Him? Show me my God unjust, and you wake in me a damnation from which no power can deliver me—least of all God Himself. It may be good news to such as are content to have a God capable of unrighteousness, if only He be on their side!

Who would not rejoice to hear from Matthew, or Mark, or Luke, what, in a few words, he meant by the word *gospel*—or rather, what in the story of Jesus made him call it *good news!* Each would probably give a different answer to the question, all the answers consistent, and each a germ from which the others might be reasoned; but in the case of John; we have his answer to the question: he gives us in one sentence of two members, not indeed the gospel according to John, but the gospel according to Jesus Christ Himself.

"This is the message," he says, "we have heard from Him, and proclaim to you, that God is light, and in Him is no darkness at all." Ah, my heart, this is indeed the good news for you! This *is* gospel! If God be light, what more, what else can I seek than God, than God Himself! Away with your doctrines! Away with your salvation from the "justice" of a God whom it is a horror to imagine! Away with your iron cages of false metaphysics! I am saved—for God is light!

My God, I come to you. That you should be yourself is enough for time and eternity, for my soul and all its endless need. Whatever seems to me darkness, that I will not believe of my God. If I would mistake, and call that darkness which is light, will He not reveal the matter to me, setting it in the light that lights every man, showing me that I saw but the husk of the thing, not the kernel? Will He not break open the shell for me, and let the truth of it, His thought, stream out upon me?

Where would the good news be if John said, "God is light, but you cannot see His light; you cannot tell, you have no notion, what light is; what God means by light, is not what you mean by light; what God calls light may be horrible darkness to you, for you are of another nature from Him!" Where, I say, would be the good news of that?

It is true, the light of God may be so bright that we see nothing; but that is not darkness, it is infinite hope of light. It is true also that to the wicked "the day of the Lord is darkness, and not light"; but is that because the conscience of the wicked man judges of good and evil oppositely to the conscience of the good man? When he says "Evil, be my good," he means by *evil* what God means by evil, and by *good* he means *pleasure*. He cannot make the meanings change places. To say that what our deepest conscience calls darkness may be light to God, is blasphemy; to say light in God and light in man are of differing kinds, is to speak against the spirit of light.

God is light far beyond what we can see, but what we mean by light, God means by light; and what is light to God is light to us, or would be light to us if we saw it, and will be light to us when we do see it. God means us to be jubilant in the fact that He is light—that He is what His children, made in His image, mean when they say *light;* that what in Him is dark to them, is dark by excellent glory, by too much cause of jubilation; that, however dark it may be to their eyes, it is light even as they mean it, light for their eyes and souls and hearts to take in the moment they are enough of eyes, enough of souls, enough of hearts, to receive it in its very being.

The Beauty of God's Light

To fear the light is to be untrue, or at least it comes of untruth. No being, for himself or for another, needs fear the light of God. Nothing can be in light inimical to our nature, which is of God, or to anything in us that is worthy. All fear of the light, all dread lest there should be something dangerous in it, comes of the darkness still in those of us who do not love the truth with all our hearts; it will vanish as we are more and more interpenetrated with the light.

In a word, there is no way of thought or action which we count admirable in man, in which God is not altogether adorable. There is no loveliness, nothing that makes man dear to his brother man, that is not in God, only it is infinitely better in God. He is God our savior. Jesus is our savior because God is our savior. He is the God of comfort and consolation. He will sooth and satisfy His children better than any mother her infant.

The only thing He will not give them is—leave to stay in the dark. If a child cry, "I want the darkness," and complain that He will not give it, yet He will not give it. He gives what His child needs—often by refusing what he asks. If His child say, "I will not be good; I prefer to die; let me die!" His dealing with that child will be as if He said—"No; I have the right to content you, not giving you your own will but mine, which is your one good. You shall not die; you shall live to thank me that I would not hear your prayer. You know what you ask, but not what you refuse."

There are good things God must delay giving until His child has a pocket to hold them—till he gets His child to make that pocket. He must first make him fit to receive and to have. There is no part of our nature that shall not be satisfied—and that not by lessening it, but by enlarging it to embrace an ever-enlarging enough.

Come to God, then, my brother, my sister, with all your desires and instincts, all your lofty ideals, all your longing for purity and unselfishness, all your yearning to love and be true, all your aspirations after self-forgetfulness and child-life in the breath of the Father; come to Him with all your weaknesses, all your shames, all your futilities; with all your helplessness over your own thoughts; with all your failure, yes, with the sick sense of having missed the tide of true affairs; come to Him with all your doubts, fears, dishonesties, meannesses, paltrinesses, misjudgments, wearinesses, disappointments, and stalenesses: be sure He will take you and all your miserable brood, whether of draggle-winged angels, or covert-seeking snakes, into His care, the angels for life, the snakes for death, and you for liberty in His limitless heart! For He is light, and in Him is no darkness at all.

If He were a king, a governor; if the name that described Him were *The Almighty,* you might well doubt whether there could be light enough in Him for you and your darkness; but He is your father, and more your father than the word can mean in any lips but His who said, "my father and your father, my God and your God"; and such a father *is* light, an infinite, perfect light. If He were any less or any other than He is, and you could yet go on growing, you must at length come to the point where you would be dissatisfied with Him; but He is light, and in Him is no darkness at all.

If anything seem to be in Him that you cannot be content with, be sure that the ripening of your love to your fellows and to Him, the source of your being, will make you at length know that anything else than just what He is would have been to you an endless loss. Be not afraid to build upon the rock Christ, as if your holy imagination might build too high and heavy for that rock, and it must give way and crumble beneath the weight of your divine idea.

Let no one persuade you that there is in Him a little darkness, because of something He has said which His creature interprets into darkness. The interpretation is the work of the enemy—a handful of tares of darkness sown in the light. Neither let your cowardly conscience receive any word as light because another calls it light, while it looks to you dark. Say either the thing is not what it seems, or God never said or did it. But, of all evils, to misinterpret what God does, and then say the thing as interpreted must be right because God does it, is of the devil.

Do not try to believe anything that affects you as darkness. Even if you mistake and refuse something true thereby, you will do less wrong to Christ by such a refusal than you would by accepting as His what you can see only as darkness. It is impossible you are seeing a true, a real thing—seeing it as it is, I mean—if it looks to you darkness. But let your words be few, lest you say with your tongue what you will afterward repent with your heart. Above all things believe in the light, that it is what you call light, though the darkness in you may give you cause at a time to doubt whether you are verily seeing the light.

John 3:19

"But there is another side to the matter: God is light indeed, but there *is* darkness; darkness is death, and men are in it."

Yes; darkness is death, but not death to him that comes out of it.

It may sound paradoxical, but no man is condemned for anything he has done; he is condemned for continuing to do wrong. He is condemned for not coming out of the darkness, for not coming to the light, the living God, who sent the light, His Son, into the world to guide him home. Let us hear what John says about the darkness.

For here also we have, I think the word of the apostle himself: at the 13th verse he begins, I think, to speak in his own person. In the 19th verse he says, "And this is the judgment"—not that men are sinners—not that they have done that which, even at the moment, they were ashamed of—not that they have committed murder, not that they have betrayed man or woman, not that they have ground the faces of the poor, making money by the groans of their fellows—not for any hideous thing are they condemned, but that they will not leave such doings behind, and do them no more: "This is the judgment, that light has come into the world, and men" would not come out of the darkness to the light, but "loved darkness rather than light, because their deeds were evil."

Choosing evil, clinging to evil, loving the darkness because it suits with their deeds, therefore turning their backs on the inbreaking light, how can they but be condemned—if God be true, if He be light, and darkness be alien to Him! Whatever of honesty is in man, whatever of judgment is left in the world, must allow that their condemnation is in the very nature of things, that it must rest on them and abide.

But it does not follow, because light has come into the world, that it has fallen upon this or that man. He has his portion of the light that lights every man, but the revelation of God in Christ may not yet have reached him. A man might see and pass the Lord in a crowd, nor be to blame like the Jews of Jerusalem for not knowing Him. A man like Nathanael might have started and stopped at the merest glimpse of Him, but all growing men are not yet like him without guile.

Everyone who has not yet come to the light is not necessarily keeping his face turned away from it. We dare not say that this or that man would not have come to the light had he seen it; we do not know that he will not come to the light the moment he does see it. God gives every man time. There is a light that lightens sage and savage, but the glory of God in the face of Jesus may not have shined on this sage or that savage.

The condemnation is of those who, having seen Jesus, refuse to come to Him, or pretend to come to Him but do not the things He says. They have all sorts of excuses at hand; but as soon as a man begins to make excuse, the time has come when he might be doing that from which he excuses himself. How many are there not who, believing there is something somewhere with the claim of light upon them, go on and on to get more out of the darkness! This consciousness, all neglected by them, gives broad ground for the expostulation of the Lord—"Yet you refuse to come to me that you may have life!"

The Unforgivable Sin

"Every sin and blasphemy," the Lord said, "will be forgiven unto men; but the blasphemy against the Spirit will not be forgiven." God speaks, as it were, in this matter: "I forgive you everything. Not a word more shall be said about your sins—only come out of them; come out of the darkness of your exile; come into the light of your home, of your birthright, and do evil no more. Lie no more; cheat no more; oppress no more; slander no more; envy no more; be neither greedy nor vain; love your neighbor as I love you; be my good child; trust in your Father. I am light; come to me, and you shall see things as I see them, and hate the evil thing. I will make you love the thing which now you call good and love not. I forgive all the past."

"I thank you, Lord, for forgiving me, but I prefer staying in the darkness: forgive me that too."

"No; that cannot be. The one thing that cannot be forgiven is the sin of choosing to be evil, of refusing deliverance. It is impossible to forgive that sin. It would be to take part in it. To side with wrong against right, with murder against life, cannot be forgiven. The thing that is past I pass, but he who goes on doing the same, annihilates this my forgiveness, makes it of no effect.

"Let a man have committed any sin whatever, I forgive him; but to choose to go on sinning—how can I forgive that? It would be to nourish and cherish evil! It would be to let my creation go to ruin. Shall I keep you alive to do things hateful in the sight of all true men? If a man refuse to come out of his sin, he must suffer the vengeance of a love that would be no love if it left him there. Shall I allow my creature to be the thing my soul hates?"

There is no excuse for this refusal. If we were punished for every fault, there would be no end, no respite; we should have no quiet wherein to repent; but God passes by all He can. He passes by and forgets a thousand sins, yea, tens of thousands, forgiving them all—only we must begin to be good, begin to do evil no more.

He who refuses must be punished and punished—punished through all the ages—punished until he gives way, yields, and comes to the light, that his deeds may be seen by himself to be what they are, and be by himself reproved, and the Father at last have His child again. For the man who in this world resists to the full, there may be, perhaps, a whole age or era in the history of the universe during which his sin shall not be forgiven; but *never* can it be forgiven until he repents. How can they who will not repent be forgiven, save in the sense that God does and will do all He can to make them repent? Who knows but such sin may need for its cure the continuous punishment of an aeon?

Selections from

THE CONSUMING FIRE

Our God is a consuming fire. Hebrews 12:29

Nothing is inexorable but love. Love which will yield to prayer is imperfect and poor. Nor is it then the love that yields, but its alloy. For if at the voice of entreaty love conquers displeasure, it is love asserting itself, not love yielding its claims. It is not love that grants a boon unwillingly; still less is it love that answers a prayer to the wrong and hurt of him who prays. Love is one, and love is changeless.

For love loves unto purity. Love has ever in view the absolute loveliness of that which it beholds. Where loveliness is incomplete, and love cannot love its fill of loving, it spends itself to make more lovely, that it may love more. It strives for perfection, even that itself may be perfected—not in itself, but in the object. As it was love that first created humanity, so even human love, in proportion to its divinity, will go on creating the beautiful for its own outpouring. There is nothing eternal but that which loves and can be loved, and love is ever climbing towards the consummation when such shall be the universe, imperishable, divine.

Therefore all that is not beautiful in the beloved, all that comes between and is not of love's kind, must be destroyed.

And our God is a consuming fire.

If this be hard to understand, it is as the simple, absolute truth is hard to understand. It may be centuries of ages before a man comes to see a truth—ages of strife, of effort, of aspiration. But when once he does see it, it is so plain that he wonders he could have lived without seeing it. That he did not understand it sooner was simply and only that he did not see it. To see a truth, to know what it is, to understand it, and to love it, are all one.

The Fire of Love

Let us look at the utterance of the apostle which is crowned with this lovely terror: "Our God is a consuming fire."

"Therefore, let us be grateful for receiving a kingdom that cannot be shaken, and thus let us offer to God acceptable worship, with reverence and awe; for our God is a consuming fire." We have received a kingdom that cannot be moved—whose nature is immovable. Let us have grace to serve the Consuming Fire, our God, with divine fear; not with the fear that cringes and craves, but with the bowing down of all thoughts, all delights, all loves before Him who is the life of them all, and will have them all pure. The kingdom He has given us cannot be moved, because it has nothing weak in it. It is of the eternal world, the world of being, of truth. We, therefore, must worship Him with a fear pure as the kingdom is unshakable. He will shake heaven and earth, that only the unshakable may remain (v. 27).

He is a consuming fire, that only that which cannot be consumed may stand forth eternal. It is the nature of God, so terribly pure that it destroys all that is not pure as fire, which demands like purity in our worship. He will have purity. It is not that the fire will burn us if we do not worship thus; but that the fire will burn us until we worship thus; yea, will go on burning within us after all that is foreign to it has yielded to its force, no longer with pain and consuming, but as the highest consciousness of life, the presence of God.

When evil, which alone is consumable, shall have passed away in His fire from the dwellers in the immovable kingdom, the nature of man shall look the nature of God in the face, and His fear shall then be pure; for an eternal, that is a holy fear, must spring from a knowledge of the nature, not from a sense of the power. But that which cannot be consumed must be one within itself, a simple existence; therefore, in such a soul the fear towards God will be one with the homeliest love.

Yea, the fear of God will cause a man to flee, not from Him, but from himself; not from Him, but to Him, the Father of himself, in terror lest he should do Him wrong or his neighbor wrong. And the first words which follow for the setting forth of that grace whereby we may serve God acceptably are these: "Let brotherly love continue." To love our brother is to worship the Consuming Fire.

The symbol of *the consuming fire* would seem to have been suggested to the writer by the fire that burned on the mountain of the old law. That fire was part of the revelation of God there made to the Israelites. Nor was it the first instance of such a revelation. The symbol of God's presence, before which Moses had to put off his shoes, and to which it was not safe for him to draw near, was a fire that did not consume the bush in which it burned.

But the same symbol employed by a writer of the New Testament should mean more, not than it meant before, but than it was before employed to express; for it could not have been employed to express more than it was possible for them to perceive. What else than terror could a nation of slaves, into whose very souls the rust of their chains had eaten, in whose memory lingered the smoke of the flesh-pots of Egypt, who, rather than not eat of the food they liked best, would have gone back to the house of their bondage—what else could such a nation see in that fire than terror and destruction? How should they think of purification by fire? They had yet no such condition of mind as could generate such a thought.

And if they had had the thought, the notion of the suffering involved would soon have overwhelmed the notion of purification. Nor would such a nation have listened to any teaching that was not supported by terror. Fear was that for which they were fit. They had no worship for any being of whom they had not to be afraid.

Was then this show upon Mount Sinai a device to move obedience, such as bad nurses employ with children? a hint of vague and false horror? Was it not a true revelation of God?

If it was not a true revelation, it was none at all, and the story is either false, or the whole display was a political trick of Moses. Those who can read the mind of Moses will not easily believe the latter, and those who understand the scope of the pretended revelation, will see no reason for supposing the former. That which would be politic, were it a deception, is not therefore excluded from the possibility of another source. Some people believe so little in a cosmos or ordered world, that the very argument of fitness is a reason for unbelief.

At all events, if God showed them these things, God showed them what was true. It was a revelation of Himself. He will not put on a mask. He puts on a face. He will not speak out of flaming fire if that flaming fire is alien to Him, if there is nothing in Him for that flaming fire to reveal. Be His children ever so brutish, He will not terrify them with a lie.

A Partial Revelation

It was a revelation, but a partial one; a true symbol, not a final vision.

No revelation can be other than partial. If for true revelation a man must be told all the truth, then farewell to revelation; yea, farewell to the sonship. For what revelation, other than a partial, can the highest spiritual condition receive of the infinite God? But it is not therefore untrue because it is partial. Because of a lower condition of the receiver, a more partial revelation might be truer than that would be which constituted a fuller revelation to one in a higher condition; for the former might reveal much to him, the latter might reveal nothing.

Only, whatever it might reveal, if its nature were such as to preclude development and growth, thus changing the man to its incompleteness, it would be but a false revelation fighting against all the divine laws of human existence. The true revelation rouses the desire to know more by the truth of its incompleteness.

Here was a nation at its lowest: could it receive anything but a partial revelation, a revelation of fear? How should the Hebrews be other than terrified at that which was opposed to all they knew of themselves, beings judging it good to honor a golden calf? Such as they were, they did well to be afraid. They were in a better condition, acknowledging a terror *above* them, flaming on that unknown mountain height, than stooping to worship the idol below them. Fear is nobler than sensuality.

Fear is better than no God, better than a god made with hands. In that fear lay deep hidden the sense of the infinite. The worship of fear is true, although very low; and though not acceptable to God in itself, for only the worship of spirit and of truth is acceptable to Him, yet even in His sight it is precious. For He regards men not as they are merely, but as they shall be; not as they shall be merely, but as they are now growing, or capable of growing, towards that image after which He made them that they might grow to it.

Therefore a thousand stages, each in itself all but valueless, are of inestimable worth as the necessary and connected gradations of an infinite progress. A condition which of declension would indicate a devil, may of growth indicate a saint. So far then the revelation, not being final any more than complete, and calling forth the best of which they were now capable, so making future and higher revelation possible, may have been a true one.

But we shall find that this very revelation of fire is itself, in a higher sense, true to the mind of the rejoicing saint as to the mind of the trembling sinner. For the former sees farther into the meaning of the fire, and knows better what it will do to him. It is a symbol which needed not to be superseded, only unfolded. While men take part *with* their sins, while they feel as if, separated from their sins, they would be no longer themselves, how can they understand that the lightning word is a Savior—that word which pierces to the dividing between the man and the evil, which will slay the sin and give life to the sinner? Can it be any comfort to them to be told that God loves them so that He will burn them clean? Can the cleansing of the fire appear to them anything beyond what it must always, more or less, be—a process of torture?

They do not want to be clean, and they cannot bear to be tortured. Can they then do other, or can we desire that they should do other, than fear God, even with the fear of the wicked, until they learn to love Him with the love of the holy? To them Mount Sinai is crowned with the signs of vengeance. And is not God ready to do unto them even as they fear, though with another feeling and a different end from any which they are capable of supposing? He is against sin: in so far as, and while, they and sin are one, He is against them—against their desires, their aims, their fears, and their hopes; and thus He is altogether and always *for them*.

That thunder and lightning and tempest, that blackness torn with the sound of a trumpet, that visible horror billowed with the voice of words, was all but a faint image to the senses of the slaves of what God thinks and feels against vileness and selfishness, of the unrest of unassuageable repulsion with which He regards such conditions. The intention was that so the stupid people, fearing somewhat to do as they would, might leave a little room for that grace to grow in them, which would at length make them see that evil, and not fire, is the fearful thing; yea, so transform them that they would gladly rush up into the trumpet-blast of Sinai to escape the flutes around the golden calf. Could they have understood this, they would have needed no Mount Sinai. It was a true, and of necessity a partial revelation—partial in order to be true.

What Is to Be Feared?

When we say that God is Love, do we teach men that their fear of Him is groundless? No. As much as they fear will come upon them, possibly far more. But there is something beyond their fear—a divine fate which they cannot withstand, because it works along with the human individuality which the divine individuality has created in them.

The wrath will consume what they *call* themselves; so that the selves God made shall appear, coming out with ten-fold consciousness of being, and bringing with them all that made the blessedness of the life the men tried to lead without God. They will know that now first are they fully themselves. The avaricious, weary, selfish, suspicious old man shall have passed away. The young, every young self, will remain—remain glorified in repentant hope. For that which cannot be shaken shall remain. That which they *thought* themselves shall have vanished: that which they *felt* themselves, though they misjudged their own feelings, shall remain—remain glorified in repentant hope. For that which cannot be shaken shall remain. That which is immortal in God shall remain in man. The death that is in them shall be consumed.

It is the law of Nature—that is, the law of God—that all that is destructible shall be destroyed. When that which is immortal buries itself in the destructible—when it receives all the messages from without, through the surrounding region of decadence, and none from within, from the eternal doors—it cannot, though immortal still, know its own immortality. The destructible must be burned out of it, or begin to be burned out of it, before it can *partake* of eternal life. When that is all burnt away and gone, then it has eternal life. Or rather, when the fire of eternal life has possessed a man, then the destructible is gone utterly, and he is pure.

Many a man's work must be burned, that by that very burning he may be saved—"so as by fire." Away in smoke go the lordships, the Rabbi-hoods of the world, and the man who acquiesces in the burning is saved by the fire; for it has destroyed the destructible, which is the vantage point of the deathly, which would destroy both body and soul in hell. If still he clings to that which can be burned, the burning goes on deeper and deeper into his bosom, till it reaches the roots of the falsehood that enslaved him—possibly by looking like the truth.

The man who loves God, and is not yet pure, courts the burning of God. Nor is it always torture. The fire shows itself sometimes only as light—still it will be fire of purifying. The consuming fire is just the original, the active form of Purity, that which makes pure, that which is indeed Love, the creative energy of God. Without purity there can be as no creation so no persistence. That which is not pure is corruptible, and corruption cannot inherit incorruption.

The man whose deeds are evil, fears the burning. But the burning will not come the less because he fears it or denies it. Escape is hopeless. For love is inexorable. Our God is a consuming fire. He shall not come out till he has paid the last penny.

The Outer Darkness

If the man resists the burning of God, the consuming fire of Love, a terrible doom awaits him, and its day will come. He shall be cast into the outer darkness who hates the fire of God. What sick dismay shall then seize upon him! For let a man think and care ever so little about God, he does not therefore exist without God. God is here with him, upholding, warming, delighting, teaching him—making life a good thing to him. God gives him Himself, though he knows it not.

But when God withdraws from a man as far as that can be without the man's ceasing to be; when the man feels himself abandoned, hanging in a ceaseless vertigo of existence upon the verge of the gulf of his being, without support, without refuge, without aim, without end—for the soul has no weapons wherewith to destroy herself—with no inbreathing of joy, with nothing to make life good; then will he listen in agony for the faintest sound of life from the closed door. If the moan of suffering humanity ever reaches the ear of the outcast of darkness, he will be ready to rush into the very heart of the Consuming Fire to know life once more, to change this terror of sick negation, of unspeakable death, for the region of painful hope.

Imagination cannot mislead us into too much horror of being without God—that one living death. But with this divine difference: that the outer darkness is but the most dreadful form of the consuming fire—the fire without light—the darkness visible, the black flame. God hath withdrawn Himself, but not lost His hold. His face is turned away, but His hand is laid upon him still. His heart has ceased to beat into the man's heart, but He keeps him alive by His fire. And that fire will go searching and burning on in him, as in the highest saint who is not yet pure as He is pure.

But at length, O God, will you not cast Death and Hell into the lake of Fire—even into your own consuming self?

Selections from
JUSTICE

*And that to thee, O Lord, belongs steadfast
love. For thou dost requite a man according
to his work*. Psalm 62:12

S ome of the translators make it *kindness* and *goodness;* but I presume
there is no real difference among them as to the character of the word
which here, in the English Bible, is translated *mercy* [RSV: steadfast love].

The religious mind, however, educated upon the theories yet prevailing in the so-called religious world, must here recognize a departure
from the presentation to which they have been accustomed. To make the
psalm speak according to prevalent theoretic modes, the verse would
have to be changed thus: "To thee, O Lord, belongs *justice*, for thou dost
requite a man according to his work."

Let us endeavour to see plainly what we mean when we use the
word *justice*, and whether we mean what we ought to mean when we use
it—especially with reference to God. Let us come nearer to knowing what
we ought to understand by justice, that is, the justice of God. For His
justice is the live, active justice, giving existence to the idea of justice in
our minds and hearts. Because He is just, we are capable of knowing
justice; it is because He is just, that we have the idea of justice so deeply
imbedded in us.

What do we most often mean by *justice?* Is it not the carrying out
of the law, the infliction of penalty assigned to offense? By a just judge
we mean a man who administers the law without prejudice, without favor

or dislike; and where guilt is manifest, punishes as much as, and no more than, the law has in the case laid down. It may not be that justice has therefore been done. The law itself may be unjust, and the judge may mistake; or, which is more likely, the working of the law may be foiled by the parasites of law for their own gain. But even if the law be good, and thoroughly administered, it does not necessarily follow that justice is done.

Illustration

Suppose my watch has been taken from my pocket. I lay hold of the thief. He is dragged before the magistrate, proved guilty, and sentenced to a just imprisonment. Must I walk home satisfied with the result? Have I had justice done me? The thief may have had justice done him—but where is my watch? That is gone, and I remain a man wronged. Who had done me the wrong? The thief. Who can set right the wrong? The thief, and only the thief; nobody but the man that did the wrong. God may be able to move the man to right the wrong, but God Himself cannot right it without the man.

Suppose my watch found and restored, is the account settled between me and the thief? I may forgive him, but is the wrong removed? By no means. But suppose the thief repents. He has, we shall say, put it out of his power to return the watch, but he comes to me and says he is sorry he stole it, and begs me to accept for the present what little he is able to bring, as a beginning of atonement. How should I then regard the matter?

Should I not feel that he had gone far to make atonement—done more to make up for the injury he had inflicted upon me, than the mere restoration of the watch, even by himself, could reach to? Would there not lie, in the thief's confession and submission and initial restoration, an appeal to the divinest in me—to the eternal brotherhood? Would it not indeed amount to a sufficing atonement as between man and man? If he offered to bear what I chose to lay upon him, should I feel it necessary, for the sake of justice, to inflict some certain suffering as demanded by righteousness? I should still have a claim upon him for my watch, but should I not be apt to forget it? He who commits the offense can make up for it—and he alone.

One thing must surely be plain—that the punishment of the wrong-doer makes no atonement for the wrong done. How could it make up to me for the stealing of my watch that the man was punished? The wrong would be there all the same. Punishment may do good to the man who does the wrong, but that is a thing as different as important.

Another thing plain is, even without the material rectification of the wrong where that is impossible, repentance removes the offense which no suffering could. I at least should feel that I had no more quarrel with the man. I should even feel that the gift he had made me, giving into my heart a repentant brother, was infinitely beyond the restitution of what he had taken from me. True, he owed me both himself and the watch, but such a greater does more than include such a less.

It may be objected, "You may forgive, but the man has sinned against God!" Then it is not a part of the divine to be merciful, I return, and a man may be more merciful than his maker! A man may do that which would be too merciful in God! Then mercy is not a divine attribute. It must not be infinite; therefore, it cannot be God's own.

What Is God's Justice?

"Mercy may be against justice." Never—if you mean by justice what I mean by justice. If anything be against justice, it cannot be called mercy, for it is cruelty. . . . *"to thee, O Lord, belongs steadfast love. For thou dost requite a man according to his work."* There is *no* opposition, *no* strife whatever, between mercy and justice. Those who say justice means the punishing of sin, and mercy the not punishing of sin, and attribute both to God, would make a schism in the very idea of God. And this brings me to the question, What is meant by divine justice?

Human justice may be a poor distortion of justice, a mere shadow of it; but the justice of God must be perfect. We cannot frustrate it in its working; are we just to sit in our idea of it? In God shall we imagine a distinction of office and character? God is one; and the depth of foolishness is reached by that theology which talks of God as if He held different offices, and differed in each. It sets a contradiction in the very nature of God Himself. It represents Him, for instance, as having to do that as a magistrate which as a father He would not do! The love of the father makes Him desire to be unjust as a magistrate!

Oh the folly of any mind that would explain God before obeying Him! that would map out the character of God, instead of crying, Lord, what would you have me to do? God is no magistrate; but, if He were, it would be a position to which His fatherhood alone gave Him the right; His rights as a father cover every right He can be analytically supposed to possess.

The justice of God is this, that—to use a boyish phrase, the best the language will now afford me because of misuse—He gives every man, woman, child, and beast—everything that has being—*fair play*. He renders to every man according to his work. And therein lies His perfect mercy, for nothing else would be merciful to the man, and nothing but mercy could be fair to him. God does nothing of which any just man, the thing set fairly and fully before him so that he understood, would not say, "That is fair."

Who would, I repeat, say a man was a just man because he insisted on prosecuting every offender? A scoundrel might do that. Yet the justice of God, forsooth, is His punishment of sin! A just man is one who cares, and tries, and always tries, to give fair play to everyone in everything. When we speak of the justice of God, let us see that we do mean justice! Punishment of the guilty may be involved in justice, but it does not constitute the justice of God one atom more than it would constitute the justice of a man.

The Lord of Life complains of men for not judging right. To say on the authority of the Bible that God does a thing no honorable man would do, is to lie against God; to say that it is therefore right, is to lie against the very Spirit of God. To uphold a lie for God's sake is to be against God, not for Him. God cannot be lied for. He is the truth. The truth alone is on His side. While His child could not see the rectitude of a thing, He would infinitely rather, even if the thing were right, have him say, "God could not do that thing," than have him believe that He did it.

If it be said by any that God does a thing, and the thing seems to me unjust, than either I do not know what the thing is, or God does not do it. The saying cannot mean what it seems to mean, or the saying is not true. If, for instance, it be said that God visits the sins of the fathers on the children, a man who takes *visits upon* to mean *punishes,* and *the children* to mean *the innocent children,* ought to say, "Either I do not understand the statement, or the thing is not true, whoever says it." God *may* do what seems to a man not right, but it must so seem to him because God works on higher, on divine, on perfect principles, too right for a selfish, unfair, or unloving man to understand. But least of all must we accept some low notion of justice in a man, and argue that God is just in doing after that notion.

Does God Punish Sin?

The common idea, then, is, that the justice of God consists in punishing sin: it is in the hope of giving a larger idea of the justice of God that I ask, *"Why is God bound to punish sin?"*

"How could He be a just God and not punish sin?"

Mercy is a good and right thing, I answer, and but for sin there could be no mercy. We are enjoined to forgive; to be merciful, to be as our Father in heaven. Two rights cannot possibly be opposed to each other. If God punish sin, it must be merciful to punish sin; and if God forgive sin, it must be just to forgive sin. We are required to forgive, with the argument that our Father forgives. It must, I say, be right to forgive. Every attribute of God must be infinite as Himself. He cannot be sometimes merciful, and not always merciful. He cannot be just, and not always just. Mercy belongs to Him, and needs no contrivance of theologic chicanery to justify it.

"Then you mean that it is wrong to punish sin; therefore, God does not punish sin?"

By no means; God does punish sin, but there is no opposition between punishment and forgiveness. The one may be essential to the possibility of the other. *Why*, I repeat, does God punish sin? That is my point.

"Because in itself sin deserves punishment."

Then how can He tell us to forgive it?

"He punishes, and having punished He forgives?"

That will hardly do. If sin demands punishment, and the righteous punishment is given, then the man is free. Why should he be forgiven?

"He needs forgiveness because no amount of punishment will meet his deserts."

(I avoid for the present, as anyone may perceive, the probable expansion of this reply.)

Then why not forgive him at once if the punishment is not essential—if part can be pretermitted? And again, can that be required which, according to your showing, is not adequate? You will perhaps answer,

"God may please to take what little He can have," and this brings me to the fault in the whole idea.

Punishment is *nowise* an *offset* to sin. Foolish people sometimes, in a tone of self-gratulatory pity, will say, "If I have sinned I have suffered." Yes, verily, but what of that? What merit is there in it? Even had you laid the suffering upon yourself, what did that do to make up for the wrong? That you may have bettered by your suffering is well for you, but what atonement is there in the suffering? The notion is a false one altogether. Punishment, or deserved suffering, is no equipoise to sin.

If it were an offset to wrong, then God would be bound to punish for the sake of the punishment; but He cannot be, for He forgives. Then it is not for the sake of the punishment, as a thing that in itself ought to be done, but for the sake of something else, as a means to an end, that God punishes. It is not directly for justice, else how could He show mercy, for that would involve injustice?

God's Obligation

Primarily, God is not bound to *punish* sin; He is bound to *destroy* sin. If He were not the Maker, He might not be bound to destroy sin—I do not know. But seeing He has created creatures who have sinned, and therefore sin has, by the creating act of God, come into the world, God is, in His own righteousness, bound to destroy sin.

"But that is to have no mercy."

You mistake. God does destroy sin; He is always destroying sin. In Him I trust that He is destroying sin in me. He is always saving the sinner from his sins, and that is destroying sin. But vengeance on the sinner, the law of a tooth for a tooth, is not in the heart of God, neither in His hand. If the sinner and the sin in him, are the concrete object of the divine wrath, then indeed there can be no mercy. Then indeed there will be an end put to sin by the destruction of the sin and the sinner together. But thus would no atonement be wrought—nothing be done to make up for the wrong God has allowed to come into being by creating man. There must be an atonement, a making-up, a bringing together—an atonement which, I say, cannot be made except by the man who has sinned.

Punishment, I repeat, is not the thing required of God, but the absolute destruction of sin. What better is the world, what better is the sinner, what better is God, what better is the truth, that the sinner should suffer—continue suffering to all eternity? Would there be less sin in the universe? Would there be any making up for sin? Would it show God justified in doing what He knew would bring sin into the world, justified in making creatures who He knew would sin? What setting-right would come of the sinner's suffering?

If justice demand it, if suffering be the equivalent for sin, then the sinner must suffer, then God is bound to exact his suffering, and not pardon; and so the making of man was a tyrannical deed, a creative cruelty. But grant that the sinner has deserved to suffer, no amount of suffering is any atonement for his sin. To suffer to all eternity could not make up for one unjust word.

Does that mean, then, that for an unjust word I deserve to suffer for all eternity? The unjust word is an eternally evil thing; nothing but God in my heart can cleanse me from the evil that uttered it; but does it follow that I saw the evil of what I did so perfectly, that eternal punishment for it would be just?

Sorrow and confession and self-abasing love will make up for the evil word; suffering will not. For evil in the abstract, nothing can be done. It is eternally evil. But I may be saved from it by learning to loathe it, to hate it, to shrink from it with an eternal avoidance. The only vengeance worth having on sin is to make the sinner himself its executioner.

Sin and punishment are in no antagonism to each other in man, any more than pardon and punishment are in God; they can perfectly co-exist. The one naturally follows the other, punishment being born of sin, because evil exists only by the life of good, and has no life of its own, being in itself death. Sin and suffering are not natural opposites; the opposite of evil is good, not suffering; the opposite of sin is not suffering but righteousness. The path across the gulf that divides right from wrong is not the fire, but repentance.

Take any of those wicked people in Dante's hell, and ask wherein is justice served by their punishment. Mind, I am not saying it is not right to punish them; I am saying that justice is not, never can be, satisfied by suffering—nay, cannot have any satisfaction in or from suffering. Human resentment, human revenge, human hate may.

Such justice as Dante's keeps wickedness alive in its most terrible forms. The life of God goes forth to inform, or at least give a home to victorious evil. Is He not defeated every time that one of those lost souls defies Him? God is triumphantly defeated, I say, throughout the hell of His vengeance. Although against evil, it is but the vain and wasted cruelty of a tyrant. There is no destruction of evil thereby, but an enhancing of its horrible power in the midst of the most agonizing and disgusting tortures a *divine* imagination can invent.

If sin must be kept alive, then hell must be kept alive; but while I regard the smallest sin as infinitely loathsome, I do not believe that any being, never good enough to see the essential ugliness of sin, could sin so as to *deserve* such punishment. I am not now, however, dealing with the question of the duration of punishment, but with the idea of punishment itself; and would only say in passing, that the notion that a creature born imperfect, nay, born with impulses to evil not of his own generating, and which he could not help having, a creature to whom the true face of God was never presented, and by whom it never could have been seen, should be thus condemned, is as loathsome a lie against God as could find place in heart too undeveloped to understand what justice is, and too low to look up into the face of Jesus. It never in truth found place in any heart, though in many a pettifogging brain. There is but one thing lower than deliberately to believe such a lie, and that is to worship the God of whom it is believed.

The Purpose of Punishment

The one deepest, highest, truest, fittest, most wholesome suffering must be generated in the wicked by a vision, a true sight, more or less adequate, of the hideousness of their lives, of the horror of the wrongs they have done. Physical suffering may be a factor in rousing this mental pain; but "I would I had never been born!" must be the cry of Judas, not because of the hell-fire around him, but because he loathes the man that betrayed his Friend, the world's Friend.

When a man loathes himself, he has begun to be saved. Punishment tends to this result. Not for its own sake, not as a make-up for sin, not for divine revenge—horrible words—not for any satisfaction to justice, can punishment exist. Punishment is for the sake of amendment and atonement. God is bound by His love to punish sin in order to deliver His creature: He is bound by His justice to destroy sin in His creation.

Love is justice—is the fulfilling of the law, for God as well as for His children. This is the reason of punishment; this is why justice requires that the wicked shall not go unpunished—that they, through the eye-opening power of pain, may come to see and do justice, may be brought to desire and make all possible amends, and so become just. Such punishment concerns justice in the deepest degree. For Justice, that is God, is bound in Himself to see justice done by His children—not in the mere outward act, but in their very being. He is bound in Himself to make up for wrong done by His children, and He can do nothing to make up for wrong done but by bringing about the repentance of the wrong-doer.

When the man says, "I did wrong; I hate myself and my deed; I cannot endure to think that I did it!" then, I say, is atonement begun. Without that, all that the Lord did would be lost. He would have made no atonement. Repentance, restitution, confession, prayer for forgiveness, righteous dealing thereafter, is the sole possible, the only true make-up for sin. For nothing less than this did Christ die.

When a man acknowledges the right he denied before; when he says to the wrong, "I abjure, I loathe you; I see now what you are; I could not see it before because I would not; God forgive me; make me clean, or let me die!" then justice, that is God, has conquered—and not till then.

What Atonement Is There?

There is every atonement that God cares for; and the work of Jesus Christ on earth was the creative atonement, because it works atonement in every heart. He brings and is bringing God and man, and man and man, into perfect unity: "I in them and thou in me, that they may be made perfect in one."

"That is a dangerous doctrine!"

More dangerous than you think to many things—to every evil, to every lie, and to every false trust in what Christ did, instead of in Christ Himself. Paul glories in the cross of Christ, but he does not trust in the cross: he trusts in the living Christ and His living Father.

Justice then requires that sin should be put an end to; and not that only, but that it should be atoned for; and where punishment can do anything to this end, where it can help the sinner to know what he has been guilty of, where it can soften his heart to see his pride and wrong and cruelty, justice requires that punishment shall not be spared. And the more we believe in God, the surer we shall be that He will spare nothing that suffering can do to deliver His child from death.

If suffering cannot serve this end, we need look for no more hell, but for the destruction of sin by the destruction of the sinner. That, however, would, it appears to me, be for God to suffer defeat, blameless indeed, but defeat.

If God be defeated, He must destroy, that is, He must withdraw life. How can He go on sending forth His life into irreclaimable souls, to keep sin alive in them throughout the ages of eternity? But then, I say, no atonement would be made for the wrongs they have done. God remains defeated, for He has created that which sinned, and which would not repent and make up for its sin.

But those who believe that God will thus be defeated by many souls, must surely be of those who do not believe He cares enough to do His very best for them. He *is* their Father; He had power to make them out of Himself, separate from Himself, and capable of being one with Him: surely He will somehow save and keep them! Not the power of sin itself can close *all* the channels between creating and created.

The Grip of False Idea

The notion of suffering as an offset for sin, the foolish idea that a man by suffering borne may get out from under the hostile claim to which his wrong-doing has subjected him, comes first of all, I think, from the satisfaction we feel when wrong comes to grief. Why do we feel this satisfaction? Because we hate wrong, but, not being righteous ourselves, more or less hate the wronger as well as his wrong, hence are not only righteously pleased to behold the law's disapproval proclaimed in his punishment, but unrighteously pleased with his suffering, because of the impact upon us of his wrong. In this way the inborn justice of our nature passes over to evil.

It is no pleasure to God, as it so often is to us, to see the wicked suffer. To regard any suffering with satisfaction, save it be sympathetically with its curative quality, comes of evil, is human because undivine, is a thing God is incapable of. His nature is always to forgive, and just because He forgives, He punishes.

Because God is so altogether alien to wrong, because it is to Him a heart-pain and trouble that one of His little ones should do the evil thing, there is, I believe, no extreme of suffering to which, for the sake of destroying the evil thing in them He would not subject them. A man might flatter, or bribe, or coax a tyrant; but there is no refuge from the love of God; that love will, for very love, insist upon the "last penny."

"That is not the sort of love I care about!"

No; how should you? I well believe it! You cannot care for it until you begin to know it. But the eternal love will not be moved to yield you to the selfishness that is killing you. You may sneer at such love, but the Son of God who took the weight of that love, and bore it through the world, is content with it, and so is everyone who knows it. The love of the Father is a radiant perfection. Love and not self-love is lord of the universe.

Justice demands your punishment, because justice demands, and will have, the destruction of sin. Justice demands your punishment because it demands that your Father should do His best for you. God, being the God of justice, that is of fair-play, and having made us what we are, apt to fall and capable of being raised again, is in Himself bound to punish in order to deliver us—else is His relation to us poor beside that of an earthly father. "To thee, O Lord, belongs steadfast love for thou dost requite a man according to his work." A man's work is his character; and God in His mercy is not indifferent, but treats him according to his work.

The notion that the salvation of Jesus is a salvation from the consequences of our sins, is a false, mean, low notion. The salvation of Christ is salvation from the smallest tendency of leaning to sin. It is a deliverance into the pure air of God's ways of thinking and feeling. It is a salvation that makes the heart pure, with the will and choice of the heart to be pure. To such a heart, sin is disgusting. It sees a thing as it is,—that is, as God sees it, for God sees everything as it is. The souls thus saved would rather sink into the flames of hell than steal into heaven and skulk there under the shadow of an imputed righteousness. No soul is saved that would not prefer hell to sin. Jesus did not die to save us from punishment; He was called Jesus because He should save His people from their sins.

MacDonald's Creed

I believe in Jesus Christ, the eternal Son of God, my elder brother, my lord and master; I believe that He has a right to my absolute obedience whereinsoever I know or shall come to know His will; that to obey Him is to ascend the pinnacle of my being; that not to obey Him would be to deny Him.

I believe that He died that I might die like Him—die to any ruling power in me but the will of God—live ready to be nailed to the cross as He was, if God will it. I believe that He is my Savior from myself, and from all that has come of loving myself, from all that God does not love, and would not have me love—all that is not worth loving; that He died that the justice, the mercy of God, might have its way with me, making me just as God is just, merciful as He is merciful, perfect as my Father in heaven is perfect.

I believe and pray that He will give me what punishment I need to set me right, or keep me from going wrong. I believe that He died to deliver me from all meanness, all pretence, all falseness, all unfairness, all poverty of spirit, all cowardice, all fear, all anxiety, all forms of self-love, all trust or hope in possession; to make me merry as a child, the child of our Father in heaven, loving nothing but what is lovely, desiring nothing I should be ashamed to let the universe of God see me desire.

I believe that God is just like Jesus, only greater yet, for Jesus said so. I believe that God is absolutely, grandly beautiful, even as the highest soul of man counts beauty, but infinitely beyond that soul's highest idea—with the beauty that creates beauty, not merely shows it, or itself exists beautiful. I believe that God has always done, is always doing His best for every man; that no man is miserable because God is forgetting him; that he is not a God to crouch before, but our Father, to whom the child-heart cries exultant, "Do with me as you will."

I believe that there is nothing good for me or for any man but God, and more and more of God, and that alone through knowing Christ can we come nigh to Him.

I believe that no man is ever condemned for any sin except one—that he will not leave his sins and come out of them, and be the child of Him who is his father.

I believe that justice and mercy are simply one and the same thing; without justice to the full there can be no mercy, and without mercy to the full there can be no justice; that such is the mercy of God that He will hold His children in the consuming fire of His distance until they pay the last penny, until they drop the purse of selfishness with all the dross that is in it, and rush home to the Father and the Son, and the many brethren—rush inside the centre of the life-giving fire whose outer circles burn. I believe that no hell will be lacking which would help the just mercy of God to redeem His children.

I believe that to him who obeys, and thus opens the doors of his heart to receive the eternal gift, God gives the Spirit of His Son, the Spirit of Himself, to be in him, and lead him to the understanding of all truth; that the true disciple shall thus always know what he ought to do, that the Spirit of the Father and the Son enlightens by teaching righteousness.

I believe that no teacher should strive to make men think as he thinks, but to lead them to the living Truth, to the Master Himself, of whom alone they can learn anything, who will make them in themselves know what is true by the very seeing of it. I believe that the inspiration of the Almighty alone gives understanding. I believe that to be the disciple of Christ is the end of being; that to persuade men to be His disciples is the end of teaching.

Atonement

"The sum of all this is that you do not believe in the atonement?"

I believe in Jesus Christ. Nowhere am I requested to believe in any thing, or in any statement, but everywhere to believe in God and in Jesus Christ. I believe that Jesus Christ *is* our atonement; that through Him we are reconciled to, made one with God. There is not one word in the New Testament about reconciling God to us; it is we that have to be reconciled to God.

I am not writing, neither desire to write, a treatise on the atonement, my business being to persuade men to be atoned to God; but I will go so far to meet my questioner as to say—without the slightest expectation of satisfying him, or the least care whether I do so or not, for his *opinion* is of no value to me, though his truth is of endless value to me and to the universe—that, even in the sense of the atonement being a making-up for the evil done by men toward God, I believe in the atonement.

Did not the Lord cast Himself into the eternal gulf of evil yawning between the children and the Father? Did He not bring the Father to us, let us look on our eternal Sire in the face of His true Son, that we might have that in our hearts which alone could make us love Him—a true sight of Him? Did He not insist on the one truth of the universe, the one saving truth, that God was just what He was? Did He not hold to that assertion to the last, in the face of contradiction and death? Did He not thus lay down His life persuading us to lay down ours at the feet of the Father? Has not His very life by which He died passed into those who have received Him, and re-created theirs, so that now they live with the life which alone is life? Did He not foil and slay evil by letting all the waves and billows of its horrid sea break upon Him, go over Him, and die without rebound—spend their rage, fall defeated, and cease? Verily, He made atonement.

We sacrifice to God!—it is God who has sacrificed His own Son to us; there was no way else of getting the gift of Himself into our hearts. Jesus sacrificed Himself to His Father and the children to bring them together—all the love on the side of the Father and Son, all the selfishness on the side of the children. If the joy that alone makes life worth living, the joy that God is such as Christ, be a true thing in my heart, how can I but believe in the atonement of Jesus Christ? I believe it heartily, as God means it.

Then again, as the power that brings about a making-up for any wrong done by man to man, I believe in the atonement. Who that believes in Jesus does not long to atone to his brother for the injury he has done him? What repentant child, feeling he has wronged his father, does not desire to make atonement? Who is the mover, the causer, the persuader, the creator of the repentance of the passion that restores fourfold?—Jesus, our propitiation, our atonement. He is the HEAD and leader, the prince of the atonement.

He could not do it without us, but He leads us up to the Father's knee: He makes us make atonement. Learning Christ, we are not only sorry for what we have done wrong, we not only turn from it and hate it, but we become able to serve both God and man with an infinitely high and true service, a soul-service. We are able to offer our whole being to God to whom by deepest right it belongs.

Have I injured anyone? With Him to aid my justice, new risen with Him from the dead, shall I not make good amends? Have I failed in love to my neighbor? Shall I not now love him with an infinitely better love than was possible to me before? That I will and can make atonement, thanks be to Him who is my atonement, making me at one with God and my fellows! He is my life, my joy, my lord, my owner, the perfecter of my being by the perfection of His own. I dare not say with

Paul that I am the slave of Christ; but my highest aspiration and desire is to be the slave of Christ.

God's Forgiving Nature

"But you do not believe that the sufferings of Christ, as sufferings, justified the Supreme Ruler in doing anything which He would not have been at liberty to do but for those sufferings?"

I do not. I believe the notion is unworthy of man's belief, as it is dishonoring to God. It has its origin doubtless in a salutary sense of sin; but sense of sin is not inspiration, though it may lie not far from the temple-door. It is indeed an opener of the eyes, but upon home-defilement, not upon heavenly truth; it is not the revealer of secrets.

Also, there is another factor in the theory, and that is unbelief—incapacity to accept the freedom of God's forgiveness; incapacity to believe that it is God's chosen nature to forgive, that He is bound in His own divinely willed nature to forgive. No atonement is necessary to Him but that men should leave their sins and come back to His heart.

But men cannot believe in the forgiveness of God. Therefore they need, therefore He has given them a mediator. And yet they will not know Him. They think of the Father of Souls as if He had abdicated His fatherhood for their sins, and assumed the judge. If He put off His fatherhood, which He cannot do, for it is an eternal fact, he puts off with it all relation to us. He cannot repudiate the essential and keep the resultant. Men cannot, or will not, or dare not see that nothing but His being our Father gives Him any right over us—that nothing but that could give Him a perfect right.

They regard the Father of their spirits as their governor! They yield the idea of the Ancient of Days, "the glad creator," and put in its stead a miserable, puritanical martinet of a God, caring not for righteousness, but for His rights; not for the eternal purities, but the goody proprieties. The prophets of such a God take all the glow, all the hope, all the color, all the worth, out of life on earth, and offer you instead what they call eternal bliss—a pale, tearless hell. Of all things, turn from a mean, poverty-stricken faith. But, if you are straitened in your own mammon-worshipping soul, how shall you believe in a God any greater than can stand up in that prison-chamber?

I desire to wake no dispute, will myself dispute with no man, but for the sake of those whom certain *believers* trouble, I have spoken my mind. I love the one God seen in the face of Jesus Christ. From all copies of Jonathan Edwards's portrait of God, however faded by time, however softened by the use of less glaring pigments, I turn with loathing. Not such a God is He concerning whom was the message John heard from Jesus, that He is light, and in Him is no darkness at all.

Selections from

THE TRUTH IN JESUS

*But you did not so learn Christ; assuming
that you have heard about Him and were
taught in Him, as the truth is in Jesus. Put
off your old nature which belongs to your
former manner of life and is corrupt through
deceitful lusts.* Ephesians 4:20, 22

How have we learned Christ? It ought to be a startling thought, that
we may have learned Him wrong. That must be far worse than not
to have learned Him at all: His place is occupied by a false Christ, hard
to exorcize! The point is, whether we have learned Christ as He taught
Himself, or as men have taught Him who thought they understood, but did
not understand Him. Do we think we know Him—with notions fleshly, after
low, mean human fancies and explanations, or do we indeed know Him—
after the spirit, in our measure as God knows Him?

The Christian religion, throughout its history, has been open to
more corrupt misrepresentation than ever the Jewish could be, for as it
is higher and wider, so must it yield larger scope to corruption. Have we
learned Christ in false statements and corrupted lessons about Him, or
have we learned *Himself*? Nay, true or false, is only our brain full of things
concerning Him, or does He dwell Himself in our hearts, a learned, and
ever being learned lesson, the power of our life?

I have been led to what I am about to say, by a certain utterance of
one in the front rank of those who assert that we can know nothing of the

"Infinite and Eternal energy from which all things proceed," and the utterance is this:

> The visiting on Adam's descendants through hundreds of generations dreadful penalties for a small transgression which they did not commit; the damning of all men who do not avail themselves of an alleged mode of obtaining forgiveness, which most men have never heard of; and the effecting a reconciliation by sacrificing a son who was perfectly innocent, to satisfy the assumed necessity for a propitiatory victim; are modes of action which, ascribed to a human ruler, would call for expressions of abhorrence; and the ascription to them to the Ultimate Cause of things even now felt to be full of difficulties, must become impossible.

I do not quote the passage with the design of opposing either clause of its statement, for I entirely agree with it. Almost it feels an absurdity to say so. Neither do I propose addressing a word to the writer of it, or to any who hold with him. The passage bears out what I have often said—that I never yet heard a word from one of the way of thinking, which even touched anything I hold. One of my earliest recollections is of beginning to be at strife with the false system here assailed. Such paganism I scorn as heartily in the name of Christ, as I scorn it in the name of righteousness.

But had I to do with the writer, I should ask how it comes that, refusing these dogmas as abominable, and in themselves plainly false, yet knowing that they are attributed to men whose teaching has done more to civilize the world than that of any men besides—how it comes that, seeing such teaching as this could not have done so, he has not taken such pains of inquiry as must surely have satisfied a man of his faculty that such was not their teaching. It was indeed so different, and so good, that even the forced companionship of such horrible lies as those he has recounted, has been unable to destroy its regenerative power.

I suppose he will allow that there was a man named Jesus, who died for the truth He taught. Can he believe He died for such alleged truth as that? Would it not be well for me to ask him to inquire what He did really teach, according to the primary sources of our knowledge of Him? If he answered that the question was uninteresting to him, I should have no more to say. Nor did I now start to speak of him save with the object of making my position plain to those to whom I would speak—those, namely, who call themselves Christians.

If of them I should ask, "How comes it that such opinions are held concerning the Holy One, whose ways you take upon you to set forth?" I should be met by most with the answer, "Those are the things He tells us Himself in His word; we have learned them from the Scriptures."

Of those whose presentation of Christian doctrine is represented in the quotation above, there are two classes—such as are content it should be so, and such to whom those things are grievous, but who do not see how to get rid of them. To the latter it may be of some little comfort to have one who has studied the New Testament for many years and loves it beyond the power of speech to express, declare to them his conviction that there is not an atom of such teaching in the whole lovely, divine utterance. Such things are all and altogether the invention of men. Honest invention, in part at least, I grant, but yet not true. Thank God, we are nowise bound to accept any man's explanation of God's ways and God's doings, however good the man may be, if it do not commend itself to our conscience. The man's conscience may be a better conscience than ours, and his judgment clearer; nothing the more can we accept while we cannot see good. To do so would be to sin.

Expostulation

I desire to address those who call themselves Christians, and expostulate with them thus:

Whatever be your *opinions* on the greatest of all subjects, is it well that the impression with regard to Christianity made upon your generation should be that of your opinions, and not of something beyond opinion? Is Christianity capable of being represented by opinion, even the best? If it were, how many of us are such as God would choose to represent His thoughts and intents by our opinions concerning them? Who is there of his friends whom any thoughtful man would depute to represent his thoughts to his fellows? If you answer, "The opinions I hold and by which I represent Christianity, are those of the Bible," I reply, that none can understand, still less represent, the opinions of another, but such as are of the same mind with him—certainly none who mistake his whole scope and intent so far as in supposing *opinion* to be the object of any writer in the Bible. Is Christianity a system of articles of belief, let them be correct as language can give them? Never. So far am I from believing it, that I would rather have a man holding, as numbers of you do, what seem to me the most obnoxious untruths, opinions the most irreverent and gross, if at the same time he *lived* in the faith of the Son of God, that is, trusted in God as the Son of God trusted in Him, than I would have a man with every one of whose formulas of belief I utterly coincided, but who knew nothing of a daily life and walk with God. The one, holding doctrines of devils, is yet a child of God; the other, holding the doctrines of Christ is of the world, yea, of the devil.

"How! a man hold the doctrine of devils, and yet be of God?"

Yes; for to hold a thing with the intellect, is not to believe it. A man's real belief is that which he lives by; and that which the man I mean lives by, is the love of God, and obedience to His law, so far as he has recognized it. What a man believes, is the thing he does. This man would shrink with loathing from actions such as he thinks God justified in doing; like God, he loves and helps and saves. Will the living God let such a man's opinions damn him? No more than He will let correct opinions of another, who lives for himself, save him. The best salvation even the latter could give would be but damnation.

What I come to and insist upon is, that—supposing your theories right, and containing all that is to be believed—yet those theories are not what makes you Christians, if Christians indeed you are. On the contrary, they are, with not a few of you, just what keeps you from being Christians. For when you say that, to be saved, a man must hold this or that, then you are leaving the living God and His will, and putting trust in some notion about Him or His will.

While the mind is occupied in inquiring, "Do I believe or feel this thing right?" the true question is forgotten: "Have I left all to follow Him?"

To the man who gives himself to the living Lord, every belief will necessarily come right: the Lord Himself will see that His disciple believe aright concerning him. If a man cannot trust Him for this, what claim can he make to faith in Him? It is because he has little or no faith, that he is left clinging to preposterous and dishonoring ideas, the traditions of men concerning His Father, and neither His teaching nor that of His apostles. The living Christ is to them but a shadow; the all but obliterated Christ of their theories no soul can thoroughly believe in. The disciple of such a Christ rests on His work, or His merits, or His atonement!

What I insist upon is, that a man's faith shall be in the living, loving, ruling, helping Christ, devoted to us as much as ever He was, and with all the powers of the Godhead for the salvation of His brethren. It is not faith that He did this, that His work wrought that—it is faith in the Man who did and is doing everything for us that will save him. Without this He cannot work to heal spiritually, any more than He would heal physically, when He was present to the eyes of men.

Do you ask, "What is faith in Him?" I answer, the leaving of your way, your objects, your self, and the taking of His and Him; the leaving of your trust in men, in money, in opinion, in character, in atonement itself, *and doing as He tells you.* I can find no words strong enough to serve the weight of this necessity—this obedience. It is the one terrible heresy of the church, that it has always been presenting something else than obedience as faith in Christ.

The work of Christ is not the Working Christ, any more than the clothing of Christ is the body of Christ. If the woman who touched the hem of His garment had trusted in the garment and not in Him who wore it, would she have been healed? And the reason that so many who believe *about* Christ rather than in Him, get the comfort they do, is that, touching thus the mere hem of His garment, they cannot help believing a little in the live man inside the garment.

Some even ponder the imponderable—whether they are of the elect, whether they have an interest in the blood shed for sin, whether theirs is a saving faith—when all the time the Man who died for them is waiting to begin to save them from every evil, and first from this self which is consuming them with trouble about its salvation. He will set them free, and take them home to the bosom of the Father—if only they will mind what He says to them—which is the beginning, middle, and end of faith. If they would but awake and arise from the dead, and come out into the light which Christ is waiting to give them, He would begin at once to fill them with the fulness of God.

The Primacy of Obedience

"But I do not know how to awake and arise!"

I will tell you. Get up, and do something the Master tells you; so make yourself His disciple at once. Instead of asking yourself whether you believe or not, ask yourself whether you have this day done one thing because He said, Do it, or once abstained because He said, Do not do it. It is simply absurd to say you believe, or even want to believe in Him, if you do not anything He tells you. If you can think of nothing He ever said as having had an atom of influence on your doing or not doing, you have too good ground to consider yourself no disciple of His.

But you can begin at once to *be* a disciple of the Living One—by obeying Him in the first thing you can think of in which you are not obeying Him. We must learn to obey Him in everything, and so must begin somewhere. Let it be at once, and in the very next thing that lies at the door of our conscience! Oh fools and slow of heart, if you think of nothing but Christ, and do not set yourselves to do His words! You but build your houses on the sand.

What have those teachers not to answer for who have turned your regard away from the direct words of the Lord Himself, which are spirit and life, to contemplate plans of salvation tortured out of the words of His apostles, even were those plans as true as they are false! There is but one plan of salvation, and that is to believe in the Lord Jesus Christ; that is, to take Him for what He is—our Master, and His words as if He meant them, which assuredly He did. To do His words is to enter into vital relation with Him, to obey Him is the only way to be one with Him.

The relation between Him and us is an absolute one; it can nohow begin to *live* but in obedience; it *is* obedience. There can be no truth, no reality, in any initiation of at-one-ment with Him, that is not obedience. What! have I the poorest notion of God, and dare think of entering into relations with Him, the very first of which is not that what He says, I will do? The thing is eternally absurd, and comes of the father of lies.

I know what Satan whispers to those to whom such teaching as this is distasteful: "it is the doctrine of works!" But one word of the Lord humbly heard and received will suffice to send all the demons of false theology into the abyss. He says the man that does not do the things He tells him, builds his house to fall in utter ruin. He instructs His messengers to go and baptize all nations, "teaching them to observe all that I have commanded you." Tell me it is faith He requires: do I not know it? and is not faith the highest act of which the human mind is capable? But faith in what? Faith in what He is, in what He says—a faith which can have no existence except in obedience—a faith which *is* obedience.

What have you done this day because it was the will of Christ? Have you dismissed, once dismissed, an anxious thought for the morrow? Have you ministered to any needy soul or body, and kept your right hand from knowing what your left hand did? Have you begun to leave all and follow Him? Did you set yourself to judge righteous judgment? Are you being wary of covetousness? Have you forgiven your enemy? Are you hungering and thirsting after righteousness? Have you given to some one that asked of you?

Tell me something that you have done, are doing, or are trying to do because He told you. If you do nothing that He says, it is no wonder that you cannot trust in Him, and are therefore driven to seek refuge in the atonement, as if something He had done, and not He Himself in His doing were the atonement. *That is not as you understand it?* What does it matter how you understand, or what you understand, so long as you are not of one mind with the Truth, so long as you and God are not *at one*, do not atone together? How should you understand?

Knowing that you do not heed His word, why should I heed your explanation of it? You do not His will, and so you cannot understand Him; you do not know Him, that is why you cannot trust in Him. It is the heart of the child that alone can understand the Father.

Do you suppose He ever gave a commandment knowing it was of no use for it could not be done? He tells us a thing knowing that we must do it, or be lost; that not His Father Himself could save us but by getting us at length to do everything He commands, for not otherwise can we know life, can we learn the holy secret of divine being. He knows that you can try, and that in your trying and failing He will be able to help you, until at length you shall do the will of God even as He does it Himself. He takes the will in the imperfect deed, and makes the deed at last perfect.

We must forsake all our fears and distrusts for Christ. We must receive His teaching heartily, nor let the interpretation of it attributed to His apostles make us turn aside from it. I say interpretation attributed to them; for what they teach is never against what Christ taught, though very often the exposition of it is—and that from no fault in the apostles; but from the grievous fault of those who would understand, and even explain, rather than obey.

We may be sure of this, that no man will be condemned for any sin that is past. If he be condemned, it will be because he would not come to the light when the light came to him; because he would not cease to do evil and learn to do well; because he hid his unbelief in the garment of a false faith, and would not obey; because he imputed to himself a righteousness that was not his; because he preferred imagining himself a worthy person, to confessing himself everywhere in the wrong, and repenting. We may be sure also of this, that, if a man becomes the disciple of Christ, He will not leave him in ignorance as to what he has to believe; he shall know the truth of everything it is needful for him to understand. If we do what He tells us, His light will go up in our hearts. Till then we could not understand even if He explained to us.

Leaving All

Is there then anything you will not leave for Christ? You cannot know Him—and yet He is the Truth, the one thing alone that can be known! Do you not care to be imperfect? Would you rather keep this or that, with imperfection, than part with it to be perfect? You cannot know Christ, for the very principle of His life was the simple absolute relation of realities; His one idea was to be a perfect child to His Father. He who will not part with all for Christ, is not worthy of Him, and cannot know Him; and the Lord is true, and cannot acknowledge him.

How could He receive to His house, as one of His kind, a man who prefers something to His Father; a man who is not for God; a man who will strike a bargain with God, and say, "I will give up so much, if you will spare me"! To yield all to Him who has only made us and given us everything, yea His very self by life and by death, such a man counts too much. His conduct says, "I never asked you to do so much for me, and I cannot make the return you demand." The man will have to be left to himself. He must find what it is to be without God! Those who know God, or have but begun to catch a far-off glimmer of His gloriousness, of what He is, regard life as insupportable save God be the All in all, the first and the last.

To let their light shine, not to force on them their interpretations of God's designs, is the duty of Christians towards their fellows. If you who set yourselves to explain the theory of Christianity, had set yourselves instead to do the will of the Master, the one object for which the Gospel was preached to you, how different would now be the condition of that portion of the world with which you come into contact! Had you given yourselves to the understanding of His word that you might do it, and not to the quarrying from it of material wherewith to buttress your systems, in many a heart by this time would the name of the Lord be loved where now it remains unknown. The word of life would then by you have been held out indeed.

Men, undeterred by your explanations of Christianity—for you would not be forcing them on their acceptance—and attracted by your behavior, would be saying to each other, as Moses said to himself when he saw the bush that burned with fire and was not consumed, "I will turn aside and see this great sight!" They would be drawing nigh to behold how these Christians loved one another, and how just and fair they were to every one that had to do with them! to note that their goods were the best, their weight surest, their prices most reasonable, their word most certain! that in their families was neither jealousy nor emulation! that their children were as diligently taught to share, as some are to save, or to lay out only upon self—their mothers more anxious lest a child should hoard than lest he should squander; that in no house of theirs was religion one thing, and the daily life another.

Obedience Leads Us to Truth

If any of you tell me my doctrine is presumptuous, that it is contrary to what is taught in the New Testament, and what the best of men have always believed, I will not therefore proceed to defend even my beliefs, the principles on which I try to live—how much less my opinions! I appeal to you instead, whether or not I have spoken the truth concerning our paramount obligation to do the word of Christ. If you answer that I have not, I have nothing more to say; there is no other ground on which we can meet. But if you allow that it is a prime, even if you do not allow it *the* prime duty, then what I insist upon is, that you should do it, so and not otherwise recommending the knowledge of Him.

I do not attempt to change your opinions; if they are wrong, the obedience alone on which I insist can enable you to set them right; I only pray you to obey, and assert that thus only can you fit yourselves for understanding the mind of Christ. I say none but he who does right, can think right; you cannot *know* Christ to be right until you do as He does, as He tells you to do; neither can you set Him forth, until you know Him as He means Himself to be known, that is, as He is.

The true heart must see at once, that, however wrong I may or may not be in other things, at least I am right in this, that Jesus must be obeyed, and at once obeyed, in the things He did say: it will not long imagine to obey Him in things He did not say. If a man does what is unpleasing to Christ, believing it His will, he shall yet gain thereby, for it gives the Lord a hold of him, which He will use; but before he can reach liberty, he must be delivered from that falsehood. The Lord will leave no man to his own way, however much he may prefer it.

The Lord did not die to provide a man with the wretched heaven he may invent for himself, or accept invented for him by others; He died to give him life, and bring him to the heaven of the Father's peace. The children must share in the essential bliss of the Father and the Son. This is and has been the Father's work from the beginning—to bring us into the home of His heart, where He shares the glories of life with the Living One, in whom was born life to light me back to the original life. This is our destiny; and however a man may refuse, he will find it hard to fight with God—useless to kick against the goads of His love.

For the Father is goading him, or will goad him, if needful, into life by unrest and trouble; hell-fire will have its turn if less will not do. Can any need it more than such as will neither enter the kingdom of heaven themselves, nor suffer them to enter it that would? The old race of the Pharisees is by no means extinct. They were St. Paul's great trouble, and are yet to be found in every religious community under the sun.

The one only thing truly to reconcile all differences is to walk in the light. So St. Paul teaches us in his epistle to the Philippians, the third chapter and sixteenth verse. After setting forth the loftiest idea of human endeavor in declaring the summit of his own aspiration, he says—not, "This must be your endeavor also, or you cannot be saved," but, "If in anything you are otherwise minded, God will reveal that also to you. Only let us hold true to what we have attained." Observe what widest conceivable scope is given by the apostle to honest opinion, even in things of grandest import! The one only essential point with him is that whereto we have attained, what we have seen to be true, *we walk by that*.

In such walking, and in such walking only, love will grow, truth will grow; the soul, then first in its genuine element and true relation towards God, will see into reality that was before but a blank to it; and He who has promised to teach, will teach abundantly. Faster and faster will the glory of the Lord dawn upon the hearts and minds of His people so walking—then His people indeed. Fast and far will the knowledge of Him spread, for truth of action, both preceding and following truth of word, will prepare the way before Him.

The man walking in that whereto he has attained, will be able to think aright. The man who does not think right, is unable because he has not been walking right. Only when he begins to do the thing he knows, does he begin to be able to think aright; then God comes to him in a new and higher way, and works along with the spirit He has created.

ABBA, FATHER

> *. . . The spirit of sonship. When we cry,*
> *'Abba, Father'. . .* Romans 8:15

The hardest, gladdest thing in the world is to cry Father! from a full heart. I would help whom I may to call thus upon the Father.

There are things in all forms of the systematic teaching of Christianity to check this outgoing of the heart—with some to render it simply impossible. Such a cold wind blowing at the very gate of heaven—thank God, *outside* the gate!—is the so-called doctrine of *Adoption.* When a heart hears—and believes, or half believes—that it is not the child of God by origin, from the first of its being, but may possibly be adopted into His family, its love sinks at once in a cold faint: where is its own father, and who is this that would adopt it?

Let us look at the passage where Paul reveals his use of the word. It is in another of his epistles, Galatians 4:1-7.

From the passage it is as plain as St. Paul could make it, that, by the word translated *adoption,* he means the raising of a father's own child from the condition of tutelage and subjection to others—a state which, he says, is no better than that of a slave—to the position and rights of a son. None but a child could become a son; the idea is—a spiritual coming of age; *only when the child is a man is he really and fully a son.*

The thing holds in the earthly relation. How many children of good parents—good children in the main too—never know those parents, never feel towards them as children might, until, grown up, they have left the house—until, perhaps, they are parents themselves, or are parted from them by death! To be a child is not necessarily to be a son or daughter. The childship is the lower condition of the upward process towards the sonship, the soil out of which the true sonship shall grow, the former without which the latter were impossible.

God can no more than an earthly parent be content to have only children: He must have sons and daughters—children of His soul, of His spirit, of His love—not merely in the sense that He loves them, or even that they love Him, but in the sense that they love like Him, love as He loves. For this He does not adopt them. He dies to give them Himself, thereby to raise His own to His heart. He gives them a birth from above; they are born again out of Himself and into Himself—for He is the one and the all.

His children are not His real, true sons and daughters until they think like Him, feel with Him, judge as He judges, are at home with him, and without fear before Him because He and they mean the same thing, love the same things, seek the same ends. Nothing will satisfy Him, or do for us, but that we be one with our Father! What else could serve! How else should life ever be a good! Because we are the sons of God, we must become the sons of God.

In my own childhood and boyhood my father was the refuge from all the ills of life, even sharp pain itself. Therefore I say to son or daughter who has no pleasure in the name *Father,* "You must interpret the word by all that you have missed in life. All that human tenderness can give or desire in the nearness and readiness of love, all and infinitely more must be true of the perfect Father—of the maker of fatherhood, the Father of all the fathers of the earth, specially the Father of those who have specially shown a father-heart."

He has made us, but we have to be. All things were made *through* the word, but that which was made *in* the Word was life, and that life is the light of men. They who live by this light, that is, live as Jesus lived—by obedience, namely, to the Father, have a share in their own making. The light becomes life in them; they are, in their lower way, alive with the life that was first born in Jesus, and through Him has been born in them—by obedience they become one with the godhead. He does not *make* them the sons of God, but He gives them power to become the sons of God: in choosing and obeying the truth, man becomes the true son of the Father of lights.

Adoption of the Body

It remains to note yet another passage.

That never in anything he wrote was it St. Paul's intention to contribute towards a system of theology, it were easy to show: one sign of the fact is, that he does not hesitate to use this word he has perhaps himself made, in different, and apparently opposing, though by no means contradictory senses. His meanings always vivify each other. At one time he speaks of the sonship as being the possession of the Israelite, at another as his who has learned to cry *Abba, Father;* and here, in the passage I have now last to consider, that from the 18th to the 25th verse of this same eighth chapter of his epistle to the Romans, he speaks of the "adoption" as yet to come—and as if it had to do, not with our spiritual, but our bodily condition. This use of the word, however, though not the same use as we find anywhere else, is nevertheless entirely consistent with his other uses of it.

The 23rd verse says, "And not only the creation, but we ourselves, who have the first fruits of the Spirit, groan inwardly as we wait for adoption as sons, the redemption of our bodies."

It is nowise difficult to discern that the ideas in this and the main use are necessarily associated and more than consistent. The putting of a son in his true, his foreordained place, has outward relations as well as inward reality. The outward depends on the inward, arises from it, and reveals it. When the child whose condition under tutors had passed away took his position as a son, he would naturally change his dress and modes of life. When God's children cease to be slaves doing right from law and duty, and become His sons doing right from the essential love of God and their neighbor, they too must change the garments of their slavery for the robes of liberty, lay aside the body of this death, and appear in bodies like that of Christ, with whom they inherit of the Father.

But many children who have learned to cry *Abba, Father,* are yet far from the liberty of the sons of God. Sons they are and no longer children, yet they groan as being still in bondage! Plainly the apostle has no thought of working out an idea; with burning heart he is writing a letter. He gives, nevertheless, lines plentifully sufficient for us to work out his idea, and this is how it takes clear shape:

We are the sons of God the moment we lift up our hearts, seeking to be sons—the moment we begin to cry *Father*. But as the world must be redeemed in a few of its thoughts and wants and ways to begin with; it takes a long time to finish the new creation of this redemption. Shall it have taken millions of years to bring the world up to the point where a few of its inhabitants shall desire God, and shall the creature of this new birth be perfected in a day? The divine process may indeed now go on with tenfold rapidity, for the new factor of man's fellow-working, for the sake of which the whole previous array of means and forces existed, is now developed; but its end is yet far below the horizon of man's vision.

The apostle speaks at one time of the thing as to come, at another time as done—when it is but commenced. Our ways of thought are such. A man's heart may leap for joy the moment when, amidst the sea-waves, a strong hand has laid hold of the hair of his head. He may cry aloud, "I am saved," and he may be safe, but he is not saved; this is far from a salvation to suffice. So are we sons when we begin to cry Father, but we are far from perfected sons. So long as there is in us the least taint of distrust, the least lingering of hate or fear, we have not received the sonship; we have not such life in us as raised the body of Jesus; we have not attained to the resurrection of the dead—by which word, in his epistle to the Philippians (3:2), St. Paul means, I think, the same thing as here he means by the sonship which he puts in apposition with the redemption of the body.

Until our outward condition is that of sons royal, sons divine; so long as the garments of our souls, these mortal bodies, are mean—torn and dragged and stained; so long as we groan under sickness and weakness and weariness, old age, forgetfulness and all heavy things; so long we have not yet received the sonship in full—we are but getting ready. We groan being burdened; we groan, waiting for the sonship—to wit, the redemption of the body—the uplifting of the body to be a fit house and revelation of the indwelling spirit—nay, like that of Christ, a fit temple and revelation of the deeper indwelling God. For we shall always need bodies to manifest and reveal us to each other—bodies, then, that fit the soul with absolute truth of presentment and revelation. Hence the revealing of the sons of God, spoken of in the 19th verse, is the same thing as the redemption of the body. The body is redeemed when it is made fit for the sons of God; then it is a revelation of them—the thing it was meant for, and always, more or less imperfectly, was. Such it shall be, when truth is strong enough in the sons of God to make it such—for it is the soul that makes the body. When we are the sons of God in heart and soul, then shall we be the sons of God in body too: "we shall be like Him, for we shall see Him as He is."

I care little to speculate on the kind of this body; two things only I will say, as needful to be believed, concerning it: first, that it will be a body to show the same self as before but, second, a body to show the being truly—without the defects, that is, and imperfections of the former bodily revelation. Even through their corporeal presence shall we then know our own infinitely better, and find in them endlessly more delight, than before. These things we must believe, or distrust the Father of our spirits.

To see how the whole utterance hangs together, read from the 18th verse to the 25th, especially noticing the 19th: "For the creation waits with eager longing for the revealing" *(the out-shining)* "of the sons of God." When the sons of God show as they are, taking, with the character, the appearance and the place that belong to their sonship; when the sons of God sit with *the* Son of God on the throne of their Father; then shall they be in potency of fact the lords of the lower creation, the bestowers of liberty and peace upon it. Then shall the creation, subjected to vanity for their sakes, find its freedom in their freedom, its gladness in their sonship. The animals will glory to serve them, will joy to come to them for help.

Let the heartless scoff, the unjust despise! the heart that cries *Abba, Father,* cries to the God of the sparrow and the oxen; nor can hope go too far in hoping what that God will do for the creation that now groans and travails in pain because our higher birth is delayed. Shall not the Judge of all the earth do right? Shall my heart be more compassionate than His?

Thus have both Jesus Christ and His love-slave Paul represented God—as a Father perfect in love, grand in self-forgetfulness, supreme in righteousness, devoted to the lives He has uttered. I will not believe less of the Father than I can conceive of glory after the lines He has given me, after the radiation of His glory in the face of His Son. He is the express image of the Father, by which we, His imperfect images, are to read and understand Him: imperfect, we have yet perfection enough to spell towards the perfect.

Summary

It comes to this then, after the grand theory of the apostle. The world exists for our education. It is the nursery of God's children, served by troubled slaves, troubled because the children are themselves slaves—children, but not good children. Beyond its own will or knowledge, the whole creation works for the development of the children of God into the sons of God. When at last the children have arisen and gone to their Father; when they are clothed in the best robe, with a ring on their hands and shoes on their feet, shining out at length in their natural, their predestined sonship; than shall the mountains and the hills break forth before them into singing, and all the trees of the field shall clap their hands.

Then shall the wolf dwell with the lamb, and the leopard lie down with the kid and the calf, and the young lion and the fatling together, and a little child shall lead them. Then shall the fables of a golden age, which faith invented, and unbelief threw into the past, unfold their essential reality, and the tale of paradise prove itself a truth by becoming a fact. Then shall every ideal show itself a necessity, aspiration although satisfied put forth yet longer wings, and the hunger after righteousness know itself blessed. Then first shall we know what was in the Shepherd's mind when He said, "I came that they may have life, and have it abundantly."

Selections from

THE TRUTH

I am . . . the truth.
John 14:6

I desire to help those whom I may to understand more of what is meant by *the truth,* not for the sake of definition, or logical discrimination, but that, when they hear the word from the mouth of the Lord, the right idea may rise in their minds. Let us endeavor to arrive at His meaning by a gently ascending stair.

A thing being so, the word that says it is so, is the truth. But the fact may be of no value in itself, and our knowledge of it of no value either. Of most facts it may be said that the truth concerning them is of no consequence. For instance, it cannot be in itself important whether on a certain morning I took one side of the street or the other. It may be of importance to someone to know which I took, but in itself it is of none. It would therefore be felt unfit if I said, "It is *a truth* that I walked on the sunny side." The correct word would be *a fact,* not *a truth.*

Let us go up now from the region of facts that seem casual, to those facts that are invariable, by us unchangeable, which therefore involve what we call *law.* It will be seen at once that the *fact* here is of more dignity, and the truth or falsehood of a statement in this region of more consequence in itself. It is a small matter whether the water in my jug was frozen on such a morning; but it is a fact of great importance that at thirty-two degrees of Fahrenheit water always freezes. Is it a truth that water freezes at thirty-two degrees? I think not. Call it a law if you will—a law of nature if you choose—that it always is so, but not a truth.

Tell us why it *must* be so, and you state a truth. When we come to see that a law is such, because it is the embodiment of a certain eternal thought, beheld by us in it, a fact of the being of God, the facts of which alone are truths, then indeed it will be to us, not a law merely, but an embodied truth. A law of God's nature is a way He would have us think of Him; it is a necessary truth of all being. When we say, "I understand that law. I see why it ought to be. It is just like God," then it rises [to become] a revelation of character, nature, and will in God. It is a picture of something in God, a word that tells a fact about God, and is therefore far nearer being called a truth than anything below it.

I believe that every fact in nature is a revelation of God, is there such as it is because God is such as He is; and I suspect that all its facts impress us so that we learn God unconsciously. From the moment when first we come into contact with the world, it is to us a revelation of God, His things seen, by which we come to know the things unseen.

How should we imagine what we may of God, without the firmament over our heads, a visible sphere, yet a formless infinitude! What idea could we have of God without the sky? The truth of the sky is what it makes us feel of the God that sent it out to our eyes.

Poet vs. Scientist

We are here in region far above that commonly claimed for science, open only to the heart of the child and the childlike man and woman—a region in which the poet is among his own things, and to which he has often to go to fetch them. For things as they are, not as science deals with them, are the revelation of God to His children.

I would not be misunderstood: there is no fact of science not yet incorporated in a law, no law of science that has got beyond the hypothetic and tentative, that has not in it the will of God, and therefore may not reveal God; but neither fact nor law is there for the sake of fact or law; each is but a means to an end; in the perfected end we find the intent, and there God—not in the laws themselves, save as His means.

For that same reason, human science cannot discover God; for human science is but the backward undoing of the tapestry-web of God's science, works with its back to Him, and is always leaving Him—His intent, that is, His perfected work—behind it, always going farther and farther away from the point where His work culminates in revelation. Doubtless it thus makes some small intellectual approach to Him, but at best it can come only to His back; science will never find the fact of God.

Analysis is well, as death is well; analysis is death, not life. It discovers a little of the way God walks to His ends, but in so doing it forgets and leaves the end itself behind. I do not say the man of science does so, but the very process of his work is such a leaving of God's ends behind.

Ask a man of mere science, what is the truth of a flower: he will pull it to pieces, show you its parts, explain how they minister each to the life of the flower; he will tell you what changes are wrought in it by scientific cultivation; where it lives originally, where it can live; the effects upon it of another climate; what part the insects bear in its varieties—and doubtless many more facts about it.

Ask the poet what is the truth of the flower, and he will answer: "Why, the flower itself, the perfect flower, and what it cannot help saying to him who has ears to hear it." The truth of the flower is, not the facts about it, be they correct as ideal science itself, but the shining, glowing, gladdening, patient thing throned on its stalk—the compeller of smile and tear from the child and prophet.

The man of science laughs at this, because he is only a man of science, and does not know what it means. The children of God must always be mocked by the children of the world. Those that hold love the only good in the world, understand and smile at the world's children, and can do very well without anything they have got to tell them. In the higher state to which their love is leading them, they will speedily outstrip the men of science, for they have that which is at the root of science, that for the revealing of which God's science exists. What shall it profit a man to know all things, and lose the bliss, the consciousness of well-being, which alone can give value to his knowledge?

The truth *of a thing*, then, is the blossom of it, the thing it is made for. Truth in a man's imagination is the power to recognize this truth of a thing. Wherever, in anything that God has made, in the glory of it, be it sky or flower or human face, we see the glory of God, there a true imagination is beholding a truth of God. And now we must advance to a yet higher plane.

Becoming a True Person

We have seen that the moment whatever goes by the name of truth comes into connection with man, the moment the knowledge of it affects or ought to affect his sense of duty, it becomes a thing of far nobler import. A fact which in itself is of no value, becomes at once a matter of life and death—moral life and death, when a man has the choice, the imperative choice of being true or false concerning it.

When the truth, the heart, the summit, the crown of a thing, is perceived by a man, he approaches the fountain of truth whence the thing came, and perceiving God by understanding what is, becomes more of a man, more of the being he was meant to be. In virtue of this truth perceived, he has relations with the universe undeveloped in him till then. But far higher will the doing of the least, the most insignificant duty raise him. He begins thereby to be a true man.

A man may delight in the vision and glory of a truth, and not himself be true. The man whose vision is weak, but who, as far as he sees, and desirous to see farther, does the thing he sees, is a true man. If a man knows what is, and says it is not, his knowing does not make him less than a liar. The man who recognizes the truth of any human relation, and neglects the duty involved, is not a true man. The man who knows the laws of nature, and does not heed them, the more he teaches them to others, the less is he a true man. But he may obey them all and be the falsest of men, because of far higher and closer duties which he neglects. The man who takes good care of himself and none of his brother and sister, is false.

Man is man only in the doing of the truth, perfect man only in the doing of the highest truth, which is the fulfilling of his relations to his origin. But he has relations with his fellow man, closer infinitely than with any of the things around him, and to many a man far plainer than his relations with God. The very nature of a man depends upon or is one with these relations. They are *truths*, and the man is a true man as he fulfils them. Fulfilling them perfectly, he is himself a *truth*, a living truth.

The man is a true man who chooses duty; he is a perfect man who at length never thinks of duty, who forgets the name of it. The duty of Jesus was the doing in lower forms than the perfect that which He loved perfectly, and did perfectly in the highest forms also. Thus He fulfilled all righteousness. One who went to the truth by mere impulse, would be a holy animal, not a true man. Relations, truths, duties, are shown to the man away beyond him, that he may choose them, and be a child of God, choosing righteousness like Him. Hence the whole sad victorious human tale, and the glory to be revealed!

The facts of human relation, then, are truths indeed, and of awfullest import. "Anyone who hates his brother is a murderer, and you know that no murderer has eternal life abiding in him!" The man who lives a hunter after pleasure, not a laborer in the fields of duty, who thinks of himself as if he were alone on the earth, is in himself a lie. Instead of being the man he looks, the man he was made to be, he lives as the beasts seem to live—with this difference, I trust, that they are rising, while he, so far as lies in himself, is sinking. But he cannot be allowed to sink beyond God's reach; hence all the holy—that is, healing—miseries that come upon him, of which he complains as so hard and unfair: they are for the compelling of the truth he will not yield—a painful persuasion to be himself, to be a truth.

The highest truth to the intellect, the abstract truth, is the relation in which man stands to the Source of his being—his will to the Will whence it became a will, his love to the Love that kindled his power to love, his intellect to the Intellect that lighted his. If a man deal with these things only as things to be dealt with, as objects of thought, as ideas to be analysed and arranged in their due order and right relation, he treats them as facts and not as truths, and is no better, probably much the worse, for his converse with them, for he knows in a measure, and is false to all that is most worthy of his faithfulness.

But when the soul, or heart, or spirit, or what you please to call that which is the man himself and not his body, sooner or later becomes aware that he needs some one above him, whom to obey, in whom to rest, from whom to seek deliverance from what in himself is despicable, disappointing, unworthy even of his own interest; when he is aware of an opposition in him, which is not harmony; that, while he hates it, there is yet present with him, and seeming to be himself, what sometimes he calls *the old Adam*, sometimes *the flesh*, sometimes *his lower nature*, sometimes *his evil self;* and sometimes recognizes as simply that part of his being where God is not; then indeed is the man in the region of truth, and beginning to come true in himself.

Nor will it be long ere he discover that there is no part in him with which he would be at strife, so God were there, so that it were true, what it ought to be—in right relation to the whole; for, by whatever name called, the old Adam, or antecedent horse, or dog, or tiger, it would then fulfil its part holily, intruding upon nothing, subject utterly to the rule of the higher, horse or dog or tiger, it would be good horse, good dog, good tiger.

When a man is, with his whole nature, loving and willing the truth, he is then a live truth. But this he has not originated in himself. He has seen it and striven for it, but not originated it. The one originating, living, visible truth, embracing all truths in all relations, is Jesus Christ. He is true; He is the live Truth. His truth, chosen and willed by Him, is His absolute obedience to His Father. The obedient Jesus is Jesus the Truth.

He is true and the root of all truth and development of truth in men. Their very being, however far from the true human, is the undeveloped Christ in them, and his likeness to Christ is the truth of a man, even as the perfect meaning of a flower is the truth of a flower. Every man, according to the divine idea of him, must come to the truth of that idea; and under every form of Christ is the Christ. The truth of every man, I say, is the perfected Christ in him. As Christ is the blossom of humanity, so the blossom of every man is the Christ perfected in him.

He gives us the will wherewith to will and the power to use it, and the help needed to supplement the power, whatever in any case the need may be. But we ourselves must will the truth, and for that the Lord is waiting, for the victory of God His Father in the heart of His child. In this alone can he see of the travail of His soul, in this alone be satisfied. The work is His, but we must take our willing share. The will, the power of willing, may be created, but the willing is begotten. Because God wills first, man wills also.

When my being is consciously and willedly in the hands of Him who called it to live and think and suffer and be glad—given back to Him by a perfect obedience—I thenceforward breathe the breath, share the life of God Himself. Then I am free, in that I am true—which means one with the Father. And freedom knows itself to be freedom.

When a man is true, if he were in hell he could not be miserable. He is right with himself because right with Him whence he came. To be right with God is to be right with the universe; one with the power, the love, the will of the mighty Father, the cherisher of joy, the lord of laughter, whose are all glories, all hopes, who loves everything, and hates nothing but selfishness, which He will not have in His kingdom.

Christ then is the Lord of life; His life is the light of men; the light mirrored in them changes them into the image of Him, the Truth; and thus the Truth, who is the Son, makes them free.

Selections from
FREEDOM

And the truth will make you free. . . . every
one who commits sin is a slave to sin. The
slave does not continue in the house for ever;
the son continues for ever. So if the Son
makes you free, you will be free indeed.
John 8:32, 34-36

Those to whom God is not all in all, are slaves. They may not commit great sins; they may be trying to do right; but so long as they *serve* God, as they call it, from duty, and do not know Him as their Father, the joy of their being, they are slaves—good slaves, but slaves.

If they did not try to do their duty, they would be bad slaves. They are by no means so slavish as those that serve from fear, but they are slaves; and because they are but slaves, they can fulfil no righteousness, can do no duty perfectly, but must ever be trying after it wearily and in pain, knowing well that if they stop trying, they are lost. They are slaves indeed, for they would be glad to be adopted by one who is their own Father!

Where then are the sons? I know none, I answer, who are yet utterly and entirely sons or daughters. There may be such—God knows; I have not known them; or, knowing them, have not been myself such as to be able to recognize them. But I do know some who are enough sons and daughters to be at war with the slave in them, who are not content to be slaves to their Father.

Nothing I have seen or known of sonship, comes near the glory of the thing. But there are thousands of sons and daughters, though their number be yet only a remnant, who are siding with the Father of their spirits against themselves, against all that divides them from Him from whom they have come. Such are not slaves; they are true though not perfect children.

They are children—with more or less of the dying slave in them; they know it is there, and what it is, and hate the slavery in them, and try to slay it. The real slave is he who does not seek to be a child; who does not desire to end his slavery; who looks upon the claim of the child as presumption; who never lifts up his heart to cry, "Father, what would you have me to do?"

The slaves of sin rarely grumble at that slavery; it is their slavery to God they grumble at; of that alone they complain—of the painful messengers He sends to deliver them from their slavery both to sin and to Himself. They must be sons or slaves. They cannot rid themselves of their owner. Whether they deny God, or mock Him by acknowledging and not heeding Him, or treat Him as an arbitrary, formal monarch; whether, taking no trouble to find out what pleases Him, they do dull things for His service He cares nothing about, or try to propitiate Him by assuming with strenuous effort some yoke the Son never wore, and never called on them to wear, they are slaves, and not the less slaves that they are slaves to God. They are so thoroughly slaves, that they do not care to get out of their slavery by becoming sons and daughters, by finding the good of life.

Could a Creator make a creature whose well-being should not depend on Himself? The whole question rests and turns on the relation of creative and created, of which relation few seem to have the consciousness yet developed. To live without the eternal creative life is an impossibility. Freedom from God can only mean an incapacity for seeing the facts of existence, an incapability of understanding the glory of the creature who makes common cause with his Creator in His creation of him, who wills that the lovely will calling him into life and giving him choice, should finish making him, should draw him into the circle of the creative heart, to joy that he lives by no poor power of his own will, but is one with the causing life of his life, in closest breathing and willing, vital and claimant oneness with the life of all life.

Such a creature knows the life of the infinite Father as the very flame of his life, and joys that nothing is done or will be done in the universe in which the Father will not make him all of a sharer that it is possible for perfect generosity to make him. If you say this is irreverent, I doubt if you have seen the God manifest in Jesus.

But one who reads may call out, in the agony and thirst of a child waking from a dream of endless seeking and no finding, "I am bound like Lazarus in his grave-clothes! what am I to do?" Here is the answer, drawn from this parable of our Lord; for the saying is much like a parable, teaching more than it utters, appealing to the conscience and heart, not to the understanding: "You are a slave; the slave has no hold on the house; only the sons and daughters have an abiding rest in the home of their father. God cannot have slaves about Him always. You must give up your slavery, and be set free from it. That is what I am here for.

"If I make you free, you shall be free indeed; for I can make you free only by making you what you were meant to be, sons like myself. That is how alone the Son can work. But it is you who must become sons; you must will it, and I am here to help you." It is as if He said, "You shall have the freedom of my Father's universe; for, free from yourselves, you will be free of His heart. Yourselves are your slavery. That is the darkness which you have loved rather than the light. You have given honor to yourselves, and not to the Father; you have sought honor from men, and not from the Father! Therefore, even in the house of your Father, you have been but sojourning slaves. We in His family are all one; we have no party-spirit; we have no self-seeking: fall in love with us, and you shall be free as we are free."

If then the poor starved child cry, "How, Lord!" the answer will depend on what he means by that *how*. If he means,"What plan will you adopt? What is your scheme for cutting my bonds and setting me free?" the answer may be a deepening of the darkness, a tightening of the bonds.

But if he means, "Lord, what would you have me to do?" the answer will not tarry. "Give yourself to me to do what I tell you, to understand what I say, to be my good, obedient little brother, and I will wake in you the heart that my Father put in you, the same kind of heart that I have, and it will grow to love the Father, altogether and absolutely, as mine does, till you are ready to be torn to pieces for Him. Then you will know that you are at the heart of the universe, at the heart of every secret—at the heart of the Father. Not till then will you be free, then free indeed!"

Christ died to save us, not from suffering, but from ourselves; not from injustice, far less from justice, but from being unjust. He died that we might live—but live as He lives, by dying as he died who died to Himself that He might live unto God.

If we do not die to ourselves, we cannot live to God, and he that does not live to God is dead. "You will know the truth," the Lord says, "and the truth will make you free. I am the truth, and you shall be free as I am free. To be free, you must be sons like me." To be free you must *be* that which you have to be, that which you are created. To be free you must give the answer of sons to the Father who calls you. To be free you must fear nothing but evil, care for nothing but the will of the Father, hold to Him in absolute confidence and infinite expectation. He alone is to be trusted.

He has shown us the Father not only by doing what the Father does, not only by loving his Father's children even as the Father loves them, but by His perfect satisfaction with Him, His joy in Him, His utter obedience to Him. He has shown us the Father by the absolute devotion of a perfect son.

He is the Son of God because the Father and He are one, have one thought, one mind, one heart. Upon this truth—I do not mean the dogma, but the truth itself of Jesus to His father—hangs the universe; and upon the recognition of this truth—that is, upon their becoming thus true— hangs the freedom of the children, the redemption of their whole world. "I and the Father are one," is the center-truth of the universe; and the circumfering truth is, "that they also may be one in us."

The only free man, then, is he who is a child of the Father. He is a servant of all, but can be made the slave of none: he is a son of the Lord of the universe. He is in himself, in virtue of his truth, free. He is in himself a king. For the Son rests his claim to royalty on this, that he was born and came into the world to bear witness to the truth.

THE WORD OF JESUS ON PRAYER

They ought always to pray.
Luke 18:1

The impossibility of doing what we would as we would, drives us to look for help. There is a reality of being in which all things are easy and plain—oneness, that is, with the Lord of Life; to pray for this is the first thing; and to the point of this prayer every difficulty hedges and directs us.

But if I try to set forth something of the reasonableness of all prayer, I beg my readers to remember that it is for the sake of action and not speculation. If prayer be anything at all, it is a thing to be done. What matter whether you agree with me or not, if you do not pray? I would not spend my labor for that. I desire it to serve for help to pray, not to understand how a man might pray and yet be a reasonable soul.

Here is a word of the Lord about prayer. It is a comfort that He recognizes difficulty in the matter—sees that we need encouragement to go on praying, that it looks as if we were not heard, that it is no wonder we should be ready to faint and leave off. He tells a parable in which the suppliant has to go often and often to the man who can help her, gaining her end only at the long last. Actual delay on the part of God, we know from what follows, He does not allow. He recognizes how the thing must look to those whom He would have go on praying. Here as elsewhere He teaches us that we must not go by the look of things, but by the reality behind the look.

A truth, a necessity of God's own willed nature, is enough to set up against a whole army of appearances. It looks as if He did not hear you. Never mind; He does. Go on as the woman did; you too will be heard. She is heard at last, and in virtue of her much going; God hears at once, and will avenge speedily. The unrighteous judge cared nothing for the woman; those who cry to God are His own chosen—plain in the fact that they cry to Him. He has made and appointed them to cry: they do cry: will He not hear them?

They exist that they may pray. He has chosen them that they may choose Him; He has called them that they may call Him—that there may be such communion, such interchange as belongs to their being and the being of their Father. The gulf of indifference lay between the poor woman and the unjust judge; God and those who seek His help, are closer than two hands clasped hard in love: He will avenge them speedily. It is a bold assertion in the face of what seems great delay—an appearance acknowledged in the very groundwork of the parable.

If there be a God, and I am His creature, there may be, there should be, there must be some communication open between Him and me. If anyone allow a God, but one scarce good enough to care about His creatures, I will yield him that it were foolish to pray to such a God; but the notion that, with all the good impulses in us, we are the offspring of a cold-hearted devil, is so horrible in its inconsistency, that I would ask that man what hideous and cold-hearted disregard to the truth makes him capable of the supposition! To such a one God's terrors, or, if not His terrors, then God's sorrow yet will speak; the divine something in him will love, and the love be left moaning.

If I find my position, my consciousness, that of one from home, nay, that of one in some sort of prison; if I find that I can neither rule the world in which I love nor my own thoughts or desires; that I cannot quiet my passions, order my likings, determine my ends, will my growth, forget when I would, or recall what I forget; that I cannot love where I would, or hate where I would; that I am no king over myself; that I cannot supply my own needs, do not even always know which of my seeming needs are to be supplied, and which treated as impostors; if, in a word, my own being is every way too much for me; if I can neither understand it, be satisfied with it, nor better it—may it not well give me pause—the pause that ends in prayer?

He that is made in the image of God must know Him or be desolate: the child must have the Father! Witness the dissatisfaction, yea desolation of my soul—wretched, alone, unfinished, without Him! It cannot act from itself, save in God; acting from what seems itself without God, is no action at all. It is a mere yielding to impulse. All within is disorder and spasm. There is a cry behind me, and a voice before. Instincts of betterment tell me I must rise above my present self—perhaps even above all my possible self. I see not how to obey, how to carry them out.

I am shut up in a world of consciousness, an unknown *I* in an unknown world. Surely this world of my unwilled, unchosen, compelled existence, cannot be shut out from Him, cannot be unknown to Him, cannot be impenetrable, impermeable, unpresent to Him from whom I am! Nay, is it not His thinking in which I think? Is it not by His consciousness that I am conscious?

Then shall I not think to Him? Shall I not tell Him my troubles—how He, even He, has troubled me by making me?—how unfit I am to be that which I am?—that my being is not to me a good thing yet?—that I need a law that shall account to me for it in righteousness—reveal to me how I am to make it a good—how I am to *be* a good, and not an evil?

If it be reasonable for me to cry thus, if I cannot but cry, it is reasonable that God should hear. He cannot but hear. A being that could not hear or would not answer prayer, could not be God.

Prayer As Experience

But, I ask, all this admitted—is what you call a necessary truth an existent fact? You say, "It must be so;" I say, "What if there is no God!" Convince me that prayer is heard, and I shall know.

I reply, What if God does not care to have you know it at second hand? What if there would be no good in that?

The sole assurance worth a man's having, even if the most incontestable evidence were open to him from a thousand other quarters, is that to be gained only from personal experience—that assurance in himself which he can least readily receive from another, and which is least capable of being transmuted into evidence for another. The evidence of Jesus Christ could not take the place of that.

A truth is of enormous import in relation to the life—that is the heart, and conscience, and will; it is of little consequence merely as a fact having relation to the understanding. God may hear all prayers that ever were offered to Him, and a man may believe that He does, nor be one whit the better for it, so long as God has no prayers of his to hear, he no answers to receive from God. Nothing in this quarter will ever be gained by investigation.

Reader, if you are in any trouble, try whether God will not help you; if you are in no need, why would you ask questions about prayer? True, he knows little of himself who does not know that he is wretched, and miserable, and poor, and blind, and naked; but until he begins at least to suspect a need, how can he pray? And for one who does not want to pray, I would not lift a straw to defeat such a one in the argument whether God hears or does not hear prayer: for me, let him think what he will! It matters nothing in heaven or in earth: whether in hell I do not know.

As to the so-called scientific challenge to prove the efficacy of prayer by the result of simultaneous petition, I am almost ashamed to allude to it. There should be light enough in science itself to show the proposal absurd. A God capable of being so moved in one direction or another, is a God not worth believing in—could not be the God believed in by Jesus Christ—and He said He knew. A God that should fail to hear, receive, attend to one single prayer, the feeblest or worst, I cannot believe in; but a God that would grant every request of every man or every company of men, would be an evil God—that is no God, but a demon.

That God should hang in the thought-atmosphere like a windmill, waiting till men enough should combine and send out prayer in sufficient force to turn His outspread arms, is an idea too absurd. God waits to be gracious, not to be tempted. A man capable of proposing such a test, could have in his mind no worthy representative idea of a God, and might well disbelieve in any. It is better to disbelieve than believe in a God unworthy.

The Problem of Unanswered Prayer

"But I want to believe in God. I want to know that there is a God that answers prayer, that I may believe in Him. There was a time when I believed in Him. I prayed to Him in great and sore trouble of heart and mind, and He did not hear me. I have not prayed since."

This only I will say: God has not to consider His children only at the moment of their prayer. Should He be willing to give a man the thing He knows he would afterwards wish He had not given him? If a man be not fit to be refused, if he be not ready to be treated with love's severity, what he wishes may perhaps be given him in order that he may wish it had not been given him; but barely to give a man what he wants because he wants it, and without further purpose of his good, would be to let a poor ignorant child take his fate into his own hands—the cruelty of a devil. Yet is every prayer heard; and the real soul of the prayer may require, for its real answer, that it should not be granted in the form in which it is requested.

"To have a thing in another shape might be equivalent to not having it at all."

If you knew God, you would leave that to Him. He is not mocked, and He will not mock. But He knows you better than you know yourself, and would keep you from fooling yourself. He will not deal with you as the child of a day, but as the child of eternal ages. You shall be satisfied, if you will but let Him have His way with the creature He has made. The question is between your will and the will of God.

He is not one of those who give readiest what they prize least. He does not care to give anything but His best, or that which will prepare for it. Not many years may pass before you confess, "you are a God who hears prayer, and gives a better answer." You may come to see that the desire of your deepest heart would have been frustrated by having what seemed its embodiment then. That God should as a loving father listen, hear, consider, and deal with the request after the perfect tenderness of His heart, is to me enough; it is little that I should go without what I pray for.

If it be granted that any answer which did not come of love, and was not for the final satisfaction of him who prayed, would be unworthy of God; that it is the part of love and knowledge to watch over the wayward, ignorant child; then the trouble of seemingly unanswered prayers begins to abate, and a lovely hope and comfort takes its place in the child-like soul. To hear is not necessarily to grant—God forbid! But to hear is necessarily to attend to—sometimes as necessarily to refuse.

"Three-times," says St. Paul, "I besought the Lord about this, that it should leave me; but He said to me, my grace is sufficient for you; for my power is made perfect in weakness." God had a better thing for Paul than granting his prayer and removing his complaint. The power of

Christ should descend and remain upon him. He would make him stronger than his suffering, make him a sharer in the energy of God. Verily, if we have God, we can do without the answer to any prayer.

Why Pray?

"But if God is so good as you represent Him, and if He knows all that we need, and better far than we do ourselves, why should it be necessary to ask Him for anything?"

I answer, What if He knows prayer to be the thing we need first and most? What if the main object in God's idea of prayer be the supplying of our great, our endless need—the need of Himself? What if the good of all our smaller and lower needs lies in this, that they help to drive us to God?

Hunger may drive the runaway child home, and he may or may not be fed at once, but he needs his mother more than his dinner. Communion with God is the one need of the soul beyond all other need; prayer is the beginning of that communion, and some need is the motive of that prayer. Our wants are for the sake of our coming into communion with God, our eternal need.

If gratitude and love immediately followed the supply of our needs, if God our Savior was the one thought of our hearts, then it might be unnecessary that we should ask for anything we need. But seeing we take our supplies as a matter of course, feeling as if they came out of nothing, or from the earth, or our own thoughts—instead of out of a heart of love and a will which alone is force—it is needful that we should be made to feel some at least of our wants, that we may seek Him who alone supplies all of them, and find His every gift a window to His heart of truth.

So begins a communion, a talking with God, a coming-to-one with Him, which is the sole end of prayer, yea, of existence itself in its infinite phases. We must ask that we may receive; but that we should receive what we ask in respect of our lower needs, is not God's end in making us pray, for He could give us everything without that. To bring His child to His knee, God withholds that man may ask.

In regard, however, to the high necessities of our nature, it is in order that He may be able to give that God requires us to ask—requires by driving us to it—by shutting us up to prayer. For how can He give into the soul of a man what it needs, while that soul cannot receive it? The ripeness for receiving is the asking.

When the soul is hungry for the light, for the truth—when its hunger has waked its higher energies, thoroughly roused the will, and brought the soul into its highest condition, that of action—its only fitness for receiving the things of God—that action is prayer. Then God can give. Then He can be as He would towards the man; for the glory of God is to give Himself. We thank you, Lord Christ, for by your pain alone do we rise towards the knowledge of this glory of your Father and our Father.

For the real good of every gift it is essential, first, that the giver be in the gift—as God always is, for He is love—and next, that the receiver know and receive the giver in the gift. Every gift of God is but a harbinger of His greatest and only sufficing gift—that of Himself. No gift unrecognized as coming from God is at its own best; therefore many things that God would gladly give us, things even that we need because we are, must wait until we ask for them, that we may know whence they come. When in all gifts we find Him, then in Him we shall find all things.

Sometimes to one praying will come the feeling rather than question: "Were it not better to abstain? If this thing be good, will He not give it me? Would He not be better pleased if I left it altogether to Him?" It comes, I think, of a lack of faith and childlikeness—taking form, perhaps, in a fear lest, asking for what was not good, the prayer should be granted. Such a thought has no place with St. Peter; he says, "Cast all your anxieties upon him, for he cares about you."

It may even come of ambition after spiritual distinction. In every request, heart and soul and mind ought to supply the low accompaniment, "Thy will be done." But the making of any request brings us near to Him, into communion with our Life. Does it not also help us to think of Him in all our affairs, and learn in everything to give thanks? Anything large enough for a wish to light upon, is large enough to hang a prayer upon: the thought of Him to whom that prayer goes will purify and correct the desire. To say, "Father, I should like this or that," would be enough at once, if the wish were bad, to make us know it and turn from it.

Such prayer about things must of necessity help to bring the mind into true and simple relation with Him; to make us remember His will even when we do not see what that will is. Surely it is better and more trusting to tell Him all without fear or anxiety. Was it not thus the Lord carried Himself towards His Father when He said, "if it be possible, let this cup pass from me"? But there was something He cared for more than His own fear—His Father's will: "Nevertheless, not my will, but thine be done."

There is no apprehension that God might be displeased with Him for saying what He would like, and not leaving it all to His Father. Neither did He regard His Father's plans as necessarily so fixed that they could not be altered to His prayer. The true son-faith is that which comes with boldness, fearless of the Father doing anything but what is right fatherly, patient, and full of loving-kindness. We must not think to please Him by any asceticism even of the spirit; we must speak straight out to Him. The true child will not fear, but lay bare his wishes to the perfect Father. The Father may will otherwise, but His grace will be enough for the child.

There could be no riches but for need. God Himself is made rich by man's necessity. By that He is rich to give; through that we are rich by receiving.

As to any notion of prevailing by entreaty over an unwilling God, that is heathenish, and belongs to such as think Him a hard master, or one like the unjust judge. What so quenching to prayer as the notion of unwillingness in the ear that hears! And when prayer is dull, what makes it flow like the thought that God is waiting to give, wants to give us everything! "Let us then with confidence draw near to the throne of grace, that we may receive mercy and find grace to help in time of need." We shall be refused our prayer if that be better; but what is good our Father will give us with divine good will. The Lord spoke His parable "to the effect that they ought always to pray, and not lose heart."

Selections from

THE LAST FARTHING

*Truly I say to you, you will never get out till
you have paid the last penny.* Matthew 5:26

There is a thing wonderful and admirable in the parables, not readily grasped, but specially indicated by the Lord Himself—their unintelligibility to the mere intellect. They are addressed to the conscience and not to the intellect, to the will and not to the imagination. They are strong and direct but not definite. They are not meant to explain anything, but to rouse a man to the feeling, "I am not what I ought to be, I do not the thing I ought to do!"

Many maundering interpretations may be given by the wise, with plentiful loss of labor, while the child who uses them for the necessity of walking in the one path will constantly receive light from them. The greatest obscuration of the words of the Lord, as of all true teachers, comes from those who give themselves to interpret rather than do them. Theologians have done more to hide the gospel of Christ than any of its adversaries.

It was not for our understandings, but our wills, that Christ came. He who does that which he sees, shall understand; he who is set upon understanding rather than doing, shall go on stumbling and mistaking and speaking foolishness. He has not that in him which can understand. The gospel itself, and in it the parables of the Truth, are to be understood only by those who walk by what they find. It is he that runs that shall read, and no other.

It is not intended by the speaker of the parables that any other should know intellectually what, known but intellectually, would be for his injury—what knowing intellectually he would imagine he had grasped, perhaps even appropriated. When the pilgrim of the truth comes on his journey to the region of the parable, he finds its interpretation. It is not a fruit or a jewel to be stored, but a well springing by the wayside.

What special meaning may be read in the different parts of magistrate, judge, and officer, beyond the general suggestion, perhaps, of the tentative approach of the final, I do not know; but I think I do know what is meant by "make friends . . . while you are going" and "the last farthing." The parable is an appeal to the common sense of those that hear it, in regard to every affair of righteousness. Arrange what claim lies against you; compulsion waits behind it. Do at once what you must do one day. As there is no escape from payment, escape at least the prison that will enforce it. Do not drive Justice to extremities. Duty is imperative; it must be done. It is useless to think to escape the eternal law of things. Yield of yourself, nor compel God to compel you.

To the honest man, to the man who would fain be honest, the word is of right gracious import. To the untrue, it is a terrible threat; to him who is of the truth, it is sweet as most loving promise. He who is of God's mind in things, rejoices to hear the word of the changeless Truth. The voice of the Right fills the heavens and the earth, and makes his soul glad; it is his salvation. If God were not inexorably just, there would be no stay for the soul of the feeblest lover of right. "You are true, O Lord: one day I also shall be true!"

"You shall render the right, cost you what it may," is a dread sound in the ears of those whose life is a falsehood. What but the last penny would those who love righteousness more than life pay? It is a joy profound as peace to know that God is determined upon such payment, is determined to have His children clean, clear, pure as very snow; is determined that not only shall they with His help make up for whatever wrong they have done, but at length be incapable, by eternal choice of good, under any temptation, of doing the thing that is not divine, the thing God would not do.

No Escape

There has been much cherishing of the evil fancy, often without its taking formal shape, that there is some way of getting out of the region of strict justice, some mode of managing to escape doing *all* that is required of us; but there is no such escape. A way to avoid any demand of righteousness would be an infinitely worse way than the road to the everlasting fire, for its end would be eternal death.

No, there is no escape. There is no heaven with a little hell in it—no plan to retain this or that of the devil in our hearts or our pockets. Out Satan must go, every hair and feather! Neither shall you think to be delivered from the necessity of being good by being made good. God is the God of the animals in a far lovelier way, I suspect, than many of us dare to think, but He will not be the God of a man by making a good beast of him. You must be good; neither death nor any admittance into good company will make you good; though, doubtless, if you be willing and try, these and all other best helps will be given you.

There is no clothing in a robe of imputed righteousness, that poorest of legal cobwebs spun by spiritual spiders. To me it seems like an invention of well-meaning dullness to soothe insanity; and indeed it has proved a door of escape out of worse imaginations. It is apparently an old "doctrine," for St. John seems to point at it where he says, "Little children, let no one deceive you. He who does right is righteous, as He is righteous."

Christ is our righteousness, not that we should escape punishment, still less escape being righteous, but as the live potent Creator of righteousness in us, so that we, with our wills receiving His spirit, shall like Him resist unto blood, striving against sin; shall know in ourselves, as He knows, what a lovely thing is righteousness. He is our righteousness, and that righteousness is no fiction, no pretense, no imputation.

One thing that tends to keep men from seeing righteousness and unrighteousness as they are, is that they have been told many things are righteous and unrighteous, which are neither the one nor the other. Righteousness is just fairness—from God to man, from man to God and to man; it is giving everyone his due—his large mighty due. He is righteous, and no one else, who does this.

And any system which tends to persuade men that there is any salvation but that of becoming righteous even as Jesus is righteous; that a man can be made good, as a good dog is good, without his own willed share in the making; that a man is saved by having his sins hidden under a robe of imputed righteousness—that system, so far as this tendency, is of the devil and not of God. Thank God, not even error shall injure the true of heart. They grow in the truth, and as love casts out fear, so truth casts out falsehood.

I read, then, in this parable, that a man had better make up his mind to be righteous, to be fair, to do what he can to pay what he owes, in any and all the relations of life—all the matters, in a word, wherein one man may demand of another, or complain that he has not received fair play. Arrange your matters with those who have anything against you, while you are yet together and things have not gone too far to be arranged; *you will have to do it,* and that under less easy circumstances than now. Putting off is of no use. You must. The thing has to be done; there are means of compelling you.

It is a very small matter *to you* whether the man give you your rights or not; it is life or death to you whether or not you give him his. Whether he pay you what you count his debt or no, you will be compelled to pay him all you owe him. If you owe him a pound and he you a million, you must pay him the pound whether he pay you the million or not; there is no business-parallel here. If, owing you love, he gives you hate, you, owing him love, have yet to pay it. We have a good while given us to pay, but a crisis will come—come soon after all—comes always sooner than those expect it who are not ready for it—a crisis when the demand unyielded will be followed by prison.

The same holds with every demand of God. By refusing to pay, the man makes an adversary who will compel him—and that for the man's own sake. If you or your life say, "I will not," then He will see to it. There is a prison, and the one thing we know about that prison is, that its doors do not open until entire satisfaction is rendered, the last penny paid.

The main debts whose payment God demands are those which lie at the root of all right, those we owe in mind, and soul, and being. Whatever in us can be or make an adversary, whatever could prevent us from doing the will of God, or from agreeing with our fellow—all must be yielded. Our every relation, both to God and our fellow, must be acknowledged heartily, met as a reality. Smaller debts, if any debt can be small, follow as a matter of course.

If a man acknowledge, and would pay if he could but cannot, the universe will be taxed to help him rather than he should continue unable. If the man accepts the will of God, he is the child of the Father, the whole power and wealth of the Father is for him, and the uttermost penny will easily be paid. If the man denies the debt, or acknowledging does nothing towards paying it, then—at last—the prison.

God in the dark can make a man thirst for the light, who never in the light sought but the dark. The cells of the prison may differ in degree of darkness; but they are all alike in this, that not a door opens but to payment. There is no day but the will of God, and he who is of the night cannot be forever allowed to roam the day. Unfelt, unprized, the light must be taken from him, that he may know what the darkness is. When the darkness is perfect, when he is totally without the light he has spent the night in slaying, then will he know darkness.

The Final Prison

I think I have seen from afar something of the final prison of all, the innermost cell of the debtor of the universe; I will endeavor to convey what I think it may be.

It is the vast outside; the ghastly dark beyond the gates of the city of which God is the light—where the evil dogs go ranging, silent as the dark, for there is no sound any more than sight. The time of signs is over. Every sense has its signs, and they were all misused: there is no sense, no sign more—nothing now by means of which to believe.

The man wakes from the final struggle of death, in absolute loneliness—such a loneliness as in the most miserable moment of deserted childhood he never knew. Not a hint, not a shadow of anything outside his consciousness reaches him. All is dark, dark and dumb; no motion—

not the breath of a wind! never a dream of change! not a scent from far-off field! nothing to suggest being or thing besides the man himself, no sign of God anywhere. God has so far withdrawn from the man, that he is conscious only of that from which He has withdrawn.

In the midst of the live world he cared for nothing but himself; now in the dead world he is in God's prison, his own separated self. But no liveliest human imagination could supply adequate representation of what it would be to be left without a shadow of the presence of God. If God gave it, man could not understand it. He knows neither God nor himself in the way of the understanding. For not he who cares least about God was in this world ever left as God could leave him. I doubt if any man could continue following his wickedness from whom God has withdrawn.

The most frightful idea of what could, to his own consciousness, befall a man, is that he should have to lead an existence with which God has nothing to do. The thing could not be; for being that is caused, the causation ceasing, must of necessity cease. It is always in, and never out of God, that we can live and do.

But I suppose the man so left that he seems to himself utterly alone, yet alas! with himself—smallest interchange of thought, feeblest contact of existence, dullest reflection from other being, impossible. In such evil case I believe the man would be glad to come in contact with the worst-loathed insect. It would be a shape of life, something beyond and besides his own huge, void, formless being! I imagine some such feeling in the prayer of the devils for leave to go into the swine.

His worst enemy, could he but be aware of him, he would be ready to worship. For the misery would be not merely the absence of all being other than his own self, but the fearful, endless, unavoidable presence of that self. Without the correction, the reflection, the support of other presences, being is not merely unsafe, it is a horror—for anyone but God, who is His own being.

For him whose idea is God's, and the image of God, his own being is far too fragmentary and imperfect to be anything like good company. It is the lovely creatures God has made all around us, in them giving us Himself, that, until we know Him, save us from the frenzy of aloneness—

for that aloneness is Self, Self, Self. The man who minds only himself must at last go mad if God did not interfere.

Release

Can there be any way out of the misery? Will the soul that could not believe in God, with all His lovely world around testifying of Him, believe when shut in the prison of its own lonely, weary all-and-nothing? It would for a time try to believe that it was indeed nothing, a mere glow of the setting sun on a cloud of dust, a paltry dream that dreamed itself—then, ah, if only the dream might dream that it was no more! that would be the one thing to hope for.

Self-loathing, and that for no sin, from no repentance, from no vision of better, would begin and grow and grow; and to what it might not come no soul can tell—of essential, original misery, uncompromising self-disgust! Only, then, if a being be capable of self-disgust, is there not some room for hope—as much as a pinch of earth in the cleft of a rock might yield for the growth of a pine? Nay, there must be hope while there is existence; for where there is existence there must be God; and God is forever good nor can be other than good.

But alas, the distance from the light! All his years in the world he received the endless gifts of sun and air, earth and sea and human face divine, as things that came to him because that was their way, and there was no one to prevent them. Now the poorest thinning of the darkness he would hail as men of old the glow of a descending angel; it would be as a messenger from God. Not that he would think of God! it takes long to think of God; but hope, not yet seeming hope, would begin to dawn in his bosom, and the thinner darkness would be as a cave of light, a refuge from the horrid self of which he used to be so proud.

A man may well imagine it impossible ever to think so unpleasantly of himself! But he has only to let things go, and he will make it the real, right, natural way to think of himself. True, all I have been saying is imaginary; but our imagination is made to mirror truth. All the things that appear in it are more or less after the model of things that are. I suspect it is the region whence issues prophecy; and when we are true it will mirror nothing but truth. I deal here with the same light and darkness the Lord dealt with, the same St. Paul and St. John and St. Peter and St. Jude dealt with. Ask yourself whether the faintest dawn of even physical light would not be welcome to such a soul as some refuge from the dark of the justly hated self.

And the light would grow and grow across the awful gulf between the soul and its haven—its repentance—for repentance is the first pressure of the bosom of God. And in the twilight, struggling and faint, the man would feel, faint as the twilight, another thought beside his, another thinking Something nigh his dreary self—perhaps the man he had most wronged, most hated, most despised—and would be glad that some one, whoever, was near him. The man he had most injured, and was most ashamed to meet, would be a refuge from himself—oh, how welcome!

So might I imagine a thousand steps up from the darkness, each a little less dark, a little nearer the light—but, ah, the weary way! He cannot come out until he have paid the last penny! Repentance once begun, however, may grow more and more rapid! If God once get a willing hold, if with but one finger He touch the man's self, swift as possibility will He draw him from the darkness into the light.

For that for which the forlorn, self-ruined wretch was made, was to be a child of God, a partaker of the divine nature, an heir of God and joint heir with Christ. Out of the abyss into which he cast himself, refusing to be the heir of God, he must rise and be raised. To the heart of God, the one and only goal of the human race—the refuge and home of all and each, he must set out and go, or the last glimmer of humanity will die from him.

Selections from

THE GOD OF THE LIVING

*Now He is not God of the dead, but of the
living: for all live to Him.* Luke 20:33

It is a recurring cause of perplexity in our Lord's teaching, that He is
too simple for us; that while we are questioning with ourselves about
the design of Solomon's carving upon some gold-plated door of the temple,
He is speaking about the foundations of Mount Zion, yea, of the earth
itself, upon which it stands. If the reader of the Gospel supposes that our
Lord was here using a verbal argument with the Sadducees, namely,
"I *am* the God of Abraham, Isaac, and Jacob; therefore they *are*," he
will be astonished that no Sadducee was found with courage enough
to reply: "All that God meant was to introduce Himself to Moses as
the same God who had aided and protected his fathers while they were
alive, saying, I am He that was the God of your fathers. They found
me faithful. You, therefore, listen to me, and you too shall find me
faithful *unto* the death."

But no such reply suggested itself even to the Sadducees of that day,
for their eastern nature could see argument beyond logic. Shall God call
Himself the God of the dead, of those who were alive once, but whom He
either could not or would not keep alive? "Trust in me, for I took care of
your fathers once upon a time, though they are gone now. Worship and
obey me, for I will be good to you for threescore years and ten, or

thereabouts; and after that, when you are not, and the world goes on all the same without you, I will call myself your God still." God changes not. Once God He is always God. If He has once said to a man, "I am your God," and that man has died the death of the Sadducee's creed, then we have a right to say that God is the God of the dead.

But "All Live to Him"

"And wherefore should He not be so far the God of the dead, if during the time allotted to them here, He was the faithful God of the living?" What God-like relation can the ever-living, life-giving, changeless God hold to creatures who partake not of His life, who have death at the very core of their being, are not worth their Maker's keeping alive? To let His creatures die would be to change, to abjure His God-hood, to cease to be that which He had made Himself. If they are not worth keeping alive, then His creating is a poor thing, and He is not so great, nor so divine as even the poor thoughts of those His dying creatures have been able to imagine Him.

But our Lord says, "All live to Him." With Him death is not. This that we call death is but a form in the eyes of men. It looks something final, an awful cessation, an utter change; it seems not probable that there is anything beyond. But if God could see us before we were, and make us after His ideal, that we shall have passed from the eyes of our friends can be no argument that He beholds us no longer. "All live to Him."

Let the change be ever so great, ever so imposing; let unseen life be ever so vague to our conception, it is not against reason to hope that God could see Abraham, after his Isaac had ceased to see him; saw Isaac after Jacob ceased to see him; saw Jacob after some of the Sadducees had begun to doubt whether there ever had been a Jacob at all. He remembers them; that is, He carries them in His mind: he of whom God thinks, lives. He takes to Himself the name of *Their God*. The Living One cannot name Himself after the dead, when the very Godhead lies in the giving of life. Therefore they must be alive. If He speaks of them, remembers His own loving thoughts of them, would He not have kept them alive if He could;

and if He could not, how could He create them? Can it be an easier thing to call into life than to keep alive?

The Nature of Resurrection

"But if they live to God, they are aware of God. And if they are aware of God, they are conscious of their own being. Why then the necessity of a resurrection?"

For their relation to others of God's children in mutual revelation; and for fresh revelation of God to all. But let us inquire what is meant by the resurrection of the body. "With what kind of body do they come?"

Let us first ask what is the use of this body of ours. It is the means of revelation to us, the *camera* in which God's eternal shows are set forth. It is by the body that we come into contact with Nature, with our fellow-men, with all their revelations of God to us. It is through the body that we receive all the lessons of passion, of suffering, of love, of beauty, of science. It is through the body that we are both trained outwards from ourselves, and driven inwards into our deepest selves to find God.

We cannot yet have learned all that we are meant to learn through the body. How much of the teaching even of this world can the most diligent and most favored man have exhausted before he is called to leave it! Is all that remains to be lost? Who that has loved this earth can but believe that the spiritual body of which St. Paul speaks will be a yet higher channel of such revelation? The meek who have found that their Lord spake true, and have indeed inherited the earth, who have seen that all matter is radiant of spiritual meaning, who would not cast a sigh after the loss of mere animal pleasure, would, I think, be the least willing to be without a body, to be unclothed without being again clothed upon.

All this revelation, however, would render only *a* body necessary, not this body. The fullness of the word *Resurrection* would be ill met if this were all. We need not only a body to convey revelation to us, but a body to reveal us to others. The thoughts, feelings, imaginations which arise in us, must have their garments of revelation whereby shall be made manifest the unseen world within us to our brothers and sisters around us; else is each left in human loneliness.

Now, if this be one of the uses my body served on earth before, the new body must be like the old. Not that only, it must be the same body, glorified as we are glorified, with all that was distinctive of each from his fellows more visible than ever before. The accidental, the non-essential, the unrevealing, the incomplete will have vanished. That which made the body what it was in the eyes of those who loved us will be tenfold there. Will not this be the resurrection of the body? of the same body though not of the same dead matter?

Every eye shall see the beloved, every heart will cry, "My own again!—more mine because more himself than ever I beheld him!" For do we not say on earth, "he is not himself today," or "She looks her own self"; "She is more like herself than I have seen her for long"? And is not this when the heart is glad and the face radiant? For we carry a better likeness of our friends in our hearts than their countenances, save at precious seasons, manifest to us.

Who will dare to call anything less than this a resurrection? Oh, how the letter kills! There are people who can believe that the dirt of their bodies will rise the same as it went down to the friendly grave, who yet doubt if they will know their friends when they rise again. And they call *that* believing in the resurrection!

What! shall a man love his neighbor as himself, and must he be content not to know him in heaven? Better be content to lose our consciousness, and know ourselves no longer. What! shall God be the God of the families of the earth, and shall the love that He has thus created towards father and mother, brother and sister, wife and child, go moaning and longing to all eternity; or worse, far worse, die out of our bosoms? Shall God be God, and shall this be the end?

No, our God is an unveiling, a revealing God. He will raise you from the dead, that I may behold you; that that which vanished from the earth may again stand forth, looking out of the same eyes of eternal love and truth, holding out the same mighty hand of brotherhood, the same delicate and gentle, yet strong hand of sisterhood, to me, this me that knew you and loved you in the days gone by.

The new shall then be dear as the old, and for the same reason, that it reveals the old love. And in the changes which, thank God, must take place when the mortal puts on immortality, shall we not feel that the nobler our friends are, the more they are themselves; that the more the idea of each is carried out in the perfection of beauty, the more like they are to what we thought them in our most exalted moods, to that which we saw in them in the rarest moments of profoundest communion, to that which we beheld through the veil of all their imperfections when we loved them the truest?

Lord, evermore give us this Resurrection, like your own in the body of your Transfiguration. Let us see and hear, and know, and be seen, and heard, and known, as you see, hear, and know. Give us glorified bodies through which to reveal the glorified thoughts which shall then inhabit us, when not only shall you reveal God, but each of us shall reveal you.

And for this, Lord Jesus, come—the child, the obedient God—that we may be one with you and with every man and woman whom you have made, in the Father.

Selections from
THE NEW NAME

*To him who conquers I will give some of the
hidden manna, and I will give him a white
stone, with a new name written on the stone
which no one knows except him who
receives it.* Revelation 2:17

Truth is truth, whether from the lips of Jesus or Balaam. But, in its deepest sense, *the truth* is a condition of heart, soul, mind, and strength towards God and towards our fellow—not an utterance, not even a *right* form of words; and therefore such truth coming forth in words is, in a sense, the person that speaks. And many of the utterances of truth in the *Revelation,* commonly called of St. John, are not merely lofty in form, but carry with them the conviction that the writer was no mere "trumpet of a prophecy," but spoke that he did know, and testified that he had seen.

In this passage about the gift of the white stone, I think we find the essence of religion.

What the notion in the mind of the writer with regard to the white stone was, is, I think, of comparatively little moment. What his mystic meaning may be, must be taken differently by different minds. I think he sees in its whiteness purity, and in its substance indestructibility. But I care chiefly to regard the stone as the vehicle of the name—as the form whereby the name is represented as passing from God to the man, and what is involved in this communication is what I wish to show. If my reader will not acknowledge my representation as St. John's meaning, I yet hope so to set it forth that he shall see the representation to be true in itself, and then I shall willingly leave the interpretation to its fate.

What a Name Expresses

I say, in brief, the giving of the white stone with the new name is the communication of what God thinks about the man to the man. It is the divine judgment, the solemn holy doom of the righteous man, the "Come, thou blessed," spoken to the individual.

In order to see this, we must first understand what is the idea of a name—that is, what is the perfect notion of a name. For, seeing the mystical energy of a holy mind here speaks of God as giving something, we must understand that the essential thing, and not any of its accidents or imitations, is intended.

A name of the ordinary kind in this world, has nothing essential in it. It is but a label by which one man and a scrap of his external history may be known from another man and a scrap of his history. The only names which have significance are those which the popular judgment or prejudice or humor bestows, either for ridicule or honor, upon a few out of the many. Each of these is founded upon some external characteristic of the man, upon some predominant peculiarity of temper, some excellence or the reverse of character, or something which he does or has done well or ill enough, or at least, singularly enough, to render him, in the eyes of the people, worthy of such distinction from other men. As far as they go, these are real names, for, in some poor measure, they express individuality.

The true name is one which expresses the character, the nature, the being, the *meaning* of the person who bears it. It is the man's own symbol—his soul's picture, in a word—the sign which belongs to him and to no one else. Who can give a man this, his own name? God alone. For no one but God sees what the man is, or even, seeing what he is, could express in a name-word the sum and harmony of what He sees.

To whom is this name given? To him that overcomes. When is it given? When he has overcome. Does God then not know what a man is going to become? As surely as he sees the oak which He put there lying in the heart of the acorn. Why then does He wait till the man has become by overcoming ere He settles what his name shall be? He does not wait; He knows his name from the first. But as—although repentance comes because God pardons—yet the man becomes aware of the pardon only in the repentance; so it is only when the man has become his name that God gives him the stone with the name upon it, for then first can he understand what his name signifies.

It is the blossom, the perfection, the completion, that determines the name; and God foresees that from the first, because He made it so; but the tree of the soul, before its blossom comes, cannot understand what blossom it is to bear, and could not know what the word meant, which, in representing its own unarrived completeness, names itself. Such a name cannot be given until the man *is* the name.

God's name for a man must then be the expression in a mystical word—a word of that language which all who have overcome understand—of His own idea of the man, that being whom He had in His thought when He began to make the child, and whom He kept in His thought through the long process of creation that went to realize the idea. To tell the name is to seal the success—to say, "In you also I am well pleased."

But we are still in the region of symbol. The mystic symbol has for its center of significance the fact of the personal individual relation of every man to his God. That every man has affairs, and those his first affairs, with God stands to the reason of every man who associates any meaning or feeling with the words, Maker, Father, God. Were we but children of a day, with the understanding that someone had given us that one holiday, there would be something to be thought, to be felt, to be done, because we knew it. For then our nature would be according to our fate, and we could worship and die. But it would be only the praise of the dead, not the praise of the living, for death would be the deepest, the lasting, the overcoming. We should have come out of nothingness, not out of God. He could only be our Maker, not our Father, our Origin. But now we know that God cannot be the God of the dead—must be the God of the living; inasmuch as to know that our death would freeze the heart of worship, and we could not say "Our God," or feel him worthy of such worth-ship as we could render.

To him who offers unto this God of the living his own self of sacrifice, to him that overcomes, who knows that he is *one* of God's children, *this* one of the Father's making, He gives the white stone. To him who climbs on the stair of all his God-born efforts and God-given victories up to the height of his being—that of looking face to face upon his ideal self in the bosom of the Father—God's *him* realized in him through the Father's love in the Elder Brother's devotion—to him God gives the new name written.

The Sanctity of Individuality

But I leave this, because that which follows embraces and intensifies this individuality of relation in a fuller development of the truth. For the name is one "which no one knows except him who receives it." Not only then has each man his individual relation to God, but each man has his peculiar relation to God. He is to God a peculiar being, made after his own fashion, and that of no one else; for when he is perfected he shall receive the new name which no one else can understand.

Hence he can worship God as no man else can worship Him—can understand God as no man else can understand Him. This or that man may understand God more, may understand God better than he, but no other man can understand God *as* he understands Him. God give me grace to be humble before you, my brother, that I drag not my simulacrum of you before the judgment seat of the unjust judge, but look up to yourself for what revelation of God you and no one else can give.

As the fir-tree lifts up itself with a far different need from the need of the palm-tree, so does each man stand before God, and lift up a different humanity to the common Father. And for each God has a different response. With every man He has a secret—the secret of the new name. In every man there is a loneliness, an inner chamber of peculiar life into which God only can enter. I say not it is *the innermost chamber*—but a chamber into which no brother, nay, no sister can come.

From this it follows that there is a chamber also—(O God, humble and accept my speech)—a chamber in God Himself, into which none can enter but the one, the individual, the peculiar man—out of which chamber that man has to bring revelation and strength for his brethren. This is that for which he was made—to reveal the secret things of the Father.

"But is there not the worst of all dangers involved in such teaching—the danger of spiritual pride?" If there be, are we to refuse the spirit for fear of the pride? Or is there any other deliverance from pride except

413

the spirit? Pride springs from supposed success in the high aim: with attainment itself comes humility.

But here there is no room for ambition. Ambition is the desire to be above one's neighbor; and here there is no possibility of comparison with one's neighbor. No one knows what the white stone contains except the man who receives it. Here is room for endless aspiration towards the unseen ideal; none for ambition. Ambition would only be higher than others; aspiration would be high. Relative worth is not only unknown— to the children of the kingdom it is unknowable. Each esteems the other better than himself.

"God has cared to make me for Himself," says the victor with the white stone, "and has called me that which I like best; for my own name must be what I would have it, seeing it is myself. What matter whether I be called a grass of the field, or an eagle of the air? a stone to build into His temple, or a Boanerges to wield His thunder? I am His; His idea, His making; perfect in my kind, yea, perfect in His sight; full of Him, revealing Him, alone with Him. Let Him call me what He will. The name shall be precious as my life. I seek no more."

Gone then will be all anxiety as to what his neighbor may think about him. It is enough that God thinks about him. To be something to God—is not that praise enough? To be a thing that God cares for and would have complete for Himself, because it is worth caring for—is not that life enough?

Neither will he thus be isolated from his fellows. For that we say of one, we say of all. It is as *one* that the man has claims amongst his fellows. Each will feel the sacredness and awe of his neighbor's dark and silent speech with his God. Each will regard the other as a prophet, and look to him for what the Lord has spoken. Each, as a high priest returning from his Holy of Holies, will bring from his communion some glad tidings, some gospel of truth, which, when spoken, his neighbors shall receive and understand. Each will behold in the other a marvel of revelation, a present son or daughter of the Most High, come forth from Him to reveal Him afresh. In God each will draw nigh to each.

Yes, there will be danger—danger as everywhere; but He gives more grace. And if the man who has striven up the heights should yet fall from them into the deeps, is there not that fire of God, the consuming fire, which burns and destroys not?

To no one who has not already had some speech with God, or who has not at least felt some aspiration towards the fount of his being, can all this appear other than foolishness. So be it.

But, Lord, help them and us, and make our being grow into your likeness. If through ages of strife and ages of growth, yet let us at last see your face, and receive the white stone from your hand.

The Imagination: Its Functions and Its Culture

To inquire into what God has made is the main function of the imagination. It is aroused by facts, is nourished by facts, seeks for higher and yet higher laws in those facts; but refuses to regard science as the sole interpreter of nature, or the laws of science as the only region of discovery.

We must begin with a definition of the word *imagination,* or rather some description of the faculty to which we give the name.

The word itself means an *imaging* or a making of likenesses. The imagination is that faculty which gives form to thought—not necessarily uttered form, but form capable of being uttered in shape or in sound, or in any mode upon which the senses can lay hold. It is, therefore, that faculty in man which is likest to the prime operation of the power of God, and has, therefore, been called the *creative* faculty, and its exercise *creation. Poet* means *maker.* We must not forget, however, that between creator and poet lies the one unpassable gulf which distinguishes—far be it from us to say *divides*—all that is God's from all that is man's; a gulf teeming with infinite revelations, but a gulf over which no man can pass to find out God, although God needs not to pass over it to find man; the gulf between that which calls, and that which is thus called into being; between that which makes in its own image and that which is made in that image. It is better to keep the word *creation* for that calling out of nothing which is the imagination of God; except it be as an occasional symbolic expression, whose daring is fully recognized, of the likeness of man's work to the work of his maker. The necessary unlikeness between the creator and the created holds within it the equally necessary likeness of the thing made to him who makes it, and so of the work of the made to the work of the maker. When therefore, refusing to employ the word *creation* of the work of man, we yet use the word *imagination* of the work of God, we cannot be said to dare at all. It is only to give the name of man's faculty to that power after which and by which it was fashioned. The imagination of man is made in the image of the imagination of God. Everything of man must have been of God first; and it will help much towards our understanding of the imagination and its functions in man if we first succeed in regarding aright the imagination of God, in which the imagination of man lives and moves and has its being.

As to *what* thought is in the mind of God ere it takes form, or what the form is to him ere he utters it; in a word, what the consciousness of God is in either case, all we can say is, that our consciousness in the resembling conditions must, afar off, resemble his. But when we come to consider the acts embodying the Divine thought (if indeed thought and act be not with him one and the same), then we enter a region of large difference. We discover at once, for instance, that where a man would make a machine, or a picture, or a book, God makes the man that makes the book, or the picture, or the machine. Would God give us a drama? He makes a Shakespeare. Or would he construct a drama more immediately his own? He begins with the building of the stage itself, and that stage is a world—a universe of worlds. He makes the actors, and they do not act,—they *are* their part. He utters them into the visible to work out their life—his drama. When he would have an epic, he sends a thinking hero into his drama, and the epic is the soliloquy of his Hamlet. Instead of writing his lyrics, he sets his birds and his maidens a-singing. All the processes of the ages are God's science; all the flow of history is his poetry. His sculpture is not in marble, but in living and speech-giving forms, which pass away, not to yield place to those that come after, but to be perfected in a nobler studio. What he has done remains, although it vanishes; and he never either forgets what he has once done, or does it even once again. As the thoughts move in the mind of a man, so move the worlds of men and women in the mind of God, and make no confusion there, for there they had their birth, the offspring of his imagination. Man is but a thought of God.

If we now consider the so-called creative faculty in man, we shall find that in no *primary* sense is this faculty creative. Indeed, a man is rather *being thought* than *thinking,* when a new thought arises in his mind. He knew it not till he found it there, therefore he could not even have sent for it. He did not create it, else how could it be the surprise that it was when it arose? He may, indeed, in rare instances foresee that something is coming, and make ready the place for its birth; but that is the utmost relation of consciousness and will he can bear to the dawning idea. Leaving this aside, however, and turning to the *embodiment* or revelation of thought, we shall find that a man no more *creates* the forms by which he would reveal this thoughts, than he creates those thoughts themselves.

For what are the forms by means of which a man may reveal his thoughts? Are they not those of nature? But although he is created in the closest sympathy with these forms, yet even these forms are not born in his mind. What springs there is the perception that this or that form is already an expression of this or that phase of thought or of feeling. For the world around him is an outward figuration of the condition of his mind; an inexhaustible storehouse of forms whence he may choose exponents—the crystal pitchers that shall protect his thought and not need to be broken that the light may break forth. The meanings are in those forms already, else they could be no garment of unveiling. God has made the world that it should thus serve his creature, developing in the service that imagination whose necessity it meets. The man has but to light the lamp within the form: his imagination is the light, it is not the form. Straightway the shining thought makes the form visible, and becomes itself visible through the form.[2] . . . For the world is—allow us the homely figure—the human being turned inside out. All that moves in the mind is symbolized in Nature. Or, to use another more philosophical, and certainly not less poetic figure, the world is a sensuous analysis of humanity, and hence an inexhaustible wardrobe for the clothing of human thought. Take any word expressive of emotion—take the word *emotion* itself—and you will find that its primary meaning is of the outer world. In the swaying of the woods, in the unrest of the "wavy plain," the imagination saw the picture of a well-known condition of the human mind; and hence the word *emotion.*[3]

But while the imagination of man has thus the divine function of putting thought into form, it has a duty altogether human, which is paramount to that function—the duty, namely, which springs from his immediate relation to the Father, that of following and finding out the divine imagination in whose image it was made. To do this, the man must watch its signs, its manifestations. He must contemplate what the Hebrew poets call the works of His hands.

"But to follow those is the province of the intellect, not of the imagination."—We will leave out of the question at present that poetic interpretation of the works of Nature with which the intellect has almost nothing, and the imagination almost everything, to do. It is unnecessary to insist that the higher being of a flower even is dependent for its reception upon the human imagination; that science may pull the snow-drop to shreds, but cannot find out the idea of suffering hope and pale confident submission, for the sake of which that darling of the spring looks out of heaven, namely, God's heart, upon us his wiser and more sinful children; for if there be any truth in this region of things acknow-ledged at all, it will be at the same time acknowledged that that region belongs to the imagination. We confine ourselves to that questioning of the works of God which is called the province of science.

"Shall, then, the human intellect," we ask, "come into readier contact with the divine imagination than that human imagination?" The work of the Higher must be discovered by the search of the Lower in degree which is yet similar in kind. Let us not be supposed to exclude the intellect from a share in every highest office. Man is not divided when the manifestations of his life are distinguished. The intellect "is all in every part." There were no imagination without intellect, however much it may appear that intellect can exist without imagination. What we mean to insist upon is, that in finding out the works of God, the Intellect must labour, workman-like, under the direction of the architect, Imagi-nation. Herein, too, we proceed in the hope to show how much more than is commonly supposed the imagination has to do with human endeavour; how large a share it has in the work that is done under the sun.

"But how can the imagination have anything to do with science? That region, at least, is governed by fixed laws."

"True," we answer. "But how much do we know of these laws? How much of science already belongs to the region of the ascertained—in other words, has been conquered by the intellect? We will not now dispute your vindication of the *ascertained* from the intrusion of the imagination; but we do claim for it all the undiscovered, all the unex-plored." "Ah, well! There it can do little harm. There let it run riot if you will." "No," we reply. "Licence is not what we claim when we assert the duty of the imagination to be that of following and finding out the work that God maketh. Her part is to understand God ere she attempts to utter man. Where is the room for being fanciful or riotous here? It is only the ill-bred, that is, the uncultivated imagination that will amuse itself where it ought to worship and work."

"But the facts of Nature are to be discovered only by observation and experiment." True. But how does the man of science come to think of his experiments? Does observation reach to the non-present, the possible, the yet unconceived? Even if it showed you the experiments which *ought* to be made, will observation reveal to you the experiments which *might* be made? And who can tell of which kind is the one that carries in its bosom the secret of the law you seek? We yield you your facts. The laws we claim for the prophetic imagination. "He had set the world *in* man's heart," not in his understanding. It is the far-seeing imagination which beholds what might be a form of things, and says to the intellect: "Try whether that may not be the form of these things;" which beholds or invents *a* harmonious relation of parts and operations, and sends the intellect to find out whether that be not *the* harmonious relation of them—that is, the law of the phenomenon it contemplates. Nay, the poetic relations themselves in the phenomenon may suggest to the imagination the law that rules its scientific life. Yea, more than this: we dare to claim for the true, childlike, humble imagination, such an inward oneness with the laws of the universe that it possesses in itself an insight into the very nature of things.

Lord Bacon tells us that a prudent question is the half of knowledge. Whence comes this prudent question? we repeat. And we answer, From the imagination. It is the imagination that suggests in what direction to make the new inquiry—which, should it cast no immediate light on the answer sought, can yet hardly fail to be a step towards final discovery. Every experiment has its origin in hypothesis; without the scaffolding of hypothesis, the house of science could never arise. And the construction of any hypothesis whatever is the work of the imagination. The man who cannot invent will never discover. The imagination often gets a glimpse of the law itself long before it is or can be *ascertained* to be a law.

The region belonging to the pure intellect is straitened: the imagination labours to extend it territories, to give it room. She sweeps across the borders, searching out new lands into which she may guide her plodding brother. The imagination is the light which redeems from the darkness for the eyes of the understanding. Novalis says, "The imagination is the stuff of the intellect"—affords, that is, the material upon which the intellect works. And Bacon, in his "Advancement of Learning," fully recognizes this its office, corresponding to the foresight of God in this, that it beholds afar off. And he says: "Imagination is much akin to miracle-working faith.". . .

This outward world is but a passing vision of the persistent true. We shall not live in it always. We are dwellers in a divine universe where no desires are in vain, if only they be large enough. Not even in this world do all disappointments breed only vain regrets.[8] And as to keeping to that which is known and leaving the rest—how many affairs of this world are so well-defined, so capable of being clearly understood, as not to leave large spaces of uncertainty, whose very correlate faculty is the imagination? Indeed it must, in most things, work after some fashion, filling the gaps after some possible plan, before action can even begin. In very truth, a wise imagination, which is the presence of the spirit of God, is the best guide that man or woman can have; for it is not the things we see the most clearly that influence us the most powerfully; undefined, yet vivid visions of something beyond, something which eye has not seen nor ear heard, have far more influence than any logical sequences whereby the same things may be demonstrated to the intellect. It is the nature of the thing, not the clearness of its outline, that determines its operation. We live by faith, and not by sight. Put the question to our mathematicians— only be sure the question reaches them—whether they would part with the well-defined perfection of their diagrams, or the dim, strange, possibly half-obliterated characters woven in the web of their being; their science, in short, or their poetry; their certainties, or their hopes; their consciousness of knowledge, or their vague sense of that which cannot be known absolutely: will they hold by their craft or by their inspirations, by their intellects or their imaginations? If they say the former in each alternative, I shall yet doubt whether the objects of the choice are actually before them, and with equal presentation.

What can be known must be known severely; but is there, therefore, no faculty for those infinite lands of uncertainty lying all about the sphere hollowed out of the dark by the glimmering lamp of our knowledge? Are they not the natural property of the imagination? there, *for* it, that it may have room to grow? there, that the man may learn to imagine greatly like God who made him, himself discovering their mysteries, in virtue of his following and worshipping imagination?

All that has been said, then, tends to enforce the culture of the imagination. But the strongest argument of all remains behind. For, if the whole power of pedantry should rise against her, the imagination will yet work; and if not for good, then for evil; if not for truth, then for falsehood; if not for life, then for death; the evil alternative becoming the more likely from the unnatural treatment she has experienced from those who ought to have fostered her. The power that might have gone forth in conceiving the noblest forms of action, in realizing the lives of the true-hearted, the self-forgetting, will go forth in building airy castles of vain ambition, of boundless riches, of unearned admiration. The imagination that might be devising how to make home blessed or to help the poor neighbour, will be absorbed in the invention of the new dress, or worse, in devising the means of procuring it. For, if she be not occupied with the beautiful, she will be occupied by the pleasant; that which goes not out to worship, will remain at home to be sensual. Cultivate the mere intellect as you may, it will never reduce the passions: the imagination, seeking the ideal in everything, will elevate them to their true and noble service. Seek not that your sons and your daughters should not see visions, should not dream dreams; seek that they should see true visions, that they should dream noble dreams. Such out-going of the imagination is one with aspiration, and will do more to elevate above what is low and vile than all possible inculcations of morality.

ENDNOTES*

2. We would not be understood to say that the man works consciously even in this. Oftentimes, if not always, the vision arises in the mind, thought and form together.

3. This passage contains only a repetition of what is far better said in the preceding extract from Carlyle, but it was written before we had read (if reviewers may be allowed to confess such ignorance) the book from which that extract is taken.

8. "We will grieve not, rather find
Strength in what remains behind;
In the primal sympathy
Which, having been, must ever be;
In the soothing thoughts that spring
Out of human suffering;
In the faith that looks through death,
In years that bring the philosophic mind."

*Notes taken from the original text of *Orts* by George MacDonald

The Fantastic Imagination

From

THE LIGHT PRINCESS AND
OTHER FAIRY TALES

That we have in English no word corresponding to the German *Mährchen*, drives us to use the word *Fairytale*, regardless of the fact that the tale may have nothing to do with any sort of fairy. The old use of the word *Fairy*, by Spenser at least, might, however, well be adduced, were justification or excuse necessary where *need must*.

Were I asked, what is a fairytale? I should reply, *Read Undine: that is a fairytale; then read this and that as well, and you will see what is a fairytale*. Were I further begged to describe the *fairytale*, or define what it is, I would make answer, that I should as soon think of describing the abstract human face, or stating what must go to constitute a human being. A fairytale is just a fairytale, as a face is just a face; and of all fairytales I know, I think *Undine* the most beautiful.

Many a man, however, who would not attempt to define *a man*, might venture to say something as to what a man ought to be: even so much I will not in this place venture with regard to the fairytale, for my long past work in that kind might but poorly instance or illustrate my now more matured judgment. I will but say some things helpful to the reading, in right-minded fashion, of such fairytales as I would wish to write, or care to read.

Some thinkers would feel sorely hampered if at liberty to use no forms but such as existed in nature, or to invent nothing save in accordance with the laws of the world of the senses; but it must not therefore be imagined that they desire escape from the region of law. Nothing lawless can show the least reason why it should exist, or could at best have more than an appearance of life.

The natural world has its laws, and no man must interfere with them in the way of presentment any more than in the way of use; but they themselves may suggest laws of other kinds, and man may, if he pleases, invent a little world of his own, with its own laws; for there is that in him which delights in calling up new forms—which is the nearest, perhaps, he can come to creation. When such forms are new embodiments of old truths, we call them products of the Imagination; when they are mere inventions, however lovely, I should call them the work of the Fancy: in either case, Law has been diligently at work.

His world once invented, the highest law that comes next into play is, that there shall be harmony between the laws by which the new world has begun to exist; and in the process of his creation, the inventor must hold by those laws. The moment he forgets one of them, he makes the story, by its own postulates, incredible. To be able to live a moment in an imagined world, we must see the laws of its existence obeyed. Those broken, we fall out of it. The imagination in us, whose exercise is essential to the most temporary submission to the imagination of another, immediately, with the disappearance of Law, ceases to act. Suppose the gracious creatures of some childlike region of Fairyland talking either cockney or Gascon! Would not the tale, however lovelily begun, sink at once to the level of the Burlesque—of all forms of literature the least worthy? A man's inventions may be stupid or clever, but if he does not hold by the laws of them, or if he makes one law jar with another, he contradicts himself as an inventor, he is no artist. He does not rightly consort his instruments, or he tunes them in different keys. The mind of man is the product of live Law; it thinks by law, it dwells in the midst of law, it gathers from law its growth; with law, therefore, can it alone work to any result. Inharmonious, unconsorting ideas will come to a man, but if he try to use one of such, his work will grow dull, and he will drop it from mere lack of interest. Law is the soil in which alone beauty will grow; beauty is the only stuff in which Truth can be clothed; and you may, if you will, call Imagination the tailor that cuts her garments to fit her, and Fancy his journeyman that puts the pieces of them together, or perhaps at most embroiders their button-holes. Obeying law, the maker works like his creator; not obeying law, he is such a fool as heaps a pile of stones and calls it a church.

In the moral world it is different: there a man may clothe in new forms, and for this employ his imagination freely, but he must invent nothing. He may not, for any purpose, turn its laws upside down. He must not meddle with the relations of live souls. The laws of the spirit of man must hold, alike in this world and in any world he may invent. It were no offence to suppose a world in which everything repelled instead of attracted the things around it; it would be wicked to write a tale representing a man it called good as always doing bad things, or a man it called bad as always doing good things: the notion itself is absolutely lawless. In physical things a man may invent; in moral things he must obey—and take their laws with him into his invented world as well.

"You write as if a fairytale were a thing of importance: must it have a meaning?"

It cannot help having some meaning; if it have proportion and harmony it has vitality, and vitality is truth. The beauty may be plainer in it than the truth, but without the truth the beauty could not be, and the fairytale would give no delight. Everyone, however, who feels the story, will read its meaning after his own nature and development: one man will read one meaning in it, another will read another.

"If so, how am I to assure myself that I am not reading my own meaning into it, but yours out of it?"

Why should you be so assured? It may be better that you should read your meaning into it. That may be a higher operation of your intellect than the mere reading of mine out of it: your meaning may be superior to mine.

"Suppose my child ask me what the fairytale means, what am I to say?"

If you do not know what it means, what is easier than to say so? If you do see a meaning in it, there it is for you to give him. A genuine work of art must mean many things; the truer its art, the more things it will mean. If my drawing, on the other hand, is so far from being a work of art that it needs THIS IS A HORSE written under it, what can it matter that neither you nor your child should know what it means? It is there not so much to convey a meaning as to wake a meaning. If it does not even wake an interest, throw it aside. A meaning may be there, but it is not for you. If, again, you do not know a horse when you see it, the name written under it will not serve you much. At all events, the business of the painter is not to teach zoology.

But indeed your children are not likely to trouble you about the meaning. They find what they are capable of finding, and more would be too much. For my part, I do not write for children, but for the childlike, whether of five, or fifty, or seventy-five.

A fairytale is not an allegory. There may be allegory in it, but it is not an allegory. He must be an artist indeed who can, in any mode, produce a strict allegory that is not a weariness to the spirit. An allegory must be Mastery or Moorditch.

A fairytale, like a butterfly or a bee, helps itself on all sides, sips at every wholesome flower, and spoils not one. The true fairytale is, to my mind, very like the sonata. We all know that a sonata means something; and where there is the faculty of talking with suitable vagueness, and choosing metaphor sufficiently loose, mind may approach mind, in the interpretation of a sonata, with the result of a more or less contenting consciousness of sympathy. But if two or three men sat down to write each what the sonata meant to him, what approximation to definite idea would be the result? Little enough—and that little more than needful. We should find it had roused related, if not identical, feelings, but probably not one common thought. Has the sonata therefore failed? Had it undertaken to convey, or ought it to be expected to impart anything defined, anything notionally recognizable?

"But words are not music; words at least are meant and fitted to carry a precise meaning!"

It is very seldom indeed that they carry the exact meaning of any user of them! And if they can be so used as to convey definite meaning, it does not follow that they ought never to carry anything else. Words are live things that may be variously employed to various ends. They can convey a scientific fact, or throw a shadow of her child's dream on the heart of a mother. They are things to put together like the pieces of a dissected map, or to arrange like the notes on a stave. Is the music in them to go for nothing? It can hardly help the definiteness of a meaning: is it therefore to be disregarded? They have length, and breadth, and outline: have they nothing to do with depth? Have they only to describe, never to impress? Has nothing any claim to their use but the definite? The cause of a child's tears may be altogether undefinable: has the mother therefore no antidote for his vague misery? That may be strong in colour which has no evident outline. A fairytale, a sonata, a gathering storm, a limitless night, seizes you and sweeps you away: do you begin at once to wrestle with it and ask whence its power over you, whither it is carrying you? The law of each is in the mind of its composer; that law makes one man feel this way, another man feel that way. To one the sonata is a world of odour and beauty, to another of soothing only and sweetness. To one, the cloudy rendezvous is a wild dance, with a terror at its heart; to another, a majestic march of heavenly hosts, with Truth in their centre pointing their course, but as yet restraining her voice. The greatest forces lie in the region of the uncomprehended.

I will go farther.—The best thing you can do for your fellow, next to rousing his conscience, is—not to give him things to think about, but to wake things up that are in him; or say, to make him think things for himself. The best Nature does for us is to work in us such moods in which thoughts of high import arise. Does any aspect of Nature wake but one thought? Does she ever suggest only one definite thing? Does she make any two men in the same place at the same moment think the same thing? Is she therefore a failure, because she is not definite? Is it nothing that she rouses the something deeper than the understanding—the power that underlies thoughts? Does she not set feeling, and so thinking at work? Would it be better that she did this after one fashion and not after many fashions? Nature is mood-engendering, thought-provoking: such ought the sonata, such ought the fairytale to be.

"But a man may then imagine in your work what he pleases, what you never meant!"

Not what he pleases, but what he can. If he be not a true man, he will draw evil out of the best; we need not mind how he treats any work of art! If he be a true man, he will imagine true things; what matter whether I meant them or not? They are there none the less that I cannot claim putting them there! One difference between God's work and man's is, that, while God's work cannot mean more than he meant, man's must mean more than he meant. For in everything that God has made, there is a layer upon layer of ascending significance; also he expresses the same thought in higher and higher kinds of that thought: it is God's things, his embodied thoughts, which alone a man has to use, modified and adapted to his own purposes, for the expression of his thoughts; therefore he cannot help his words and figures falling into such combinations in the mind of another as he had himself not foreseen, so many are the thoughts allied to every other thought, so many are the relations involved in every figure, so many the facts hinted in every symbol. A man may well himself discover truth in what he wrote; for he was dealing all the time with things that came from thoughts beyond his own.

"But surely you would explain your idea to one who asked you?"

I say again, if I cannot draw a horse, I will not write THIS IS A HORSE under what I foolishly meant for one. Any key to a work of imagination would be nearly, if not quite, as absurd. The tale is there, not to hide, but to show: if it show nothing at your window, do not open your door to it; leave it out in the cold. To ask me to explain, is to say, "Roses! Boil them, or we won't have them!" My tales may not be roses, but I will not boil them.

So long as I think my dog can bark, I will not sit up to bark for him.

If a writer's aim be logical conviction, he must spare no logical pains, not merely to be understood, but to escape being misunderstood; where his object is to move by suggestion, to cause to imagine, then let him assail the soul of his reader as the wind assails an æolian harp. If there be music in my reader, I would gladly wake it. Let fairytale of mine go for a firefly that now flashes, now is dark, but may flash again. Caught in a hand which does not love its kind, it will turn to an insignificant, ugly thing, that can neither flash nor fly.

The best way with music, I imagine, is not to bring the forces of our intellect to bear upon it, but to be still and let it work on that part of us for whose sake it exists. We spoil countless precious things by intellectual greed. He who will be a man, and will not be a child, must—he cannot help himself—become a little man, that is, a dwarf. He will, however, need no consolation, for he is sure to think himself a very large creature indeed.

If any strain of my "broken music" make a child's eyes flash, or his mother's grow for a moment dim, my labour will not have been in vain.

THE END

COMPLETE PRIMARY
BIBLIOGRAPHY

This is MacDonald's bibliography as given by John Malcolm Bulloch, *A Centennial Bibliography of George MacDonald* (Aberdeen: The University Press; 1925), reprinted in Mary Nance Jordan, *George MacDonald: A Bibliographical Catalog and Record* (privately published for The Marion E. Wade Collection, Wheaton College, Wheaton, Illinois, in Fairfax, Virginia, 1984).

Adela Cathcart. Contains many fairytales, parables, and poems. London: Hurst & Blackett, 1864.

Alec Forbes of Howglen. London: Hurst & Blackett, 1865.

Annals of a Quiet Neighbourhood. London: Hurst & Blackett, 1867.

At the Back of the North Wind. London: Strahan & Company, 1871.

Awakening. Chicago Pulpit (1873), iii, 151-58.

A Book of Strife in the Form of a Diary of an Old Soul. London: Unwin Brothers, 1880.

The Broken Swords. Monthly Christian Spectator (October 1854).

A Cabinet of Gems Cut and Polished by Sir Philip Sidney Now for the More Radiance Presented without Their Setting by George MacDonald (ed.). London: Elliot Stock, 1892.

The Carasoyn. (See *Works of Fancy and Imagination.*)

The Castle. (See *Adela Cathcart*.)

Castle Warlock. More often entitled *Warlock O'Glenwarlock*. London: Sampson Low, Marston, Searle and Rivington, 1882.

Cross Purposes. (See *Dealings with the Fairies*.)

The Cruel Painter. (See *Adela Cathcart*.)

David Elginbrod. London: Hurst & Blackett, 1863.

The Day Boy and the Night Girl. (Another title for *The History of Photogen and Nycteris*.)

Dealings with the Fairies. London: Alexander Strahan, 1867.

The Disciple and Other Poems. London: Strahan & Co., 1867.

A Dish of Orts. 1893 edition of *Orts,* containing the essay "The Fantastic Imagination."

Donal Grant. London: Kegan Paul, 1883.

A Double Story. (Another title for *The Wise Woman* or *The Lost Princess*.)

Dramatic and Miscellaneous Poems. New York: Scribner, 1876.

The Elect Lady. London: Kegan Paul, 1888.

England's Antiphon. London: Macmillan & Co., 1868.

Exotics: A Translation of the Spiritual Songs of Novalis. London: Strahan, 1876.

The Fairy Fleet. Argosy (April, 1866), i., 417-32.

Far Above Rubies. New York: Dodd, Mead & Company, 1899.

The Flight of the Shadow. London: Kegan Paul, 1891.

The Giant's Heart. (See *Adela Cathcart.)*

The Gifts of the Child Christ. London: Sampson Low, Marston, Searle & Rivington, 1882.

The Golden Key. (See *Dealings with the Fairies.)*

The Gray Wolf. (See *Works of Fancy and Imagination.)*

Guild Court. London: Hurst & Blackett, 1868.

Gutta Percha Willie: The Working Genius. London: Henry S. King & Company, 1873.

Heather and Snow. London: Chatto & Windus, 1893.

A Hidden Life. (See *Poems.).*

The History of Photogen and Nycteris. Graphic, 1879 (xx, 4-5, 8-9. See *The Gifts of the Child Christ.)*

Home Again. London: Kegan Paul, 1887.

The Hope of the Gospel. London: Ward, Lock, Bowden, & Company, 1892.

The Hope of the Universe. Sunday Magazine, (1892), xxi, 659-64, 770-73.

Hymns. ed., G.B. Bubier. Manchester: Fletcher & Tibbs, 1855. MacDonald contributed ten of the 318 hymns.

If I Had a Father. (See *Gifts of the Child Christ.)*

Imagination and Other Essays. (Another title for *Orts.*)

A Journey Rejourneyed. Argosy (December 1865-January 1866), i, 53-63, 127-33.

The Light Princess. (See *Adela Cathcart.)*

Lilith. London: Chatto & Windus, 1895.

Little Daylight. (See *Works of Fancy and Imagination.)*

The Lost Princess. (Another title for *The Wise Woman* or *A Double Story.)*

Malcolm. London: Henry S. King & Co., 1875.

The Marquis of Lossie. London: Hurst & Blackett, 1877.

Mary Marston. London: Sampson Low, Marston, Searle & Rivington, 1881.

The Miracles of Our Lord. London: Strahan & Company, 1870.

My Uncle Peter. The Queen (December 21, 1861), i, 298-99.

Orts. London: Sampson Low, Marston, Searle & Rivington, 1882.

Papa's Story. Illustrated London News (December 23, 1865), xlvii, 626-28.

Paul Faber, Surgeon. London: Hurst & Blackett, 1879.

Phantastes: A Fairie Romance for Men and Women. London: Smith, Elder, 1858.

Poems. London: Longman, Brown, Green, Longmans & Roberts, 1857.

The Poetical Works of George MacDonald. 2 vols. London: Chatto & Windus, 1893.

Port in a Storm. Argosy (November, 1866), ii, 477-86.

The Portent. London: Smith, Elder, 1864.

The Princess and Curdie. London: Chatto & Windus, 1883.

The Princess and the Goblin. London: Strahan & Company, 1872.

Rampolli. London: Longmans, Green & Co., 1897.

Ranald Bannerman's Boyhood. London: Strahan & Company, 1871.

Robert Falconer. London: Hurst & Blackett, 1868.

A Rough Shaking. London: Blackie & Sons, Ltd., 1891.

St. George and St. Michael. London: Henry S. King, 1876.

Salted with Fire. London: Hurst & Blackett, 1897.

Scotch Songs and Ballads. Aberdeen: John Rae Smith, 1893.

The Seaboard Parish. London: Tinsley Brothers, 1868.

The Shadows. (See *Adela Cathcart.*)

Sir Gibbie. London: Hurst & Blackett, 1879.

The Snow Fight. Good Words for the Young (November and December, 1872) iv, 9-12, 66-70.

There and Back. London: Kegan Paul, Trench, Trubner & Company, 1891.

Thomas Wingfold, Curate. London: Hurst & Blackett, 1876.

A Threefold Cord: Poems by Three Friends. London: Unwin Brothers, 1883. (See *Poetical Works.)*

The Tragedie of Hamlet. London: Longmans, Green & Company, 1885.

Twelve of the Spiritual Songs of Novalis. Privately printed, Christmas Day, 1851.

Uncle Cornelius, His Story. (See *Works of Fancy and Imagination.)*

The Unexpected Guest. Chicago Pulpit (1873), iii, 35-40.

Unspoken Sermons. London: Alexander Strahan, 1867.

Unspoken Sermons: Second Series. London: Longmans, Green & Company, 1886.

Unspoken Sermons: Third Series. London: Longmans, Green & Company, 1889.

The Vicar's Daughter. London: Tinsley Brothers, 1872.

Weighed and Wanting. London: Sampson Low, Marston, Searle & Rivington, 1882.

What's Mine's Mine. London: Kegan Paul, Trench & Company, 1886.

Wilfrid Cumbermede. Londona: Hurst & Blackett, 1872.

The Wise Woman. (Another title for *A Double Story* or *The Lost Princess.)* London: Strahan & Company, 1875.

Within and Without: A Dramatic Poem. Longman, Brown, Green & Longmans, 1855.

Works of Fancy and Imagination. 10 vols. London: Strahan & Company, 1871.

The Wow o' Rivven, or the Idiot's Home. London, Strahan & Company, 1868.